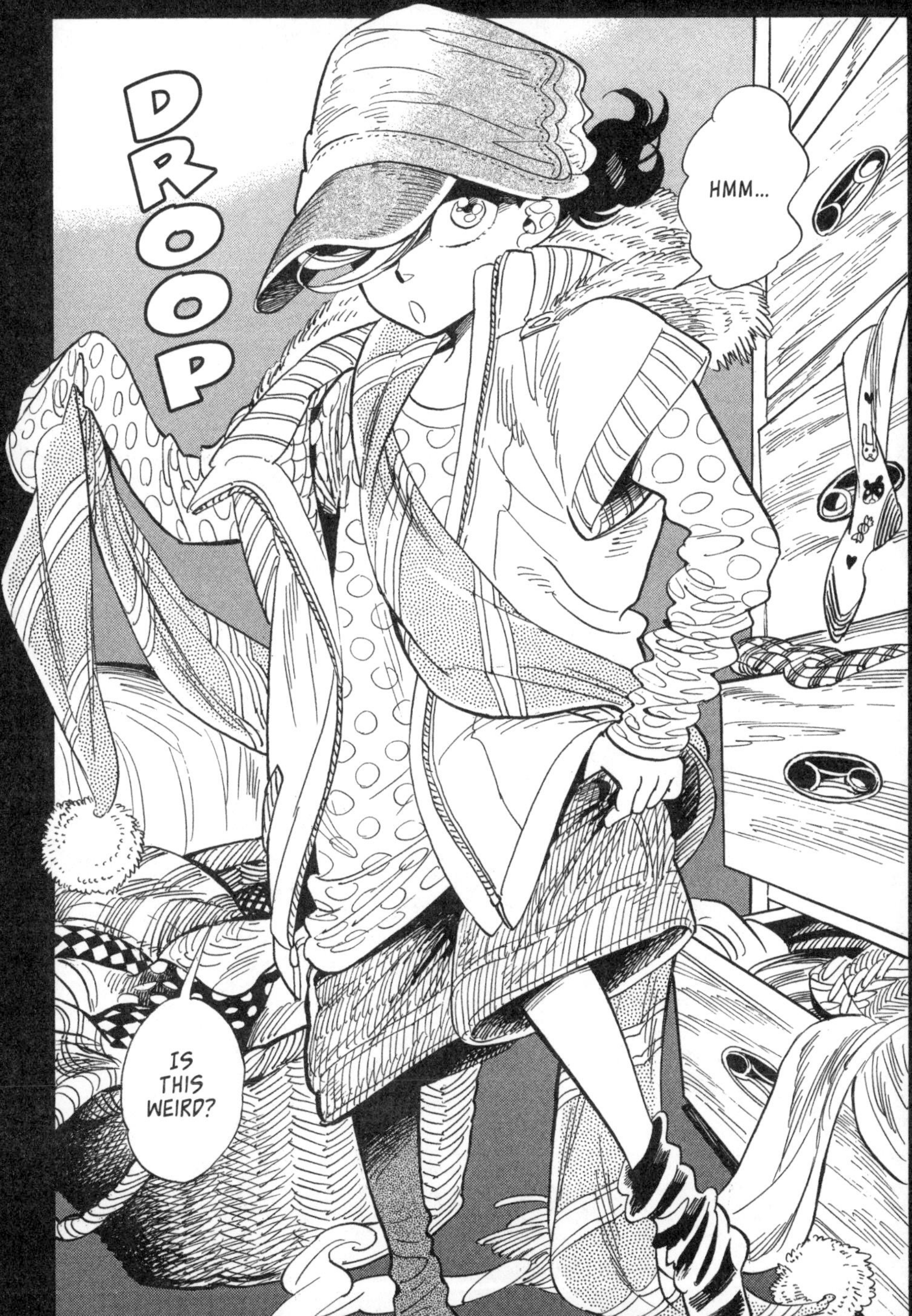
HMM...
DROOP
IS THIS WEIRD?

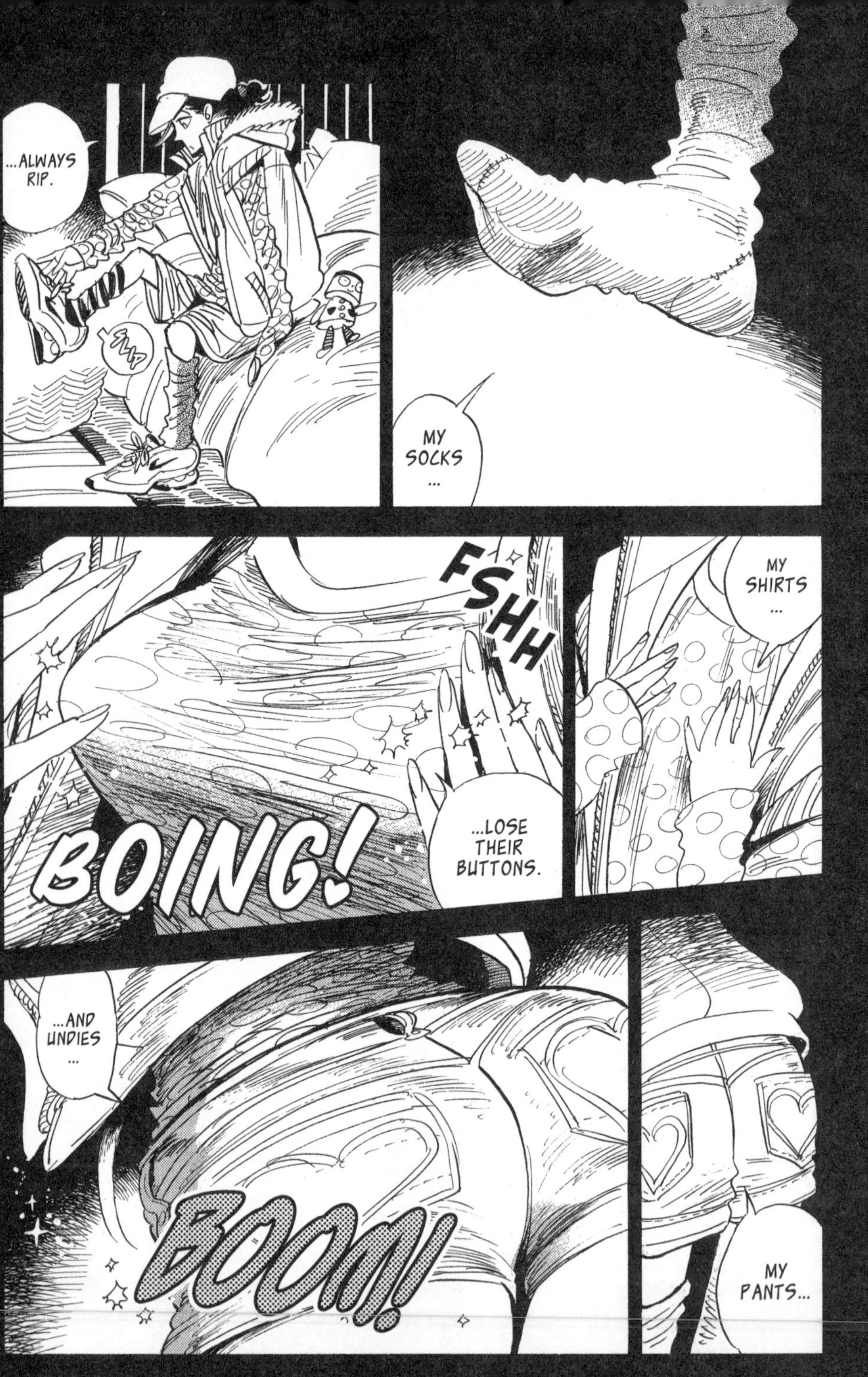
MY SOCKS ...
...ALWAYS RIP.
MY SHIRTS ...
FSHH
...LOSE THEIR BUTTONS.
BOING!
MY PANTS...
...AND UNDIES ...
BOOM!

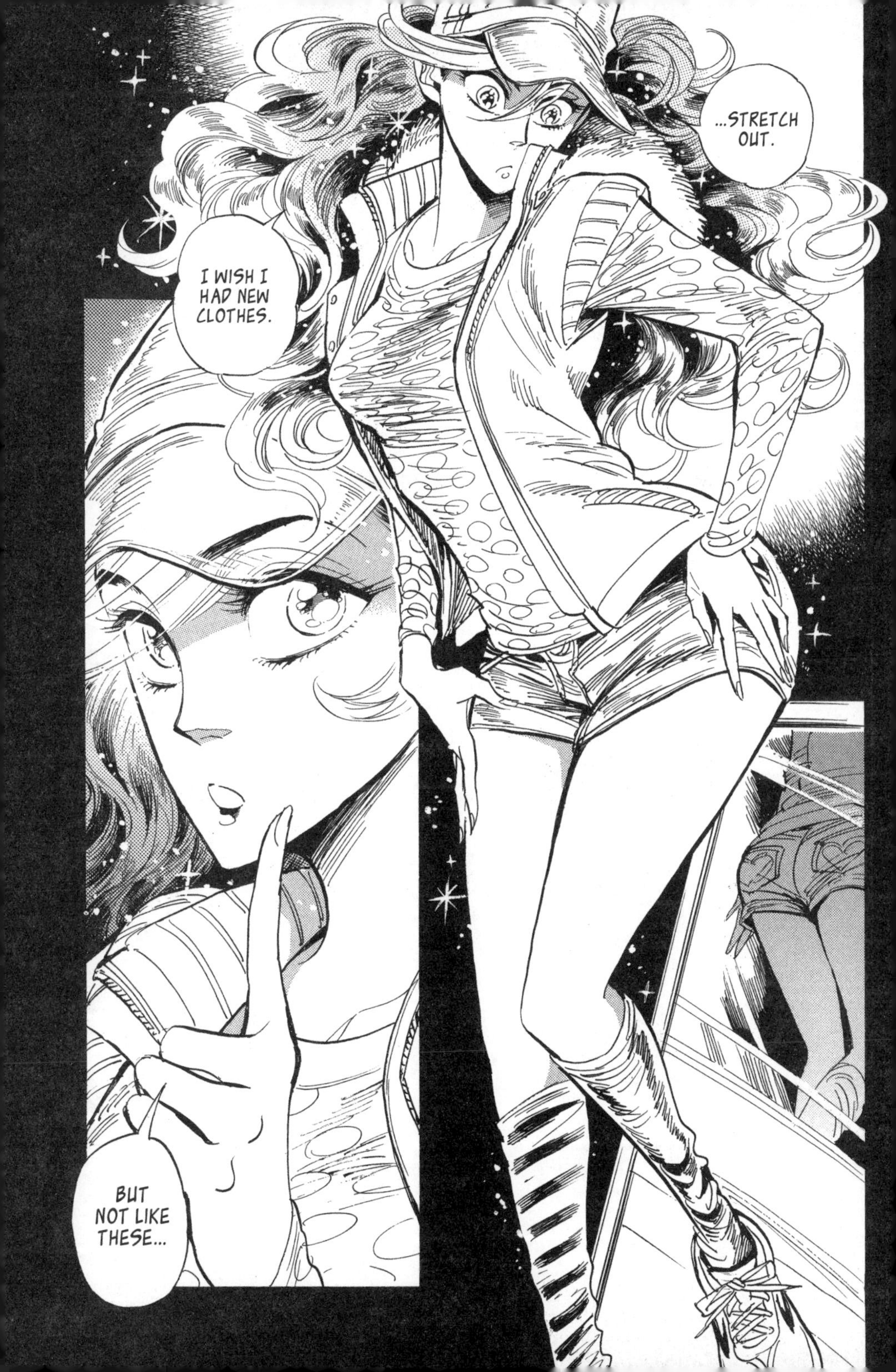
...STRETCH OUT.
I WISH I HAD NEW CLOTHES.
BUT NOT LIKE THESE...

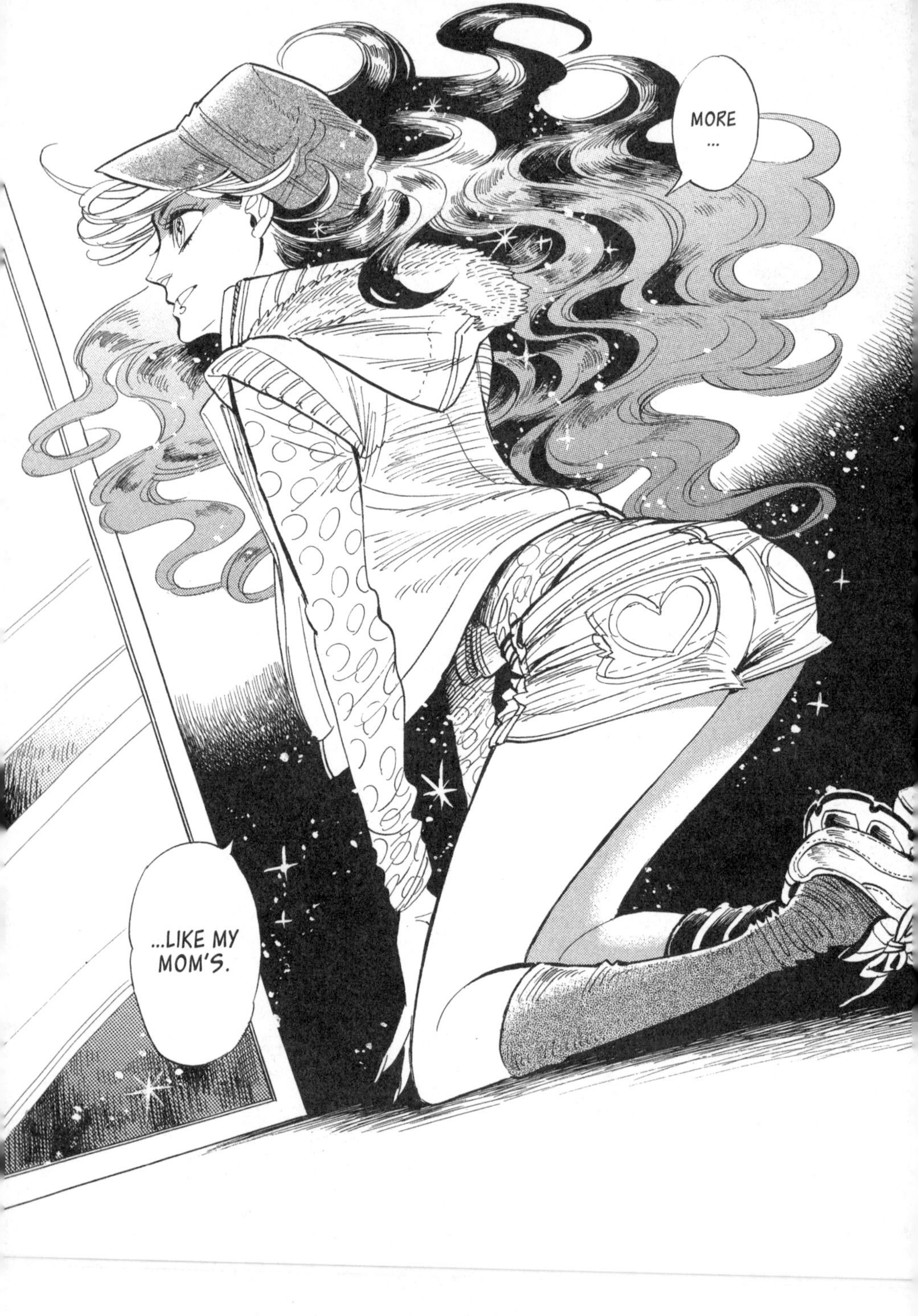
MORE ...
...LIKE MY MOM'S.

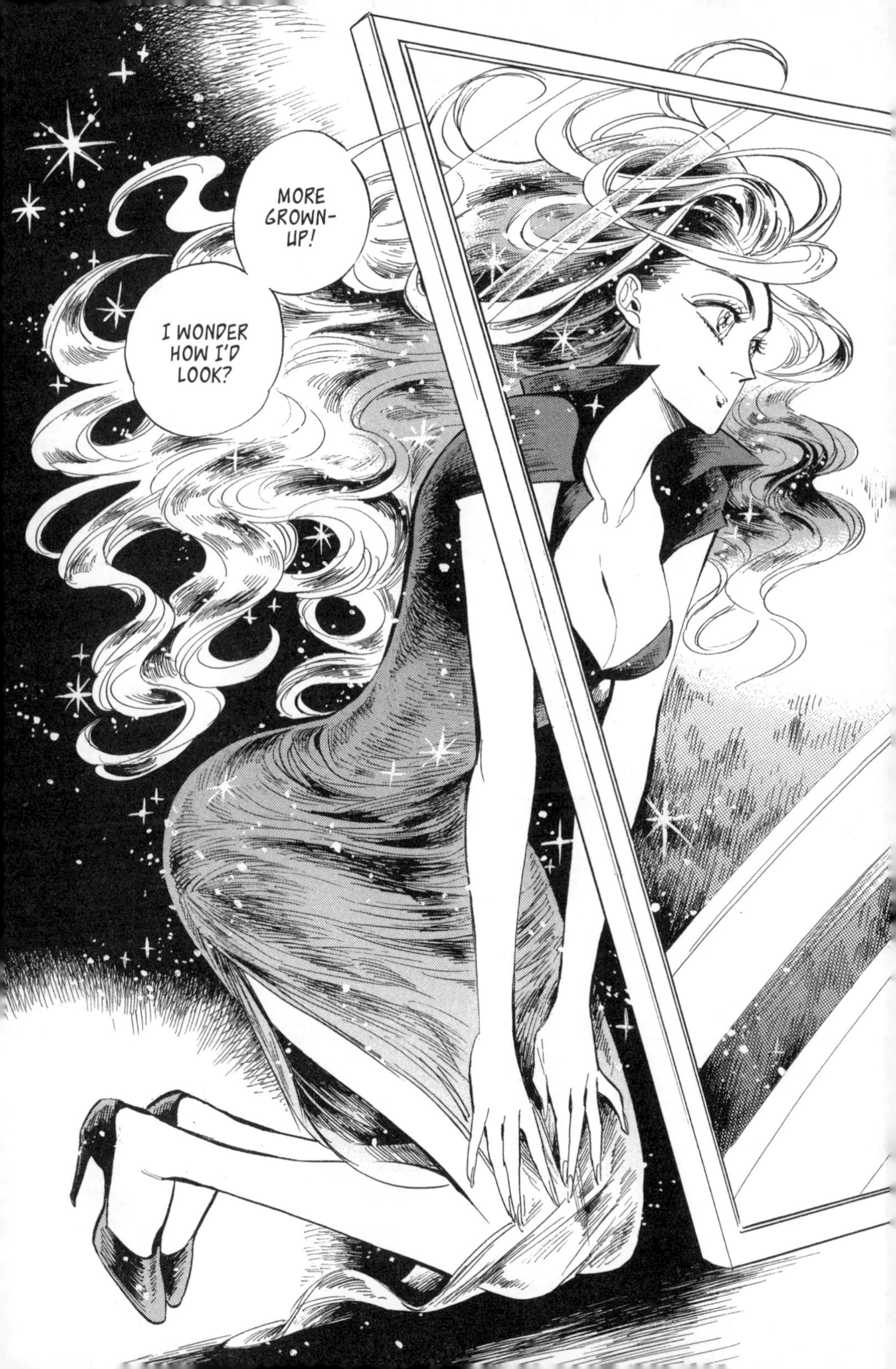
MORE GROWN-UP!
I WONDER HOW I'D LOOK?

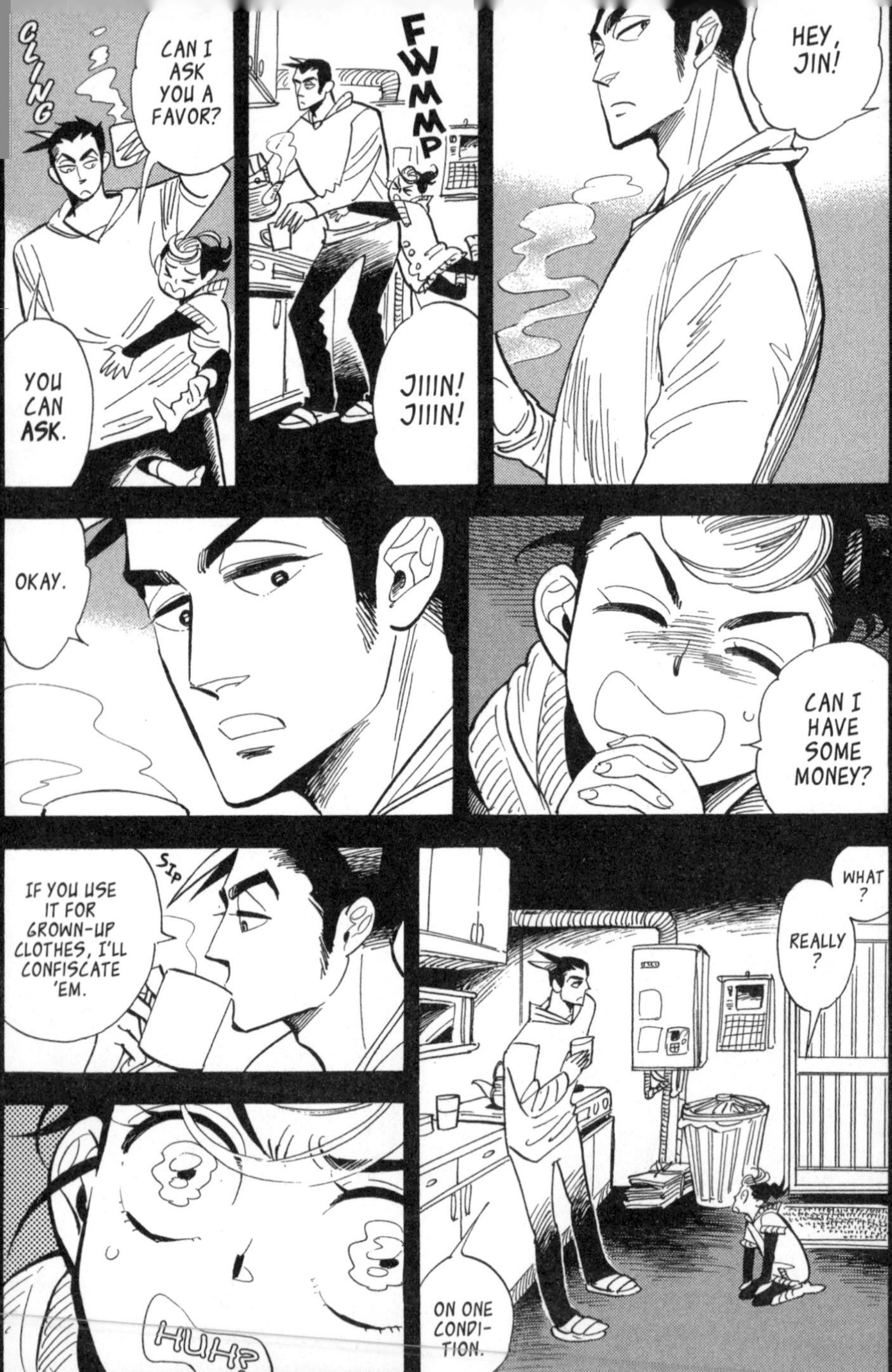
HEY, JIN!
FWMMP
JIIIN! JIIIN!
CLING
CAN I ASK YOU A FAVOR?
YOU CAN ASK.
CAN I HAVE SOME MONEY?
OKAY.
WHAT?
REALLY?
ON ONE CONDITION.
SIP
IF YOU USE IT FOR GROWN-UP CLOTHES, I'LL CONFISCATE 'EM.
HUH?

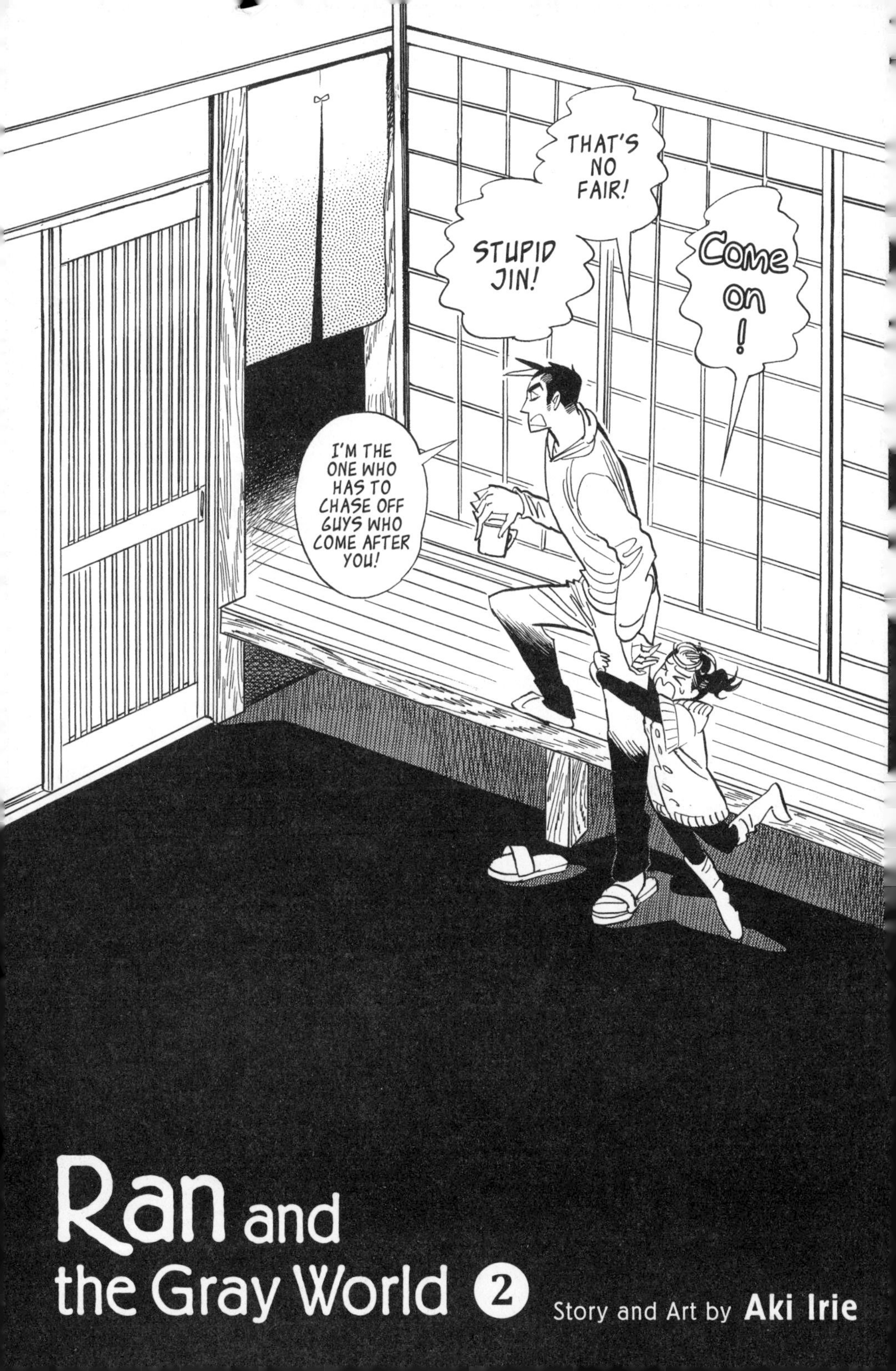
Come on!
THAT'S NO FAIR!
STUPID JIN!
I'M THE ONE WHO HAS TO CHASE OFF GUYS WHO COME AFTER YOU!

Ran and the Gray World 2

Story and Art by **Aki Irie**

Contents

Chapter 7

Tamao Arrives

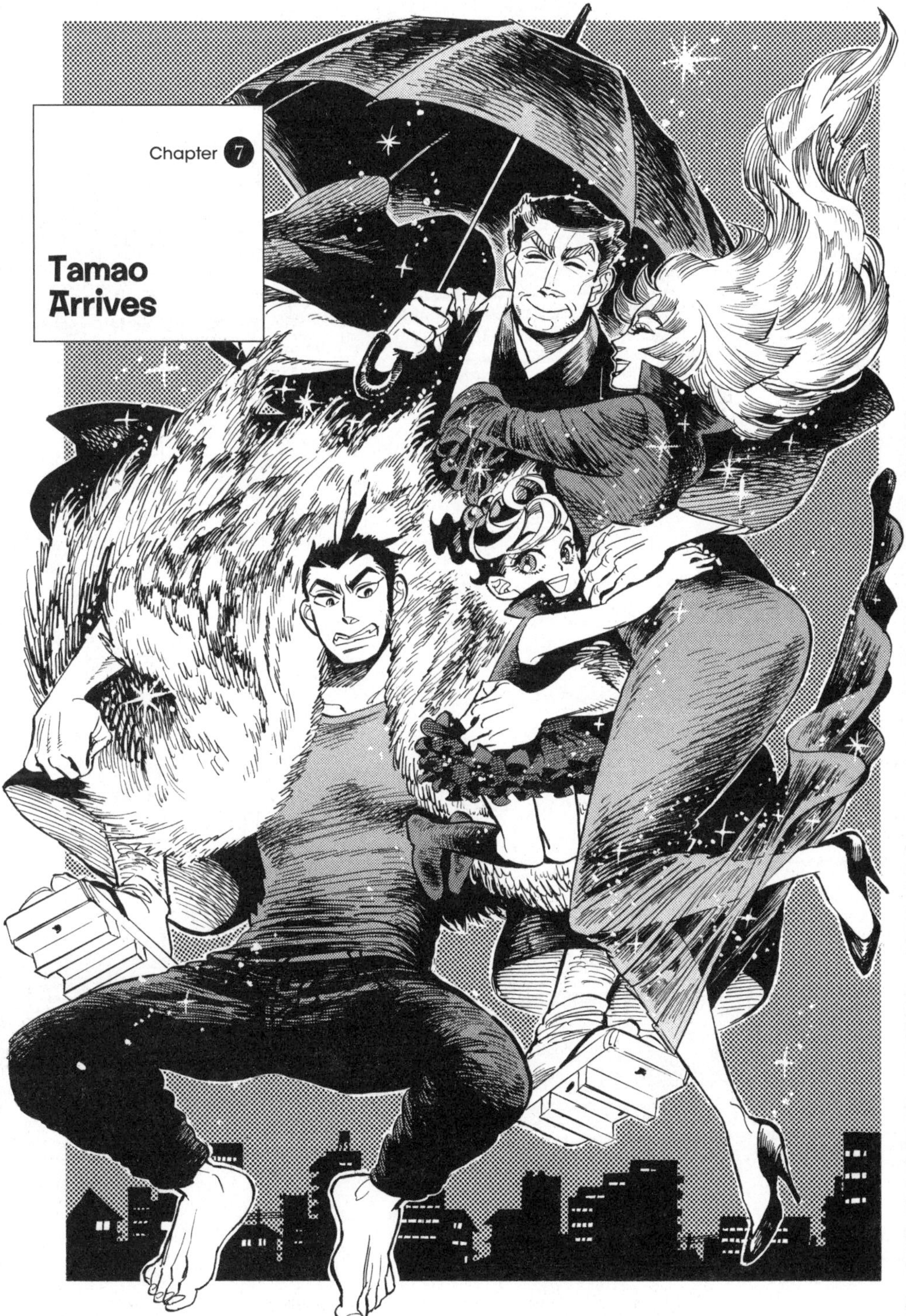

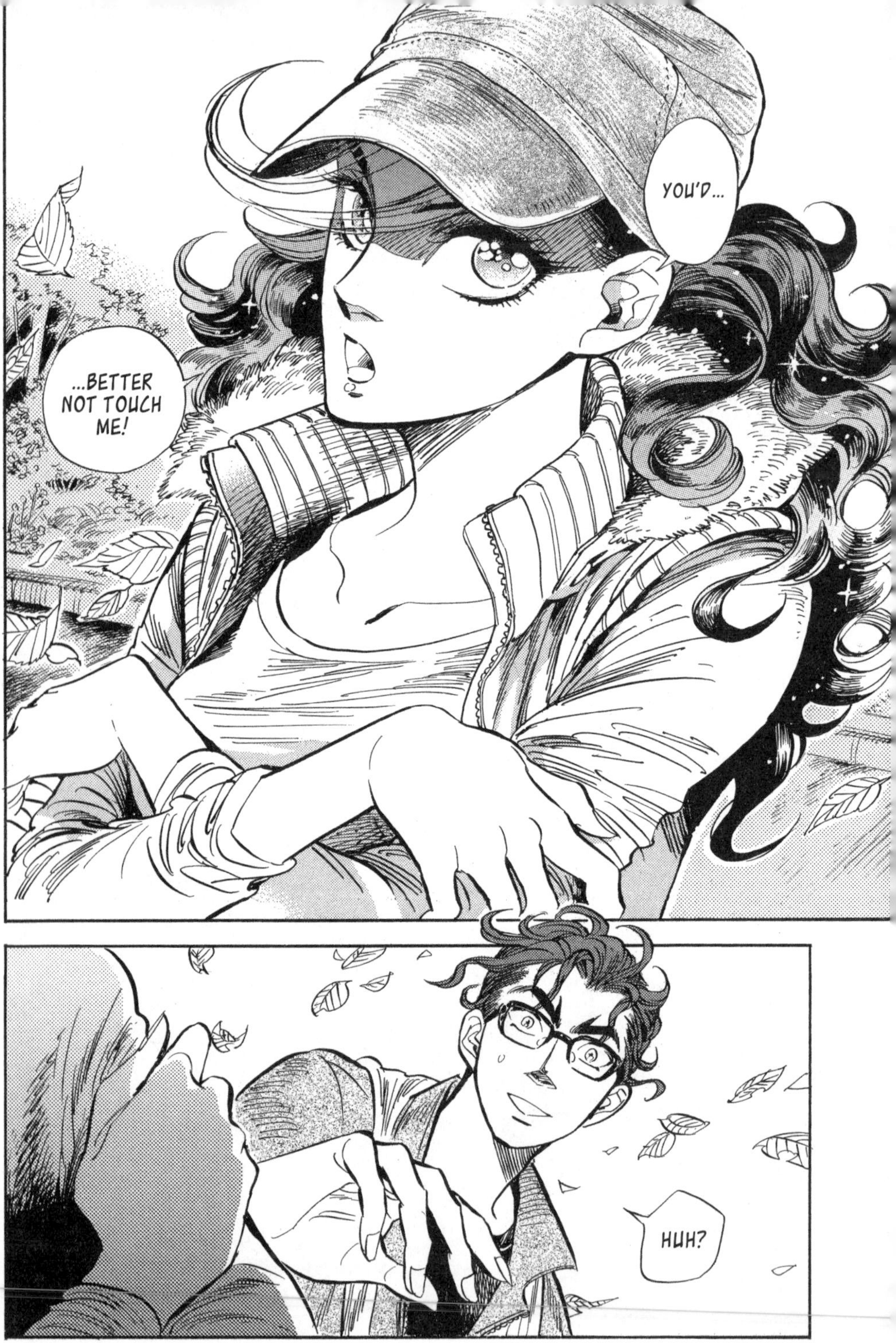
YOU'D...
...BETTER NOT TOUCH ME!
HUH?

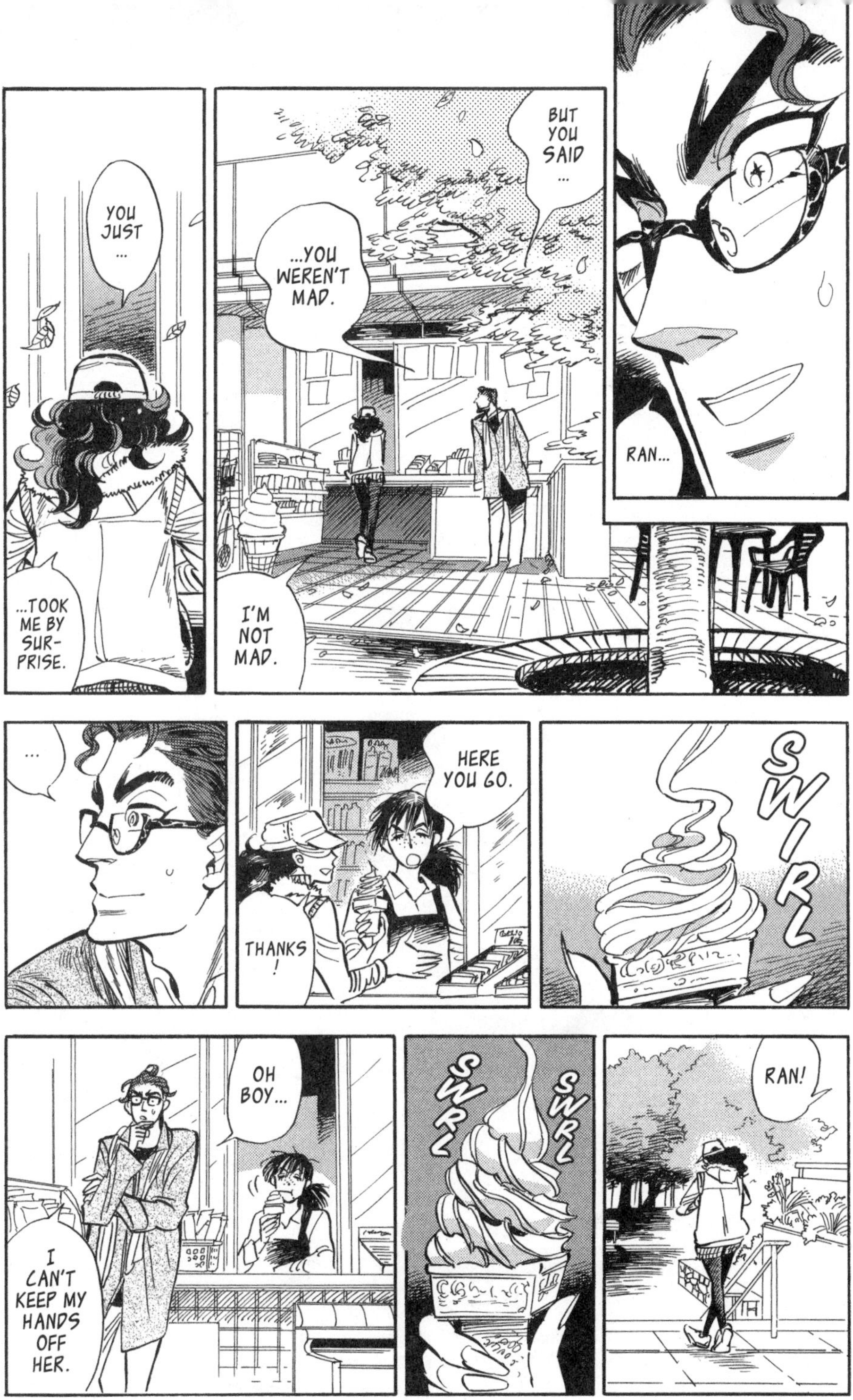
RAN...
BUT YOU SAID ...
...YOU WEREN'T MAD.
I'M NOT MAD.
YOU JUST ...
...TOOK ME BY SUR-PRISE.
SWIRL
HERE YOU GO.
THANKS!
...
RAN!
SWRL
SWRL
OH BOY...
I CAN'T KEEP MY HANDS OFF HER.

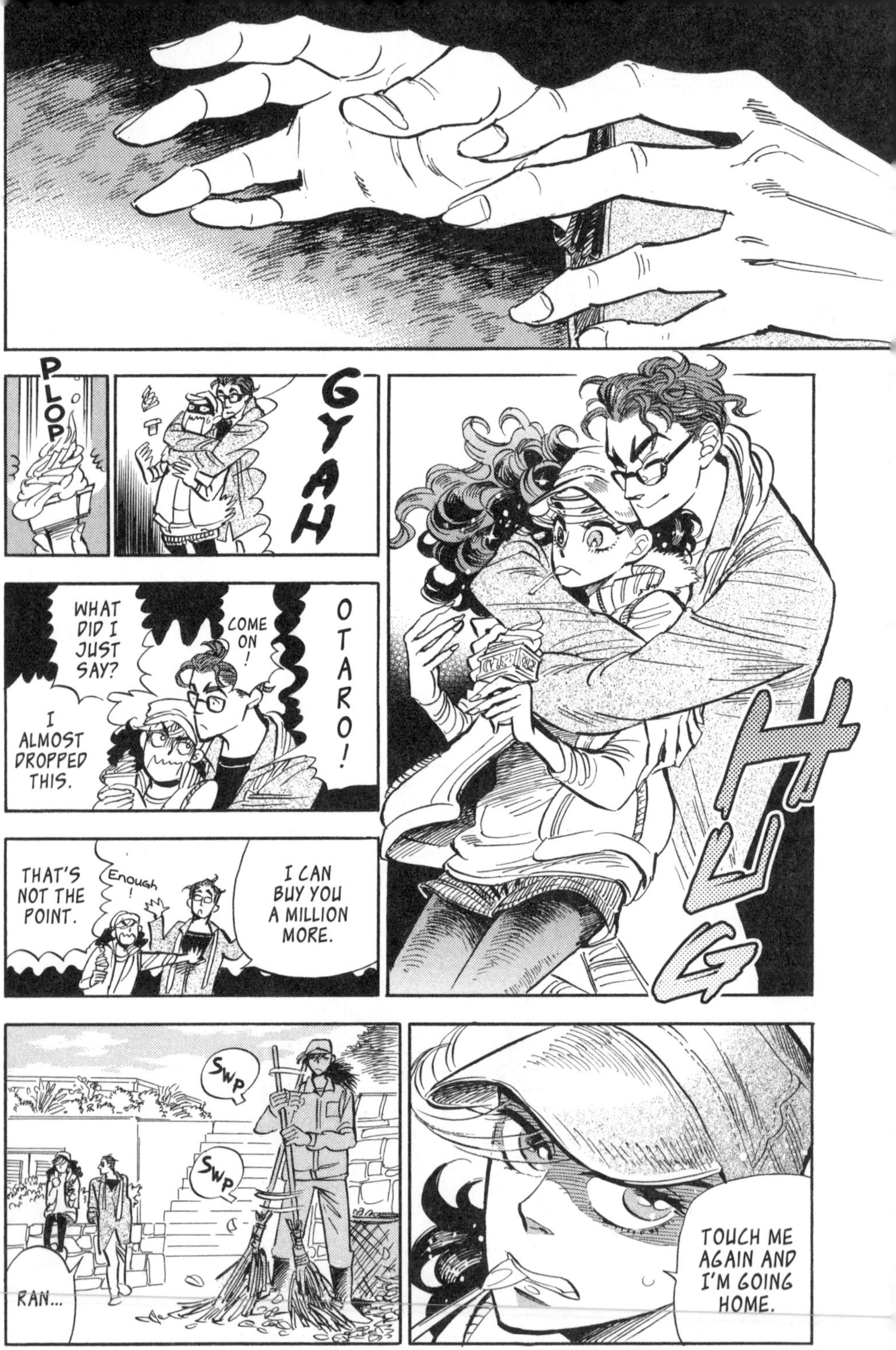
HUG
GYAH
PLOP
OTARO!
COME ON!
WHAT DID I JUST SAY?
I ALMOST DROPPED THIS.
I CAN BUY YOU A MILLION MORE.
Enough!
THAT'S NOT THE POINT.
TOUCH ME AGAIN AND I'M GOING HOME.
SWP
SWP
RAN...

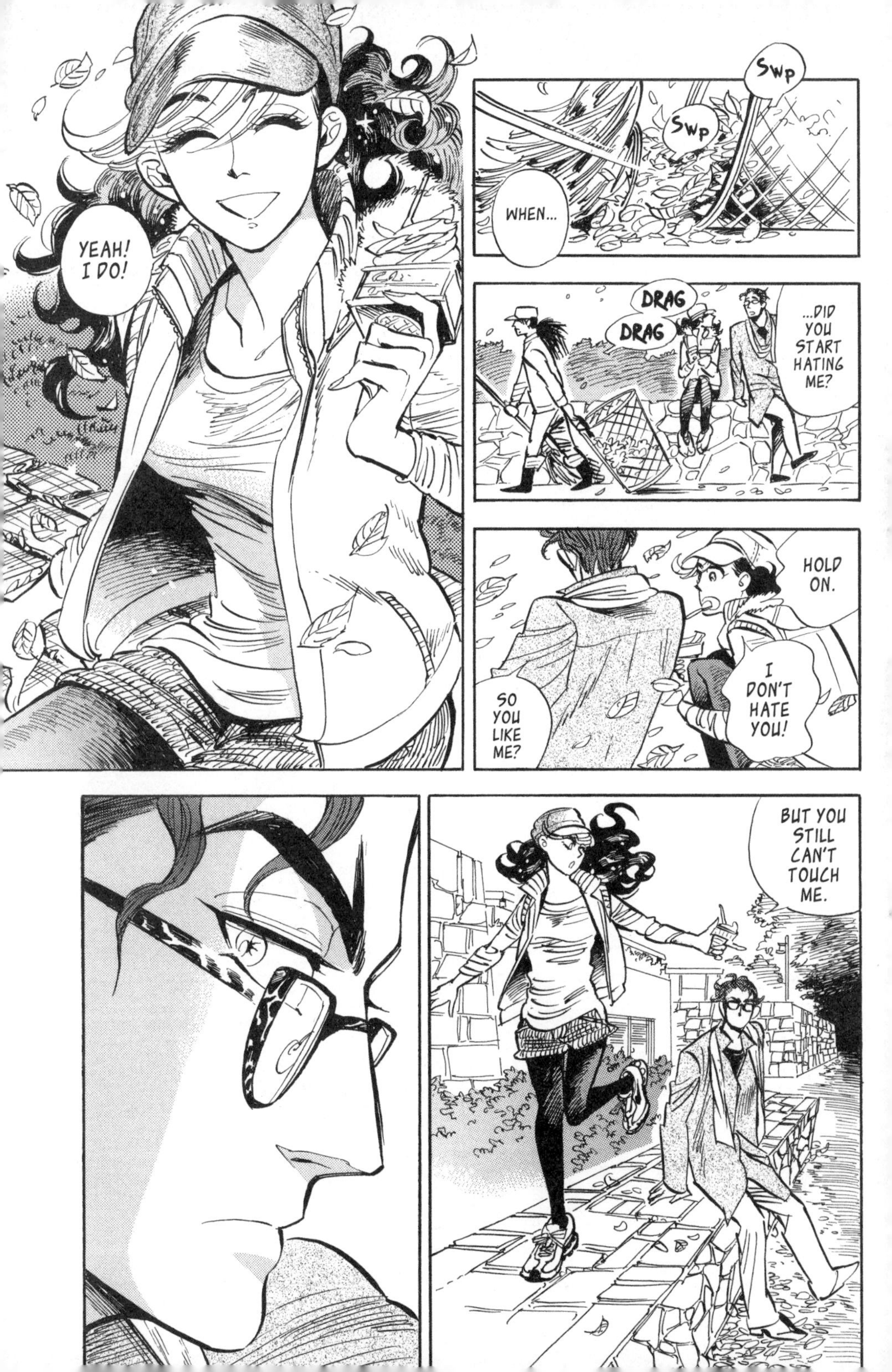
Swp
Swp
WHEN...
DRAG
DRAG
...DID YOU START HATING ME?
HOLD ON.
I DON'T HATE YOU!
SO YOU LIKE ME?
YEAH! I DO!
BUT YOU STILL CAN'T TOUCH ME.

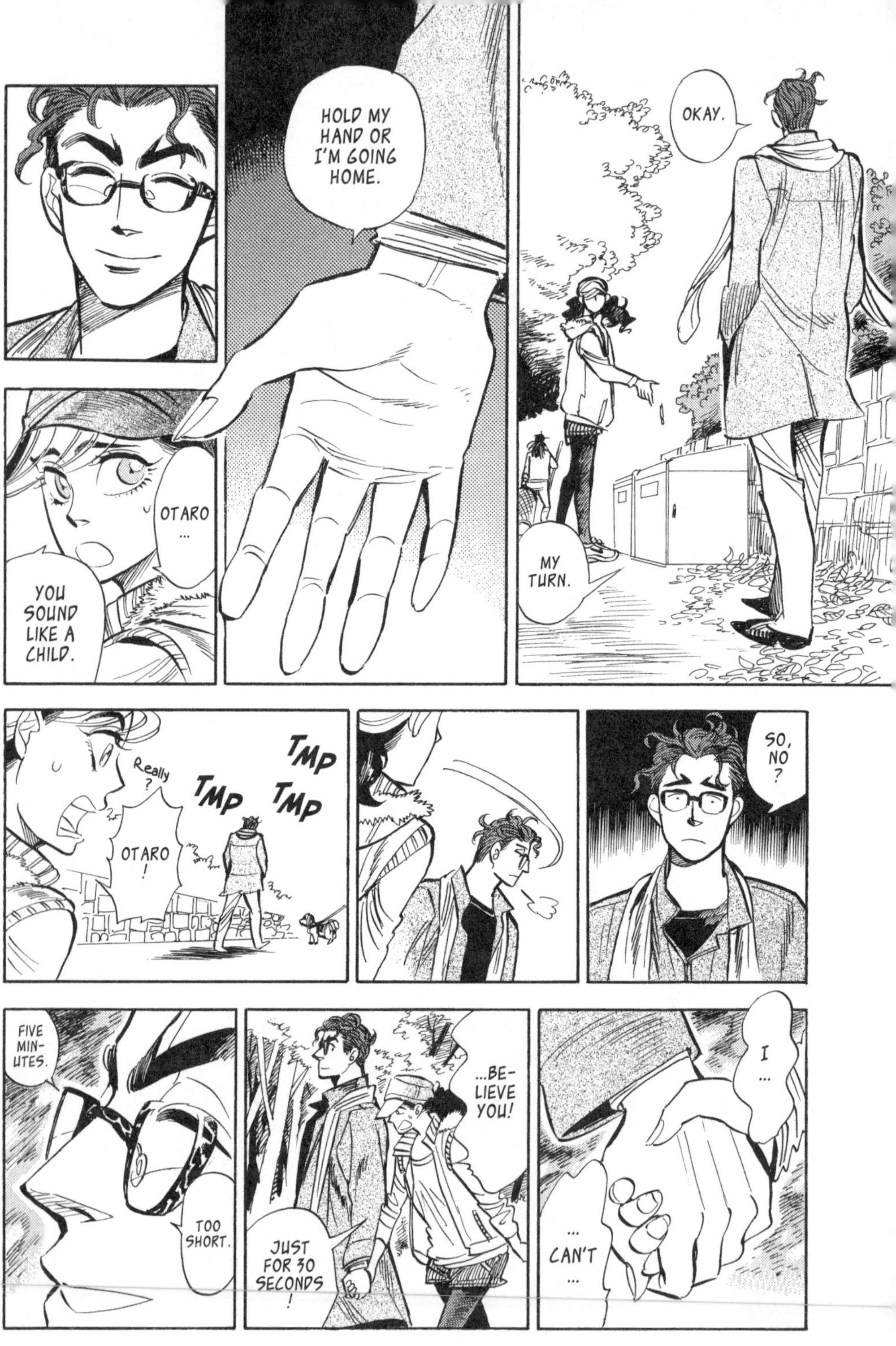
OKAY.
MY TURN.
HOLD MY HAND OR I'M GOING HOME.
OTARO ...
YOU SOUND LIKE A CHILD.
SO, NO?
TMP TMP TMP
Really?
OTARO!
I ...
... CAN'T ...
...BE-LIEVE YOU!
JUST FOR 30 SECONDS!
FIVE MIN-UTES.
TOO SHORT.

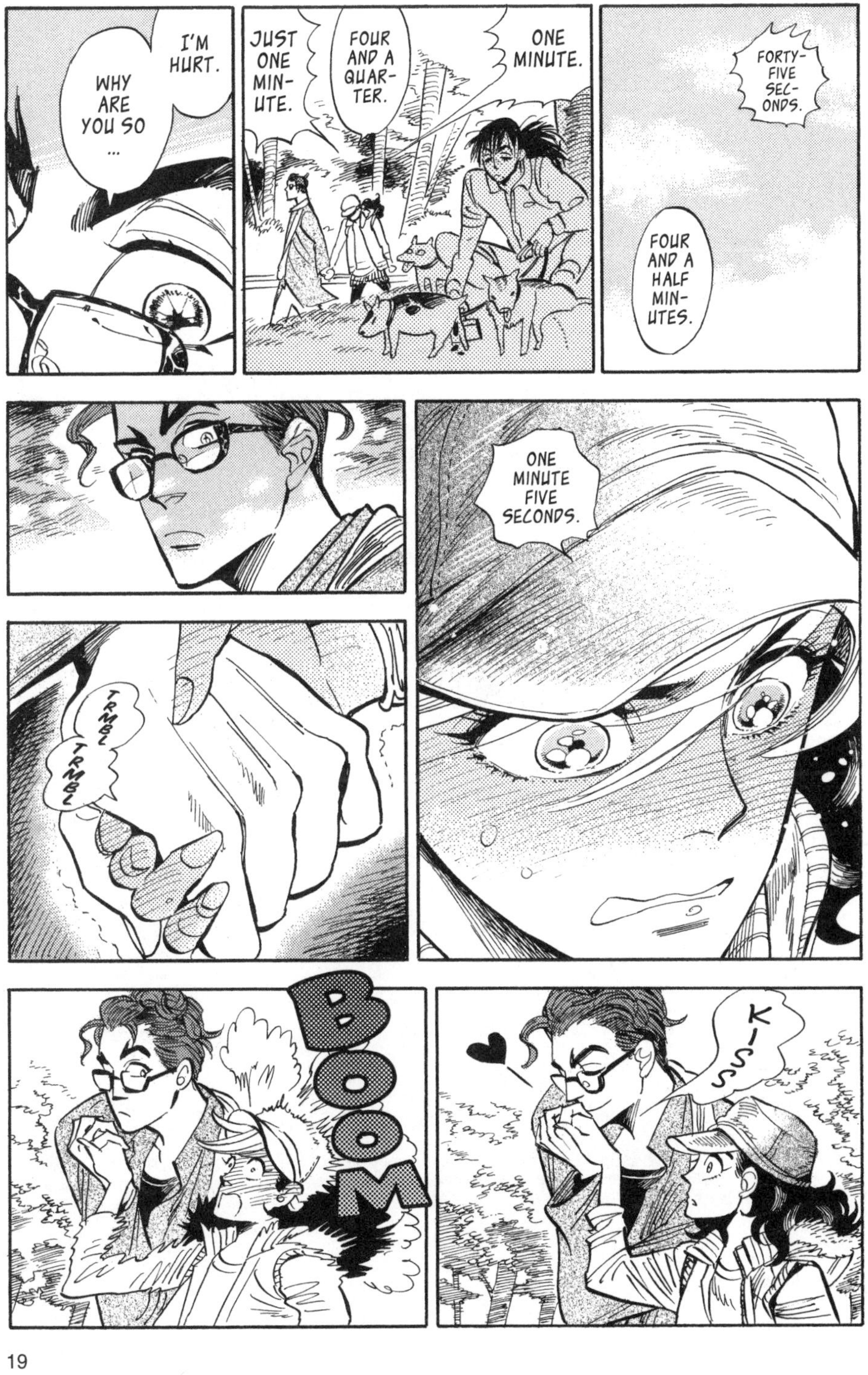
FORTY-FIVE SECONDS.
FOUR AND A HALF MINUTES.
ONE MINUTE.
FOUR AND A QUARTER.
JUST ONE MINUTE.
I'M HURT.
WHY ARE YOU SO ...
ONE MINUTE FIVE SECONDS.
TRMBL TRMBL
KISS
BOOM

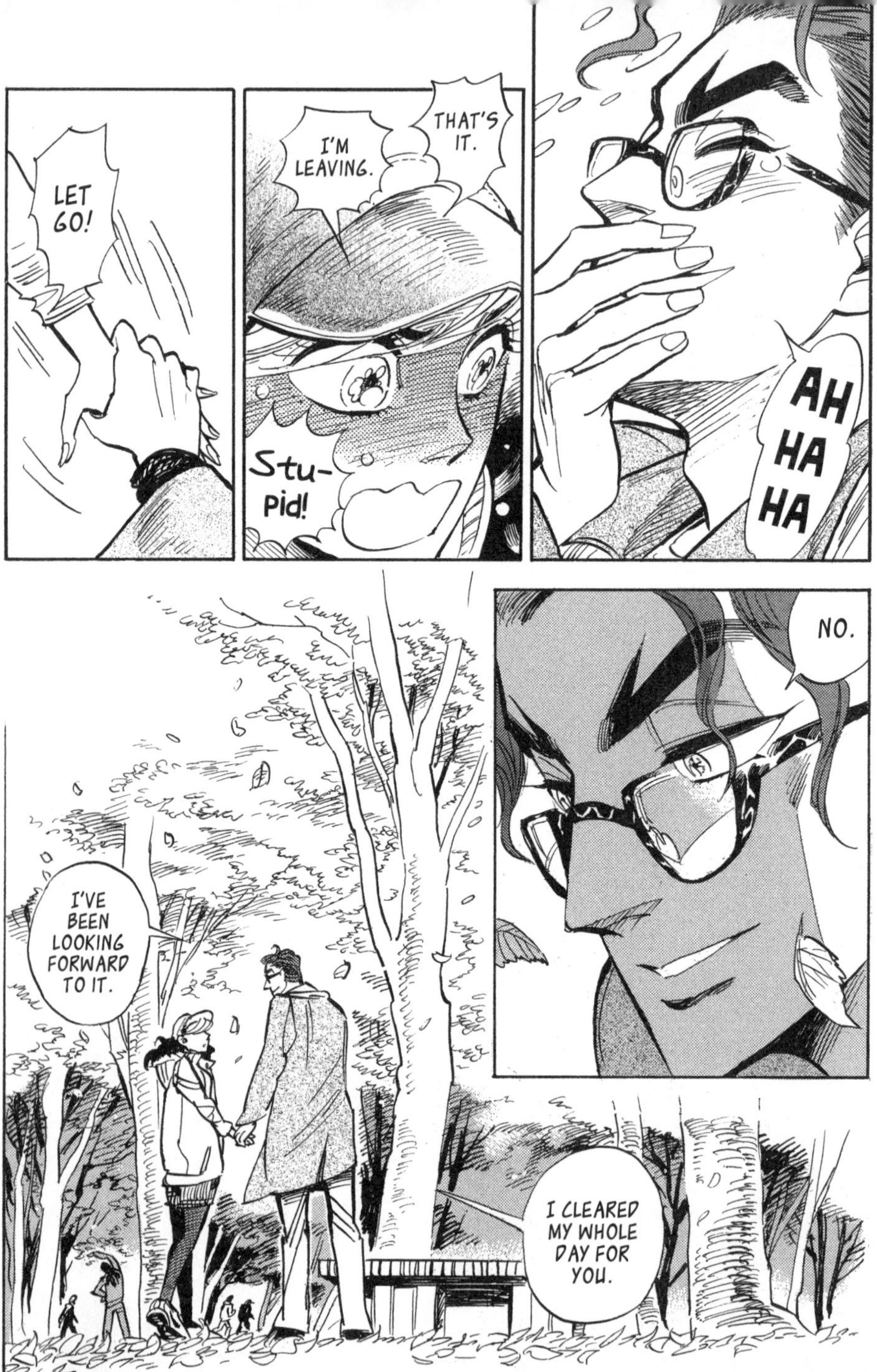
AH HA HA
THAT'S IT.
I'M LEAVING.
Stu-pid!
LET GO!
NO.
I'VE BEEN LOOKING FORWARD TO IT.
I CLEARED MY WHOLE DAY FOR YOU.

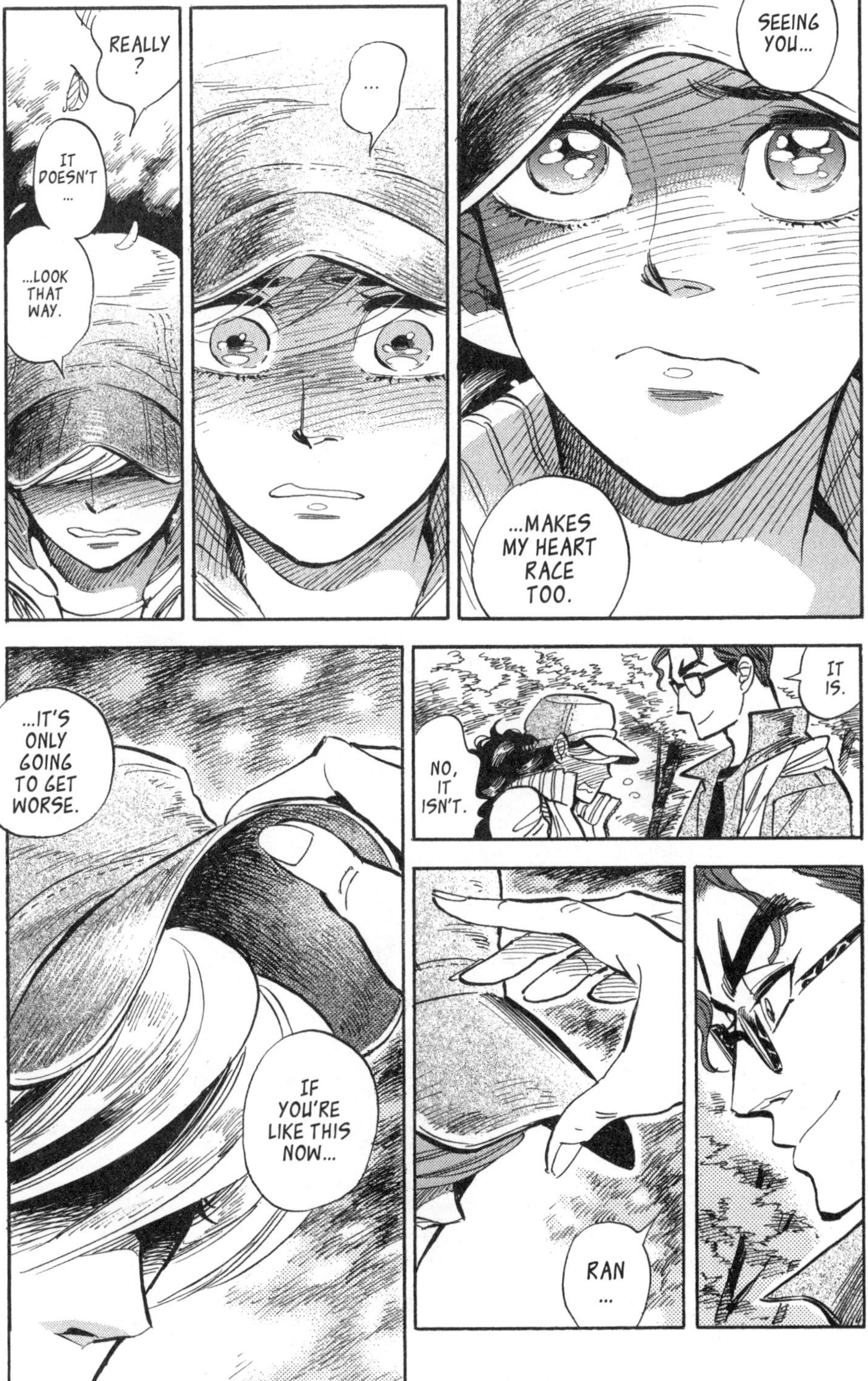
SEEING YOU...
...MAKES MY HEART RACE TOO.
...
REALLY?
IT DOESN'T...
...LOOK THAT WAY.
IT IS.
NO, IT ISN'T.
RAN...
IF YOU'RE LIKE THIS NOW...
...IT'S ONLY GOING TO GET WORSE.

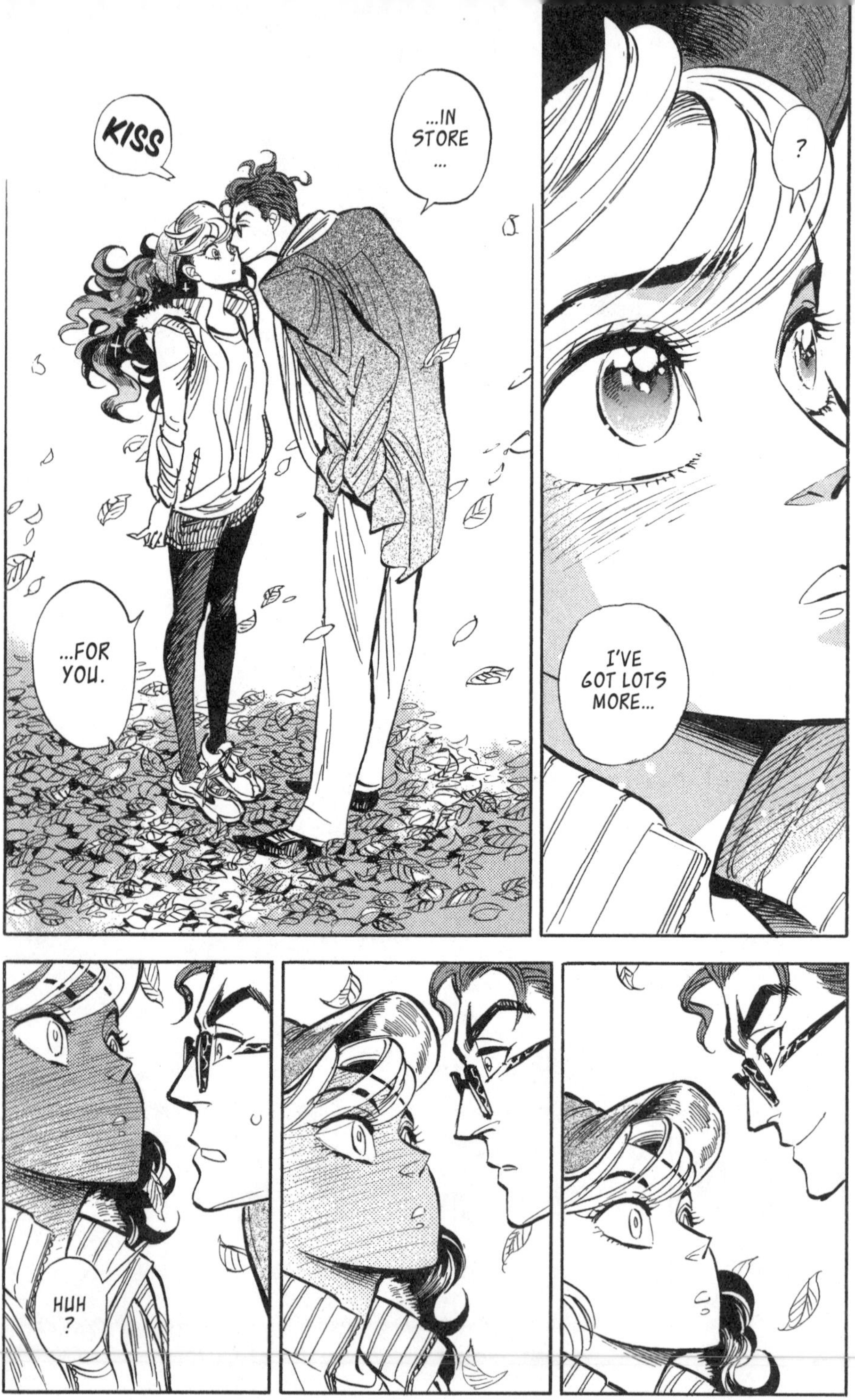
?
I'VE GOT LOTS MORE...
...IN STORE ...
KISS
...FOR YOU.
HUH ?

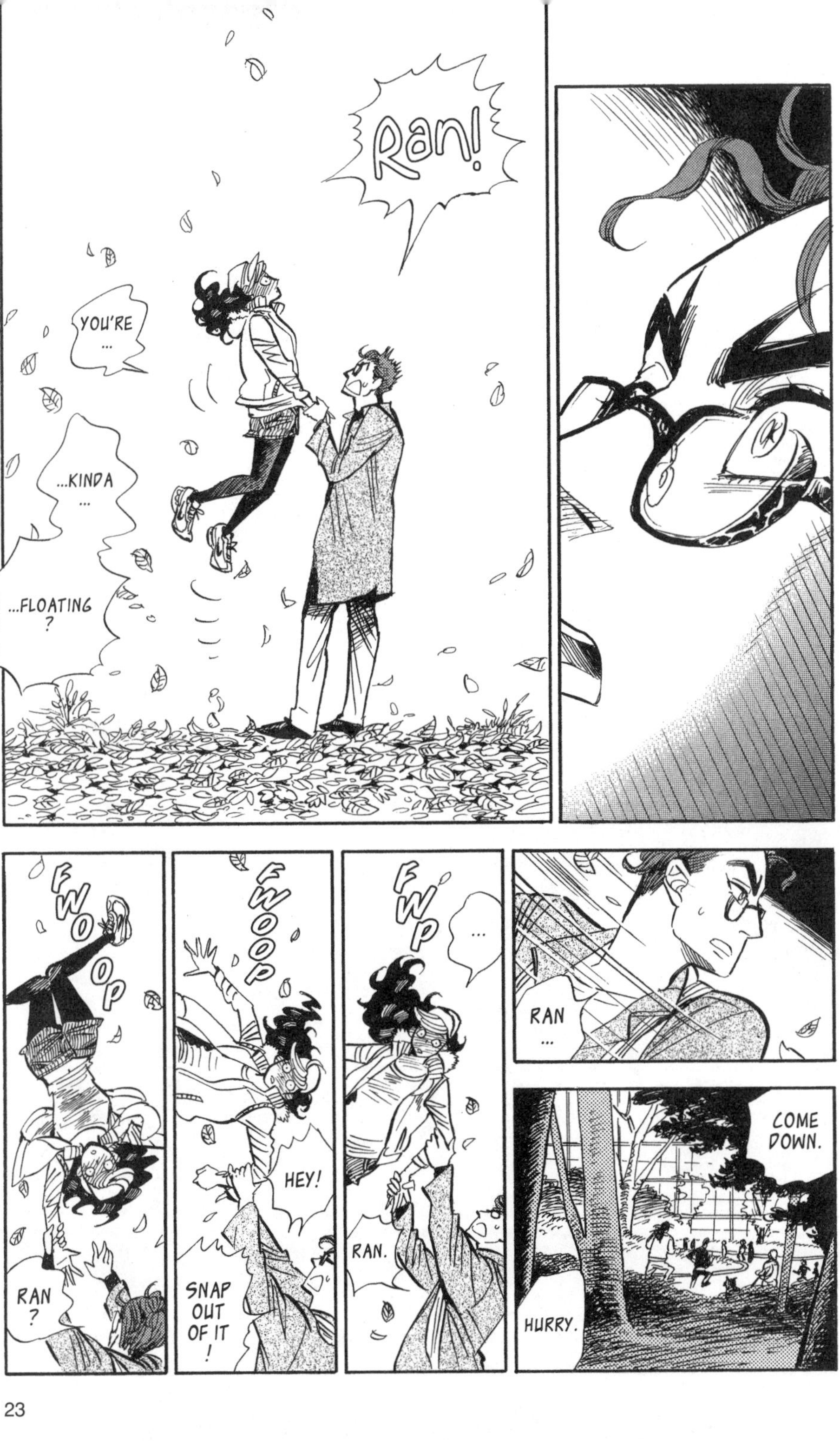
RAN!
YOU'RE ...
...KINDA ...
...FLOATING ?
RAN ...
COME DOWN.
HURRY.
FWP
...
RAN.
FWOOOP
HEY!
SNAP OUT OF IT !
FWOOOP
RAN ?

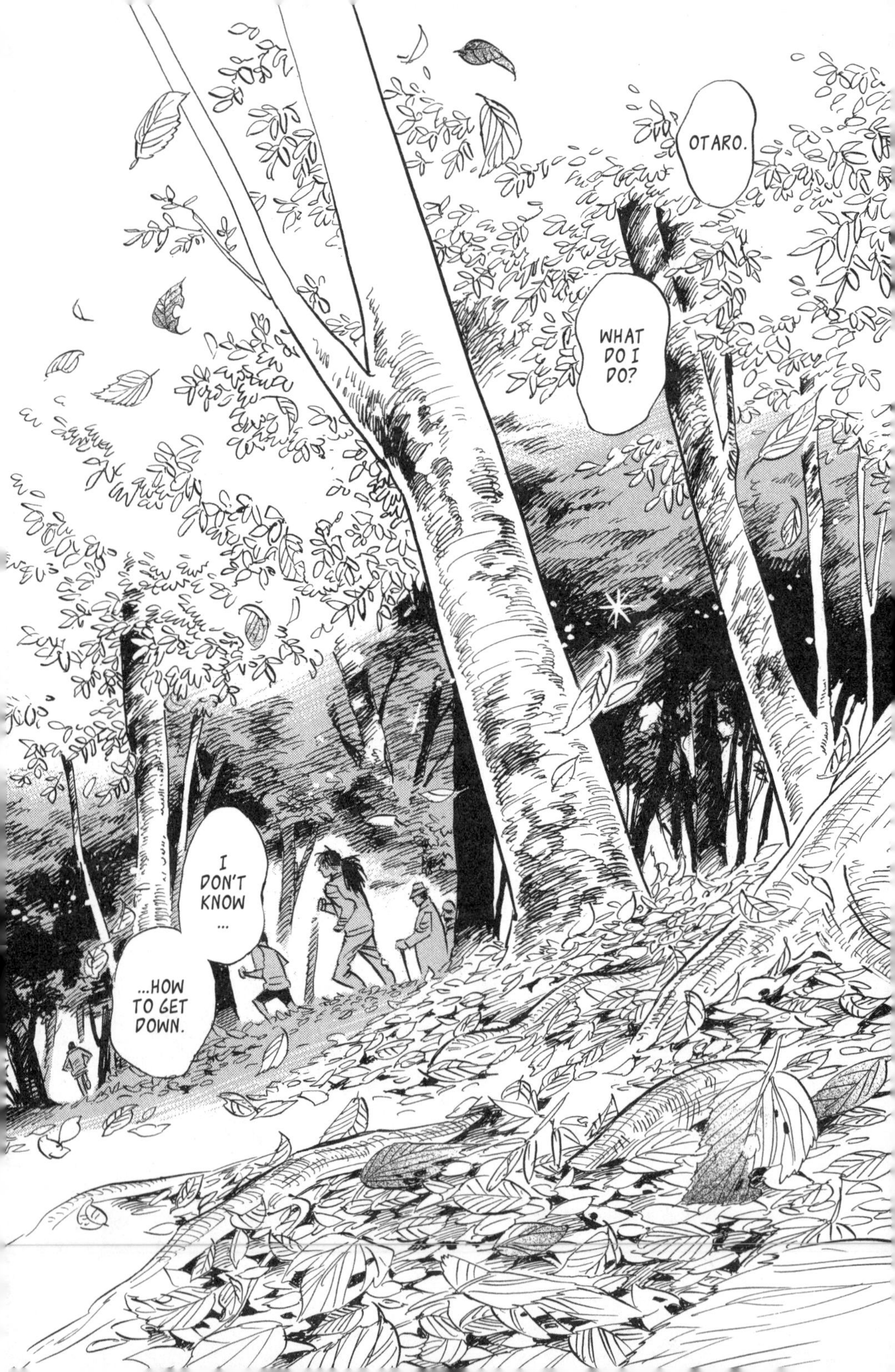
OTARO.
WHAT DO I DO?
I DON'T KNOW ...
...HOW TO GET DOWN.

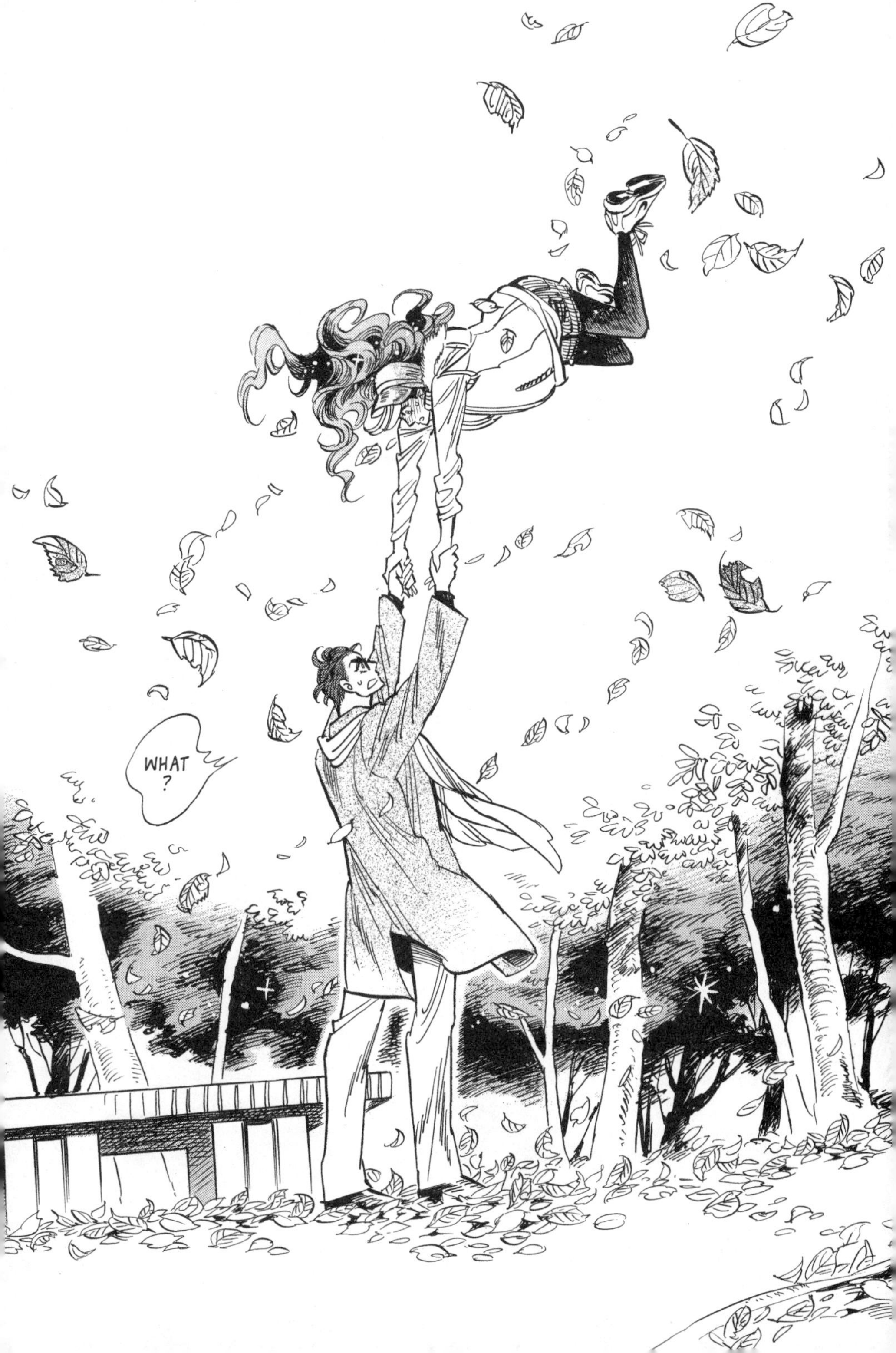
WHAT?

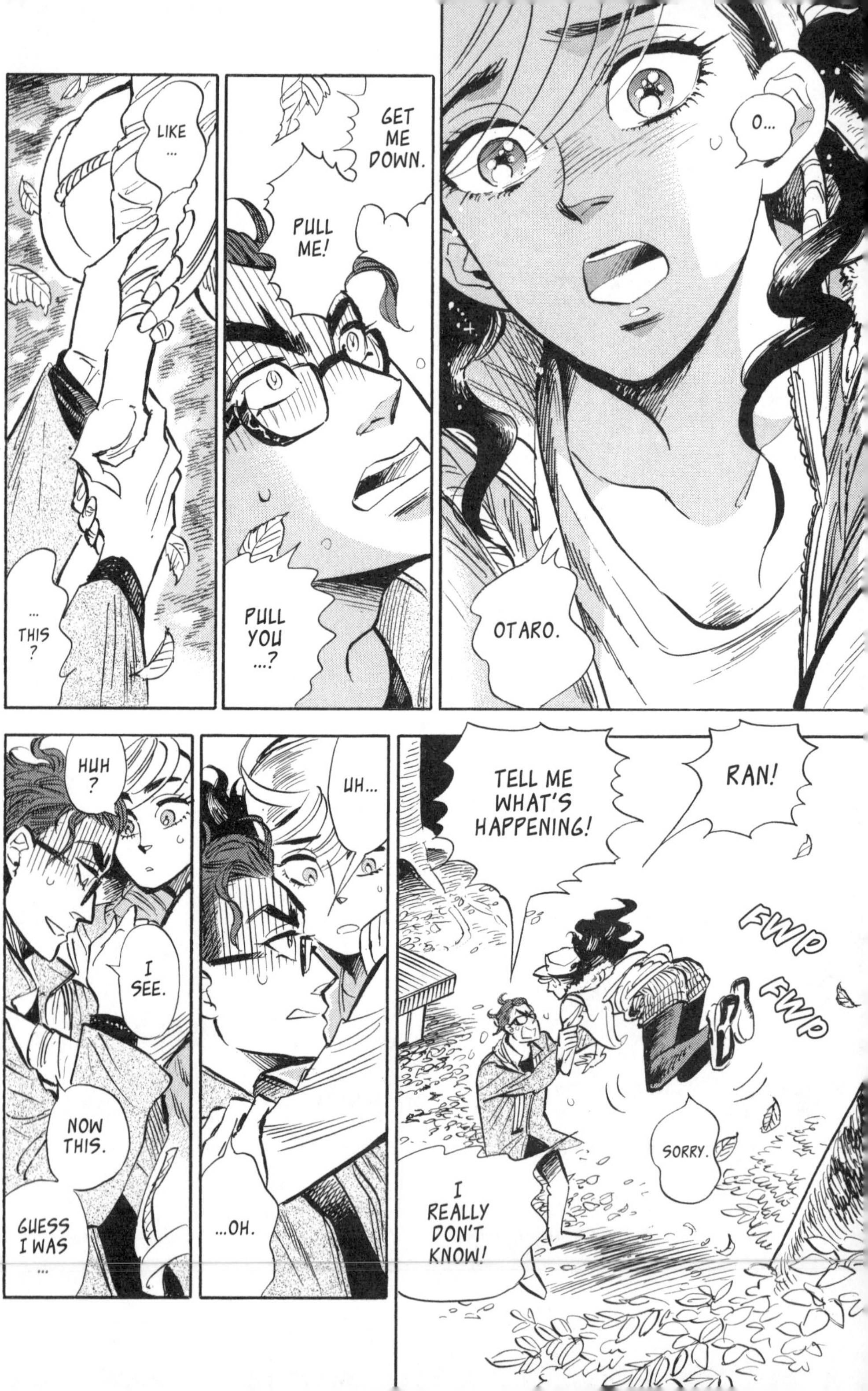
O...
OTARO.
GET ME DOWN.
PULL ME!
PULL YOU ...?
LIKE ...
... THIS ?
RAN!
TELL ME WHAT'S HAPPENING!
FWP
FWP
SORRY.
I REALLY DON'T KNOW!
UH...
...OH.
HUH ?
I SEE.
NOW THIS.
GUESS I WAS ...

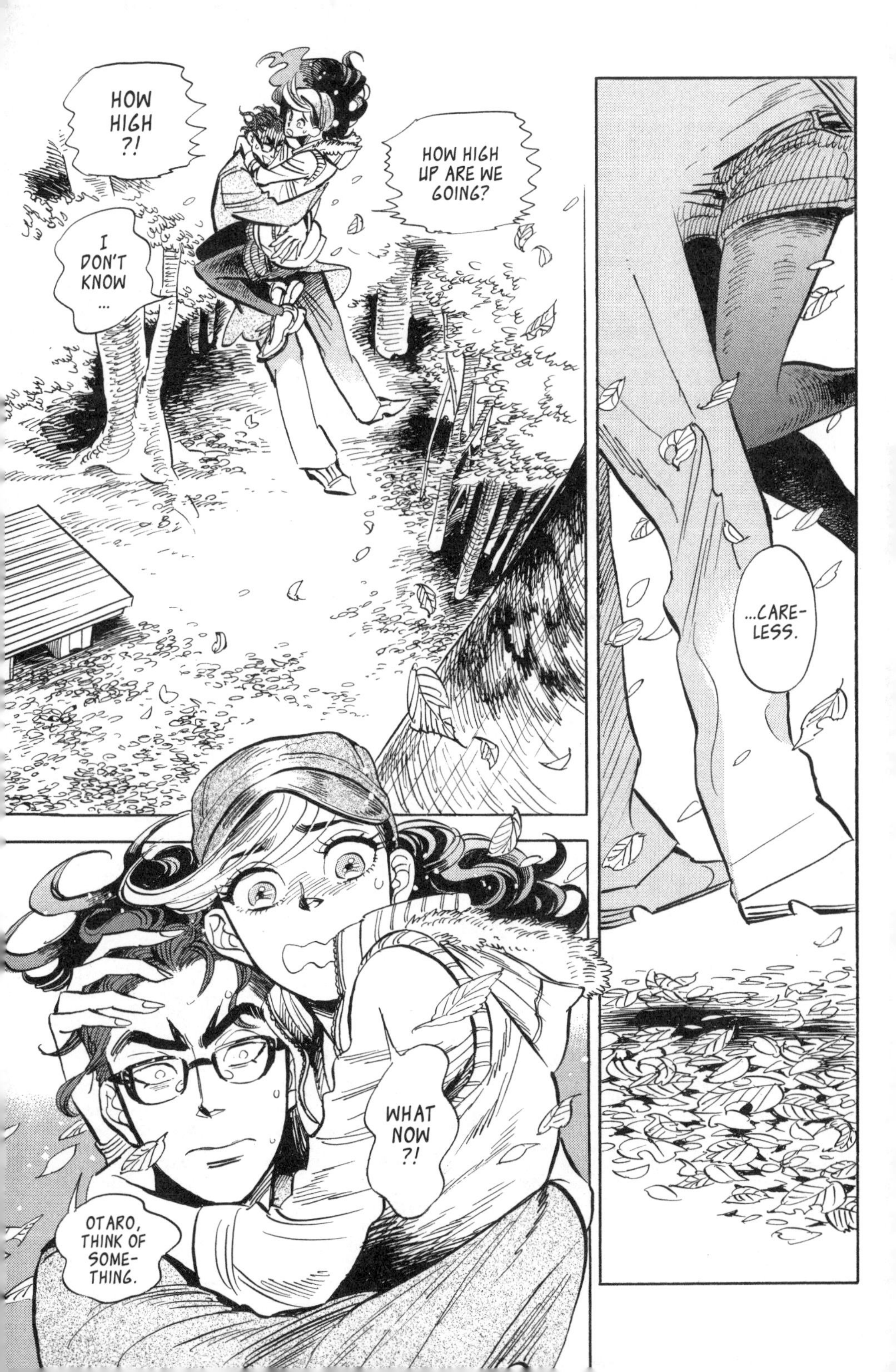
...CARE-LESS.
HOW HIGH UP ARE WE GOING?
HOW HIGH ?!
I DON'T KNOW ...
WHAT NOW ?!
OTARO, THINK OF SOME-THING.

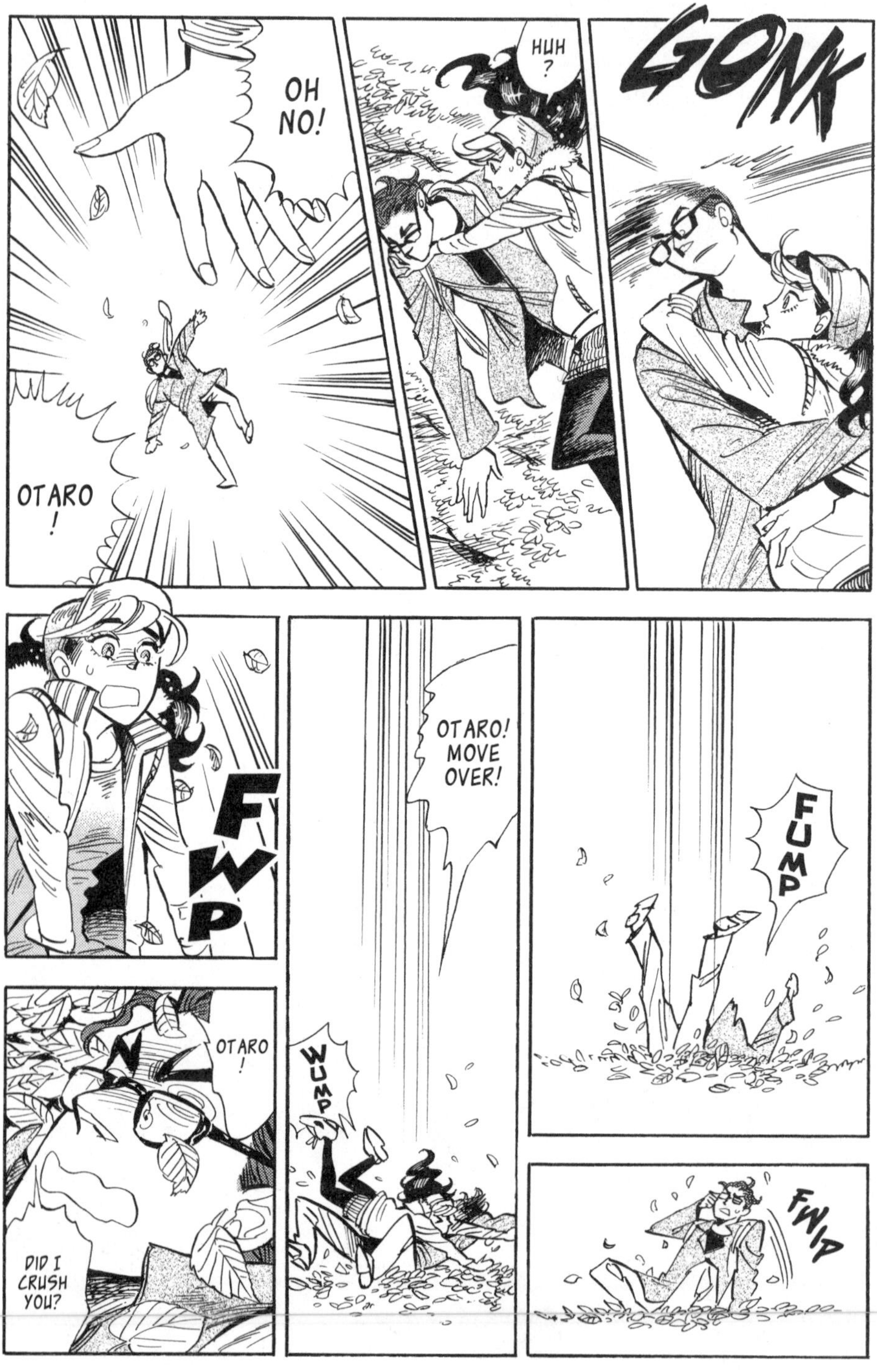
GONK
HUH ?
OH NO!
OTARO !
FUMP
FWIP
OTARO! MOVE OVER!
WUMP
FWP
OTARO !
DID I CRUSH YOU?

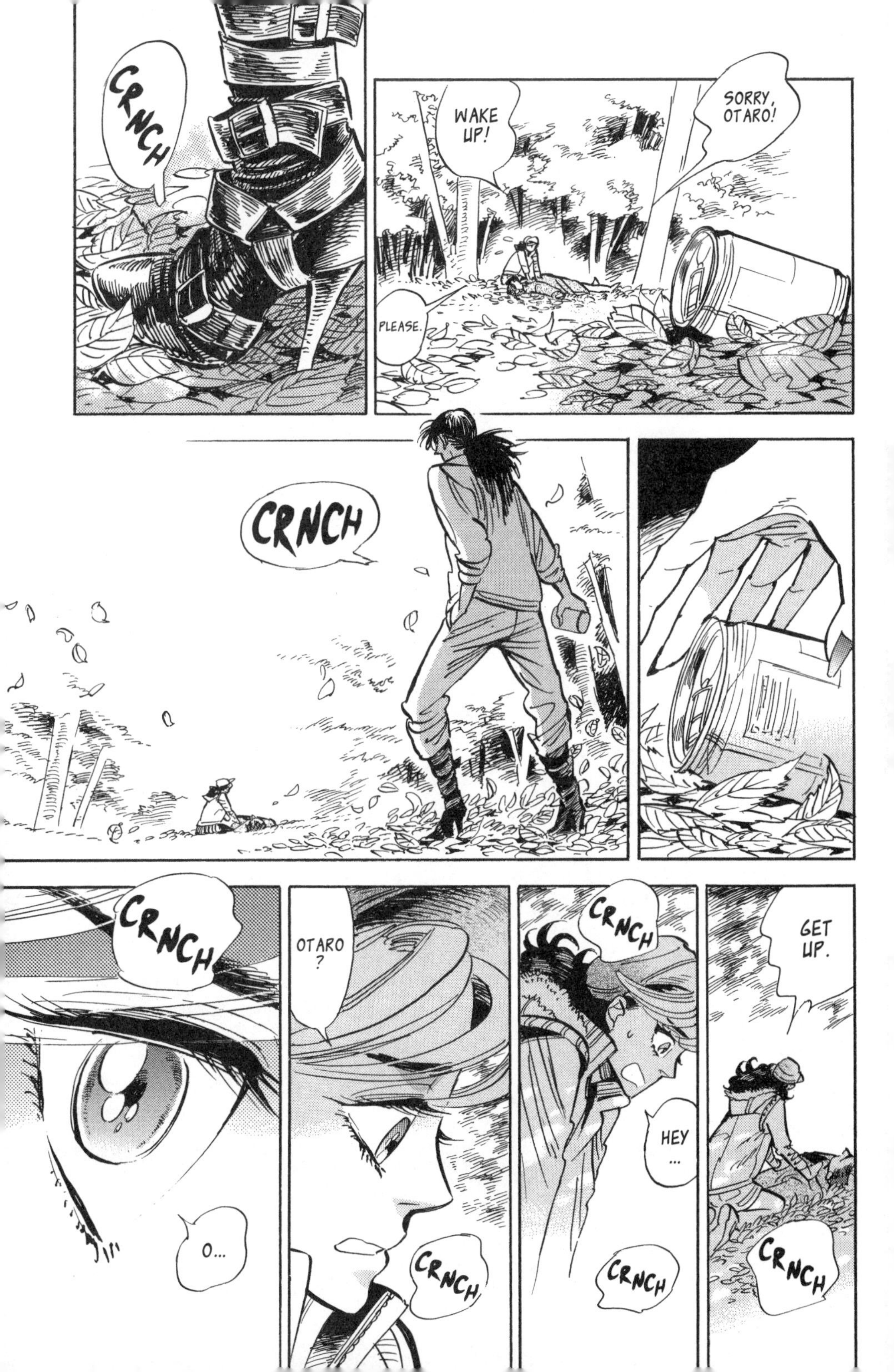
SORRY, OTARO!
WAKE UP!
PLEASE.
CRNCH
CRNCH
GET UP.
CRNCH
CRNCH
HEY ...
CRNCH
OTARO ?
CRNCH
CRNCH
O...

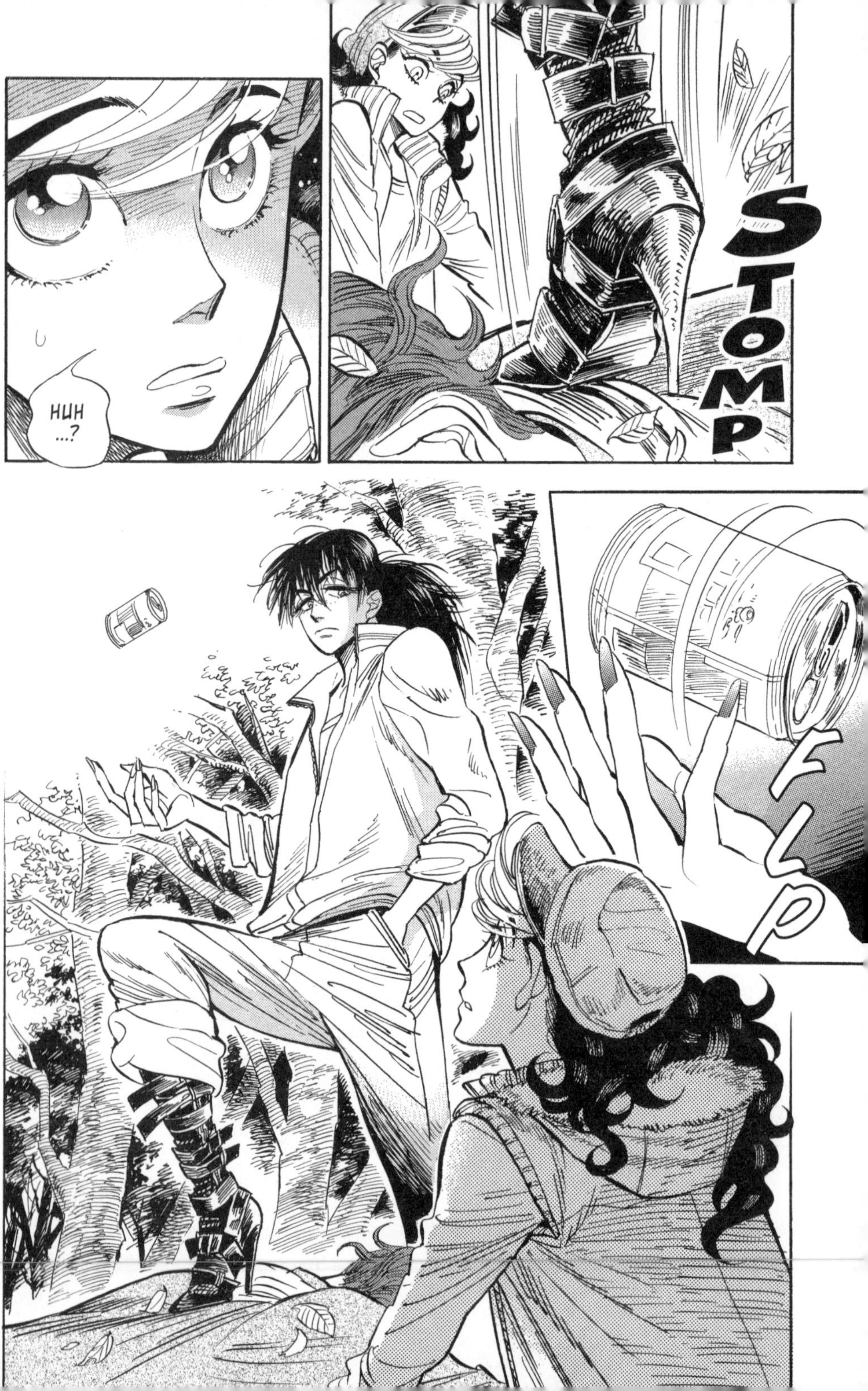
STOMP
HUH ...?

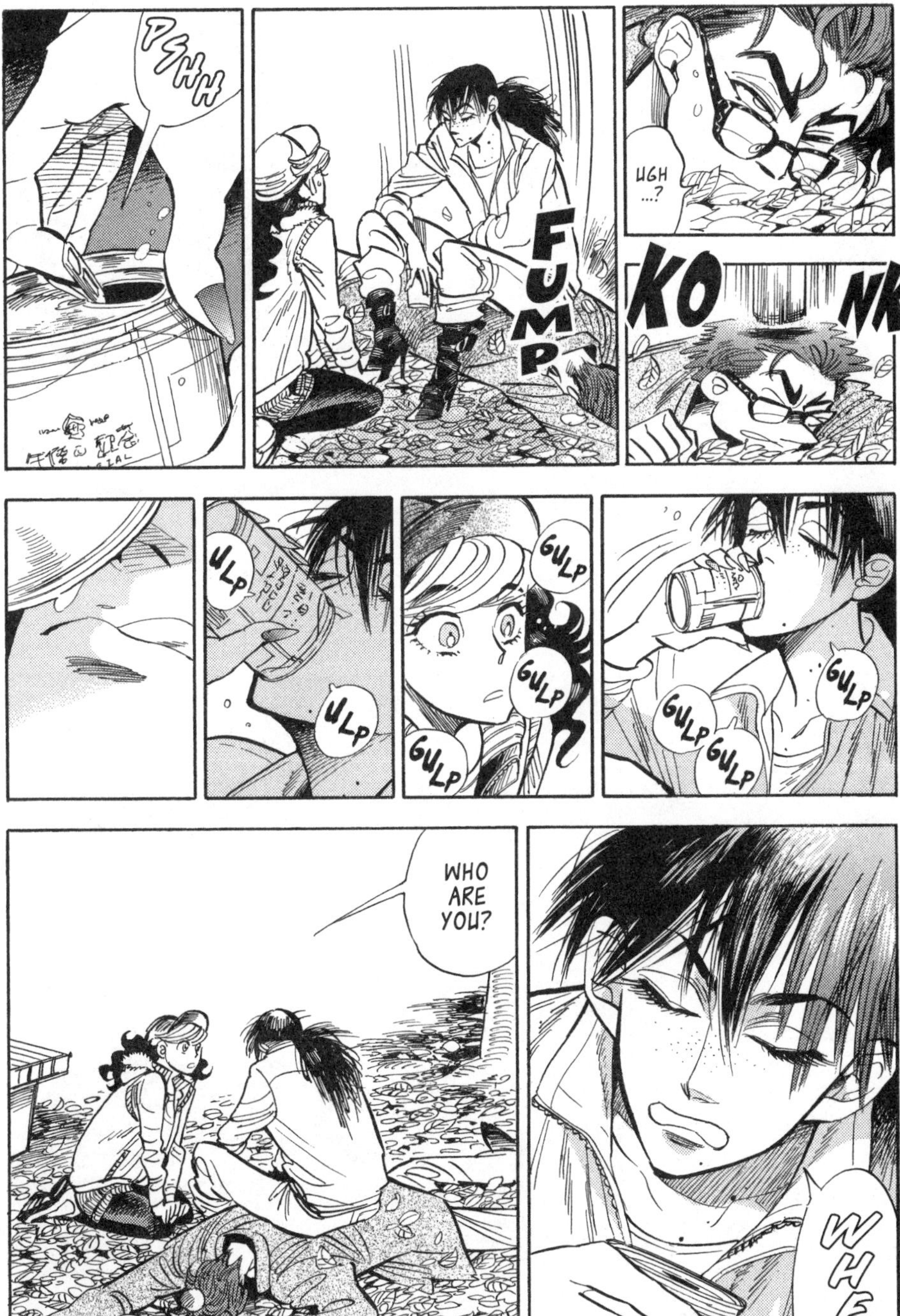
UGH ...?
KONK
FUMP
PSHH
GULP
GULP GULP
GULP
GULP
GULP
ULP
ULP
WHEW
WHO ARE YOU?

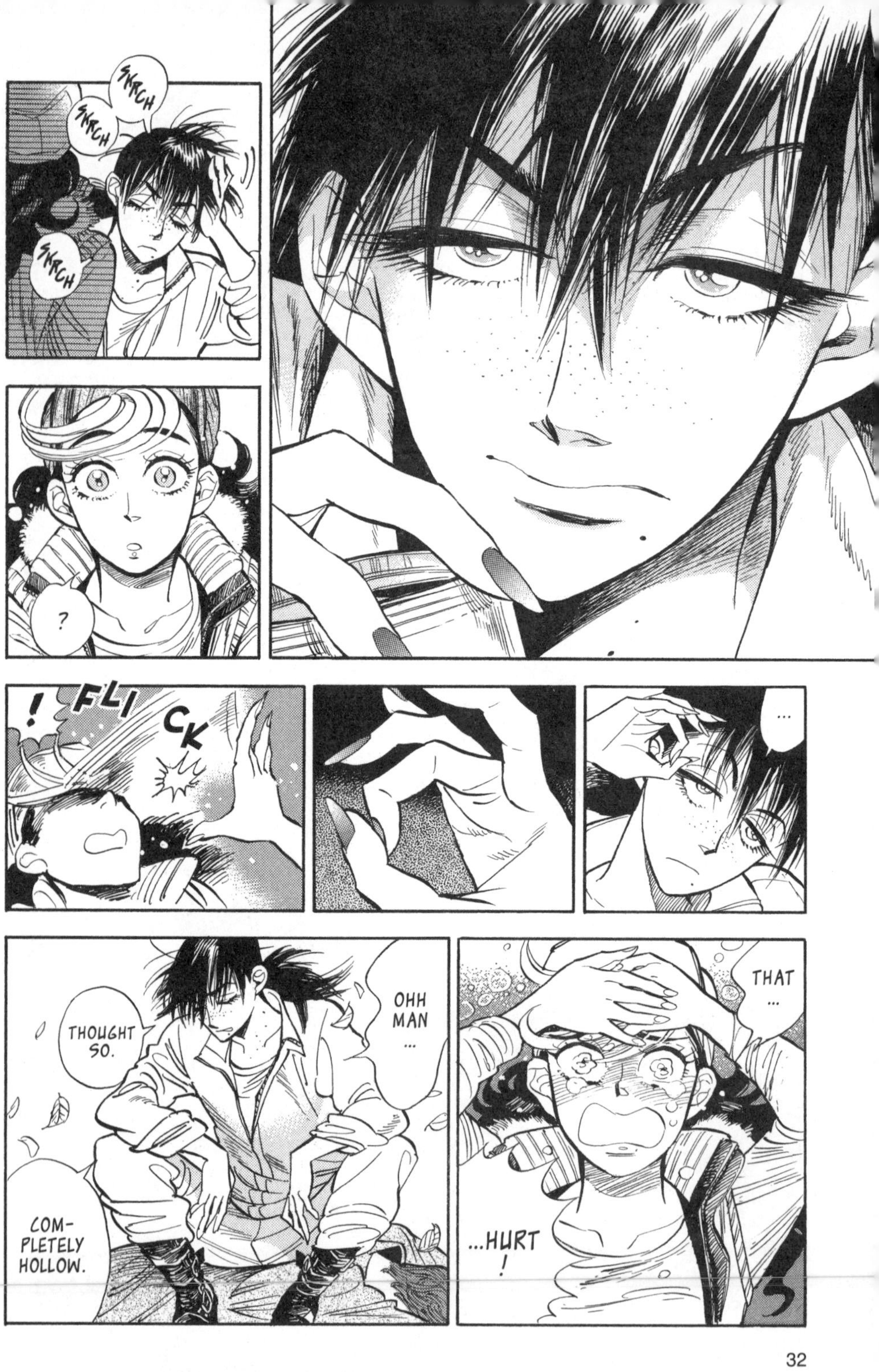
SKRCH
SKRCH
SKRCH
?
...
!
FLICK
THAT...
...HURT!
OHH MAN...
THOUGHT SO.
COMPLETELY HOLLOW.

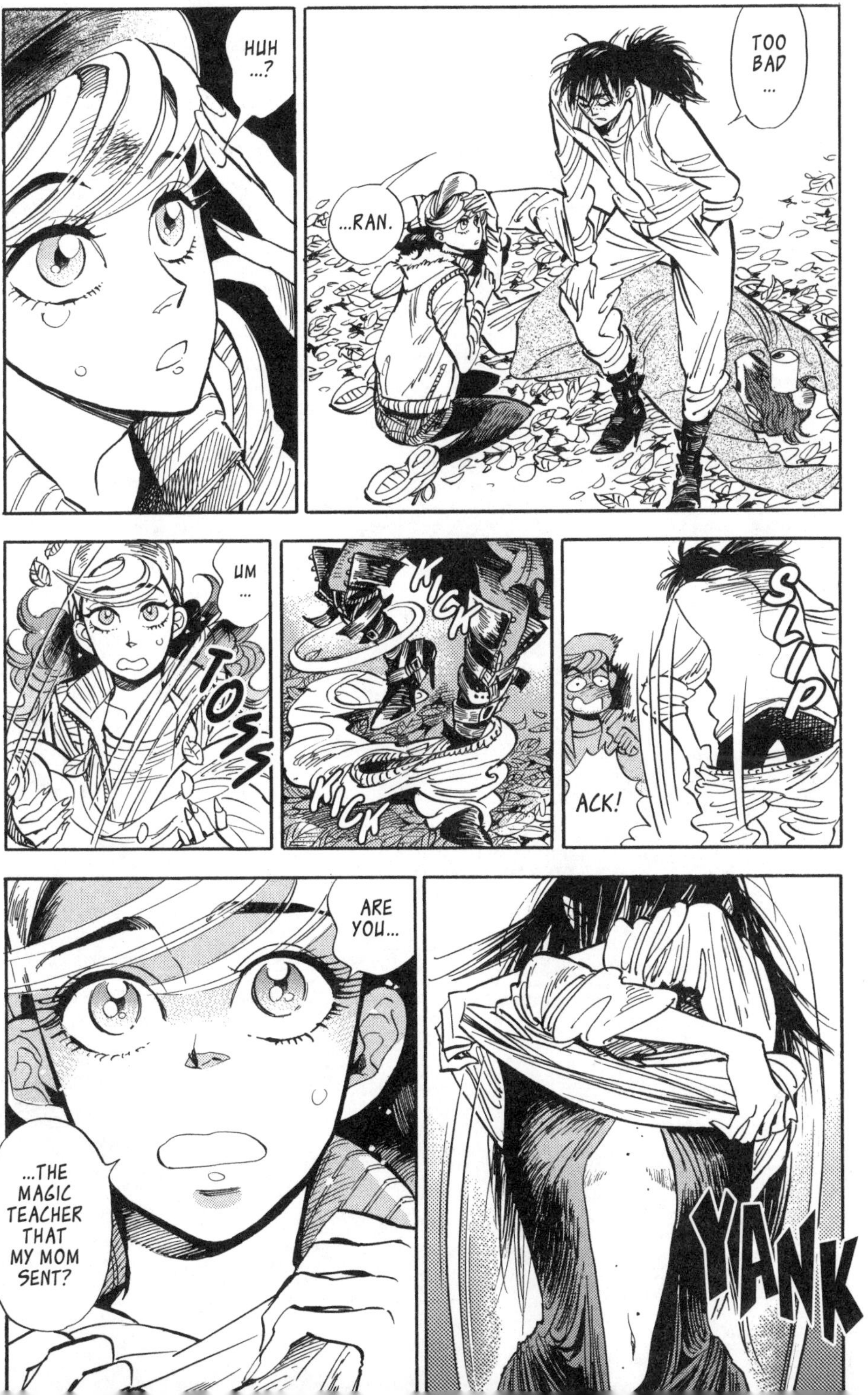
TOO BAD ...
...RAN.
HUH ...?
SLIP
ACK!
KICK
KICK
UM ...
TOSS
YANK
ARE YOU...
...THE MAGIC TEACHER THAT MY MOM SENT?

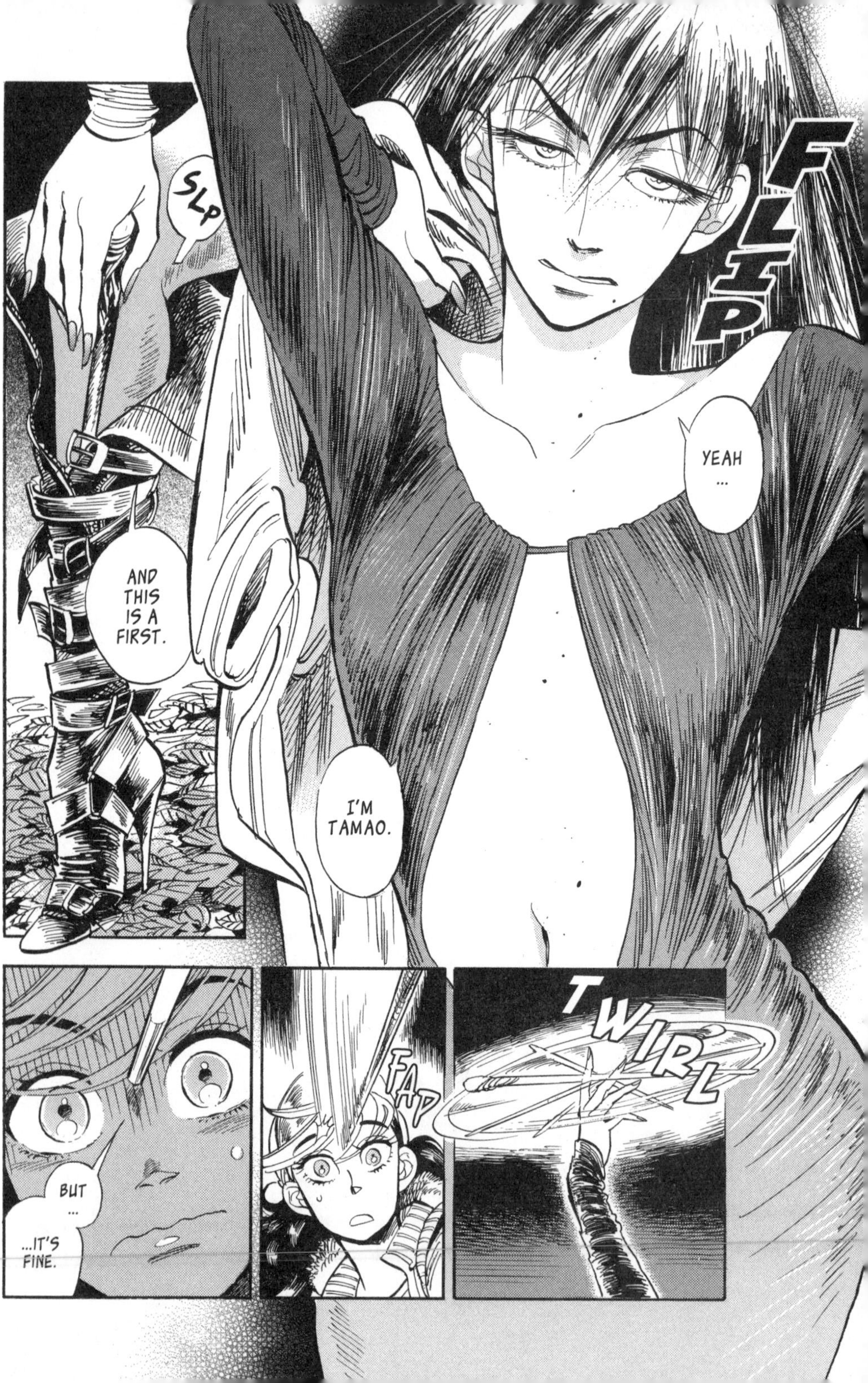
FLIP
YEAH ...
I'M TAMAO.
SLP
AND THIS IS A FIRST.
TWIRL
FAP
BUT ...
...IT'S FINE.

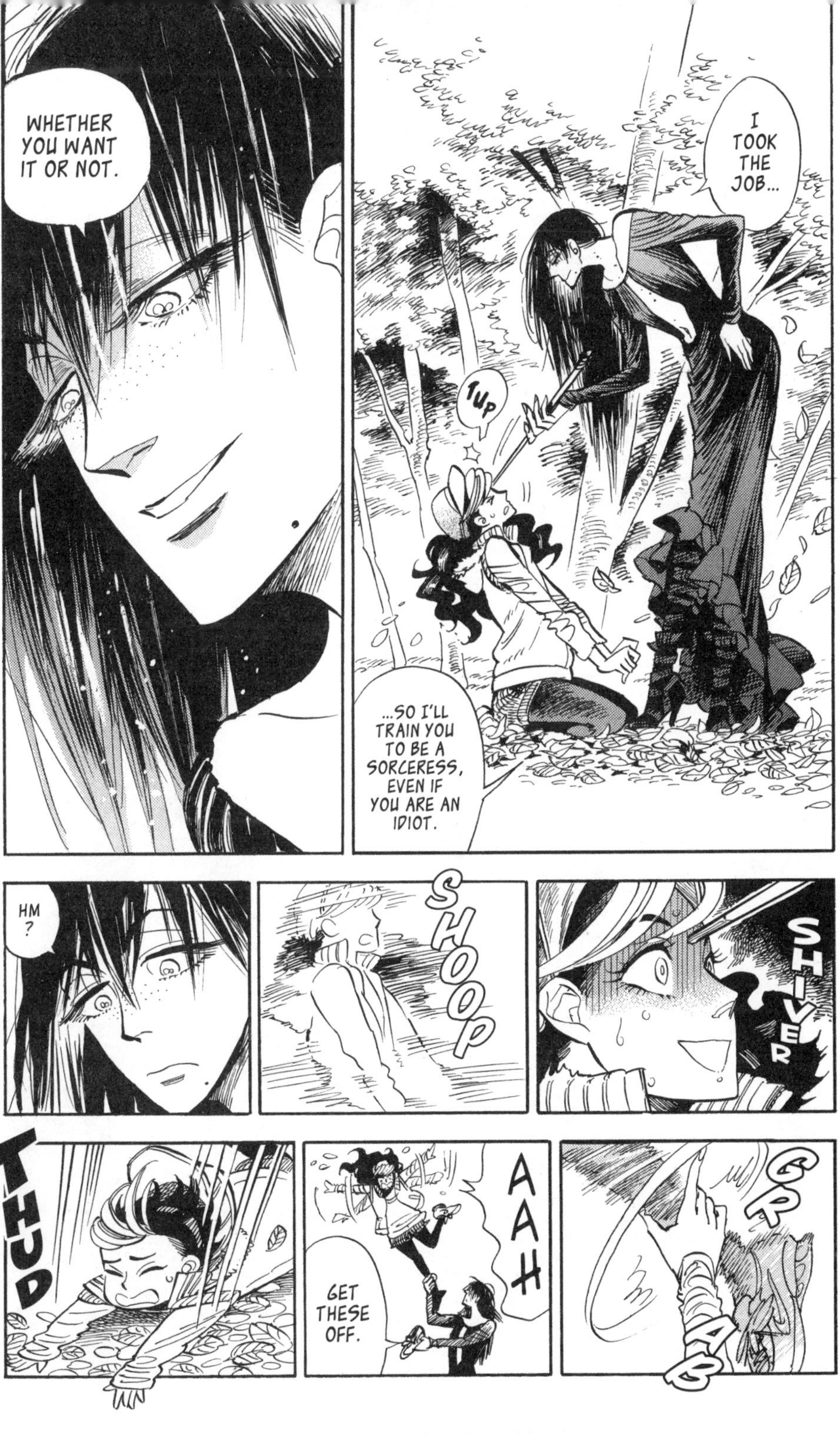
I TOOK THE JOB...
TUP
...SO I'LL TRAIN YOU TO BE A SORCERESS, EVEN IF YOU ARE AN IDIOT.
WHETHER YOU WANT IT OR NOT.
SHIVER
SHOOP
HM?
GRAB
AAH
GET THESE OFF.
THUD

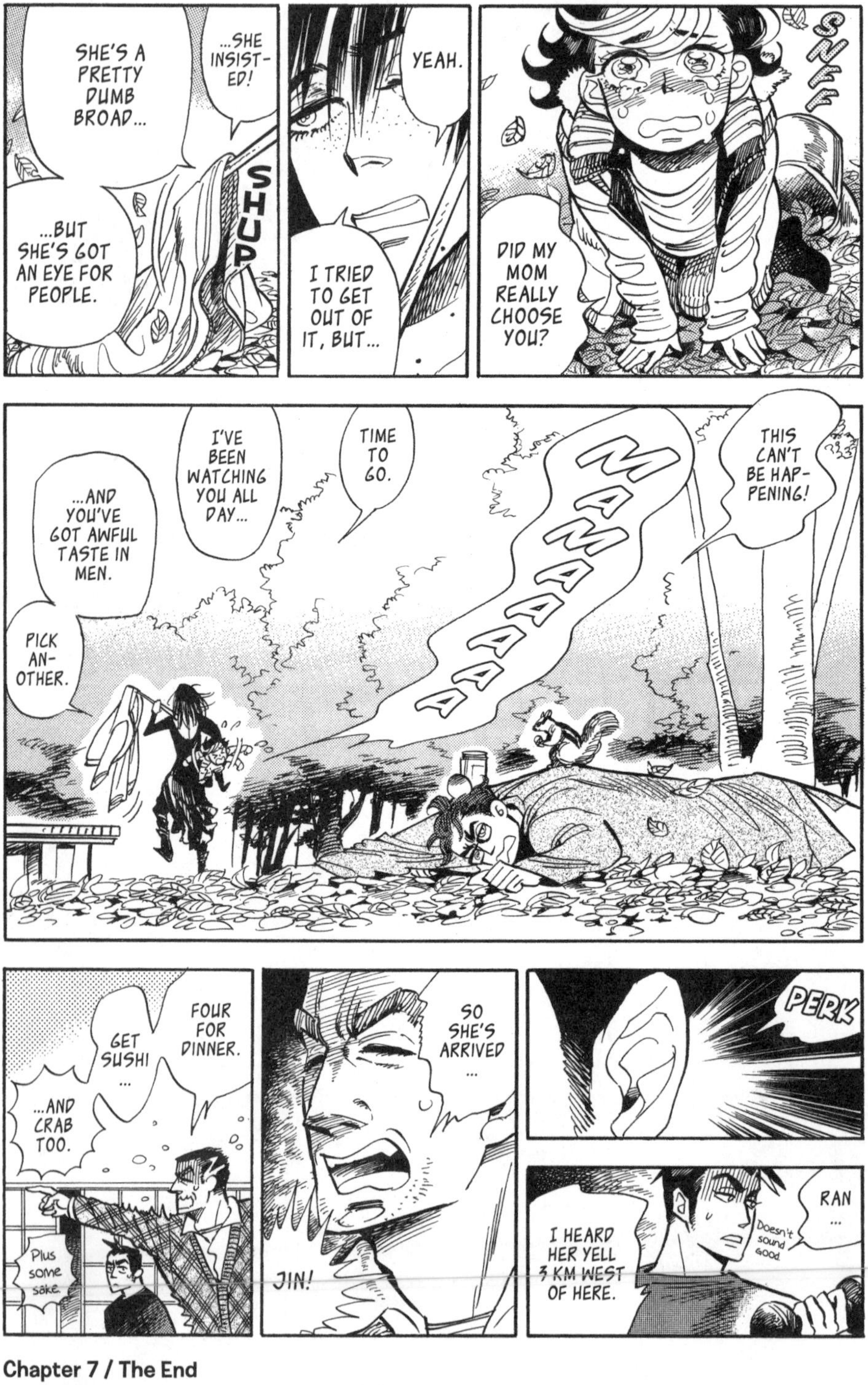
SNFF
DID MY MOM REALLY CHOOSE YOU?
YEAH.
I TRIED TO GET OUT OF IT, BUT...
...SHE INSISTED!
SHE'S A PRETTY DUMB BROAD...
...BUT SHE'S GOT AN EYE FOR PEOPLE.
SHUP
THIS CAN'T BE HAPPENING!
MAMAAAAAA
TIME TO GO.
I'VE BEEN WATCHING YOU ALL DAY...
...AND YOU'VE GOT AWFUL TASTE IN MEN.
PICK ANOTHER.
PERK
RAN...
Doesn't sound good.
I HEARD HER YELL 3 KM WEST OF HERE.
SO SHE'S ARRIVED...
JIN!
FOUR FOR DINNER.
GET SUSHI...
...AND CRAB TOO.
Plus some sake.

Chapter 7 / The End

Chapter 8

Guests

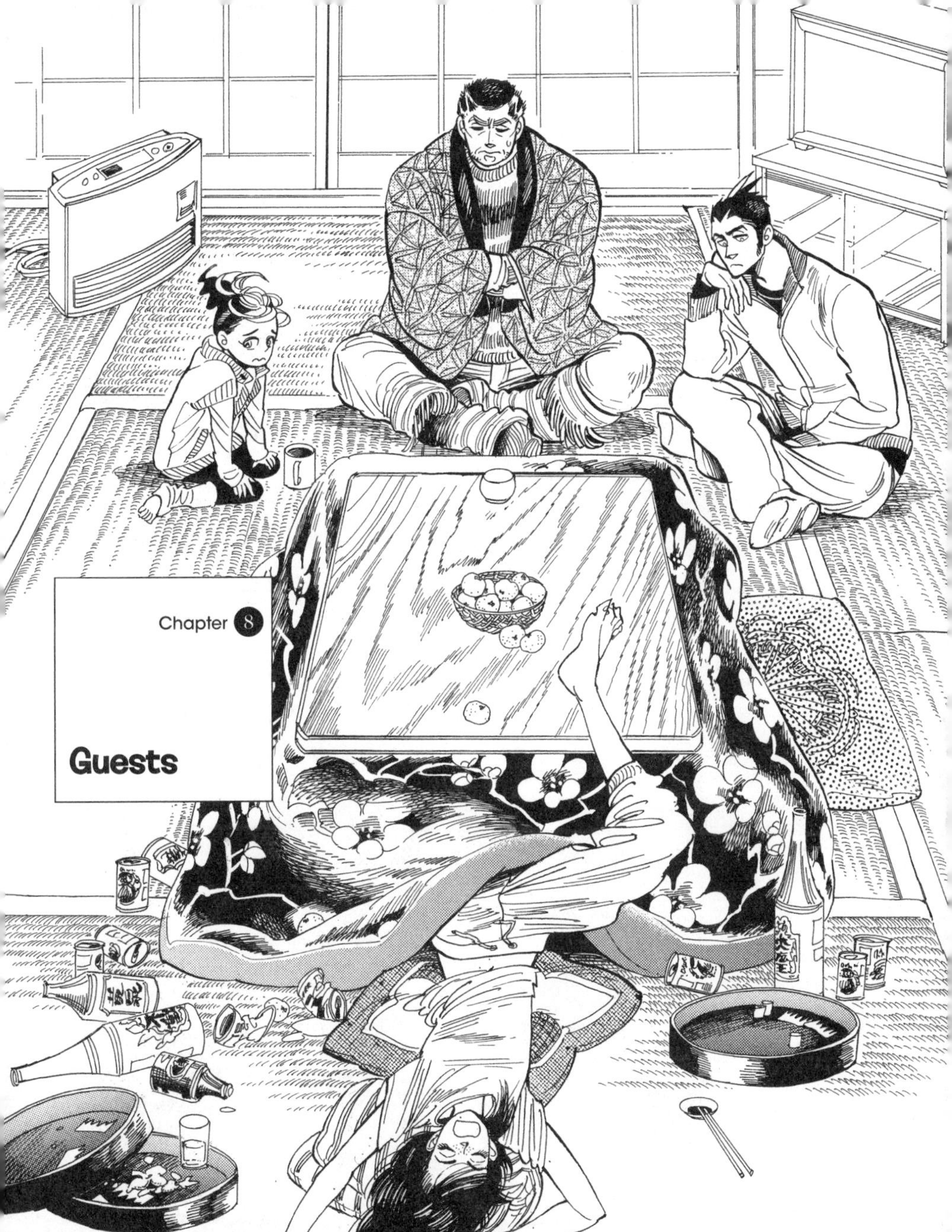

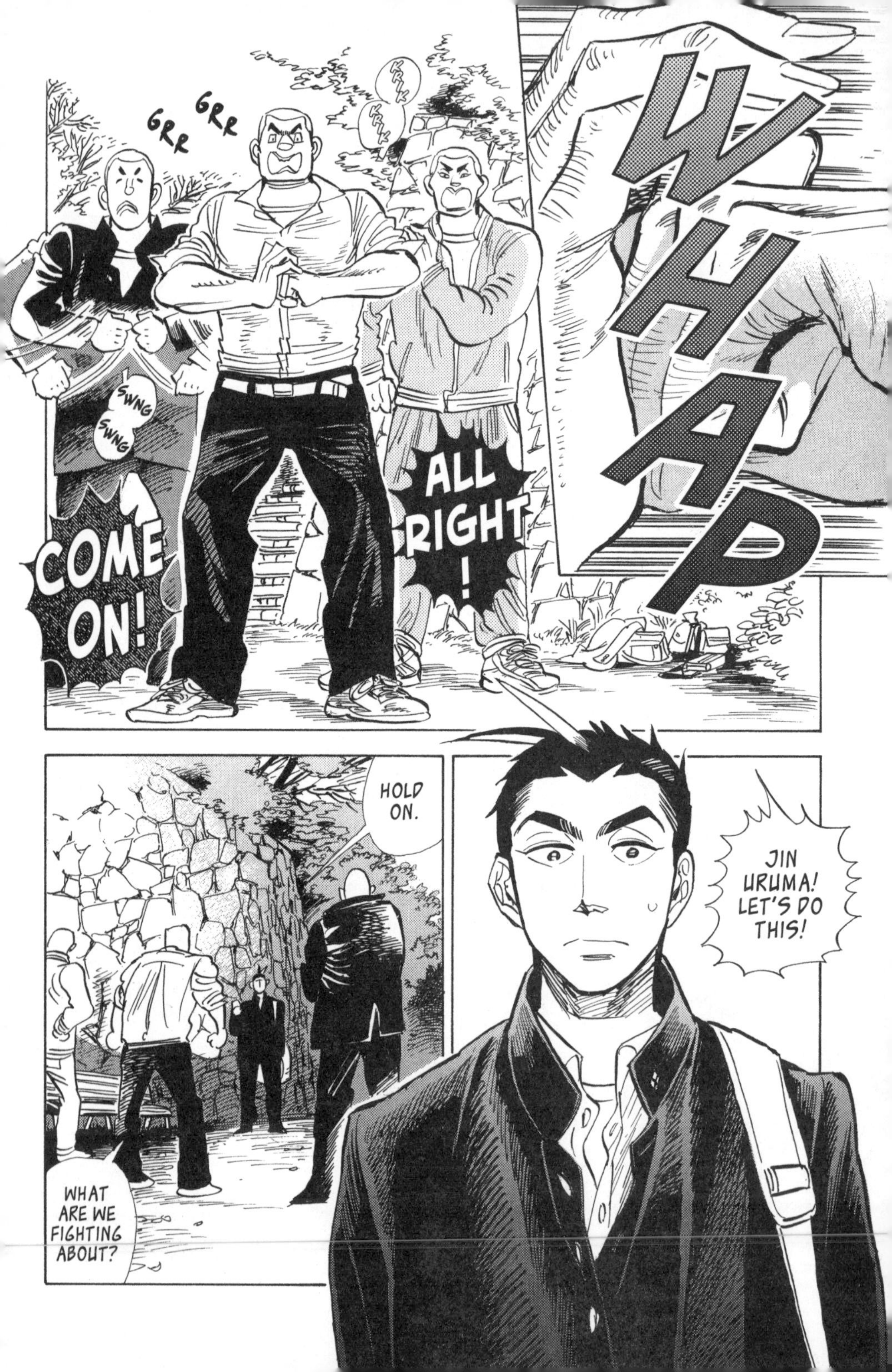
WHAP
GRR GRR
ALL RIGHT!
SWNG SWNG
COME ON!
JIN URUMA! LET'S DO THIS!
HOLD ON.
WHAT ARE WE FIGHTING ABOUT?

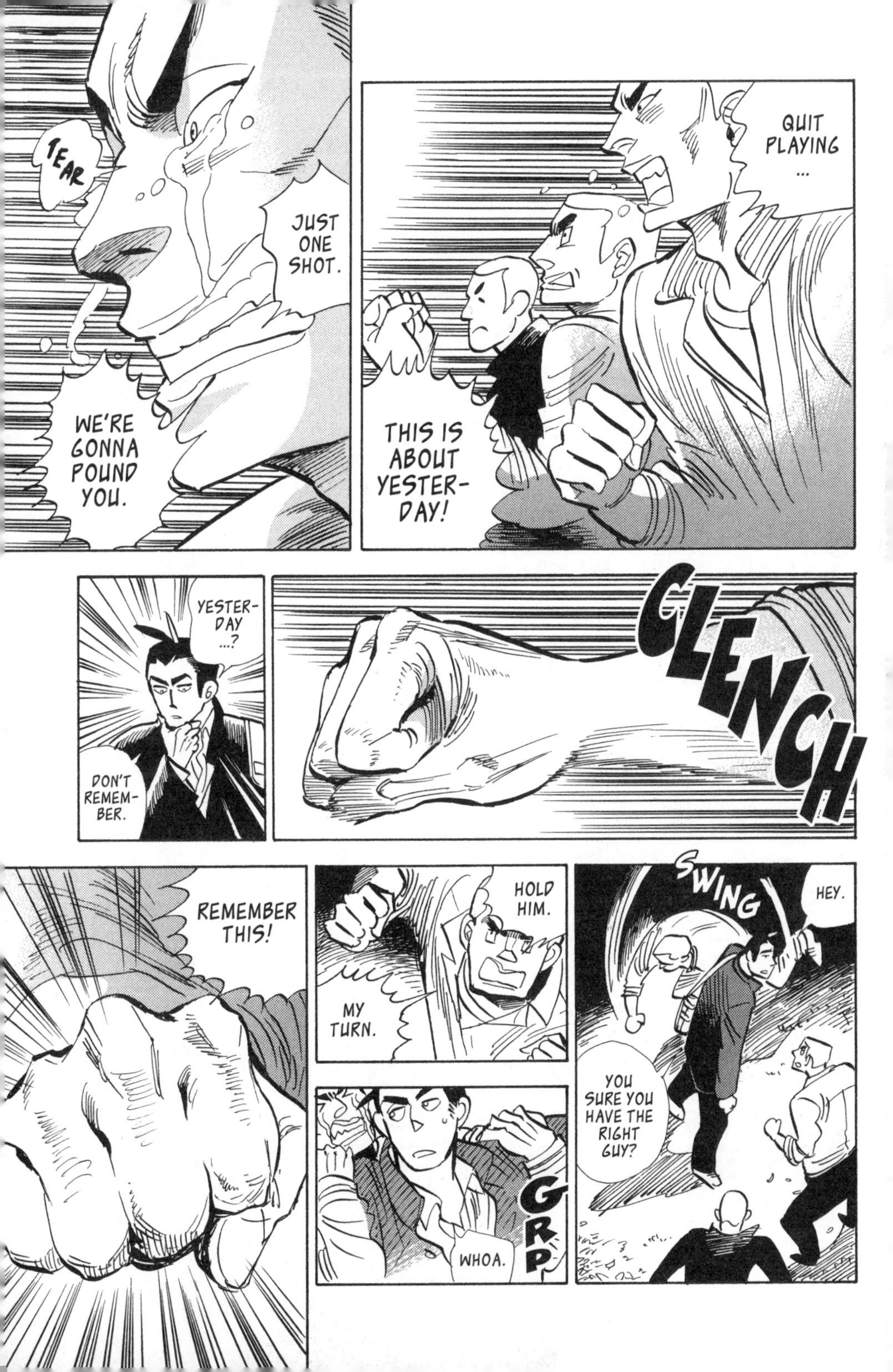
QUIT PLAYING ...
THIS IS ABOUT YESTER-DAY!
TEAR
JUST ONE SHOT.
WE'RE GONNA POUND YOU.
CLENCH
YESTER-DAY ...?
DON'T REMEM-BER.
SWING
HEY.
YOU SURE YOU HAVE THE RIGHT GUY?
HOLD HIM.
MY TURN.
GRP
WHOA.
REMEMBER THIS!

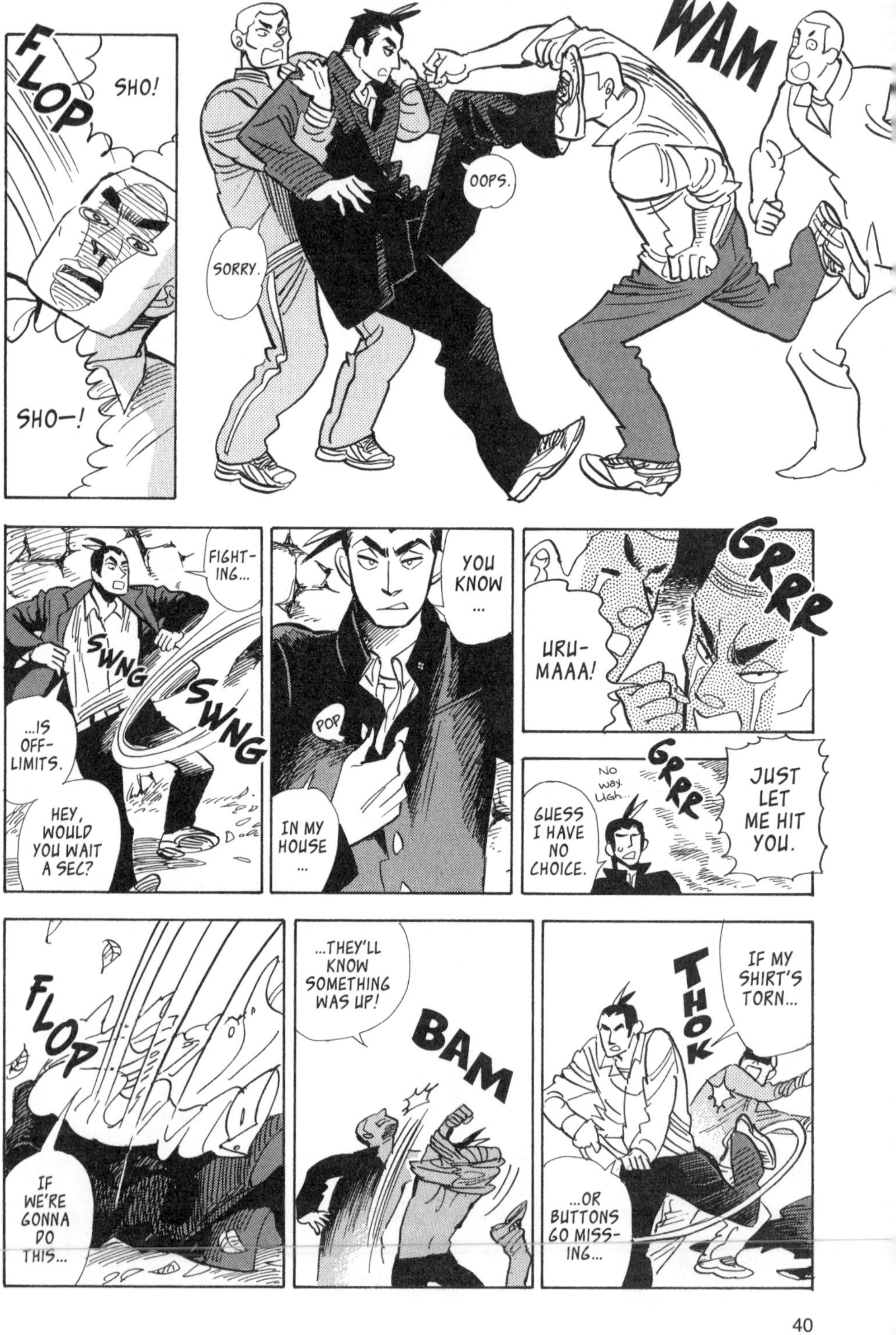
WAM
OOPS.
SORRY.
FLOP
SHO!
SHO—!
GRRR
URU-MAAA!
JUST LET ME HIT YOU.
GRRR
No way. Ugh...
GUESS I HAVE NO CHOICE.
YOU KNOW ...
POP
IN MY HOUSE ...
FIGHTING...
SWNG
SWNG
...IS OFF-LIMITS.
HEY, WOULD YOU WAIT A SEC?
IF MY SHIRT'S TORN...
THOK
...OR BUTTONS GO MISSING...
...THEY'LL KNOW SOMETHING WAS UP!
BAM
FLOP
IF WE'RE GONNA DO THIS...

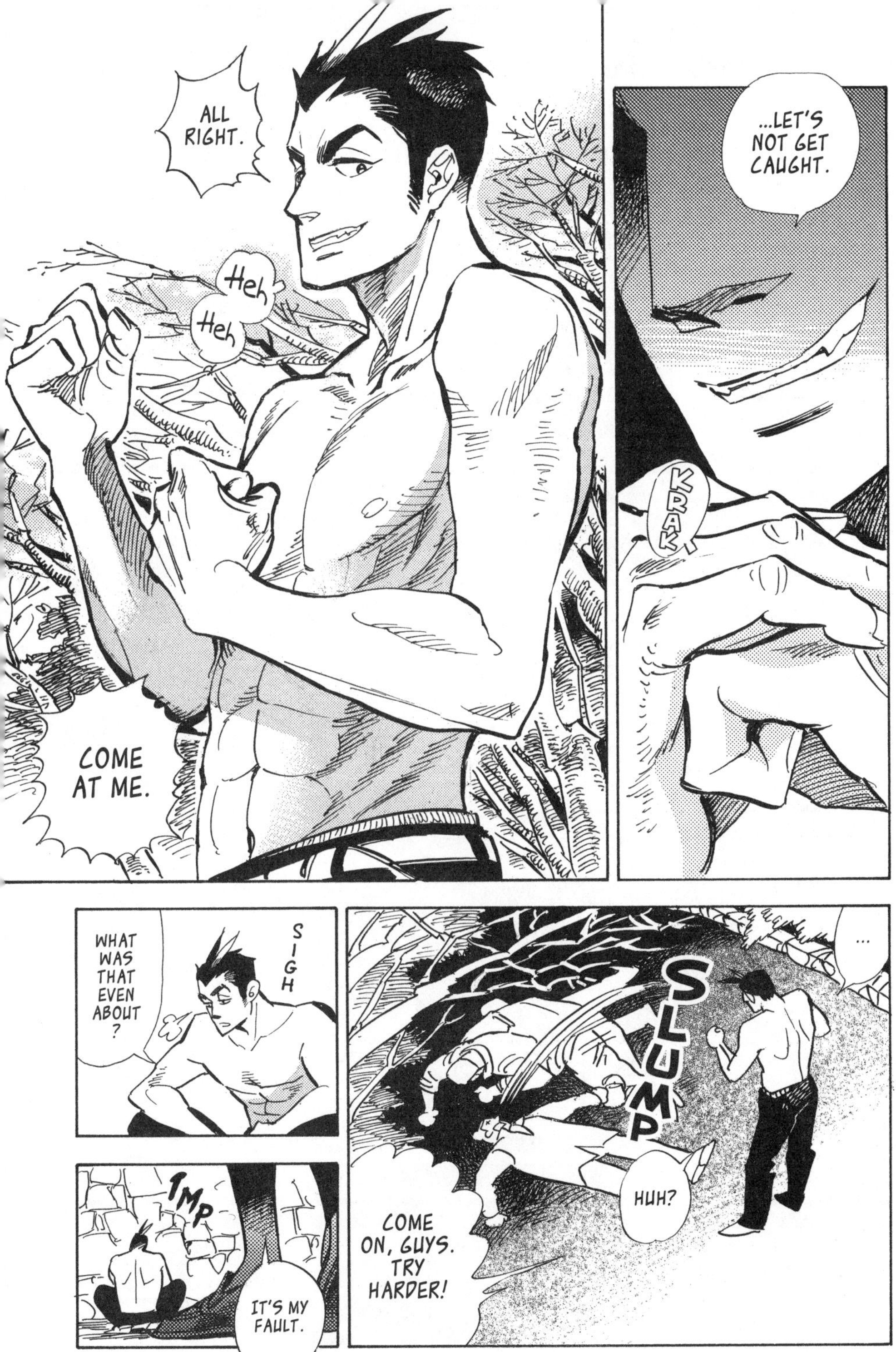
...LET'S NOT GET CAUGHT.
KRAK
ALL RIGHT.
Heh Heh
COME AT ME.
...
SLUMP
HUH?
COME ON, GUYS. TRY HARDER!
SIGH
WHAT WAS THAT EVEN ABOUT?
TMP
IT'S MY FAULT.

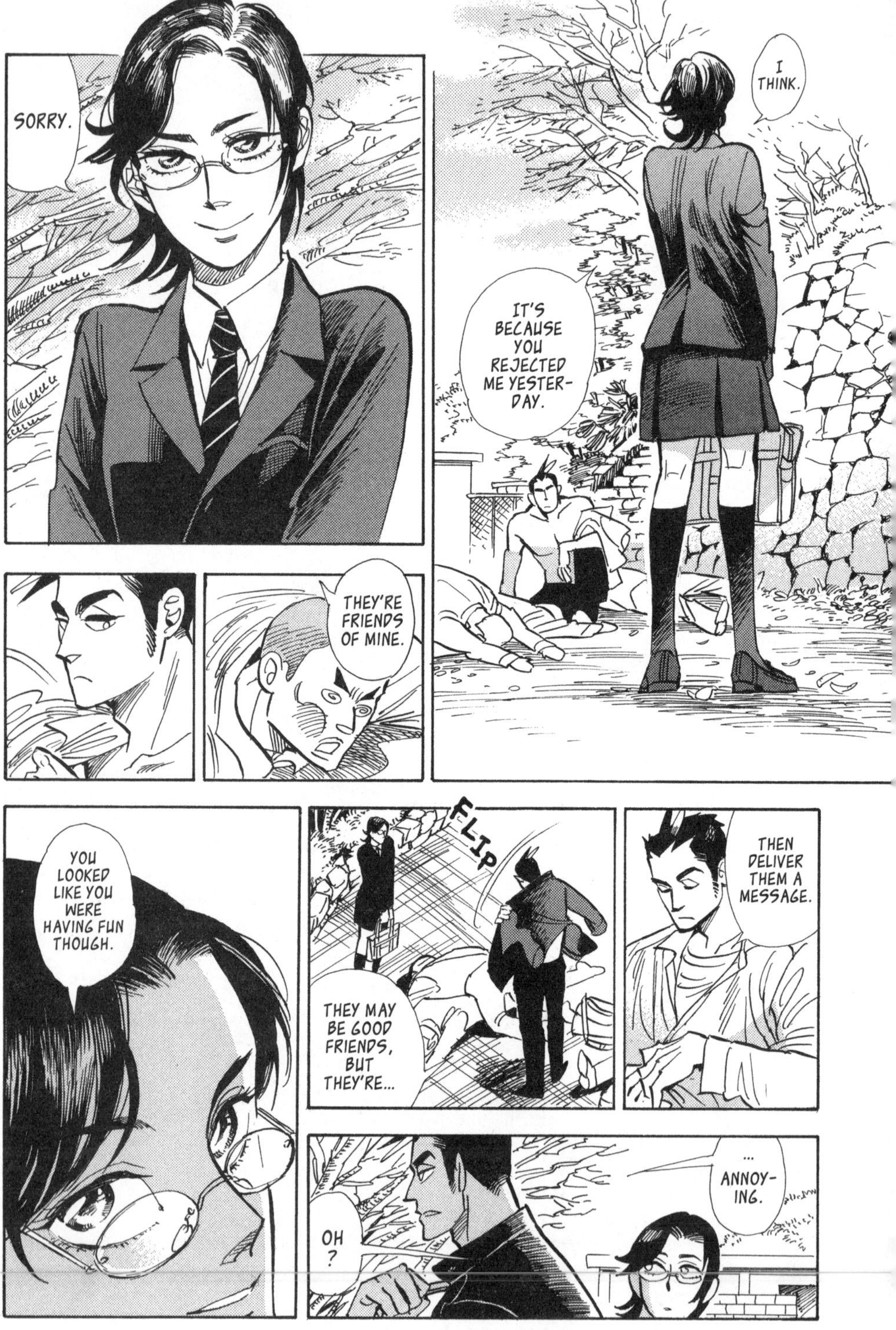
I THINK.
IT'S BECAUSE YOU REJECTED ME YESTER-DAY.
SORRY.
THEY'RE FRIENDS OF MINE.
THEN DELIVER THEM A MESSAGE.
FLIP
THEY MAY BE GOOD FRIENDS, BUT THEY'RE...
... ANNOY-ING.
OH ?
YOU LOOKED LIKE YOU WERE HAVING FUN THOUGH.

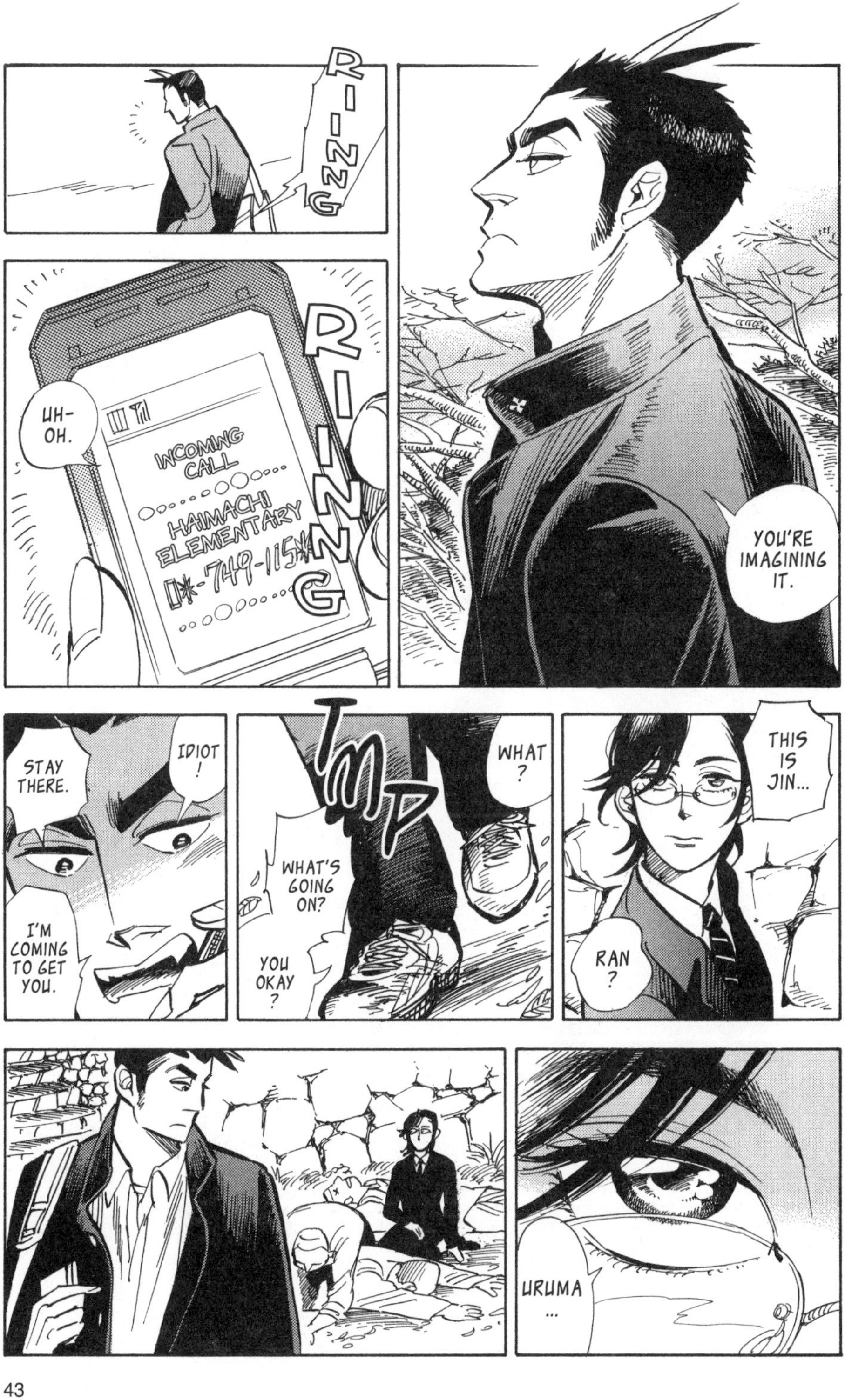
YOU'RE IMAGINING IT.
RIIINNG
RIIINNG
UH-OH.
INCOMING CALL
HAIMACHI ELEMENTARY
0*-749-115*
THIS IS JIN...
RAN?
WHAT?
TMP
WHAT'S GOING ON?
YOU OKAY?
IDIOT!
STAY THERE.
I'M COMING TO GET YOU.
URUMA...

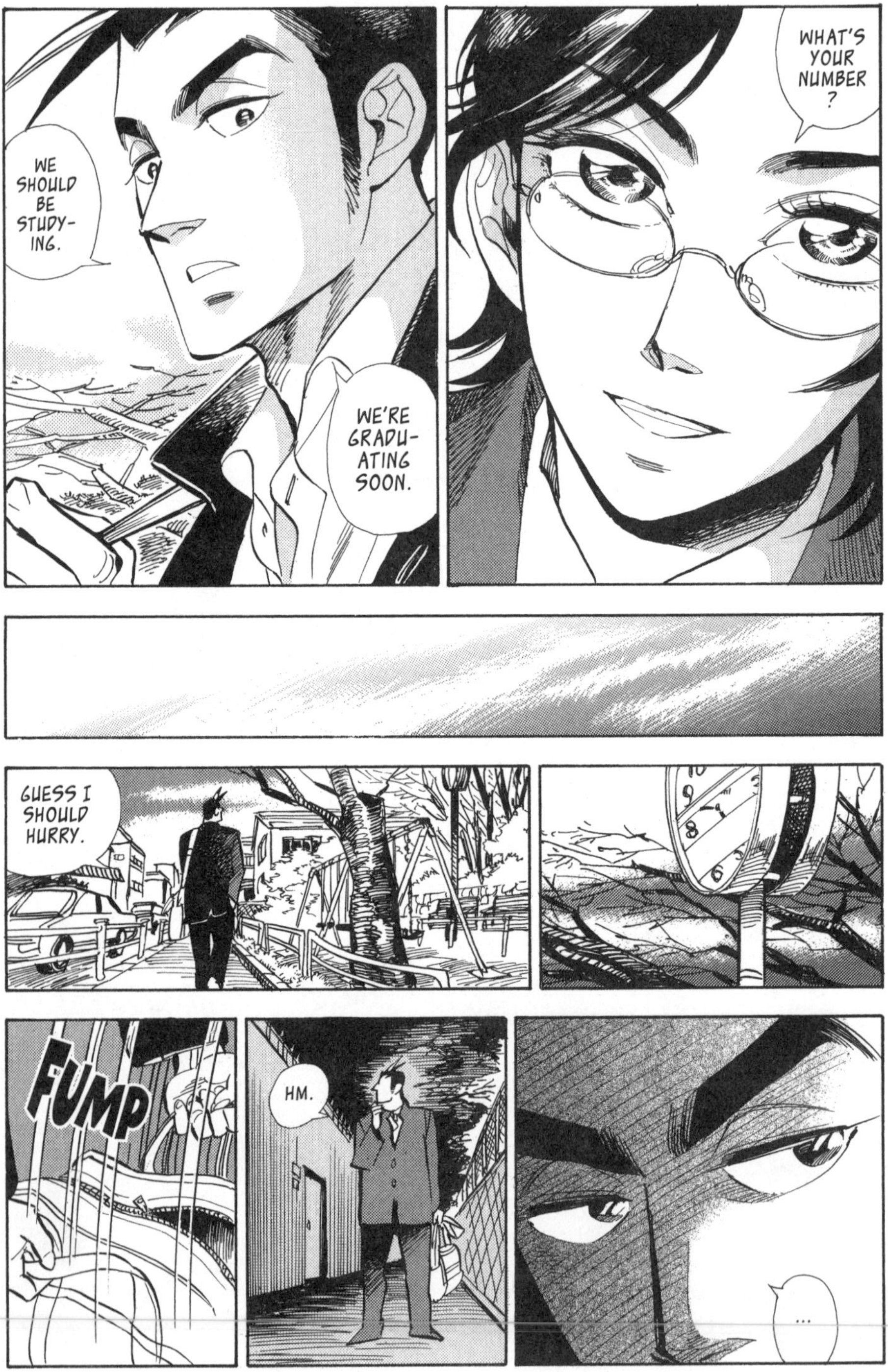
WHAT'S YOUR NUMBER?
WE SHOULD BE STUDYING.
WE'RE GRADUATING SOON.
GUESS I SHOULD HURRY.
...
HM.
FUMP

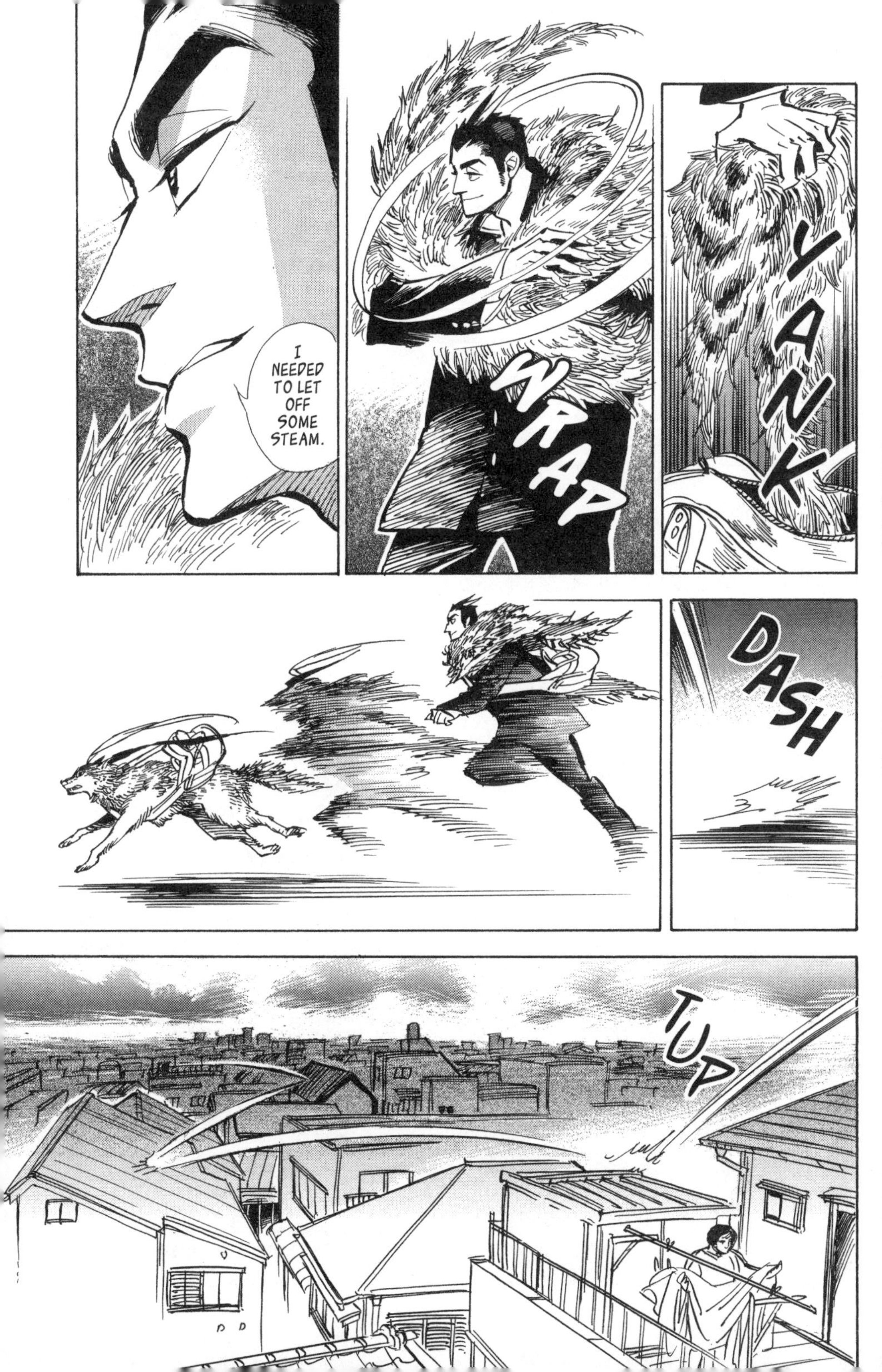
YANK
WRAP
I NEEDED TO LET OFF SOME STEAM.
DASH
TUP

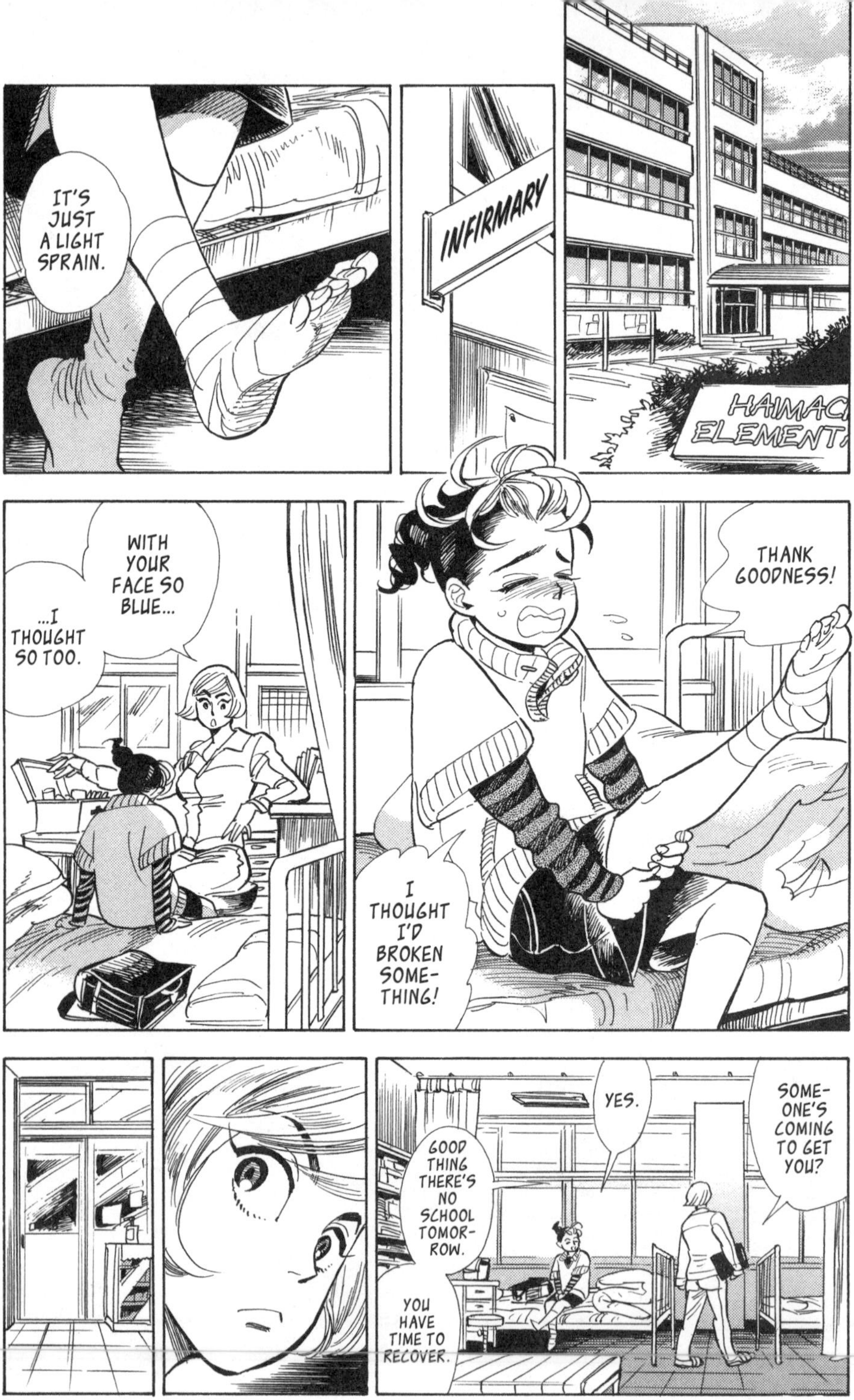
HAIMAC ELEMENT
INFIRMARY
IT'S JUST A LIGHT SPRAIN.
THANK GOODNESS!
I THOUGHT I'D BROKEN SOME-THING!
WITH YOUR FACE SO BLUE...
...I THOUGHT SO TOO.
SOME-ONE'S COMING TO GET YOU?
YES.
GOOD THING THERE'S NO SCHOOL TOMOR-ROW.
YOU HAVE TIME TO RECOVER.

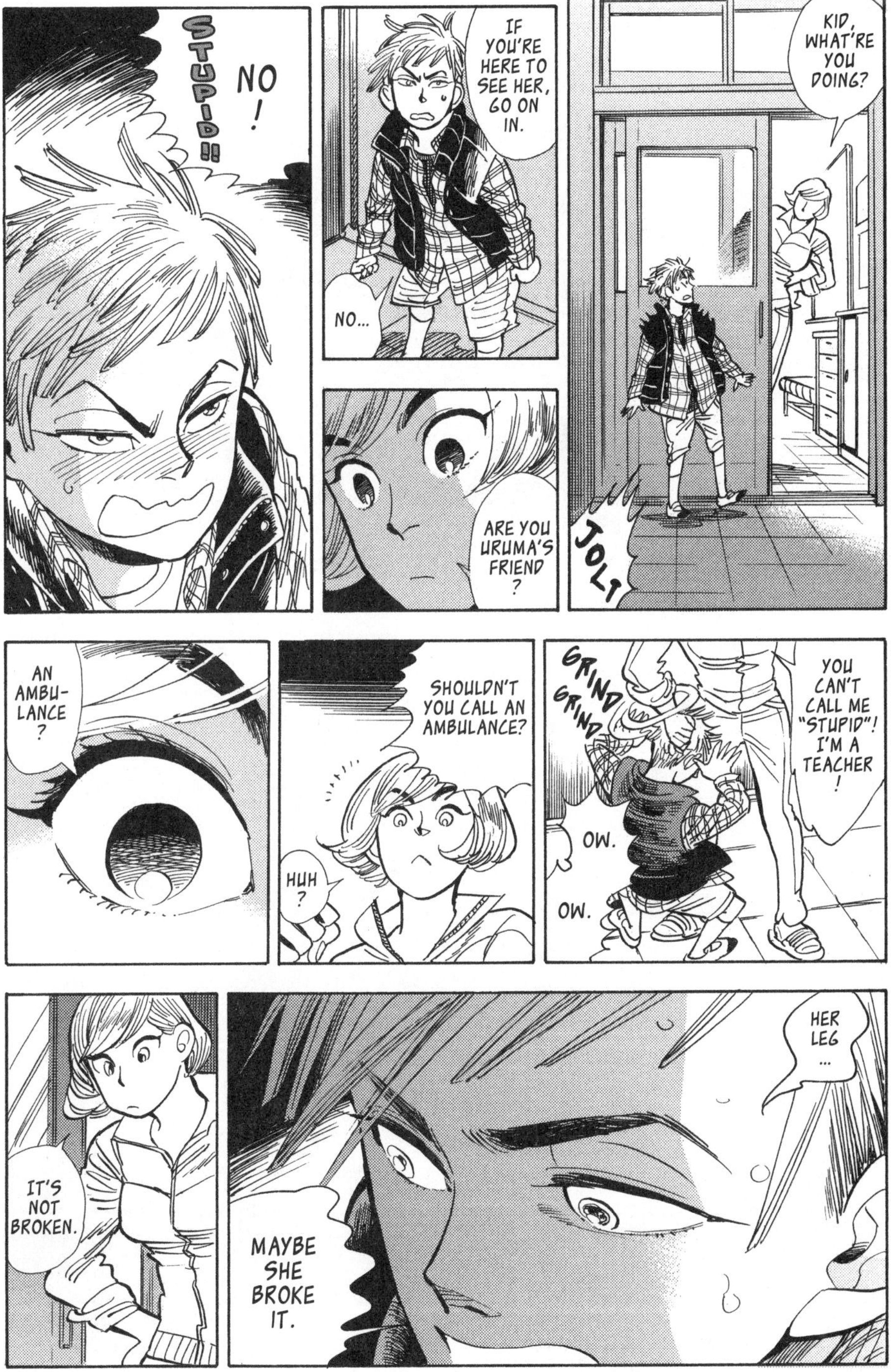

KID, WHAT'RE YOU DOING?
JOLT
IF YOU'RE HERE TO SEE HER, GO ON IN.
NO...
ARE YOU URUMA'S FRIEND?
NO!
STUPID!!
YOU CAN'T CALL ME "STUPID"! I'M A TEACHER!
GRIND GRIND
OW.
OW.
SHOULDN'T YOU CALL AN AMBULANCE?
HUH?
AN AMBULANCE?
HER LEG...
MAYBE SHE BROKE IT.
IT'S NOT BROKEN.

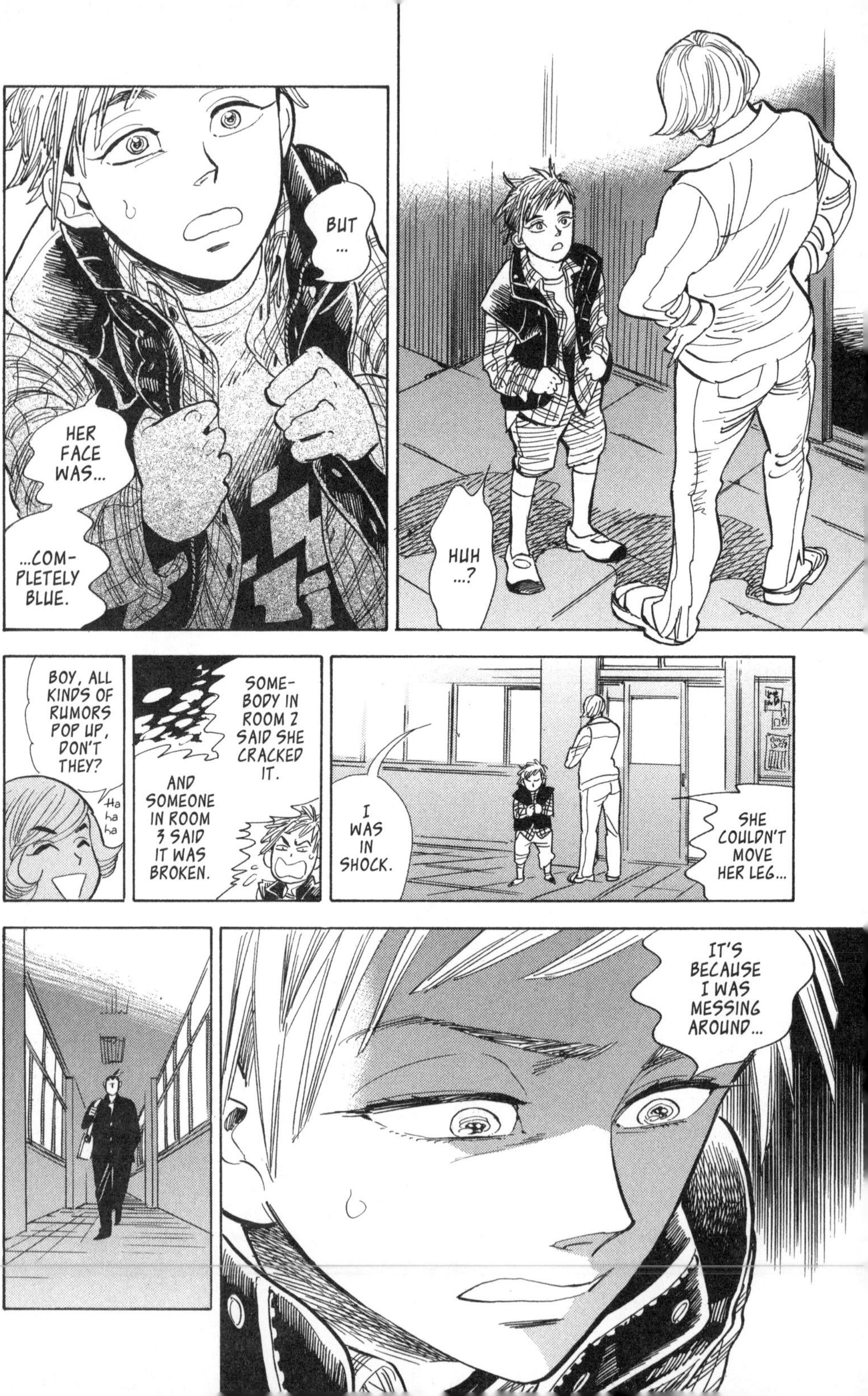
HUH ...?
BUT ...
HER FACE WAS...
...COMPLETELY BLUE.
SHE COULDN'T MOVE HER LEG...
I WAS IN SHOCK.
SOMEBODY IN ROOM 2 SAID SHE CRACKED IT.
AND SOMEONE IN ROOM 3 SAID IT WAS BROKEN.
BOY, ALL KINDS OF RUMORS POP UP, DON'T THEY?
Ha ha ha
IT'S BECAUSE I WAS MESSING AROUND...

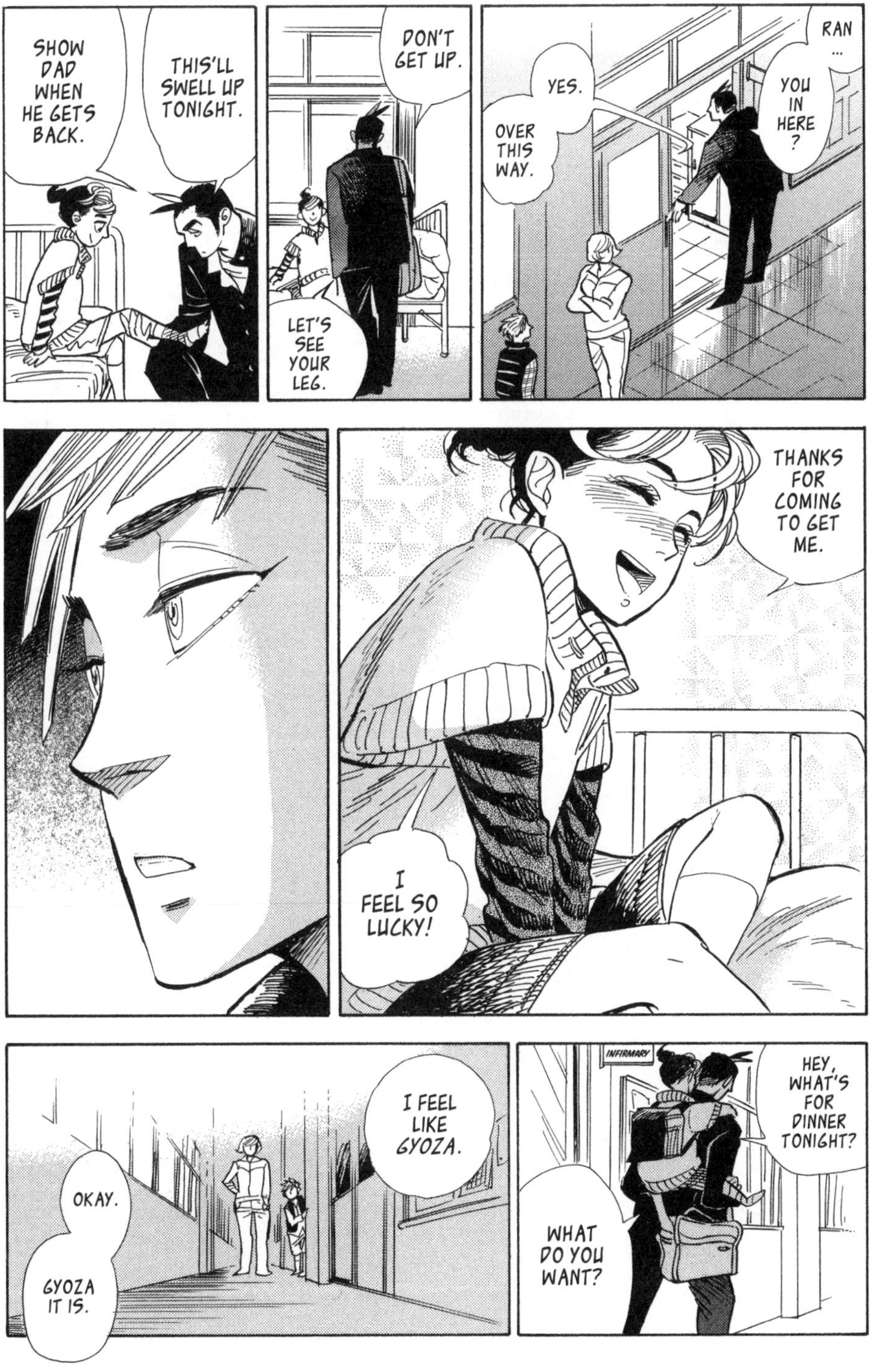
RAN ...
YOU IN HERE?
YES.
OVER THIS WAY.
DON'T GET UP.
LET'S SEE YOUR LEG.
THIS'LL SWELL UP TONIGHT.
SHOW DAD WHEN HE GETS BACK.
THANKS FOR COMING TO GET ME.
I FEEL SO LUCKY!
INFIRMARY
HEY, WHAT'S FOR DINNER TONIGHT?
WHAT DO YOU WANT?
I FEEL LIKE GYOZA.
OKAY.
GYOZA IT IS.

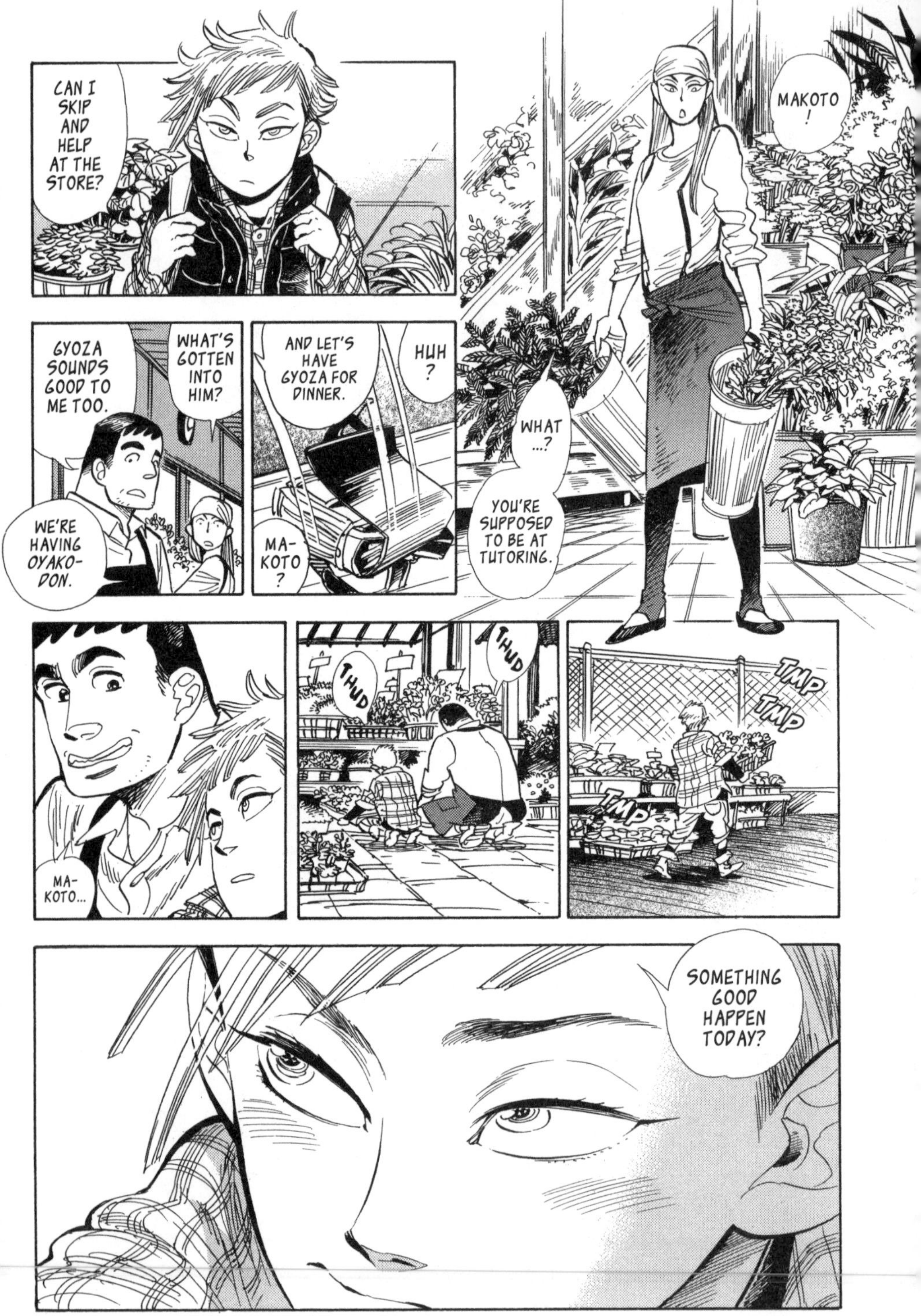
MAKOTO!
WHAT...?
YOU'RE SUPPOSED TO BE AT TUTORING.
CAN I SKIP AND HELP AT THE STORE?
HUH?
AND LET'S HAVE GYOZA FOR DINNER.
MA-KOTO?
WHAT'S GOTTEN INTO HIM?
GYOZA SOUNDS GOOD TO ME TOO.
WE'RE HAVING OYAKO-DON.
TMP
TMP
TMP
THUD
THUD
MA-KOTO...
SOMETHING GOOD HAPPEN TODAY?

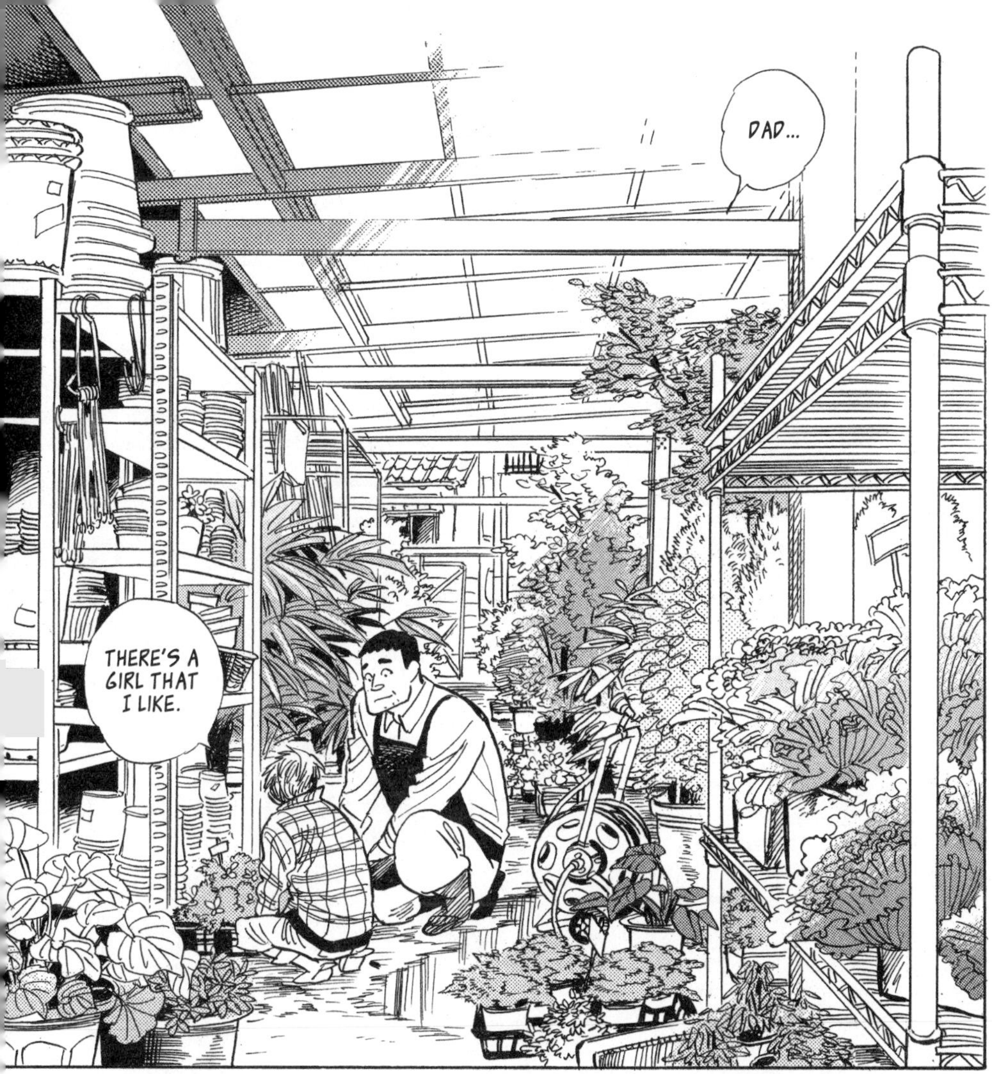
DAD...
THERE'S A GIRL THAT I LIKE.

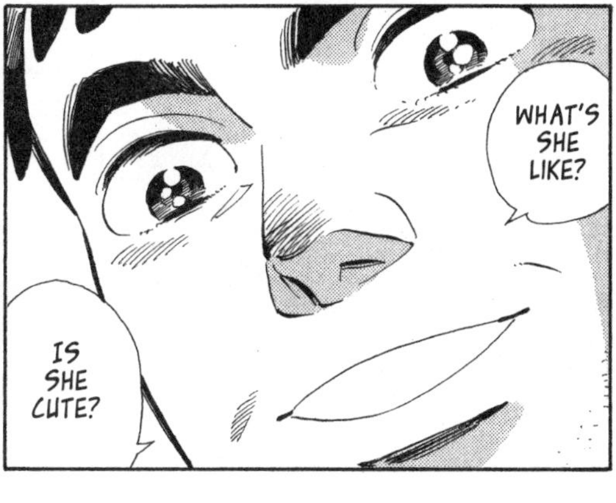
WHAT'S SHE LIKE?
IS SHE CUTE?

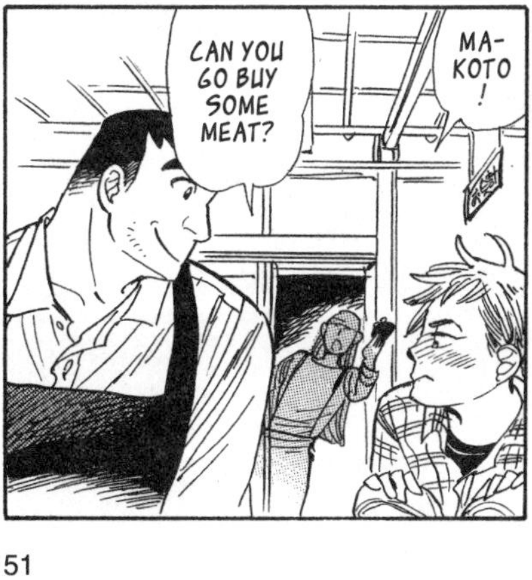
MA-KOTO!
CAN YOU GO BUY SOME MEAT?

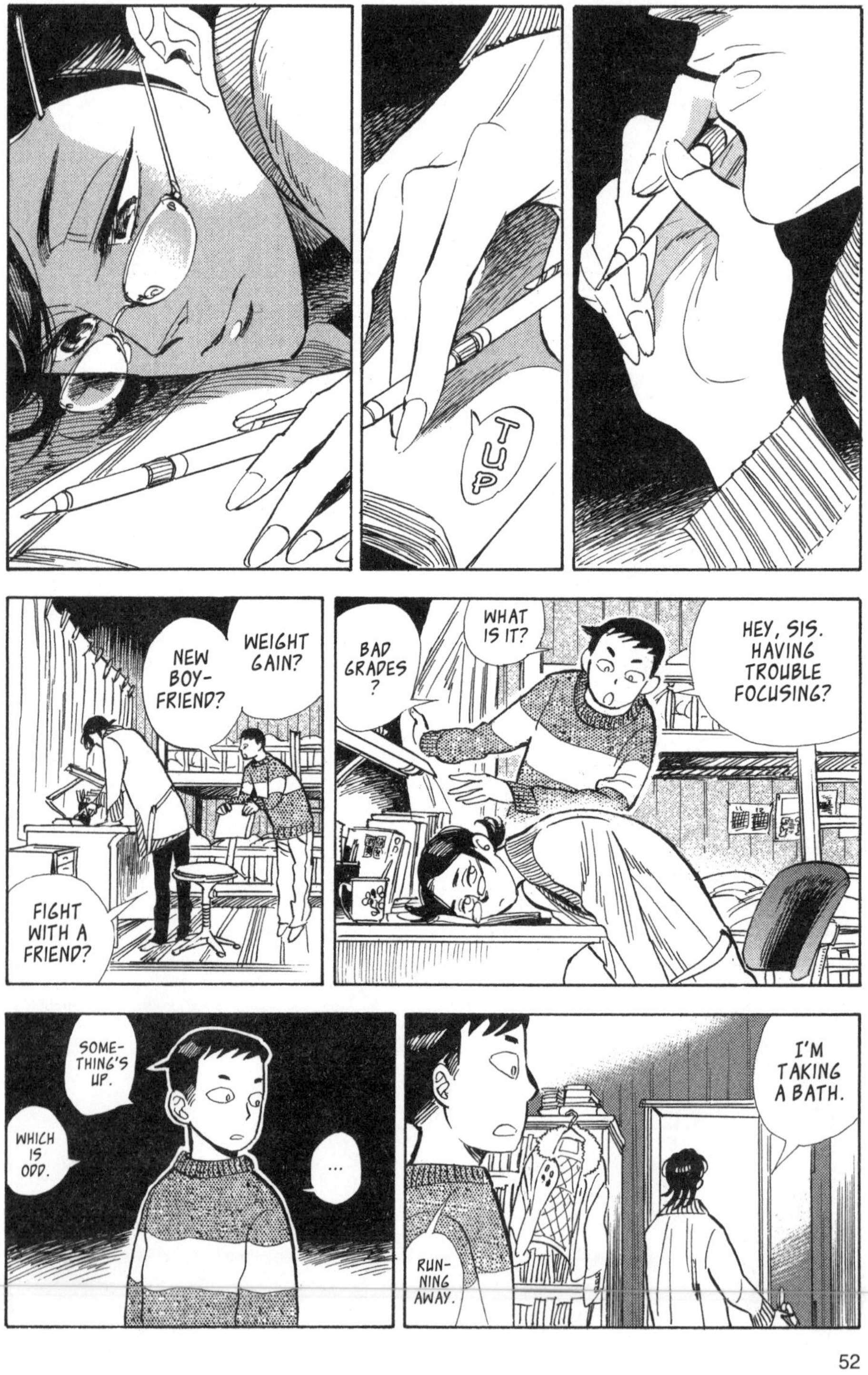
TUP
HEY, SIS. HAVING TROUBLE FOCUSING?
WHAT IS IT?
BAD GRADES?
WEIGHT GAIN?
NEW BOY-FRIEND?
FIGHT WITH A FRIEND?
I'M TAKING A BATH.
RUN-NING AWAY.
SOME-THING'S UP.
WHICH IS ODD.
...

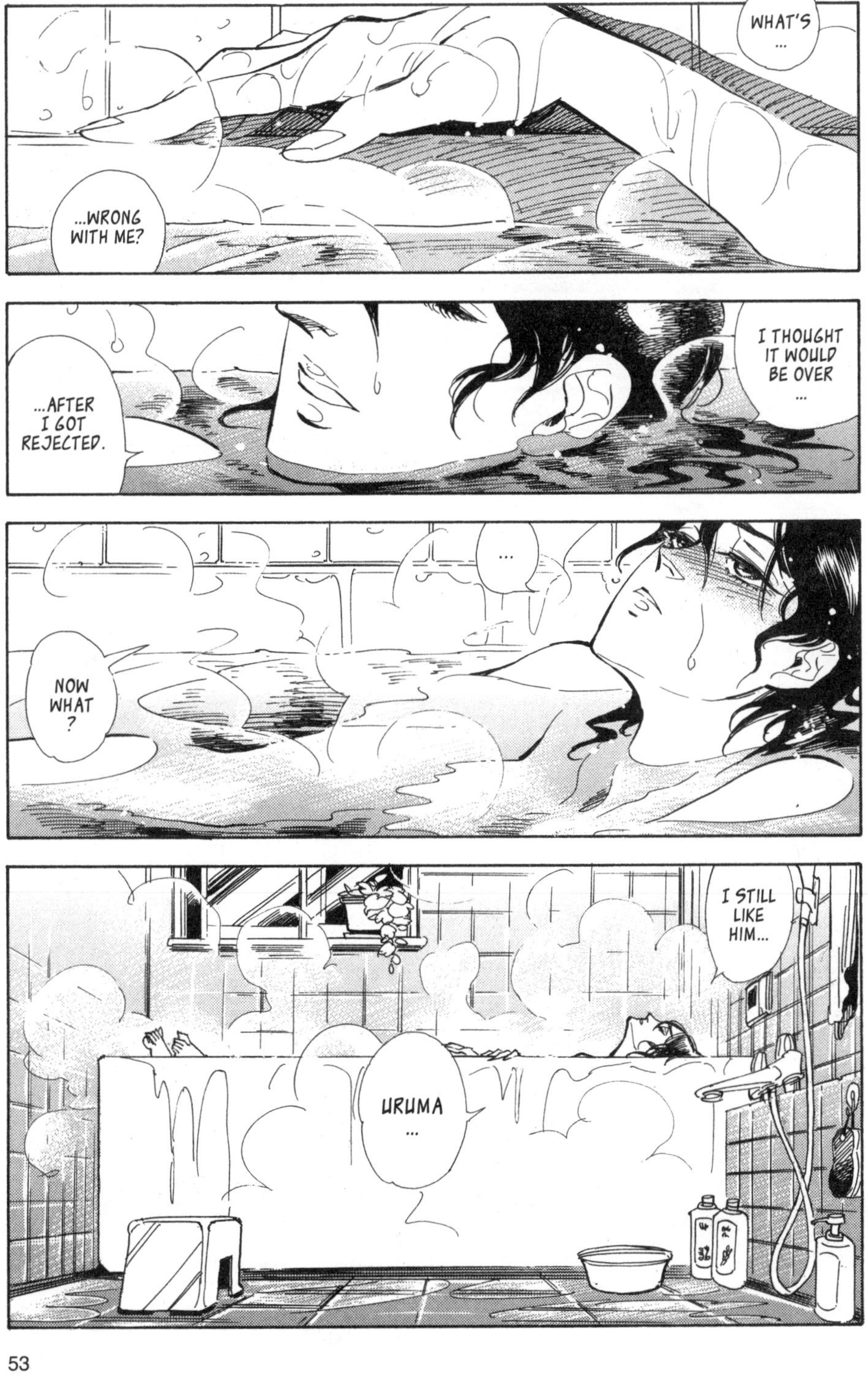
WHAT'S ...
...WRONG WITH ME?
I THOUGHT IT WOULD BE OVER ...
...AFTER I GOT REJECTED.
...
NOW WHAT ?
I STILL LIKE HIM...
URUMA ...

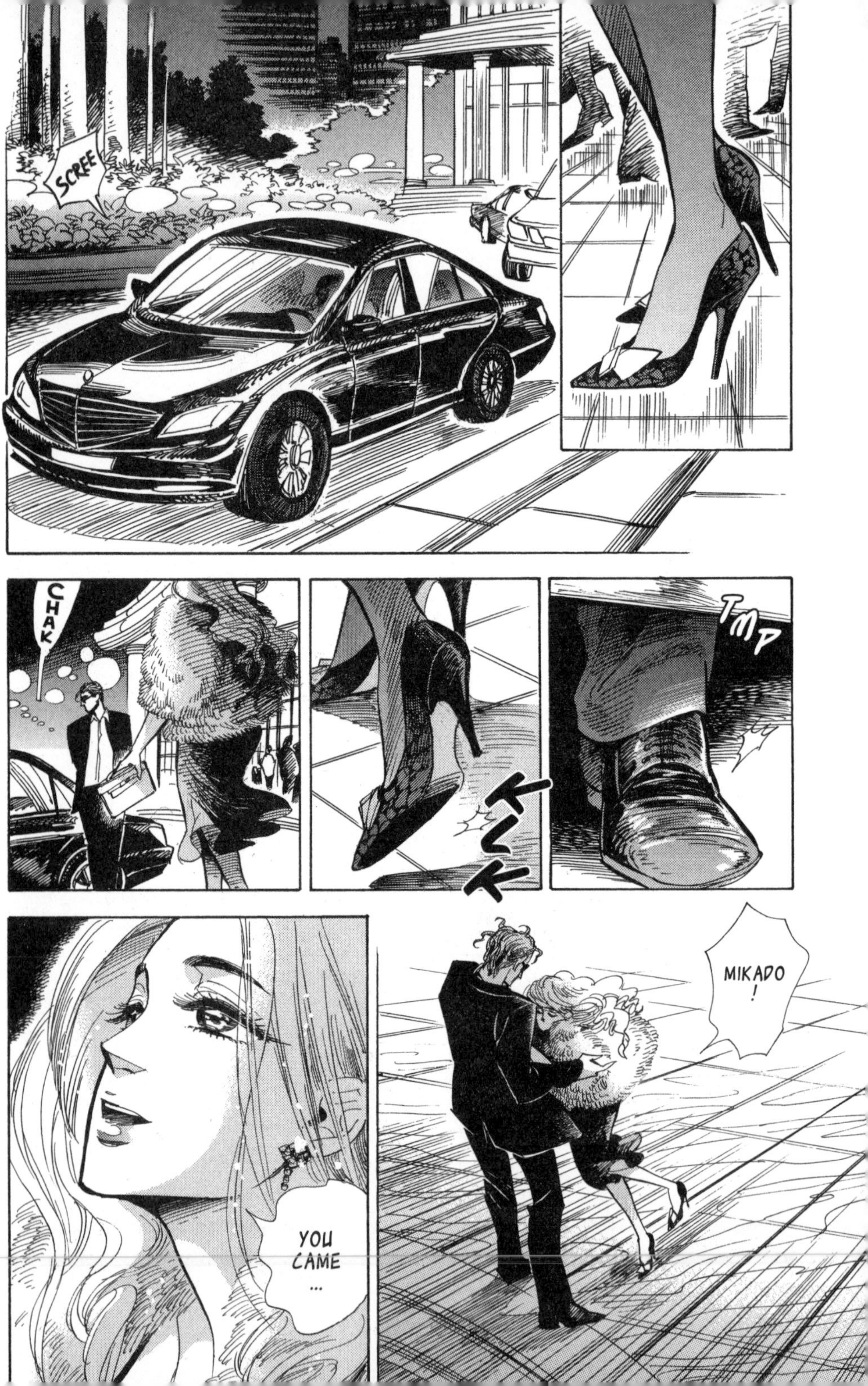
SCREE
TMP
KLK
CHAK
MIKADO!
YOU CAME...

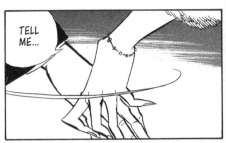

TELL ME...

...THAT YOU...

...FORGIVE ME?

...SUR-PRISED.

I WAS SO...

I DIDN'T THINK YOU'D LEAVE NAKED.

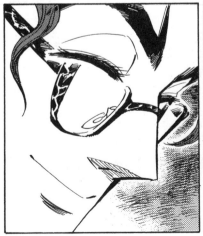

NO...

NOT YET.

LET'S GO INSIDE.

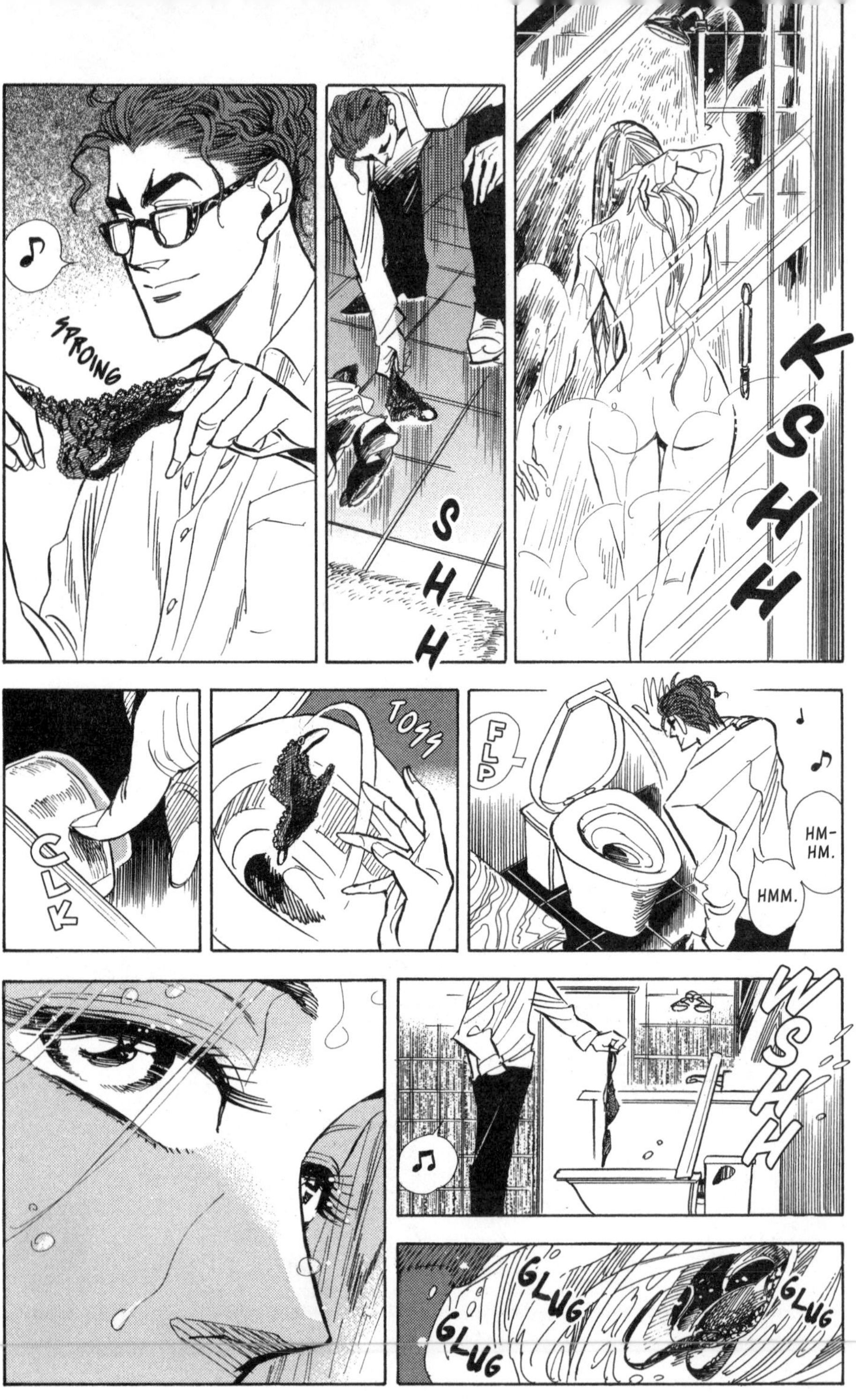
KSHHH
SHHH
♪
SPROING
FLP
♪
♪
HM-HM.
HMM.
TOSS
CLK
WSHHH
♪
GLUG
GLUG
GLUG

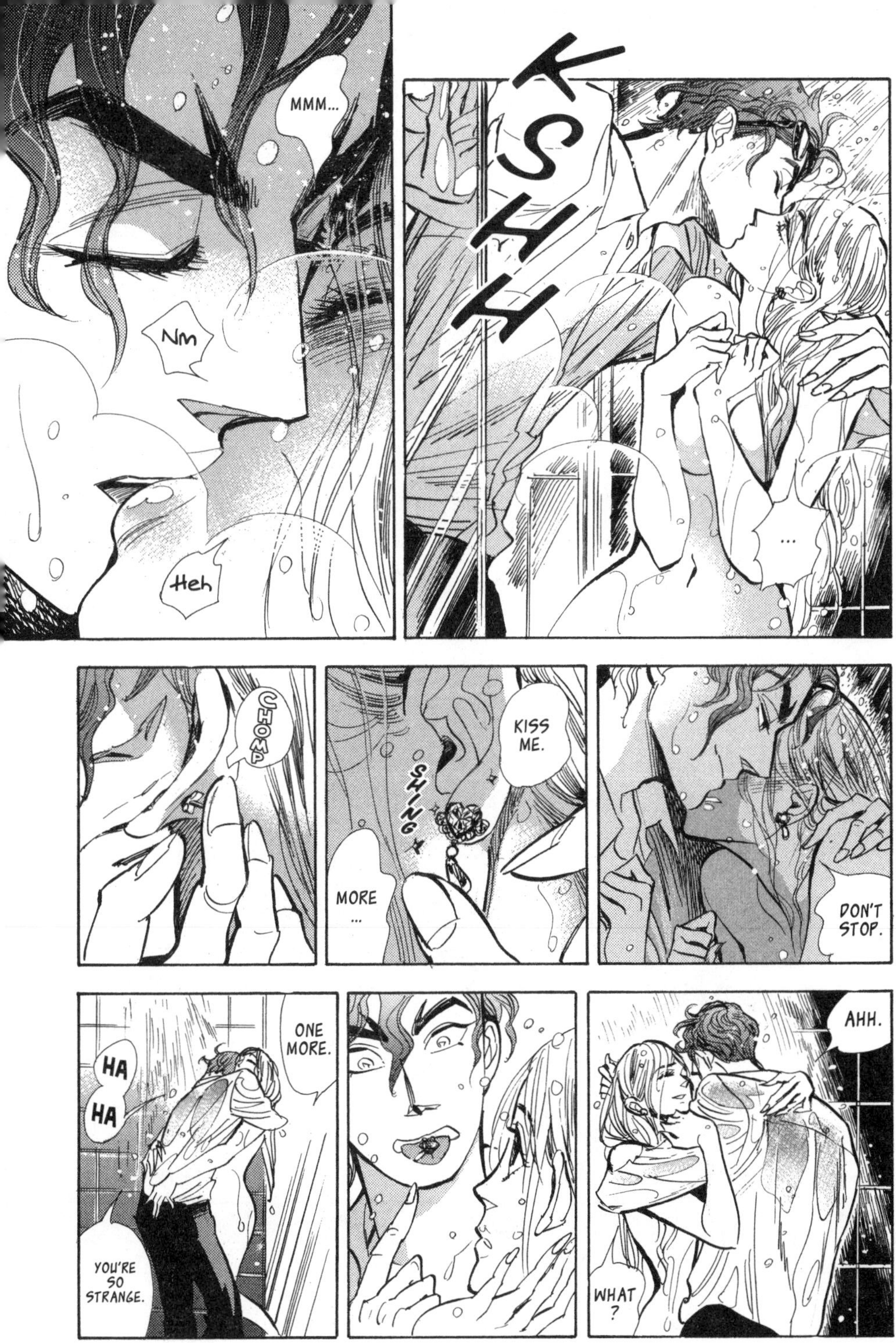
KSHH
...
MMM...
Nm
Heh
DON'T STOP.
KISS ME.
SHING
MORE ...
CHOMP
AHH.
WHAT ?
ONE MORE.
HA HA
YOU'RE SO STRANGE.

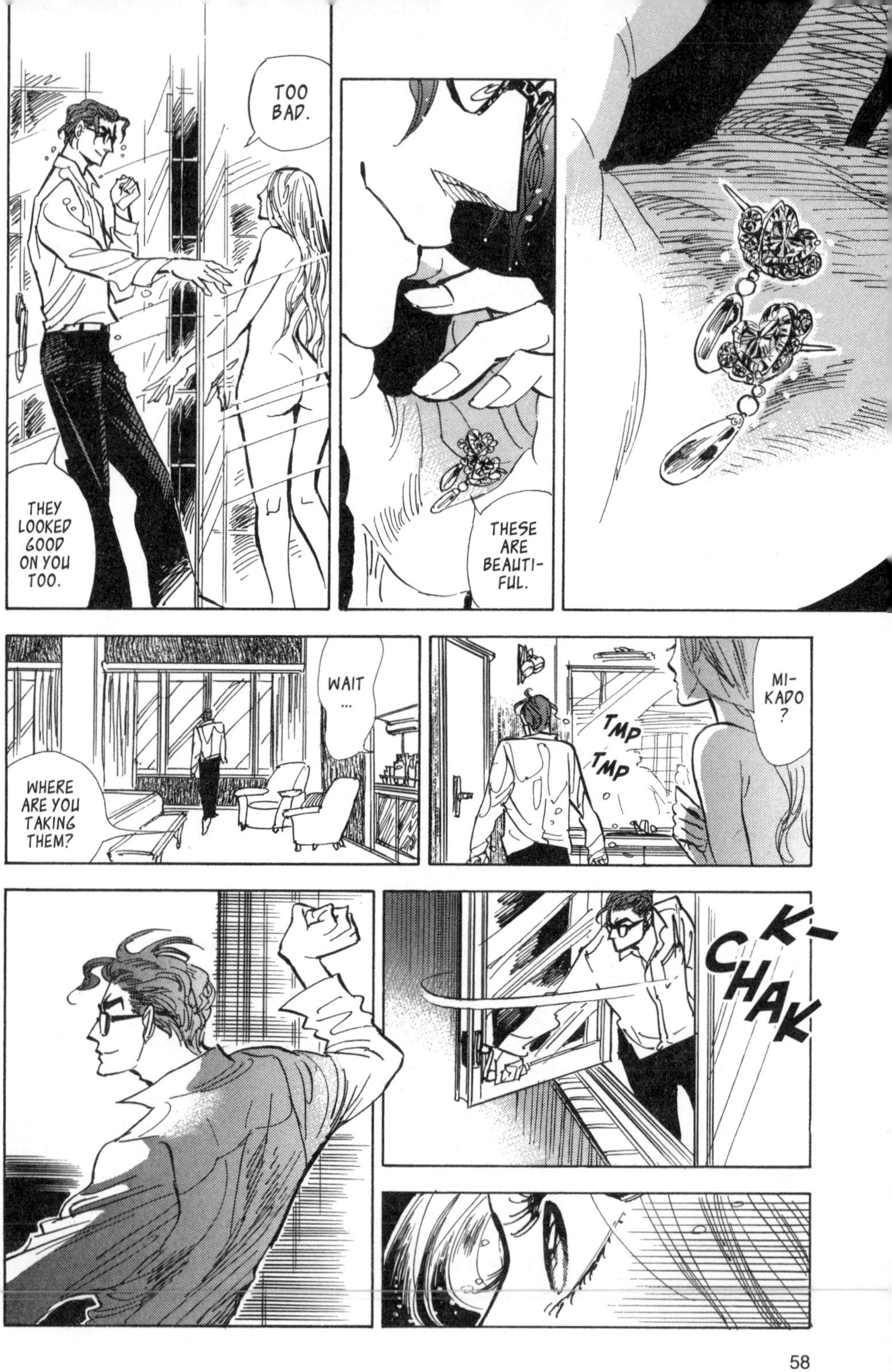
THESE ARE BEAUTI-FUL.
TOO BAD.
THEY LOOKED GOOD ON YOU TOO.
MI-KADO?
TMP
TMP
WAIT ...
WHERE ARE YOU TAKING THEM?
K-CHAK

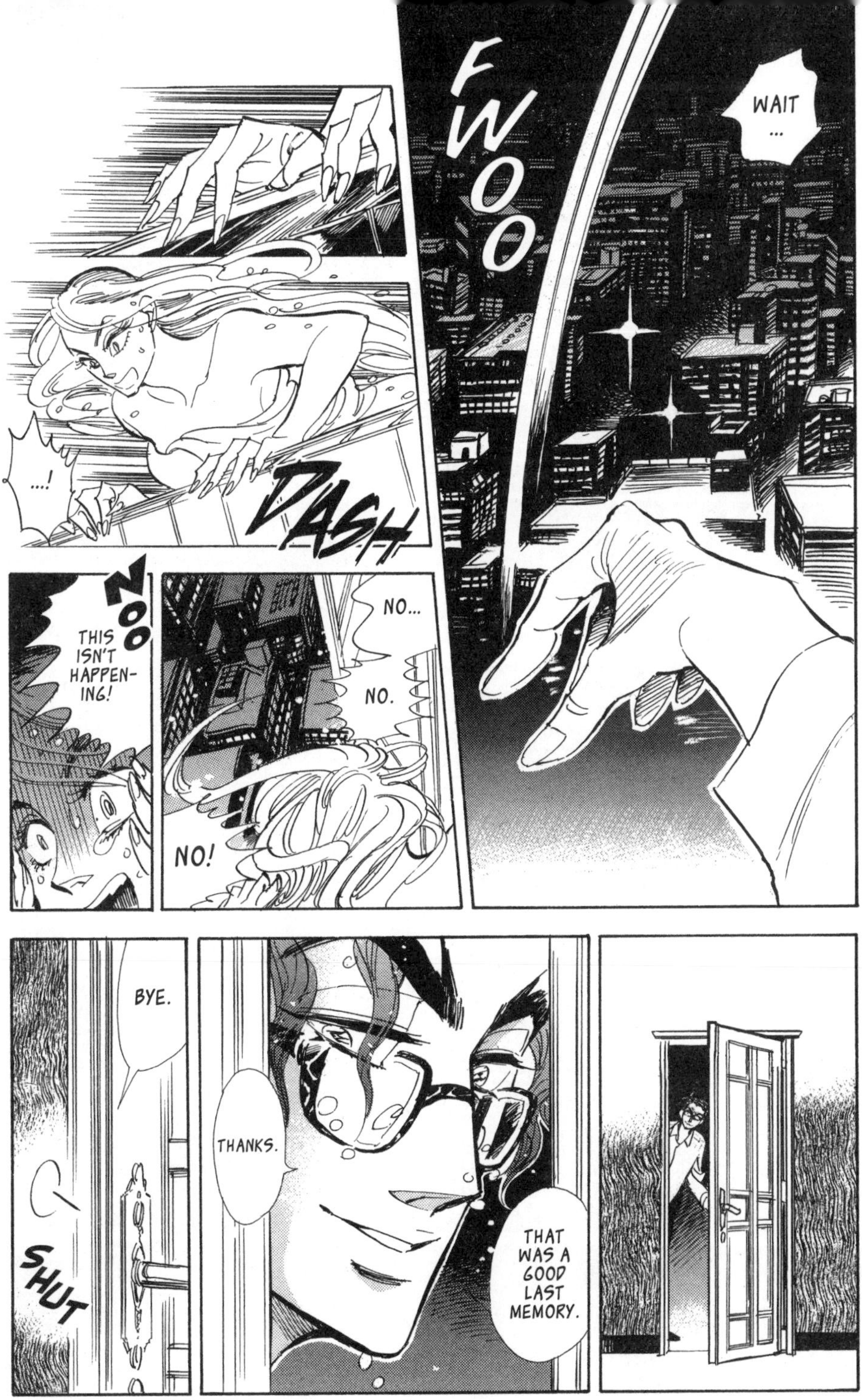
FWOO
WAIT ...
DASH
...!
NO...
NO.
NO!
NOO
THIS ISN'T HAPPENING!
THANKS.
THAT WAS A GOOD LAST MEMORY.
BYE.
SHUT

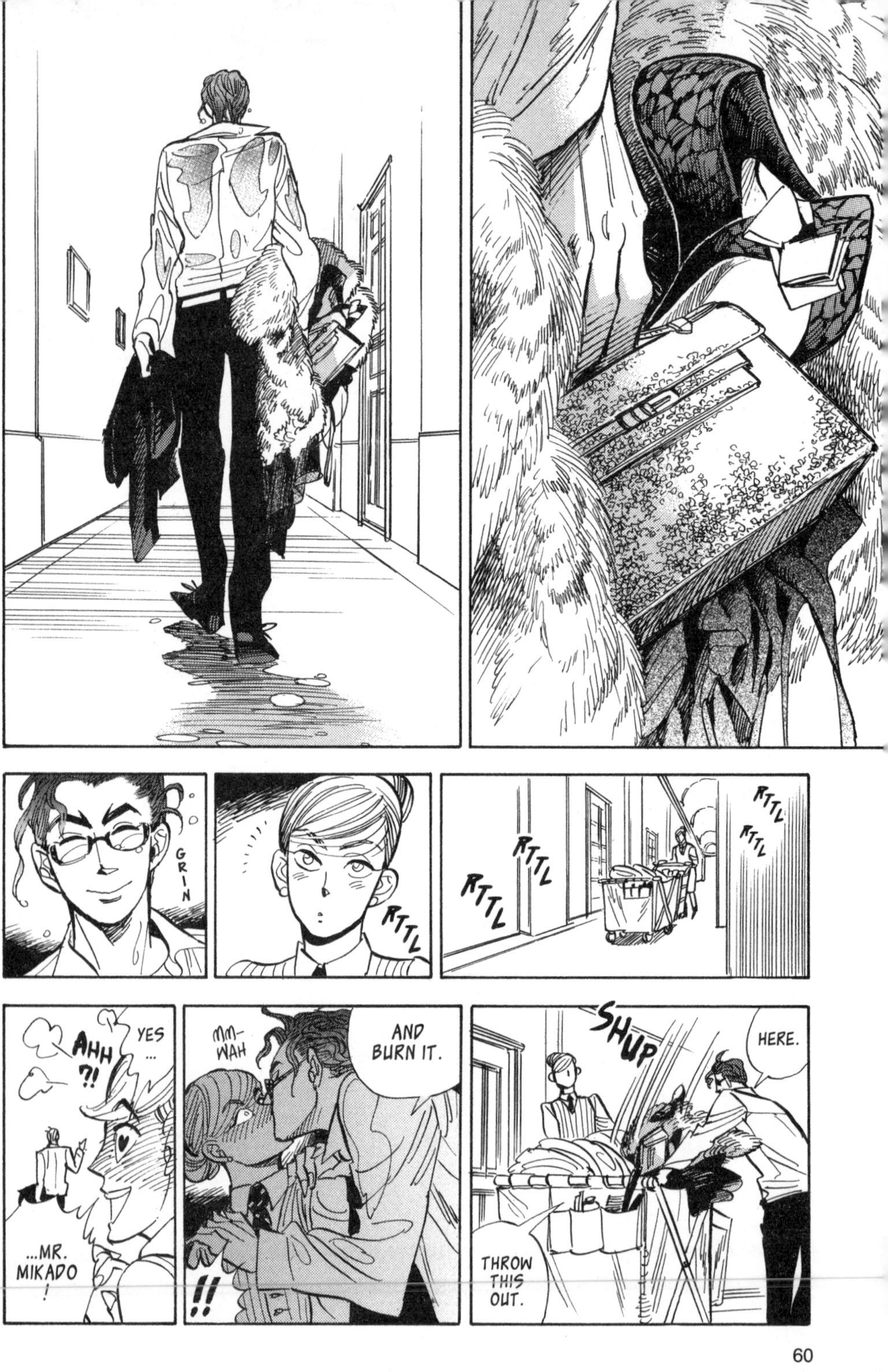
RTTL
RTTL
RTTL
RTTL
RTTL
GRIN
SHUP
HERE.
THROW THIS OUT.
AND BURN IT.
MM-WAH
!!
YES ...
AHH ?!
...MR. MIKADO!

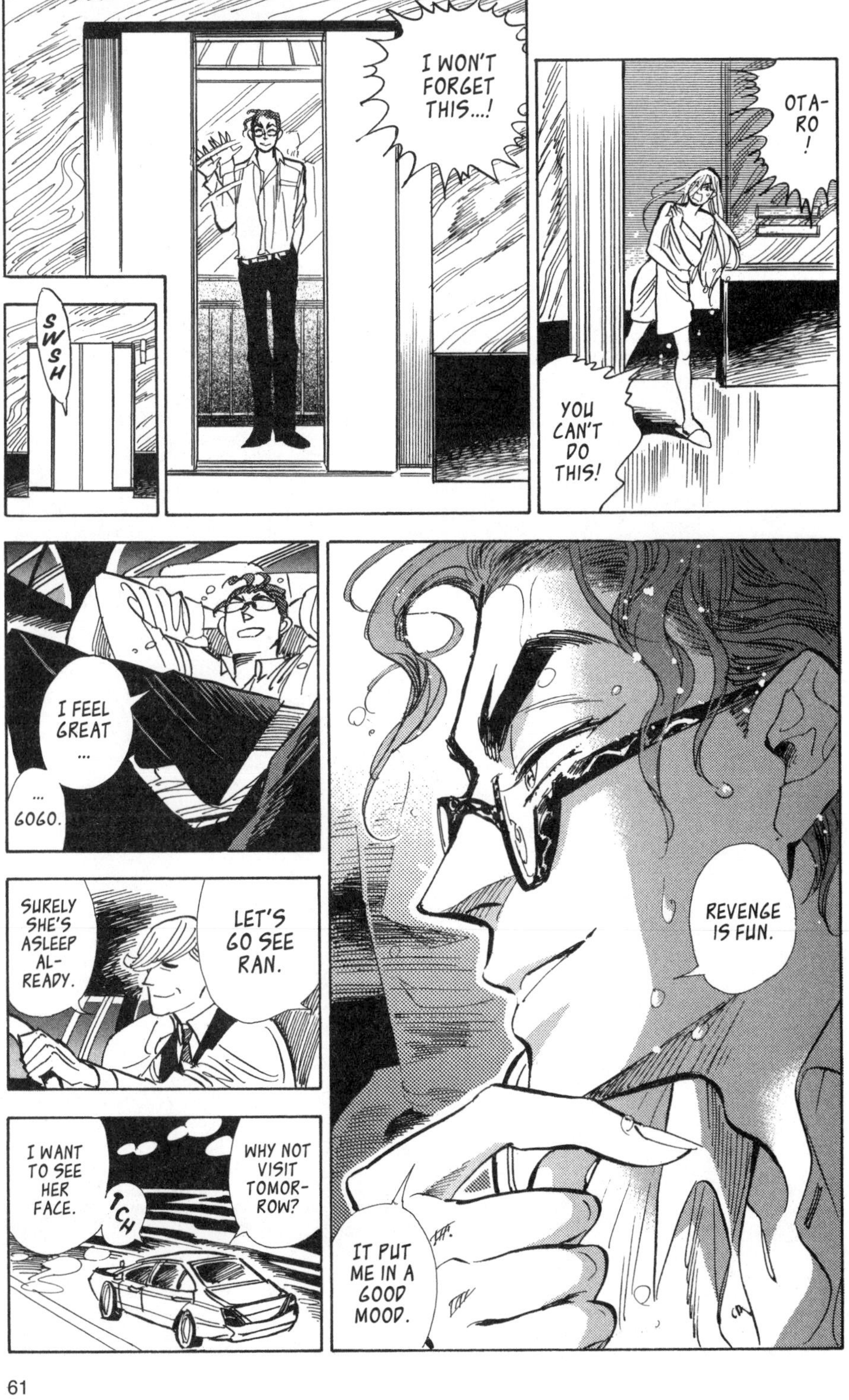
OTA-RO!
YOU CAN'T DO THIS!
I WON'T FORGET THIS...!
SWSH
REVENGE IS FUN.
IT PUT ME IN A GOOD MOOD.
I FEEL GREAT ...
... GOGO.
LET'S GO SEE RAN.
SURELY SHE'S ASLEEP AL-READY.
WHY NOT VISIT TOMOR-ROW?
TCH
I WANT TO SEE HER FACE.

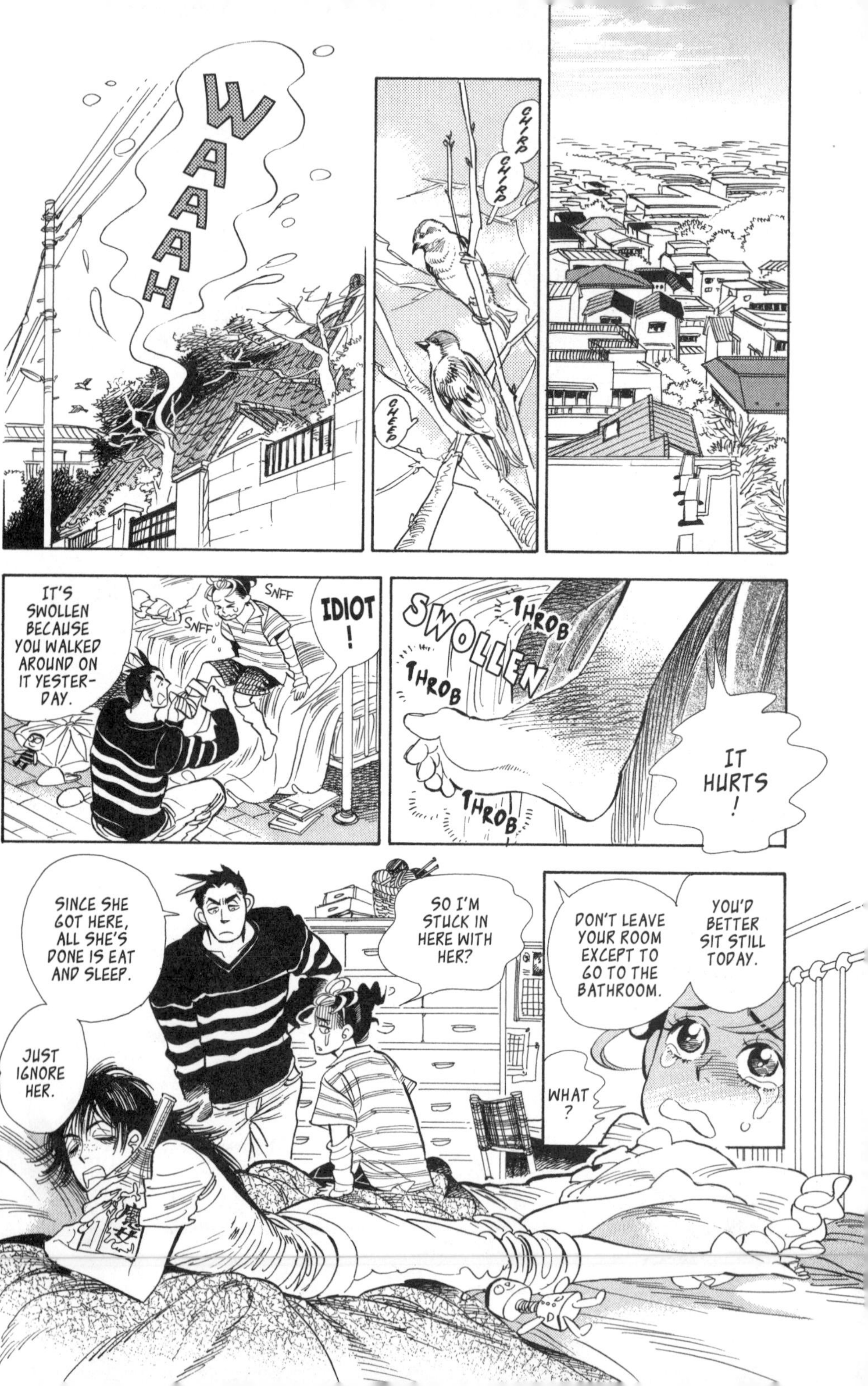
CHIRP CHIRP
CHEEP
WAAAAH
SWOLLEN
THROB
THROB
THROB
IT HURTS!
IDIOT!
SNFF
SNFF
IT'S SWOLLEN BECAUSE YOU WALKED AROUND ON IT YESTER-DAY.
YOU'D BETTER SIT STILL TODAY.
DON'T LEAVE YOUR ROOM EXCEPT TO GO TO THE BATHROOM.
WHAT?
SO I'M STUCK IN HERE WITH HER?
SINCE SHE GOT HERE, ALL SHE'S DONE IS EAT AND SLEEP.
JUST IGNORE HER.

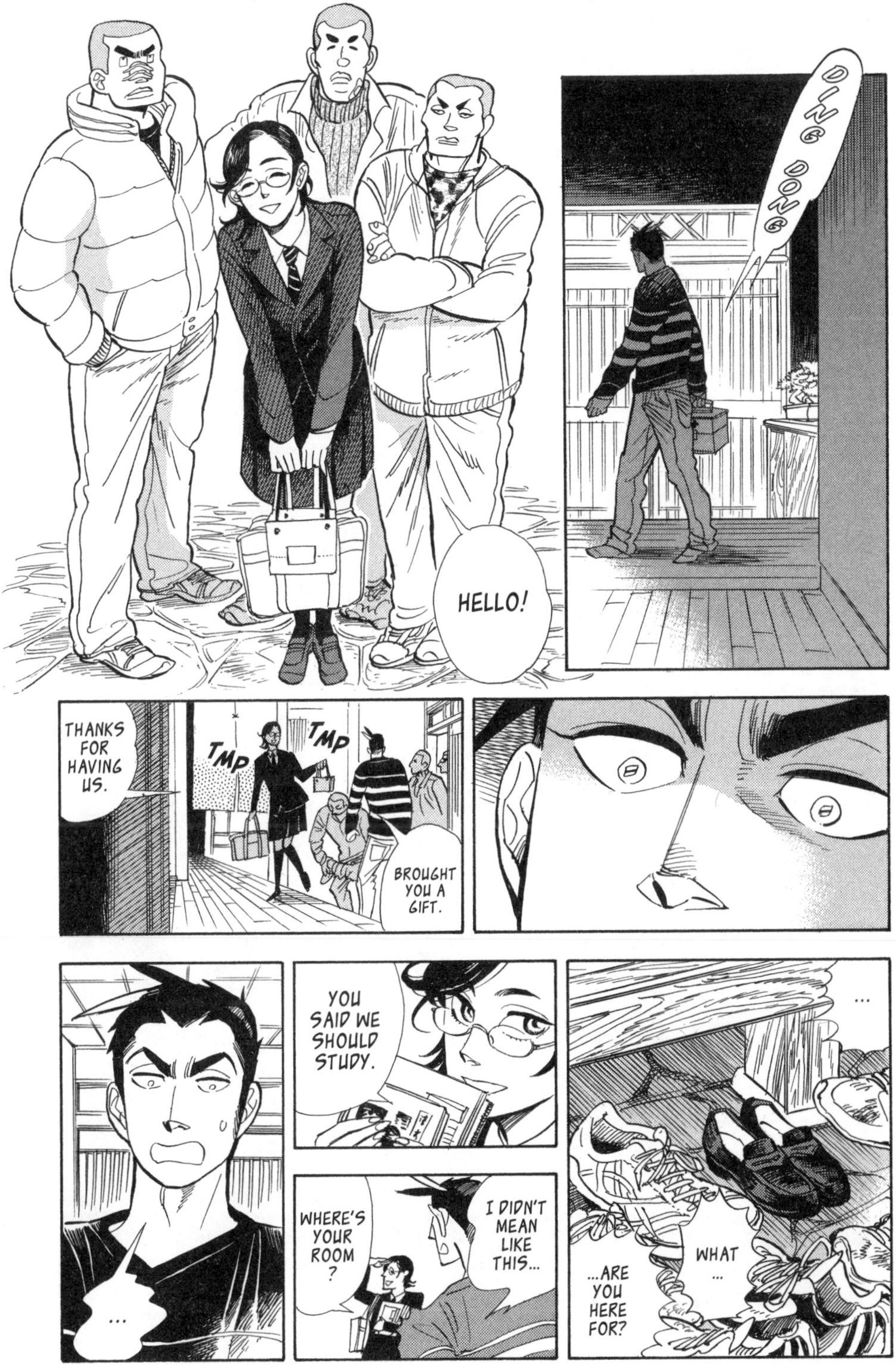
DING DONG
HELLO!
TMP
TMP
THANKS FOR HAVING US.
BROUGHT YOU A GIFT.
...
WHAT ...
...ARE YOU HERE FOR?
YOU SAID WE SHOULD STUDY.
I DIDN'T MEAN LIKE THIS...
WHERE'S YOUR ROOM?
...

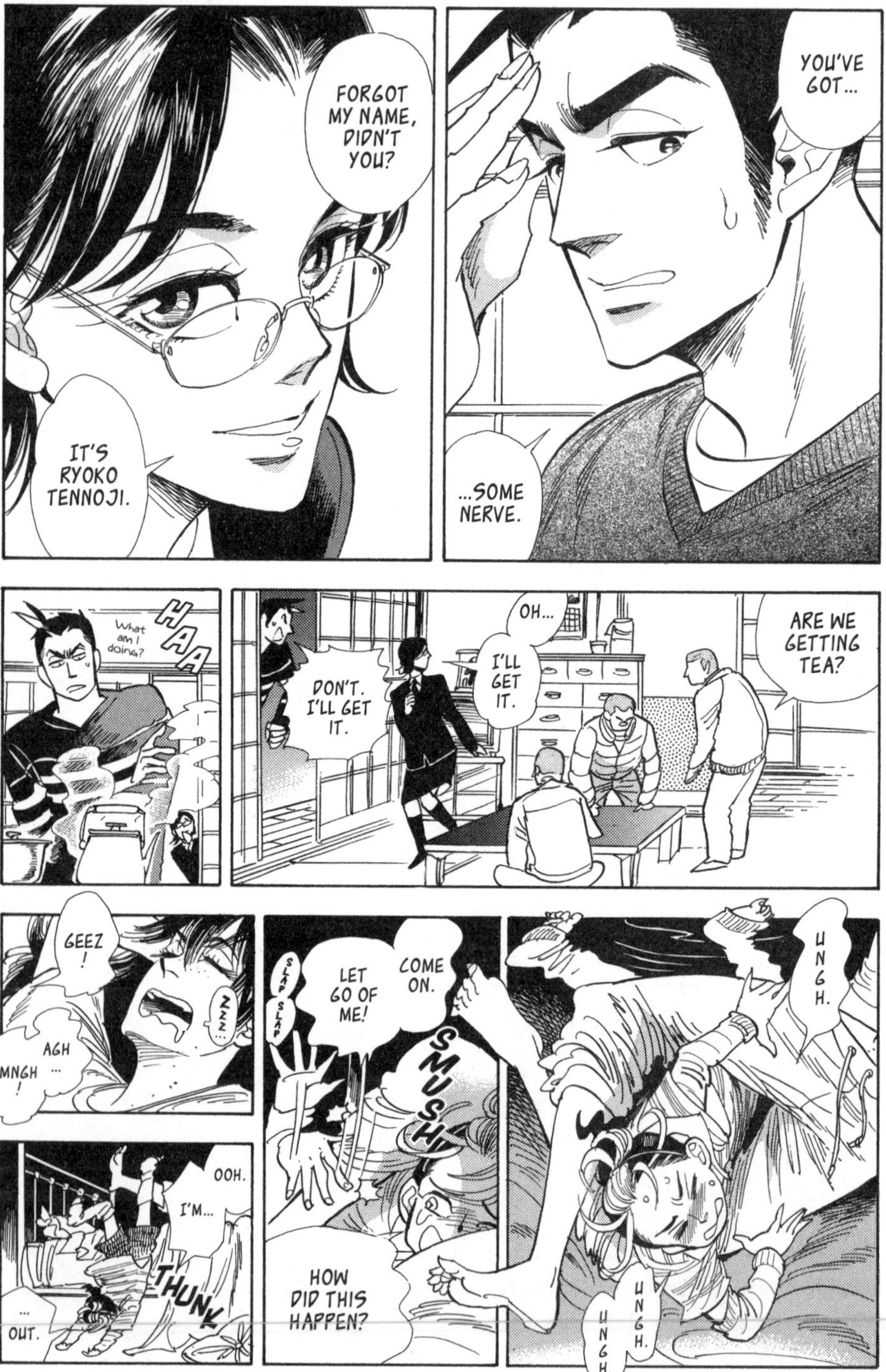
YOU'VE GOT...
...SOME NERVE.
FORGOT MY NAME, DIDN'T YOU?
IT'S RYOKO TENNOJI.
ARE WE GETTING TEA?
OH...
I'LL GET IT.
DON'T. I'LL GET IT.
HAA
What am I doing?
UNGH.
COME ON.
LET GO OF ME!
SLAP SLAP
SMUSH
HOW DID THIS HAPPEN?
UNGH.
UNGH.
GEEZ!
ZZZ...
AGH...
MNGH!
OOH.
I'M...
THUNK
...OUT.

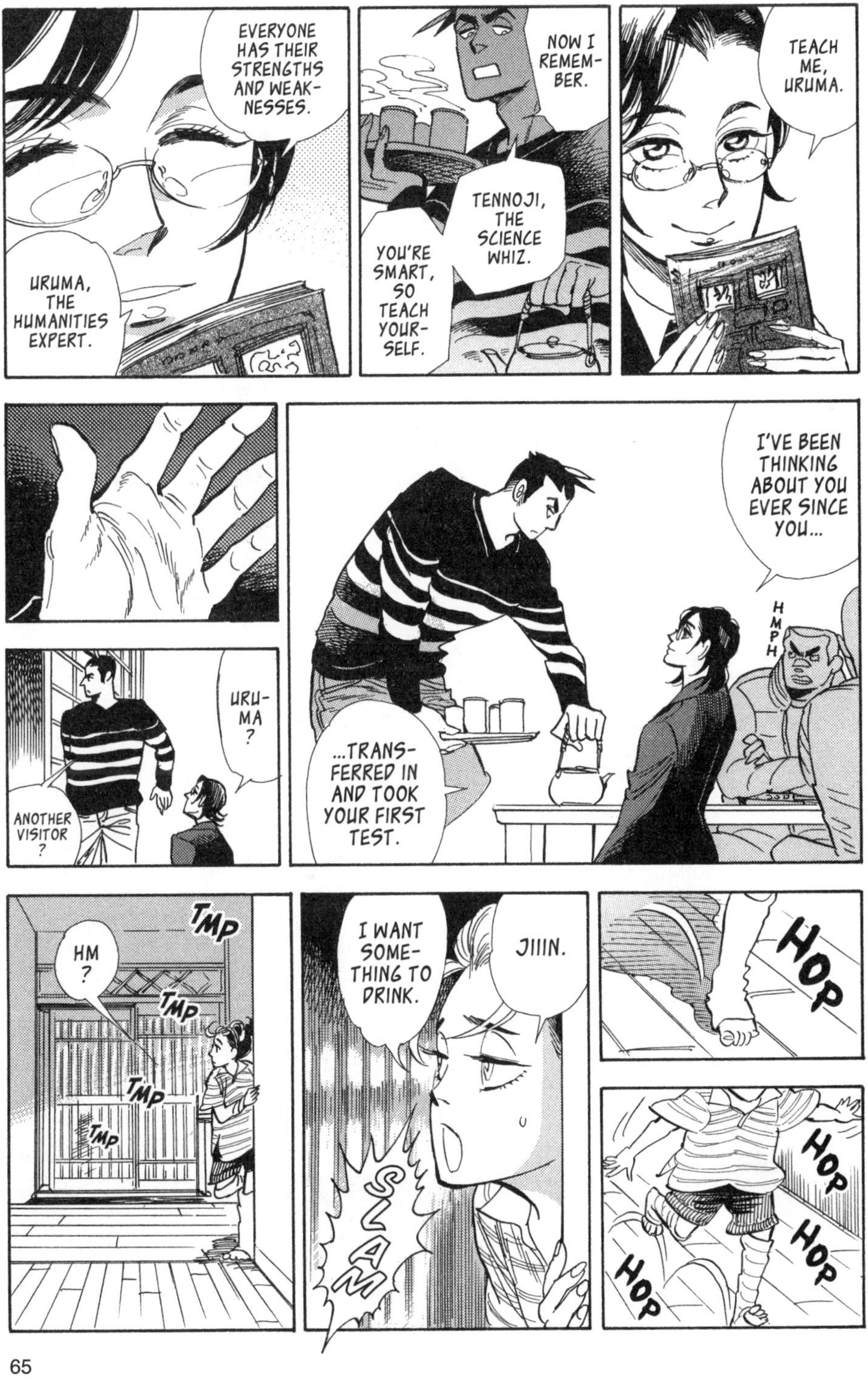
TEACH ME, URUMA.
NOW I REMEMBER.
TENNOJI, THE SCIENCE WHIZ.
YOU'RE SMART, SO TEACH YOURSELF.
EVERYONE HAS THEIR STRENGTHS AND WEAKNESSES.
URUMA, THE HUMANITIES EXPERT.
I'VE BEEN THINKING ABOUT YOU EVER SINCE YOU...
HMPH
...TRANSFERRED IN AND TOOK YOUR FIRST TEST.
URUMA?
ANOTHER VISITOR?
HOP
HOP
HOP
HOP
HOP
JIIIN.
I WANT SOMETHING TO DRINK.
SLAM
TMP
HM?
TMP
TMP
TMP

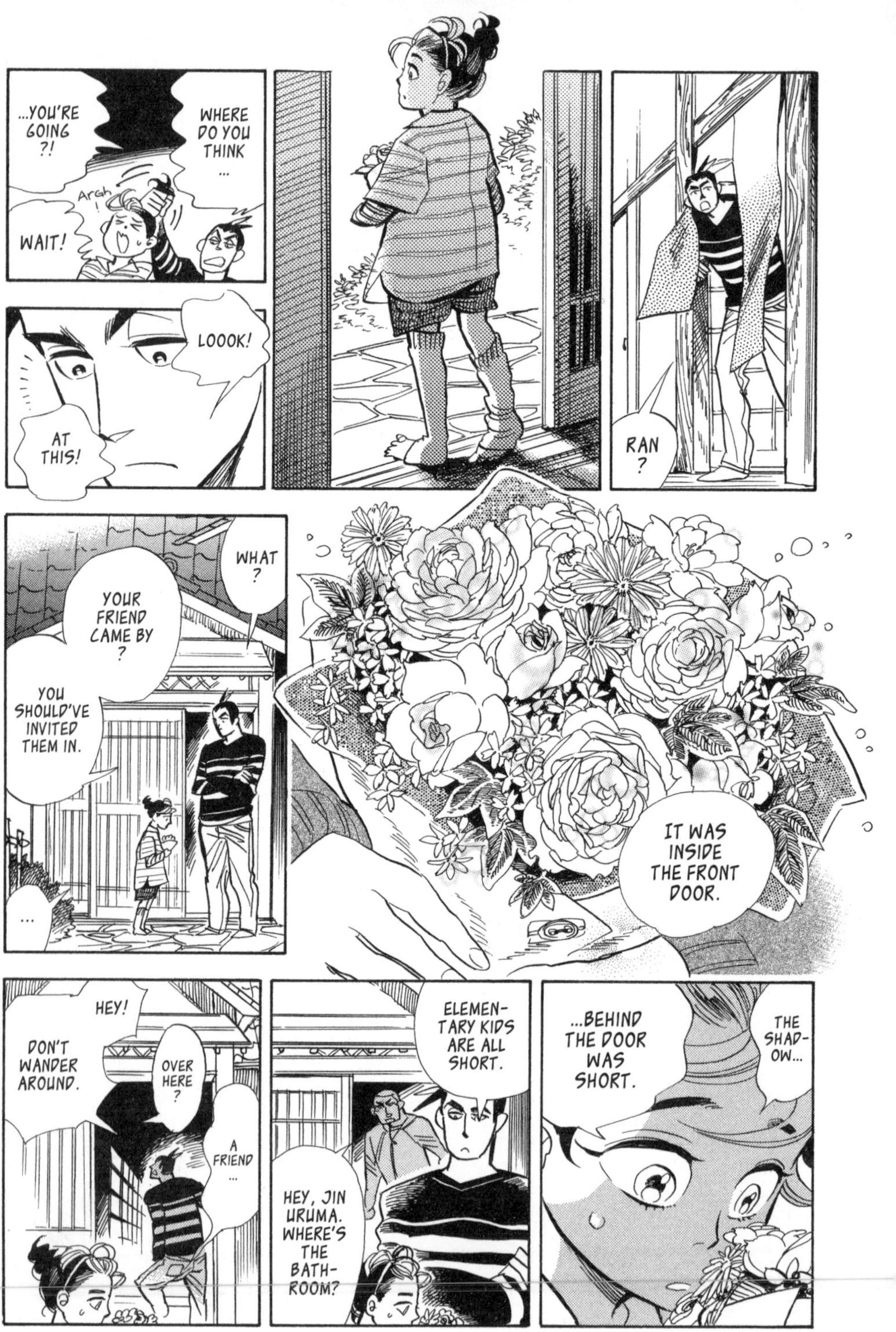
RAN ?
WHERE DO YOU THINK ...
...YOU'RE GOING ?!
Argh !
WAIT!
LOOOK!
AT THIS!
IT WAS INSIDE THE FRONT DOOR.
WHAT ?
YOUR FRIEND CAME BY ?
YOU SHOULD'VE INVITED THEM IN.
...
THE SHADOW...
...BEHIND THE DOOR WAS SHORT.
ELEMENTARY KIDS ARE ALL SHORT.
HEY, JIN URUMA. WHERE'S THE BATHROOM?
HEY!
DON'T WANDER AROUND.
OVER HERE ?
A FRIEND ...

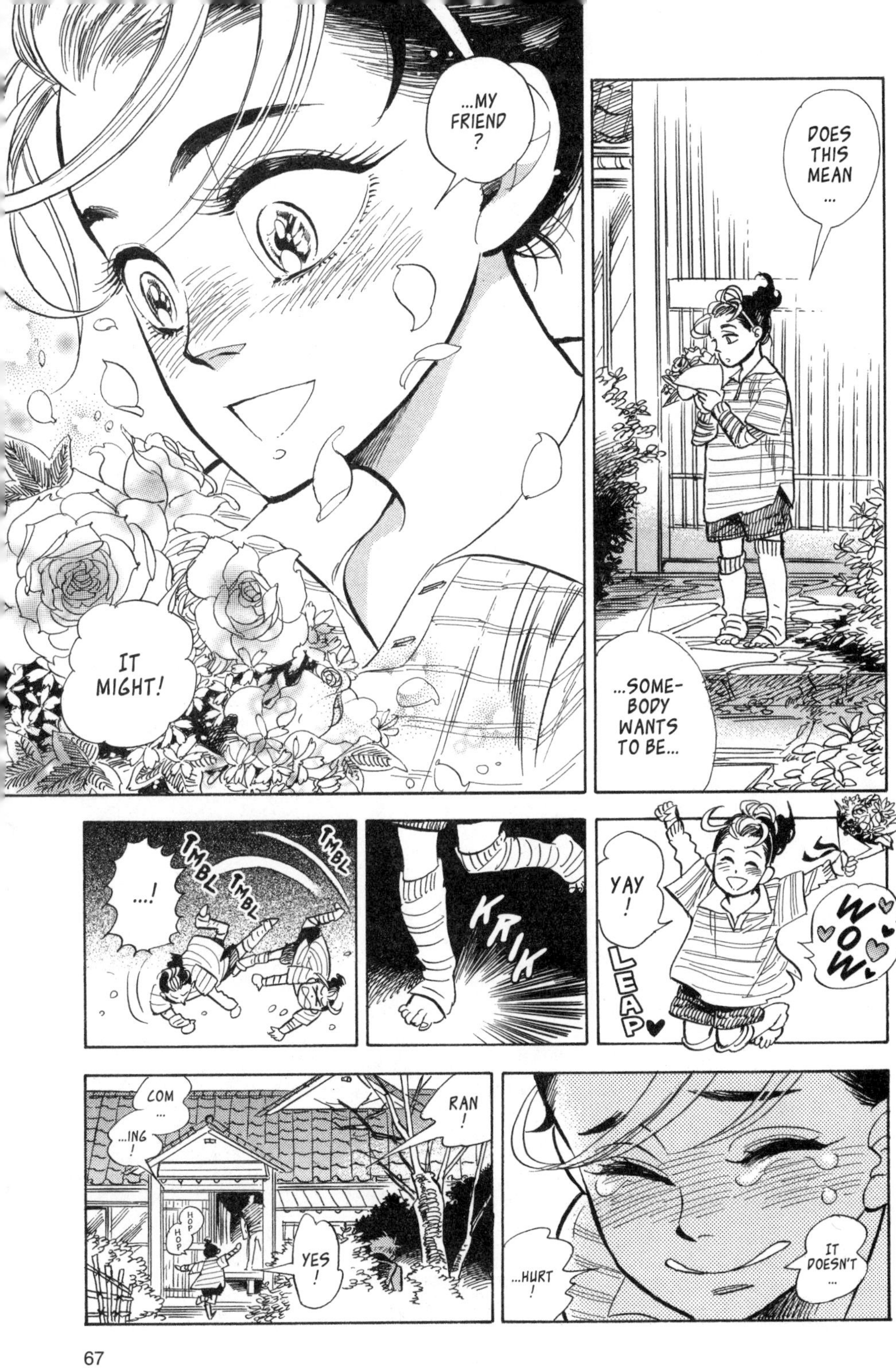
DOES THIS MEAN ...
...SOME-BODY WANTS TO BE...
...MY FRIEND ?
IT MIGHT!
YAY !
LEAP
WOW
KRIK
...!
TMBL
TMBL
TMBL
IT DOESN'T ...
...HURT !
RAN !
COM ...
...ING !
YES !
HOP
HOP

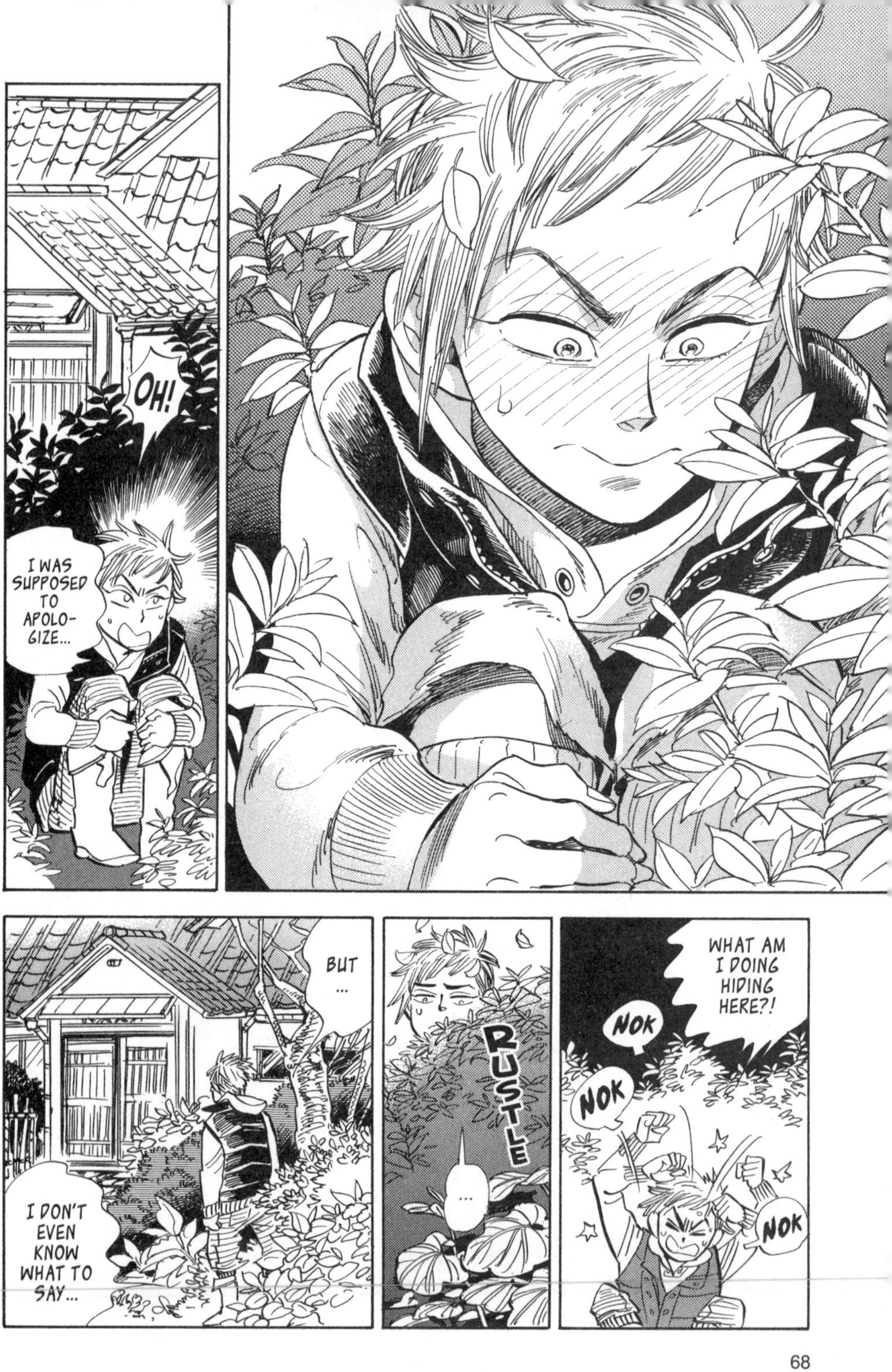
OH!
I WAS SUPPOSED TO APOLOGIZE...
WHAT AM I DOING HIDING HERE?!
NOK
NOK
NOK
RUSTLE
...
BUT ...
I DON'T EVEN KNOW WHAT TO SAY...

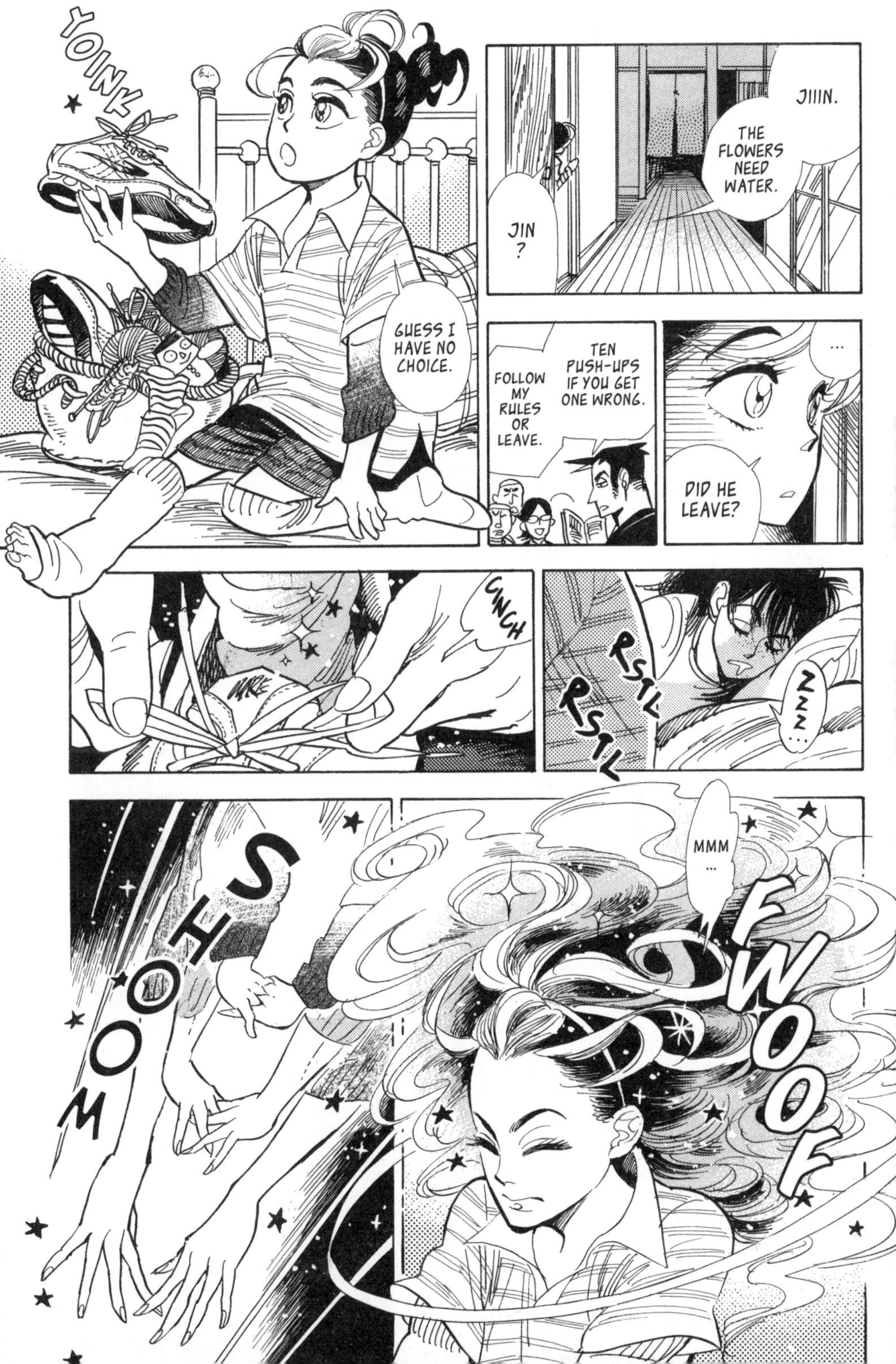
JIIN.
THE FLOWERS NEED WATER.
JIN?
...
DID HE LEAVE?
TEN PUSH-UPS IF YOU GET ONE WRONG.
FOLLOW MY RULES OR LEAVE.
YOINK
GUESS I HAVE NO CHOICE.
RSTL
RSTL
ZZZ...
CINCH
MMM...
FWOOF
SHOOOM

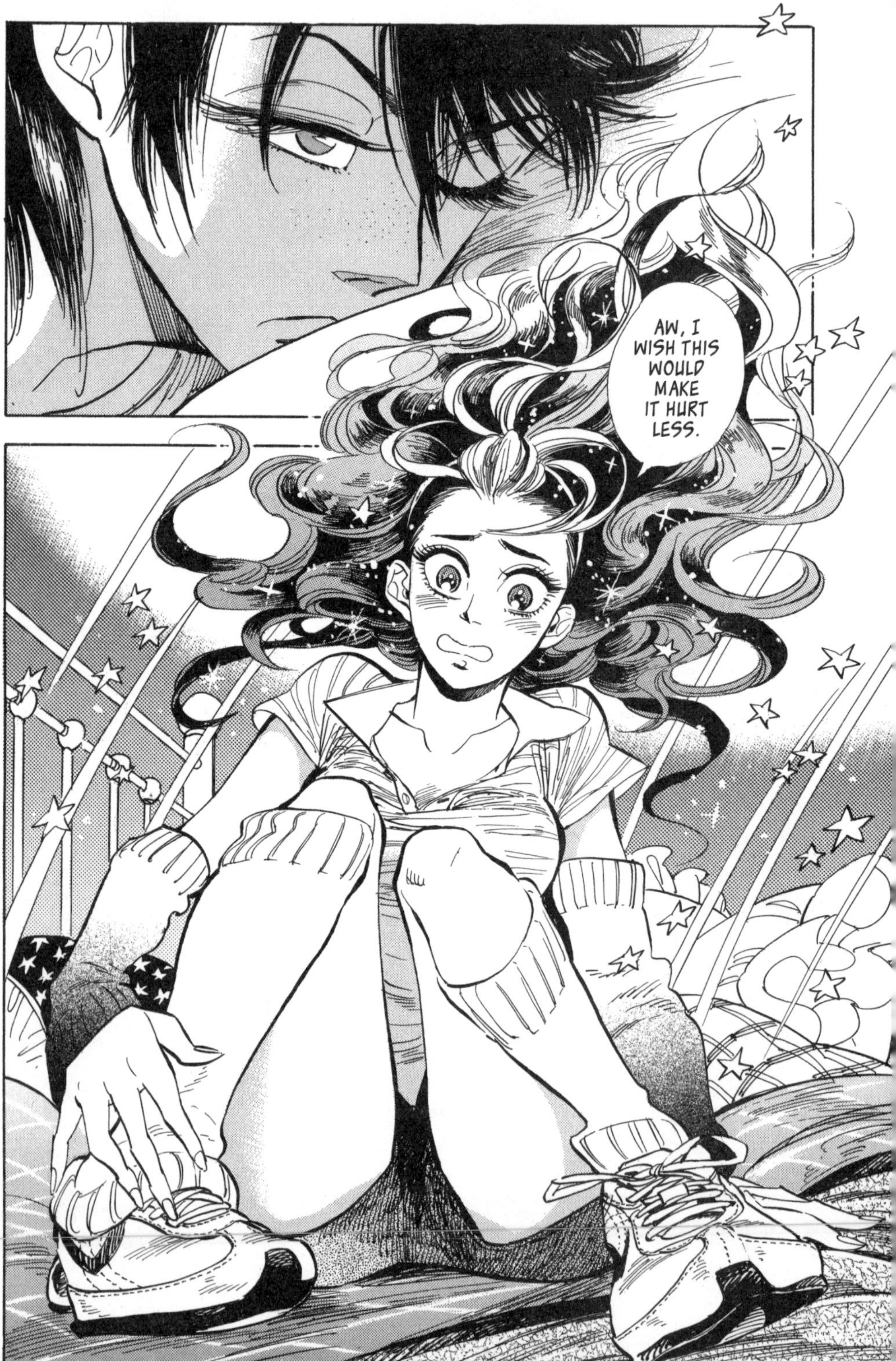
AW, I WISH THIS WOULD MAKE IT HURT LESS.

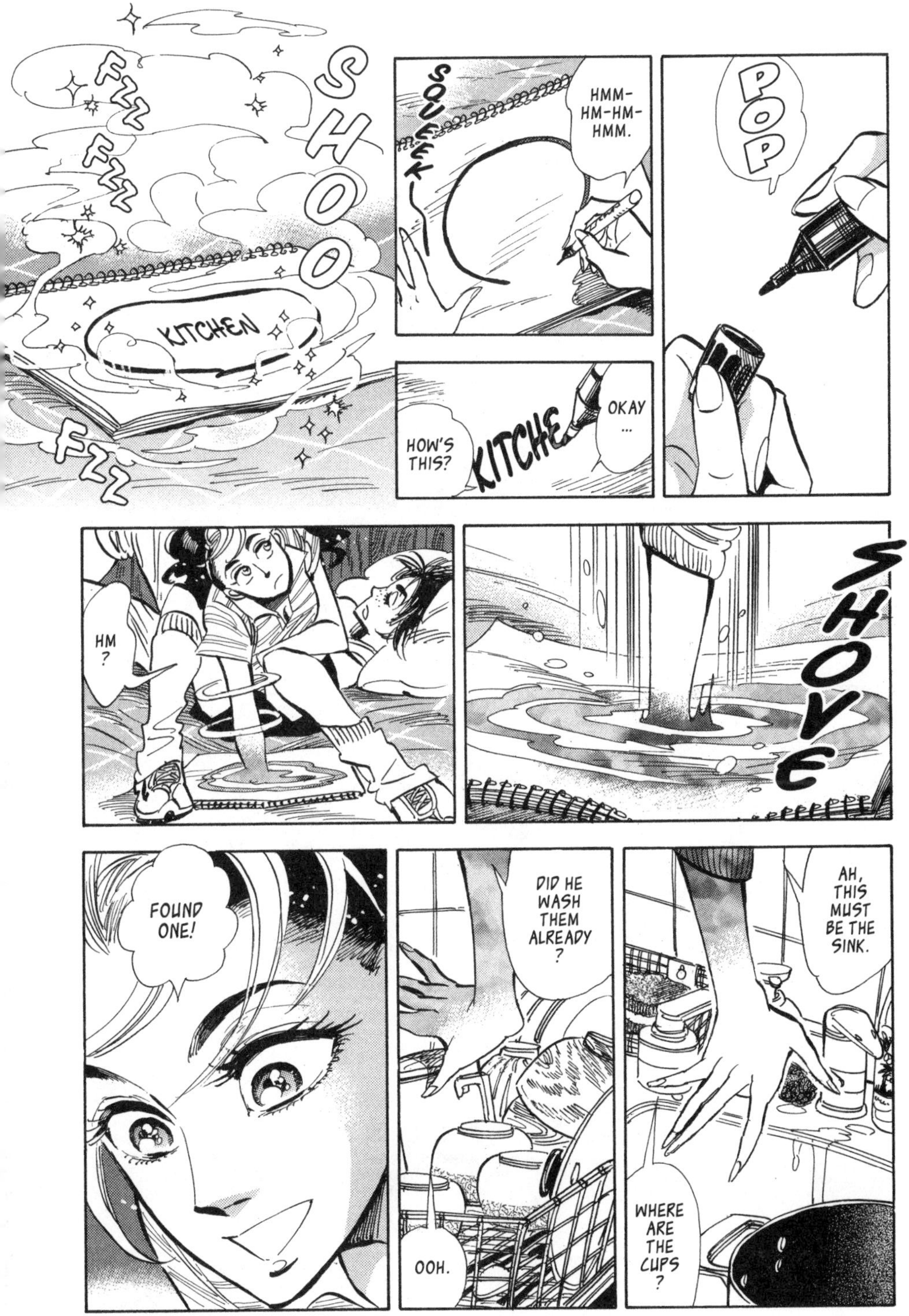
POP
HMM-HM-HM-HMM.
SQUEEK
OKAY ...
KITCHE
HOW'S THIS?
SHOO
FZZ
FZZ
KITCHEN
FZZ
SHOVE
HM?
AH, THIS MUST BE THE SINK.
WHERE ARE THE CUPS?
DID HE WASH THEM ALREADY?
OOH.
FOUND ONE!

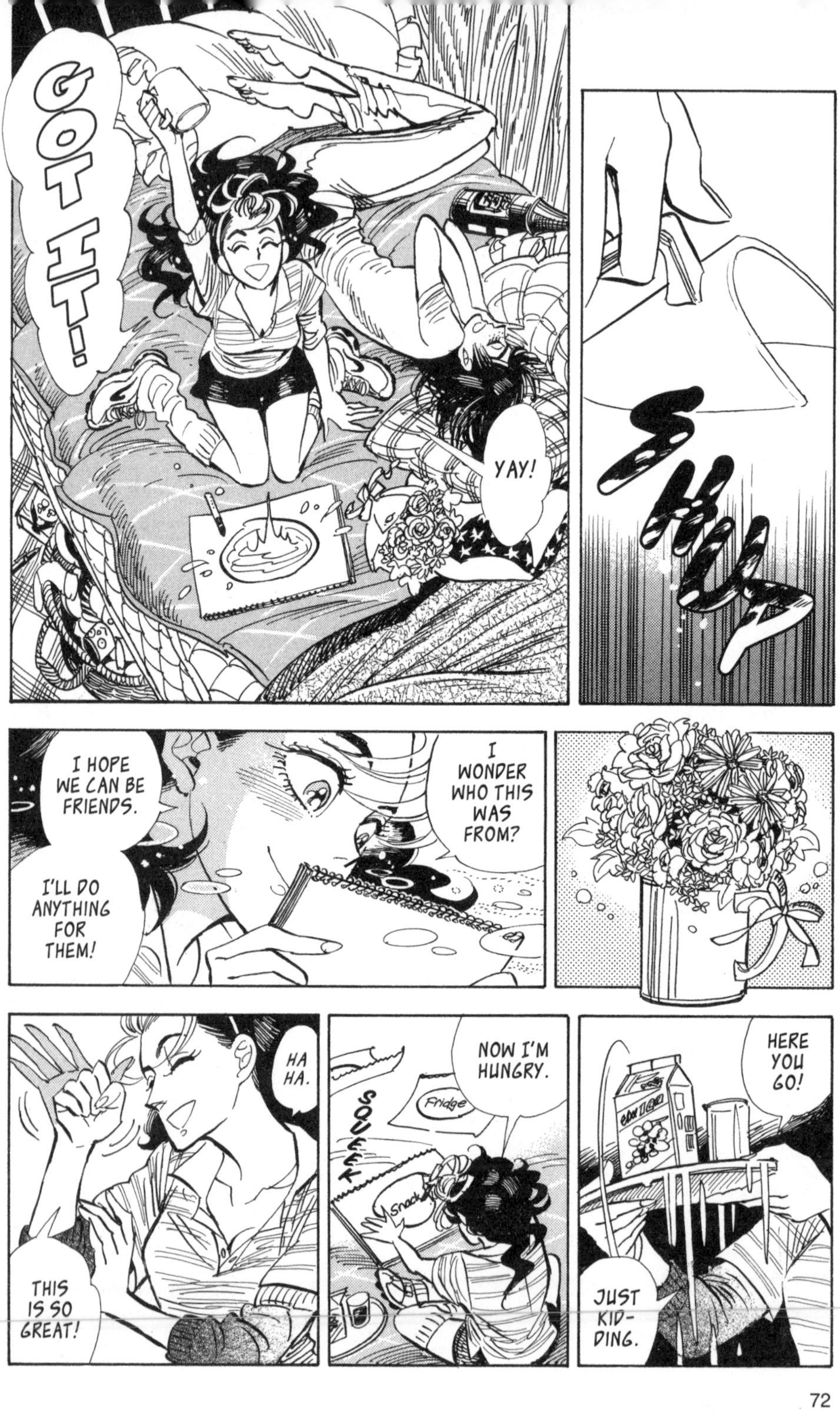
GOT IT!
YAY!
I WONDER WHO THIS WAS FROM?
I HOPE WE CAN BE FRIENDS.
I'LL DO ANYTHING FOR THEM!
HERE YOU GO!
JUST KID-DING.
NOW I'M HUNGRY.
Fridge
SQUEEK
Snack
HA HA.
THIS IS SO GREAT!

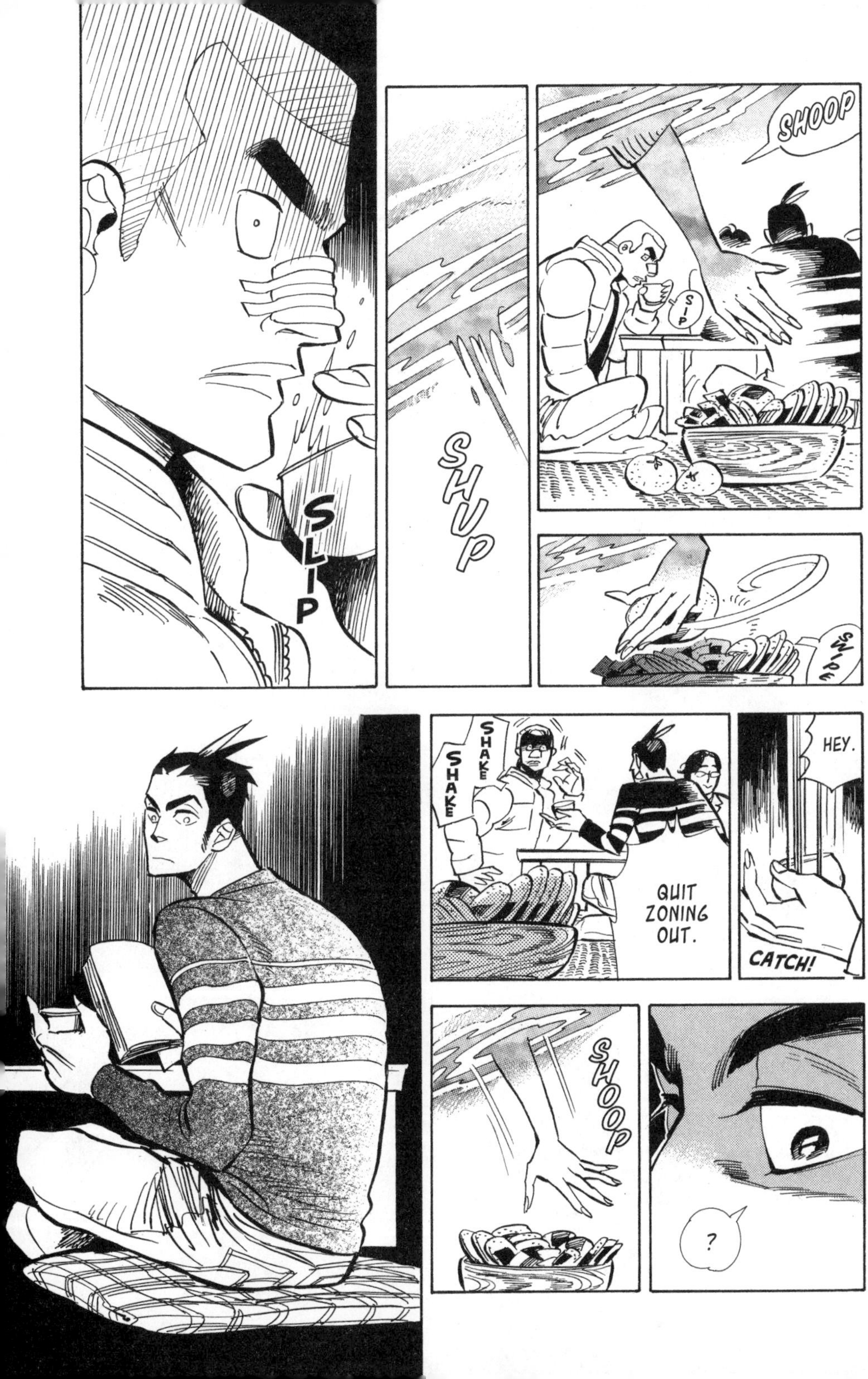
SHOOP
SIP
SWIPE
SHUP
SLIP
HEY.
CATCH!
SHAKE
SHAKE
QUIT ZONING OUT.
?
SHOOP

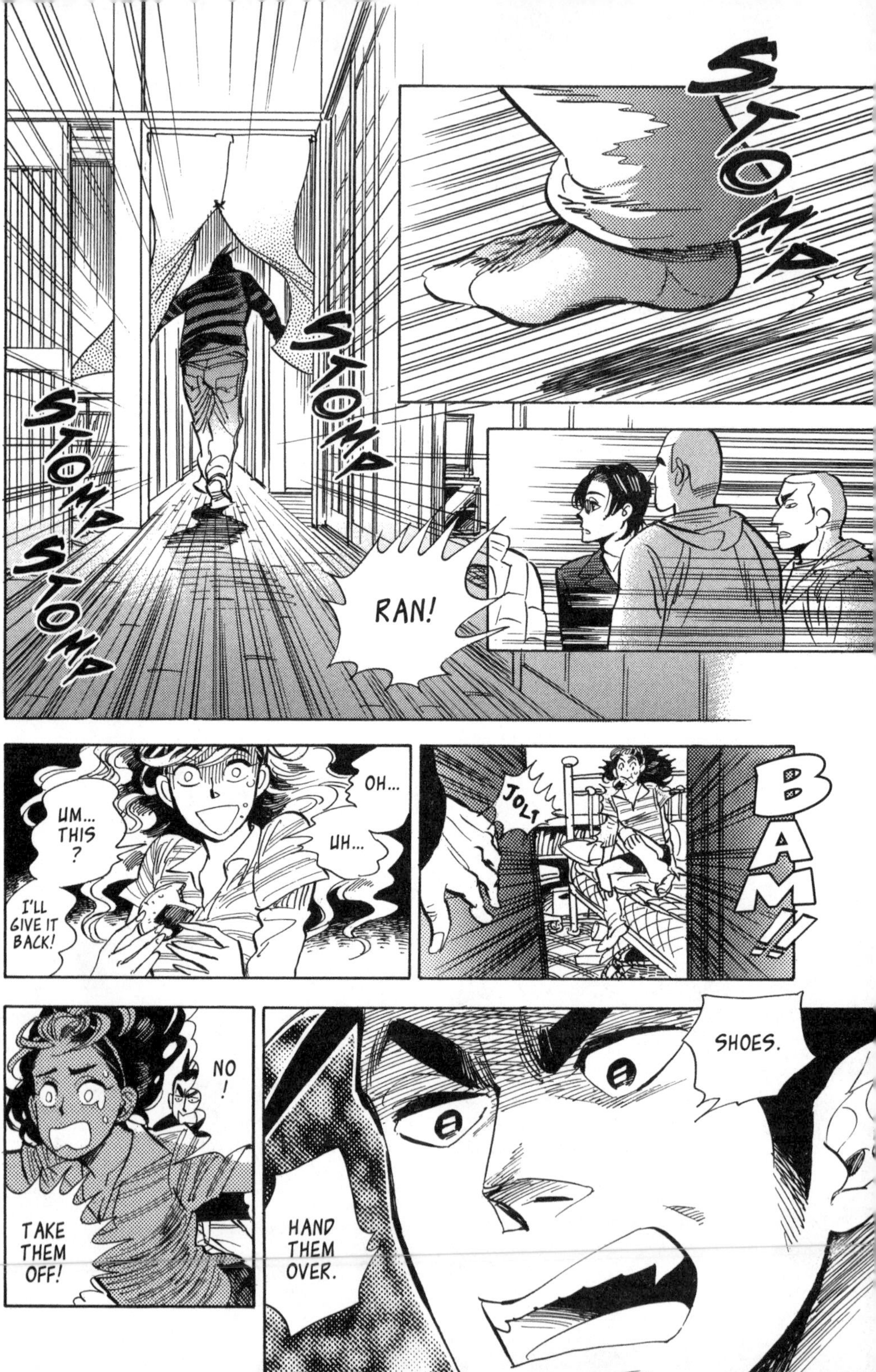
STOMP
RAN!
STOMP
STOMP
STOMP
STOMP
JOLT
BAM!!
OH...
UH...
UM... THIS?
I'LL GIVE IT BACK!
SHOES.
HAND THEM OVER.
NO!
TAKE THEM OFF!

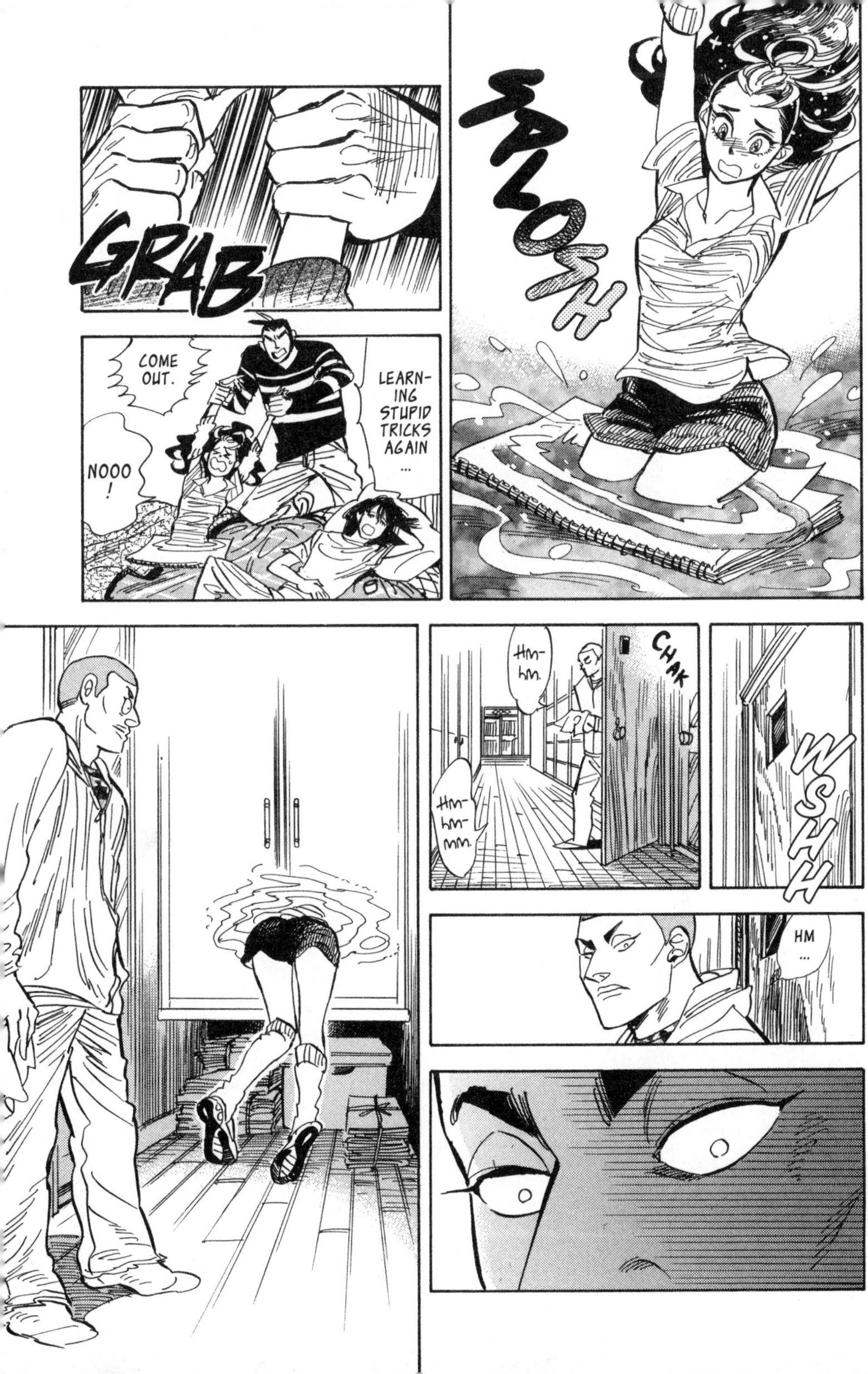
SPLOSH
GRAB
LEARNING STUPID TRICKS AGAIN ...
COME OUT.
NOOO!
WSHH
CHAK
Hm-hm.
Hm-hm-mm.
HM ...

THMP

...

ULP

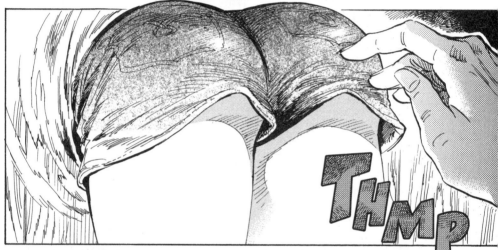

THMP

NOW WHO IS IT?

DING DONG

WHO JUST POKED ME?!

RAN!

SPLSH

HUH ?

HAAH ?!

!!

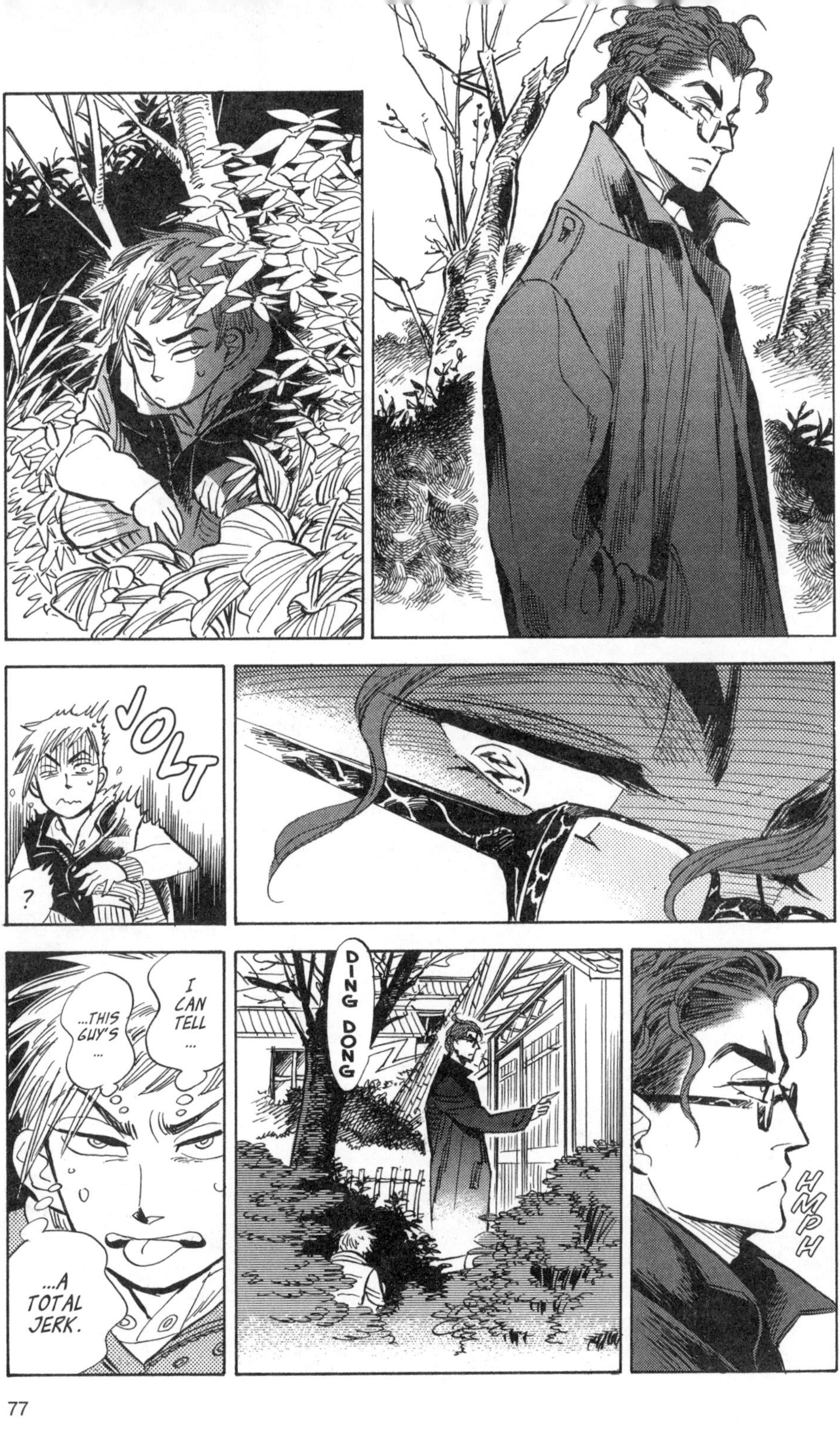
JOLT
?
HMPH
DING DONG
I CAN TELL ...
...THIS GUY'S ...
...A TOTAL JERK.

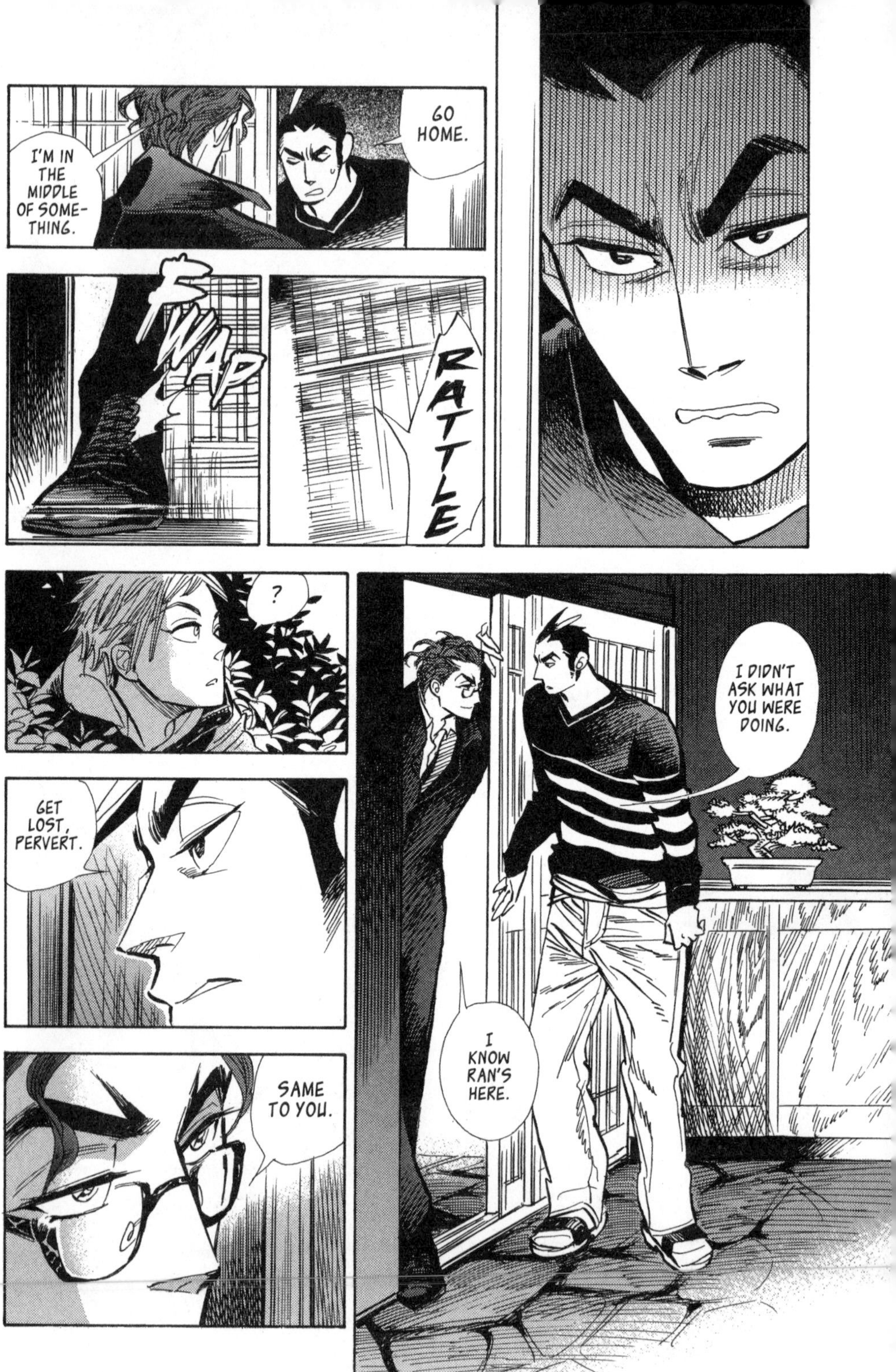
GO HOME.
I'M IN THE MIDDLE OF SOME-THING.
RATTLE
FWAP
I DIDN'T ASK WHAT YOU WERE DOING.
I KNOW RAN'S HERE.
?
GET LOST, PERVERT.
SAME TO YOU.

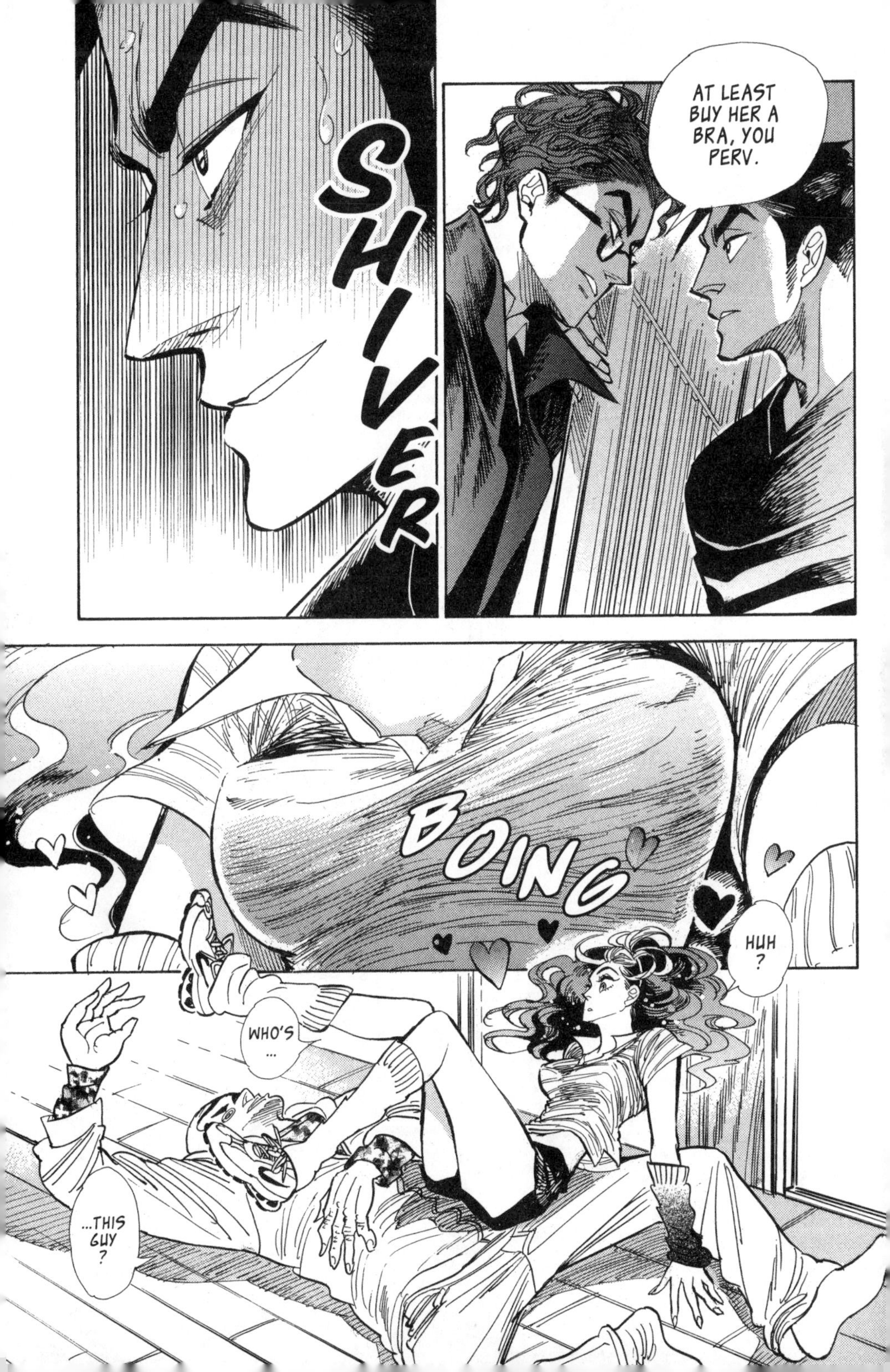
AT LEAST BUY HER A BRA, YOU PERV.
SHIVER
BOING
HUH?
WHO'S...
...THIS GUY?

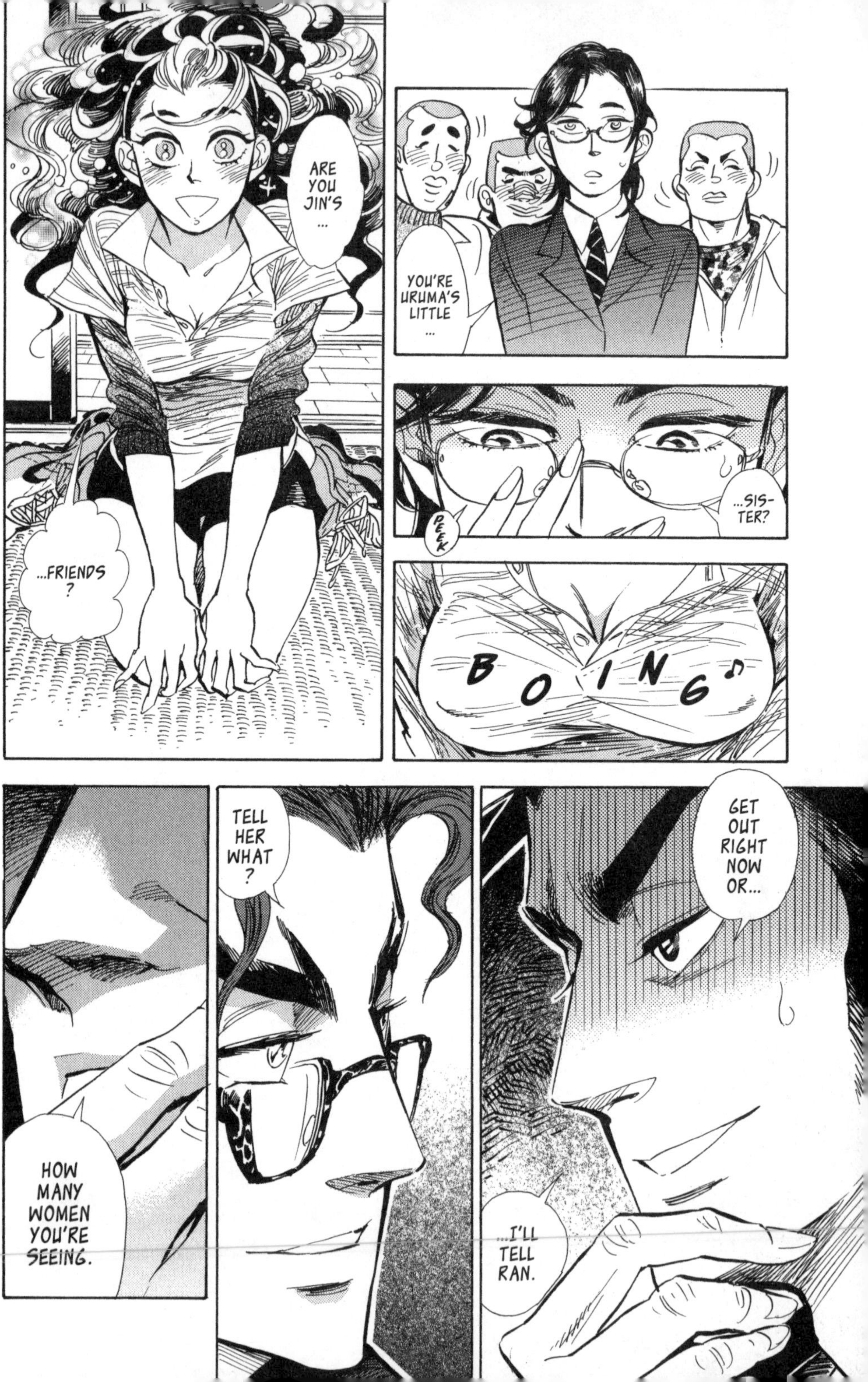
YOU'RE URUMA'S LITTLE ...
...SIS-TER?
PEEK
BOING♪
ARE YOU JIN'S ...
...FRIENDS?
GET OUT RIGHT NOW OR...
...I'LL TELL RAN.
TELL HER WHAT?
HOW MANY WOMEN YOU'RE SEEING.

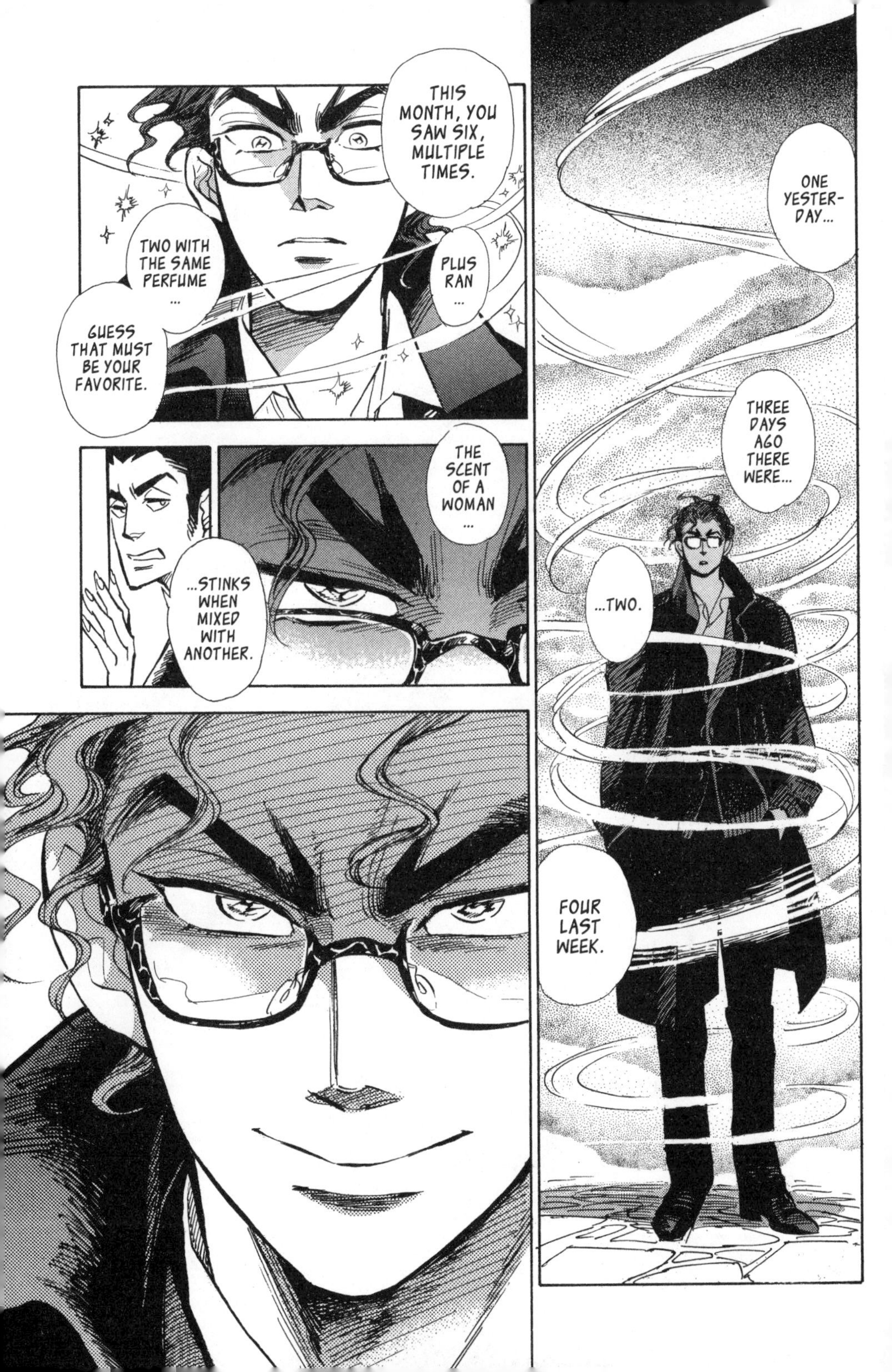
ONE YESTER-DAY...
THREE DAYS AGO THERE WERE...
...TWO.
FOUR LAST WEEK.
THIS MONTH, YOU SAW SIX, MULTIPLE TIMES.
PLUS RAN ...
TWO WITH THE SAME PERFUME ...
GUESS THAT MUST BE YOUR FAVORITE.
THE SCENT OF A WOMAN ...
...STINKS WHEN MIXED WITH ANOTHER.

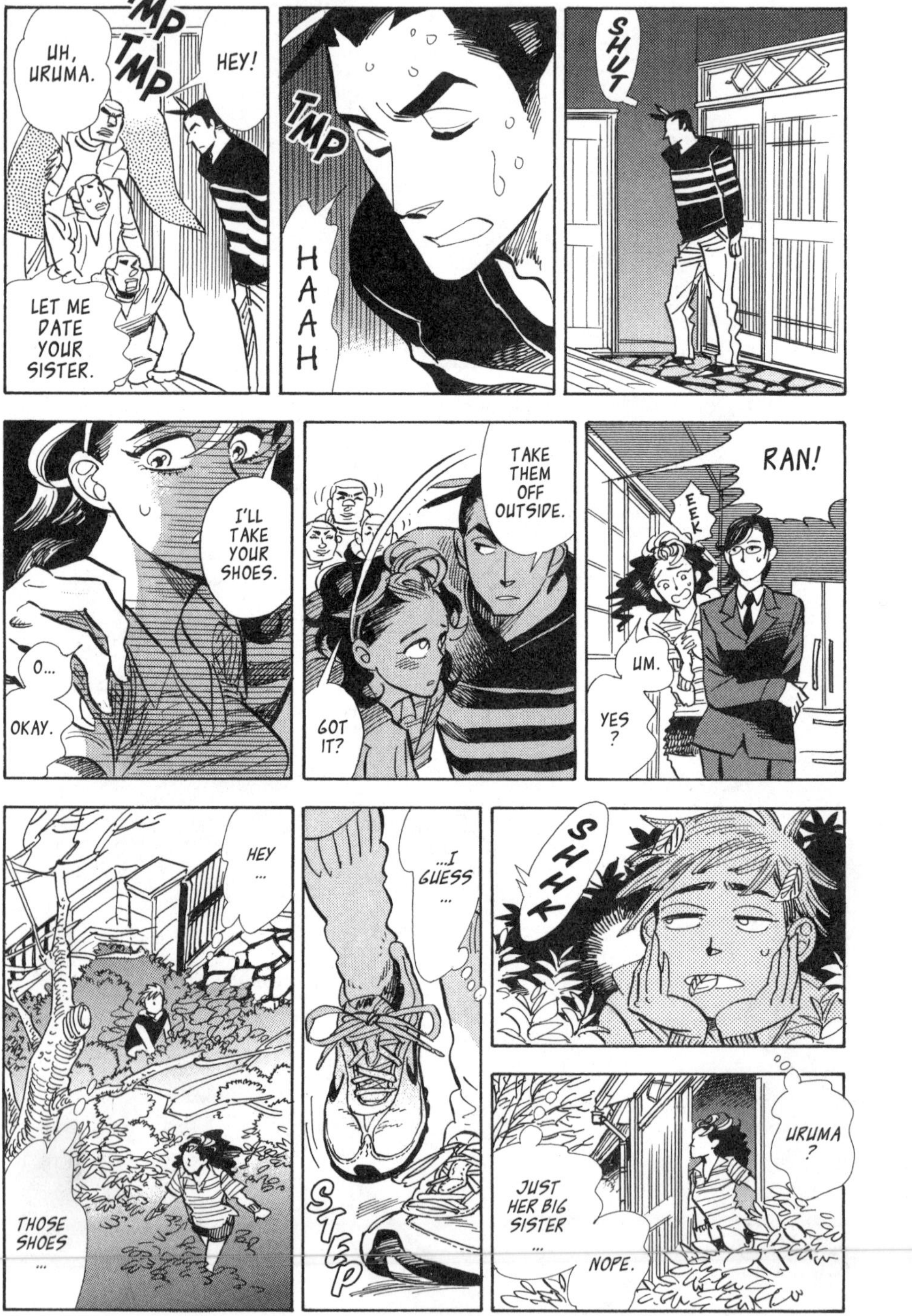
SHUT
TMP
HAAH
HEY!
TMP TMP
UH, URUMA.
LET ME DATE YOUR SISTER.
RAN!
EEK
UM.
YES?
TAKE THEM OFF OUTSIDE.
GOT IT?
I'LL TAKE YOUR SHOES.
O...
OKAY.
SHHK
URUMA?
JUST HER BIG SISTER...
NOPE.
...I GUESS...
STEP
HEY...
THOSE SHOES...

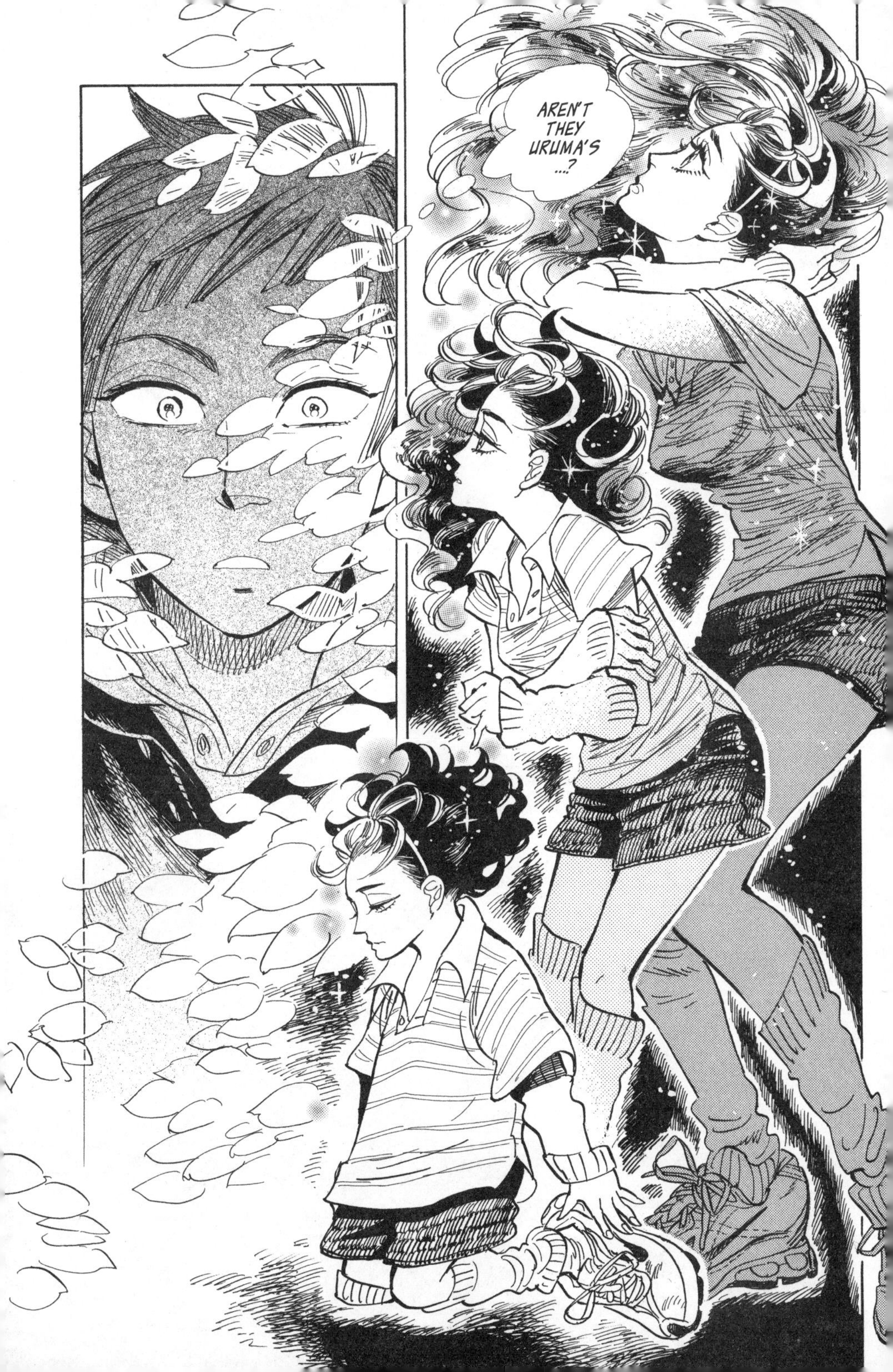
AREN'T THEY URUMA'S ...?

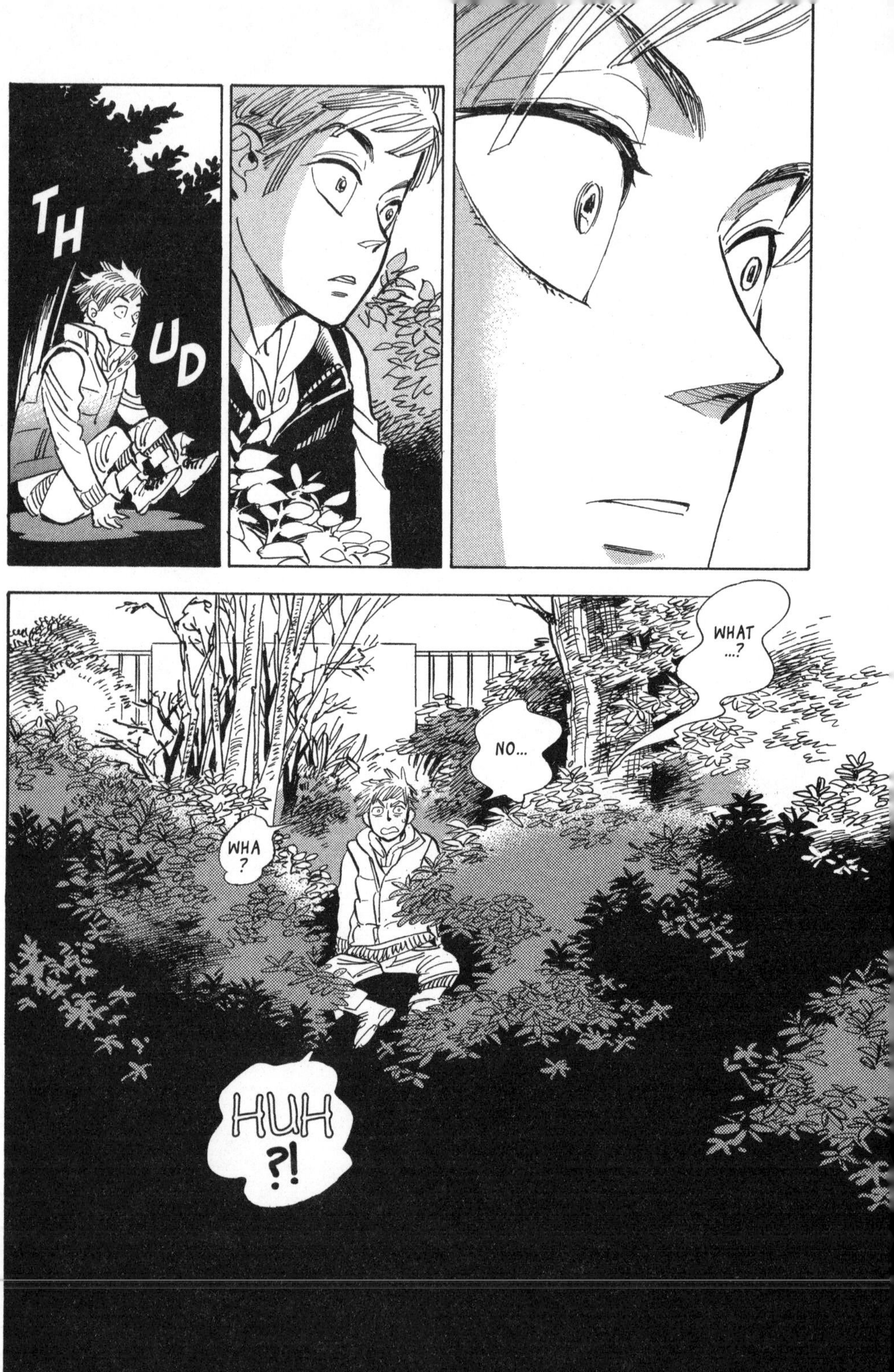
THUD
WHAT ...?
NO...
WHA ?
HUH ?!

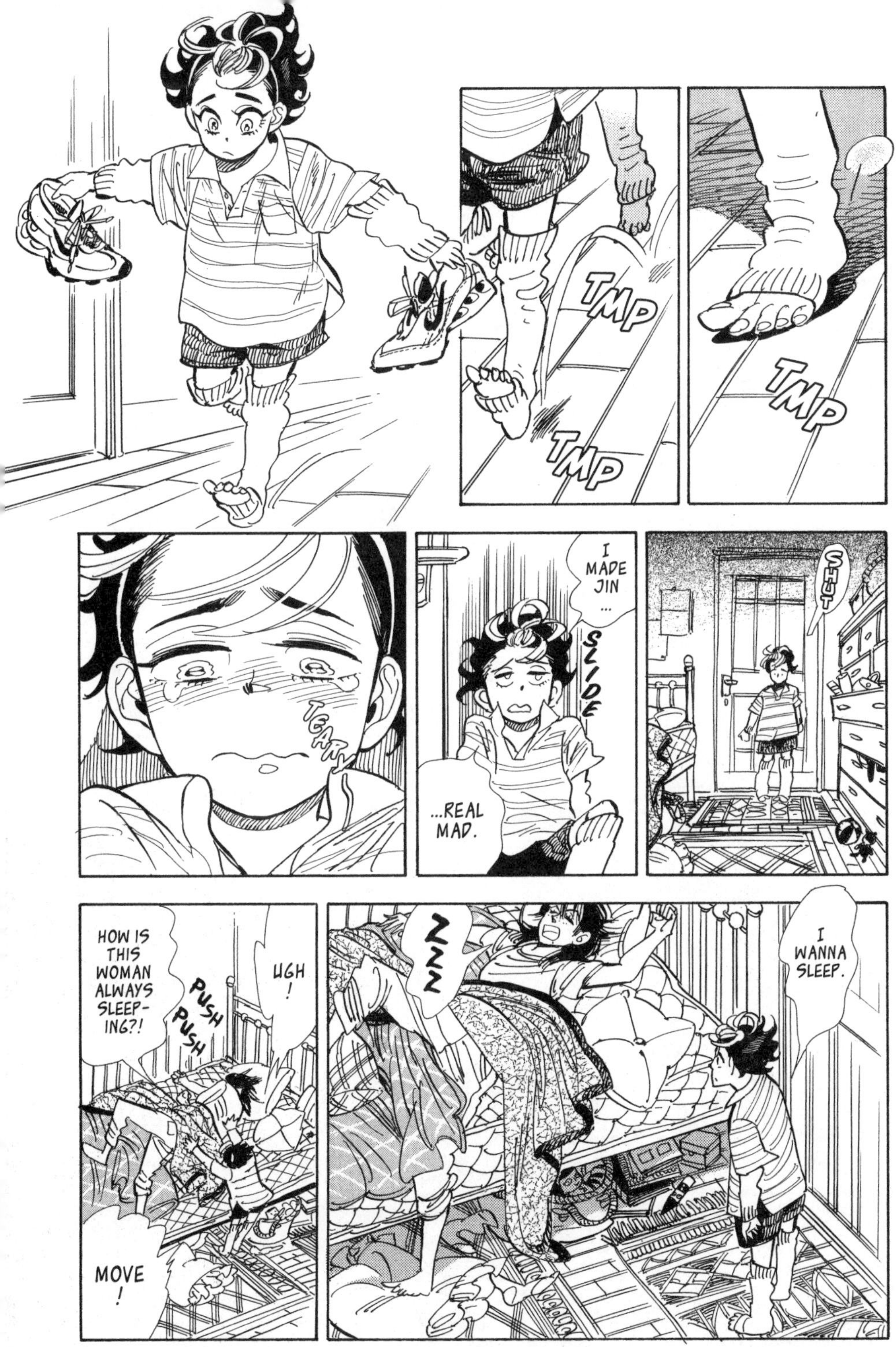
TMP
TMP
TMP
SHUT
I MADE JIN ...
SLIDE
...REAL MAD.
TEARY
I WANNA SLEEP.
ZZZ
UGH!
HOW IS THIS WOMAN ALWAYS SLEEPING?!
PUSH PUSH
MOVE!

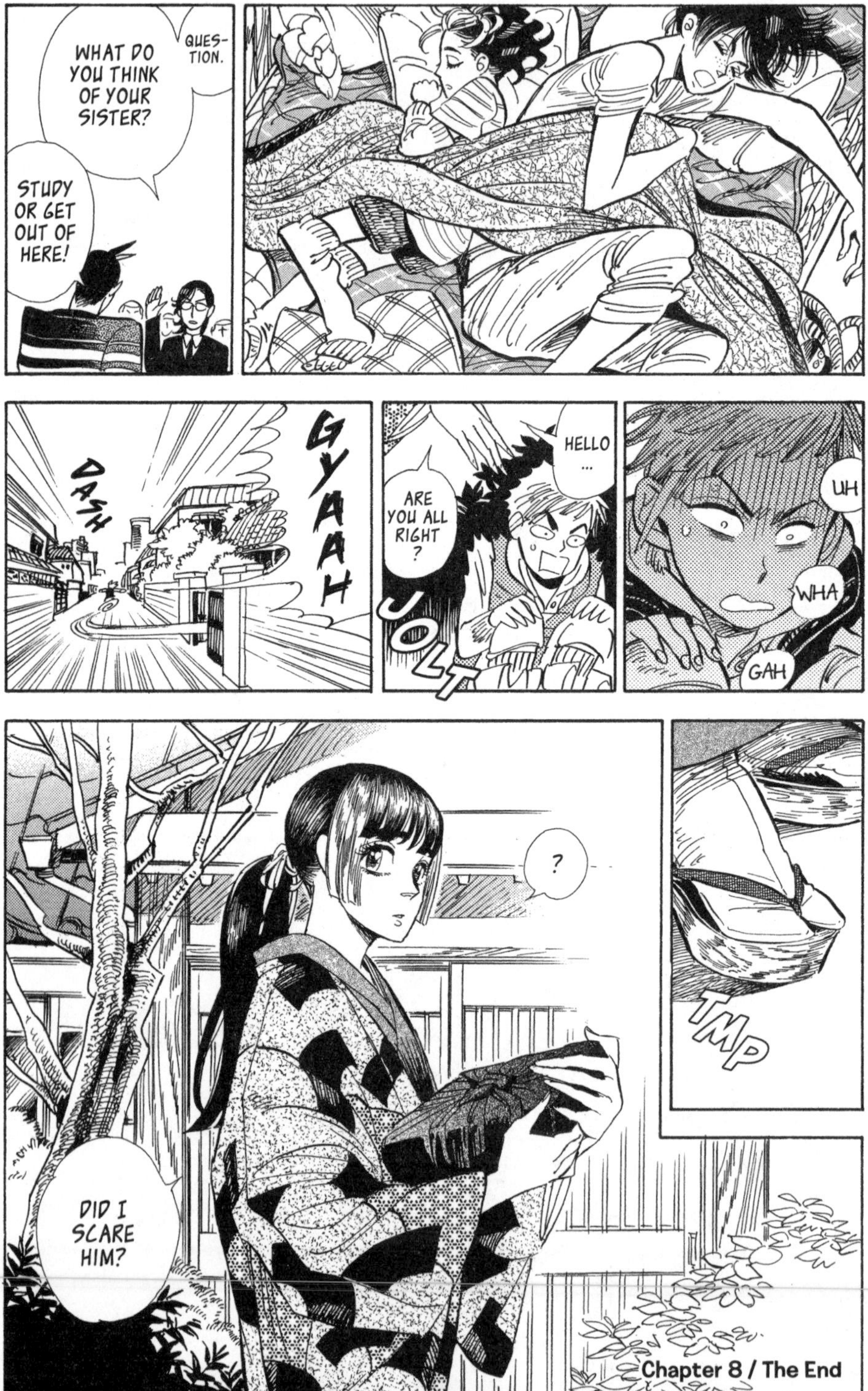
QUESTION.
WHAT DO YOU THINK OF YOUR SISTER?
STUDY OR GET OUT OF HERE!
UH
WHA
GAH
HELLO ...
ARE YOU ALL RIGHT ?
JOLT
GYAAH
DASH
TMP
?
DID I SCARE HIM?

Chapter 8 / The End

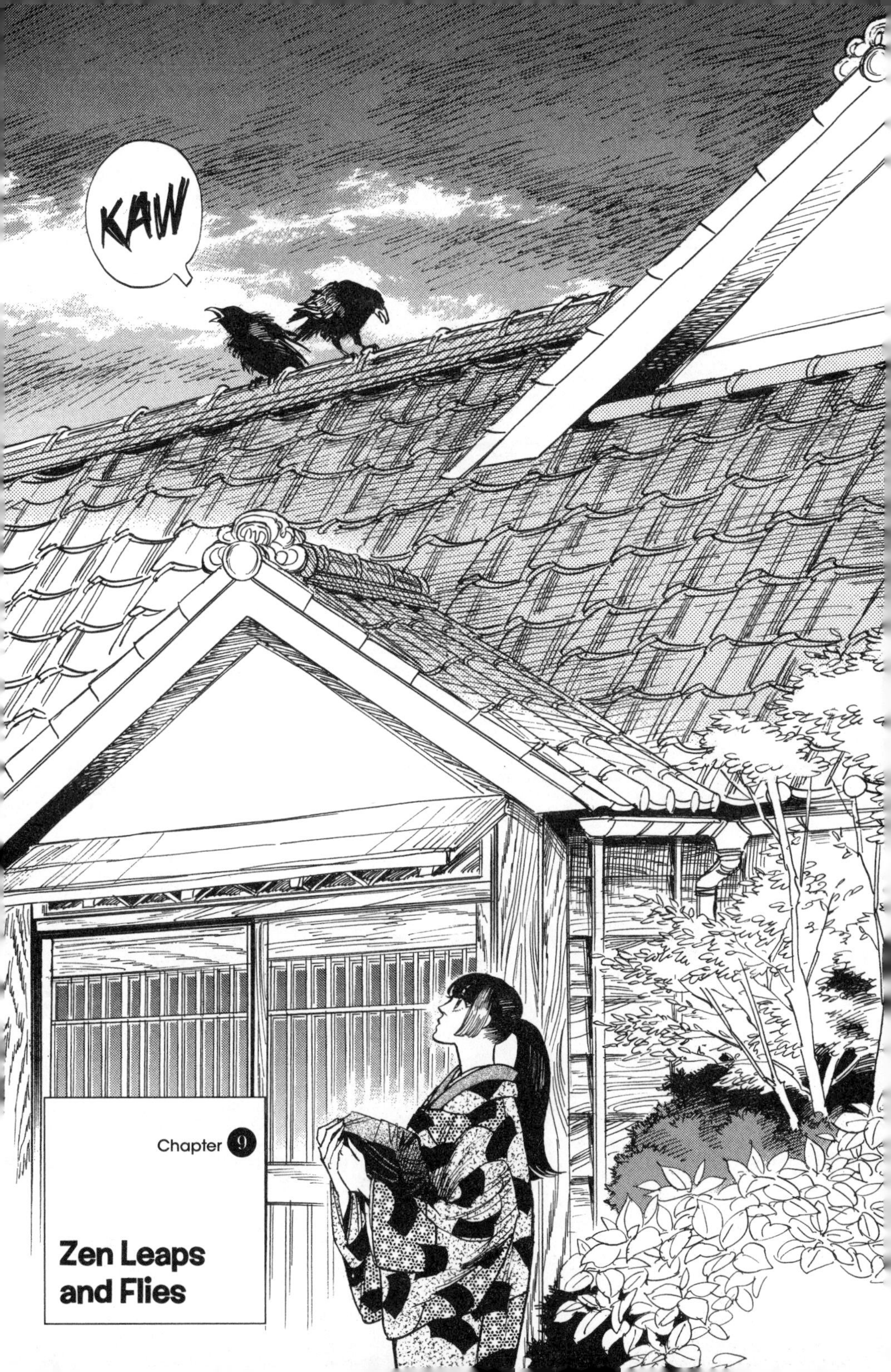
KAW
Chapter 9
Zen Leaps and Flies

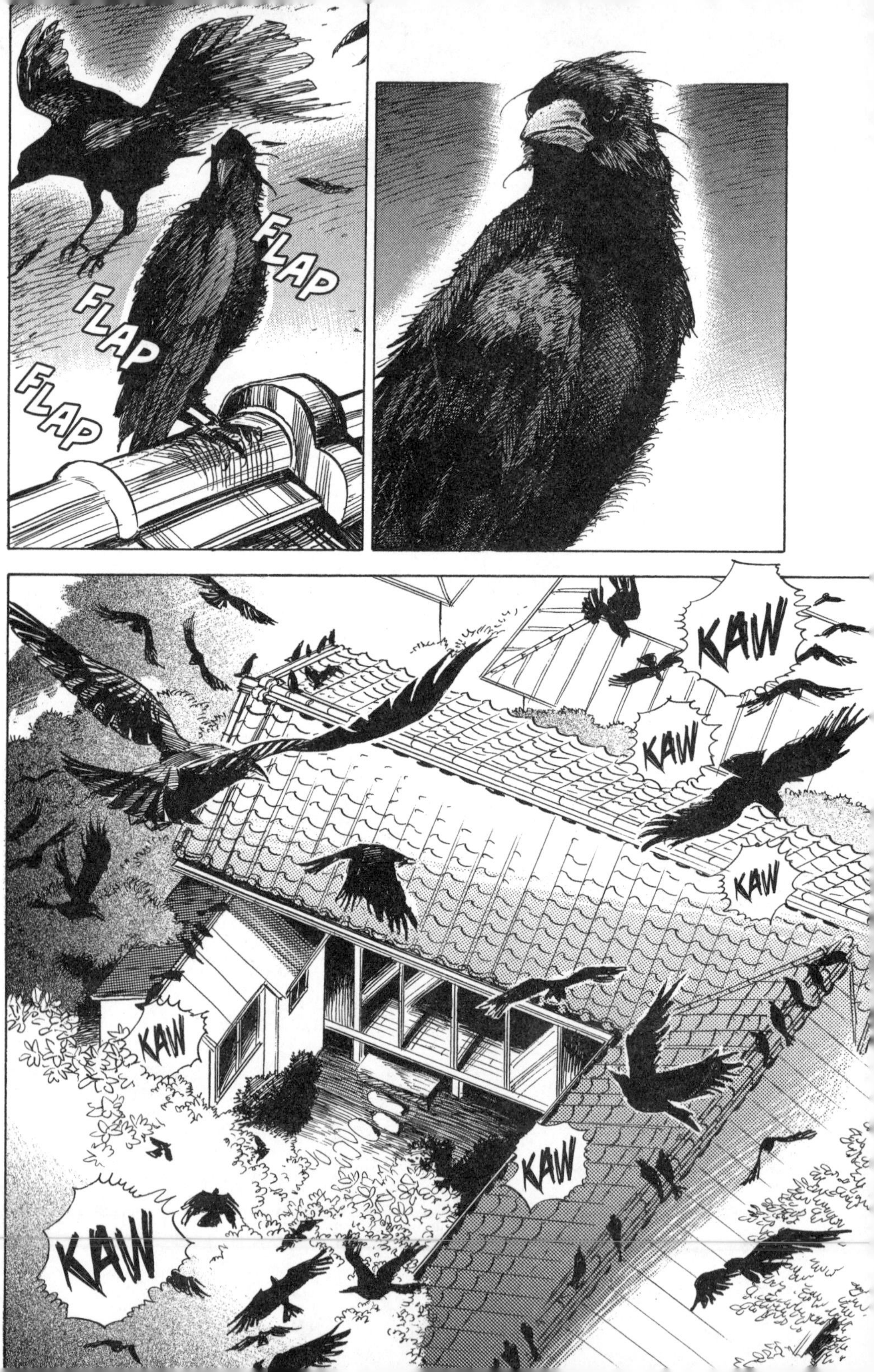
FLAP
FLAP
FLAP
KAW
KAW
KAW
KAW
KAW
KAW

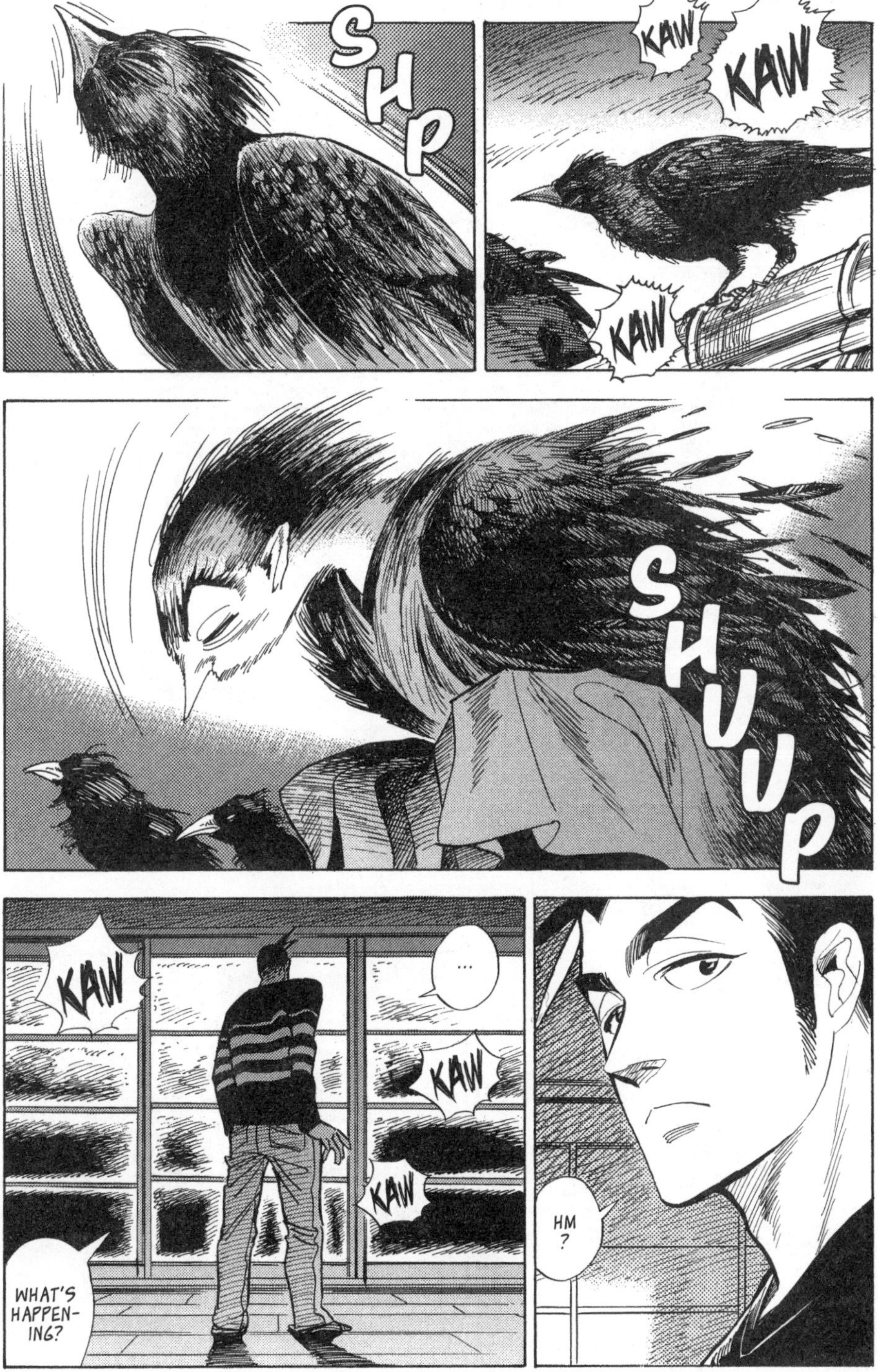
KAW
KAW
KAW
SHP
SHUUUP
HM ?
...
KAW
KAW
KAW
WHAT'S HAPPEN-ING?

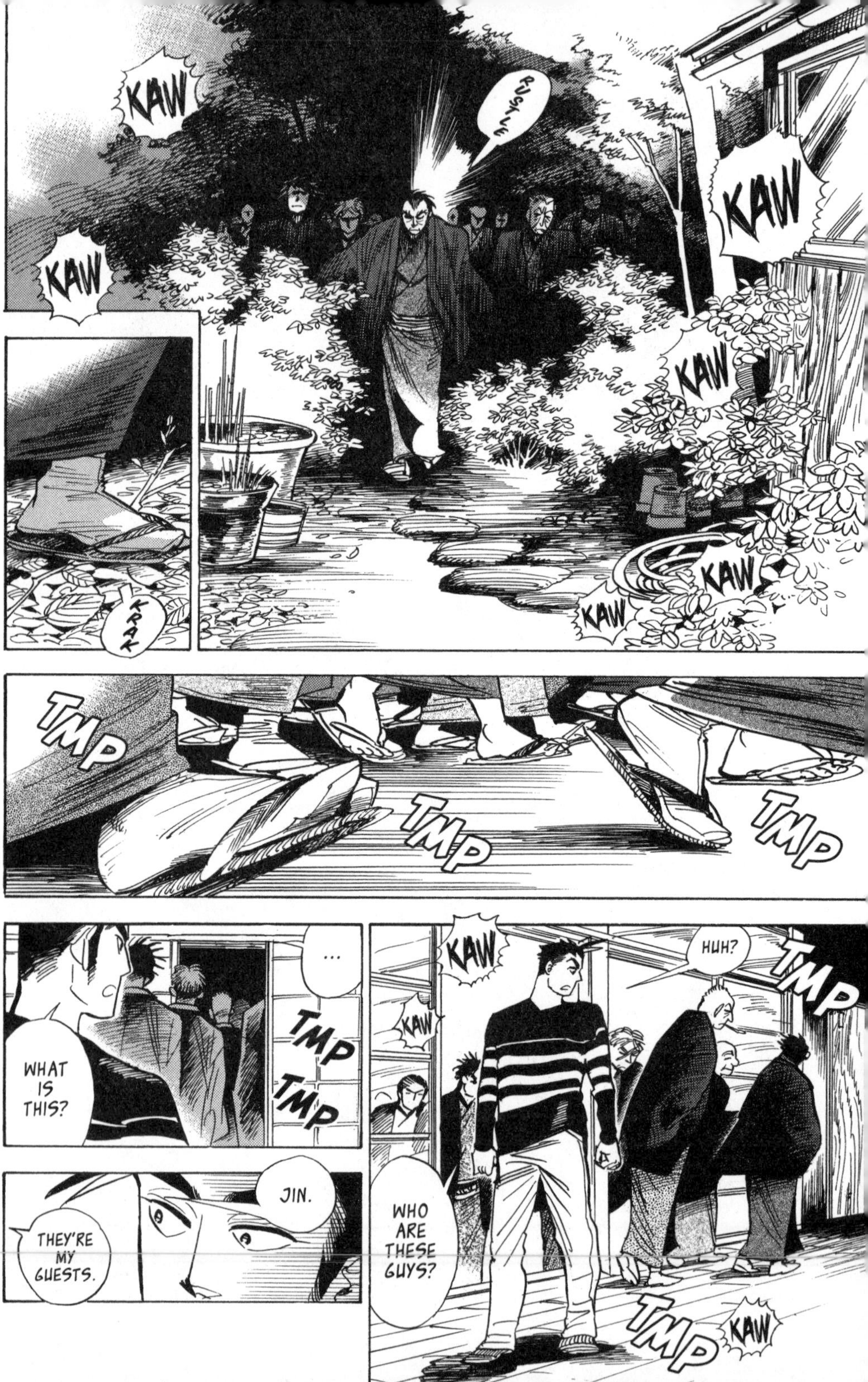
KAW
RUSTLE
KAW
KAW
KAW
KAW
KAW
KRAK
TMP
TMP
TMP
KAW
HUH?
TMP
KAW
WHO ARE THESE GUYS?
TMP
KAW
...
TMP
TMP
WHAT IS THIS?
JIN.
THEY'RE MY GUESTS.

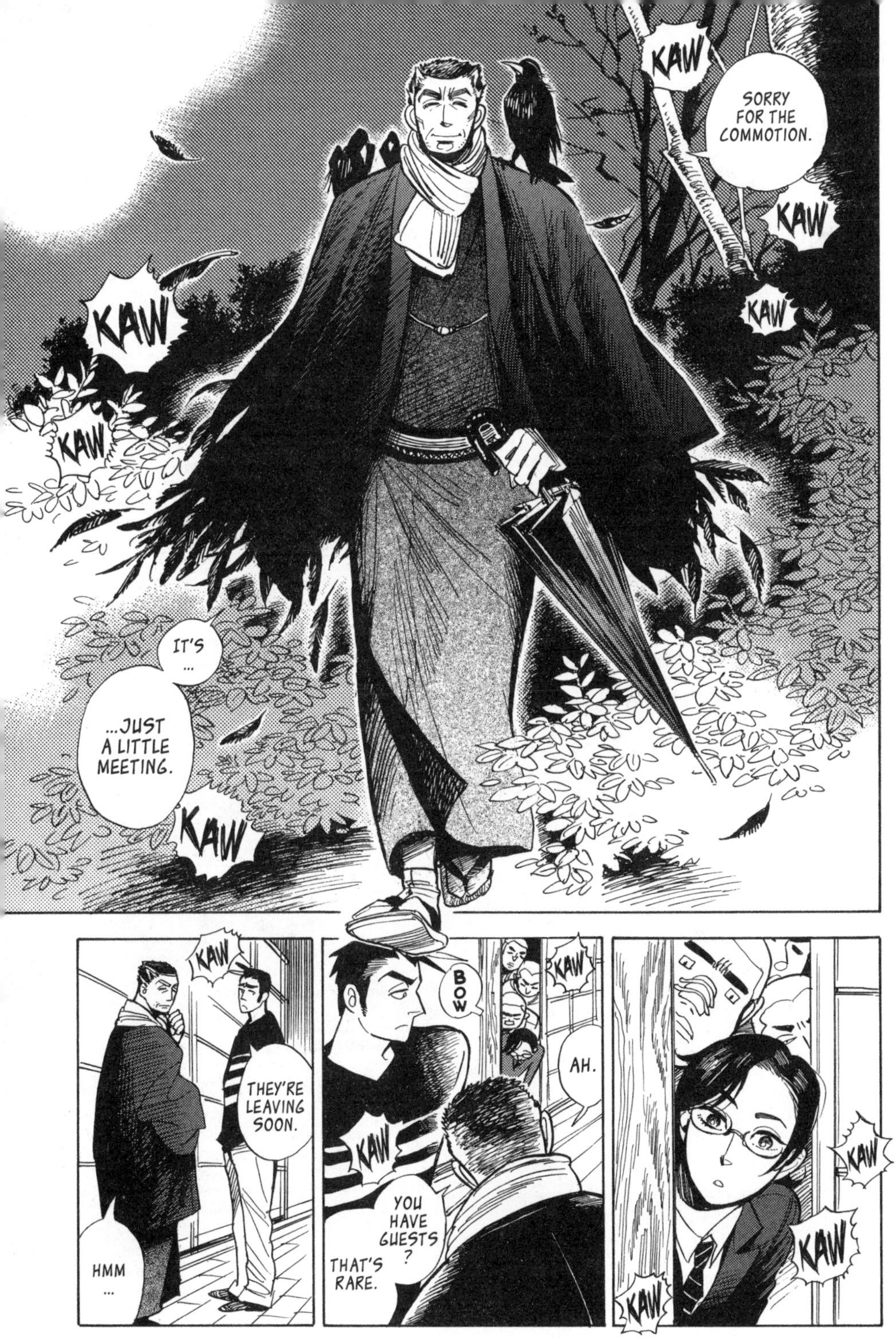
KAW
SORRY FOR THE COMMOTION.
KAW
KAW
KAW
KAW
IT'S ...
...JUST A LITTLE MEETING.
KAW
KAW
KAW
KAW
BOW
KAW
AH.
KAW
YOU HAVE GUESTS?
THAT'S RARE.
KAW
THEY'RE LEAVING SOON.
HMM ...

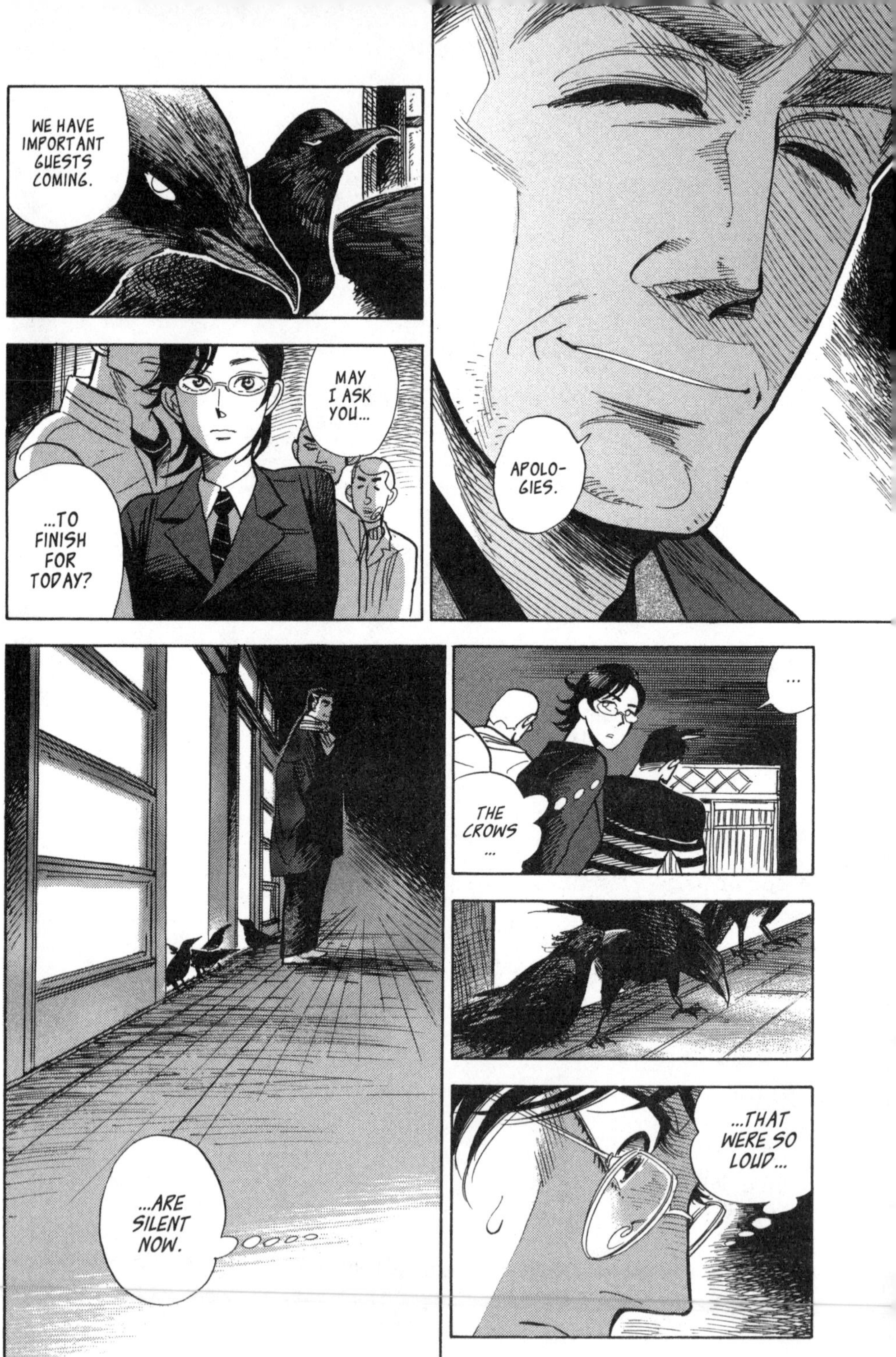
APOLO-GIES.
WE HAVE IMPORTANT GUESTS COMING.
MAY I ASK YOU...
...TO FINISH FOR TODAY?
...
THE CROWS ...
...THAT WERE SO LOUD...
...ARE SILENT NOW.

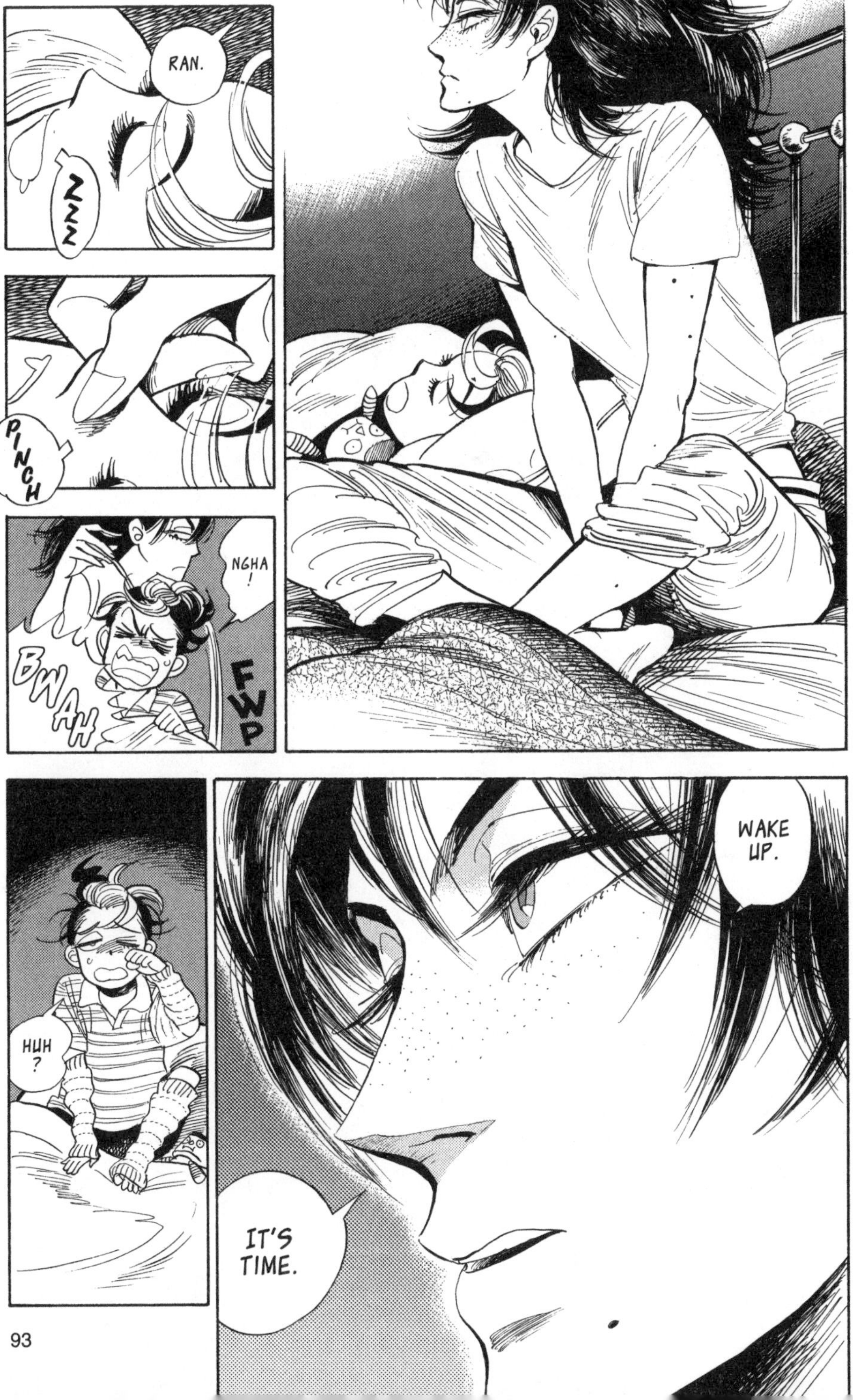
RAN.
ZZZ
PINCH
NGHA!
FWP
BWAH
WAKE UP.
IT'S TIME.
HUH?

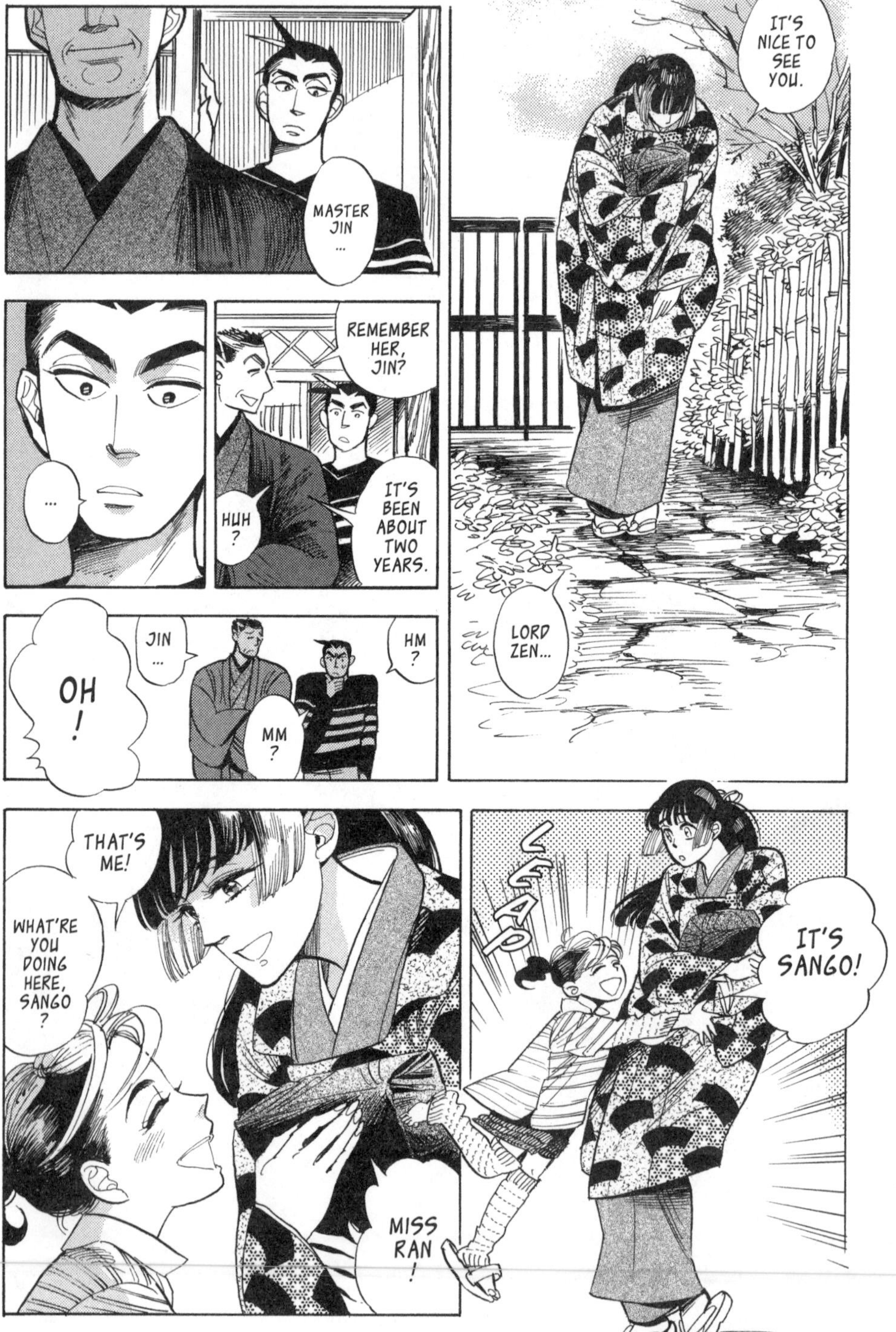
IT'S NICE TO SEE YOU.
LORD ZEN...
MASTER JIN ...
REMEMBER HER, JIN?
IT'S BEEN ABOUT TWO YEARS.
HUH ?
...
HM ?
JIN ...
MM ?
OH !
IT'S SANGO!
LEAP
THAT'S ME!
WHAT'RE YOU DOING HERE, SANGO ?
MISS RAN !

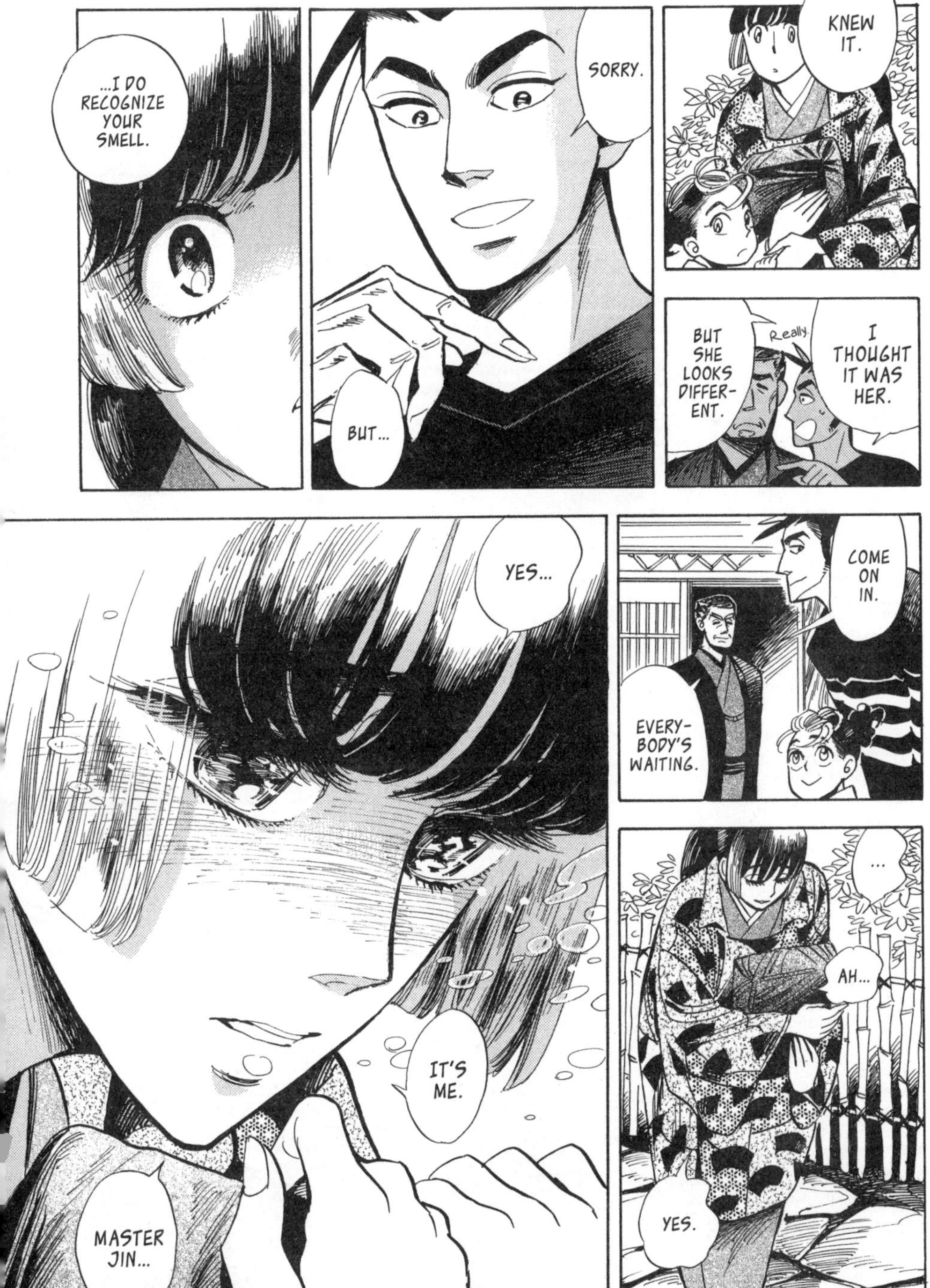
KNEW IT.
I THOUGHT IT WAS HER.
Really.
BUT SHE LOOKS DIFFERENT.
SORRY.
BUT...
...I DO RECOGNIZE YOUR SMELL.
COME ON IN.
EVERYBODY'S WAITING.
...
AH...
YES.
YES...
IT'S ME.
MASTER JIN...

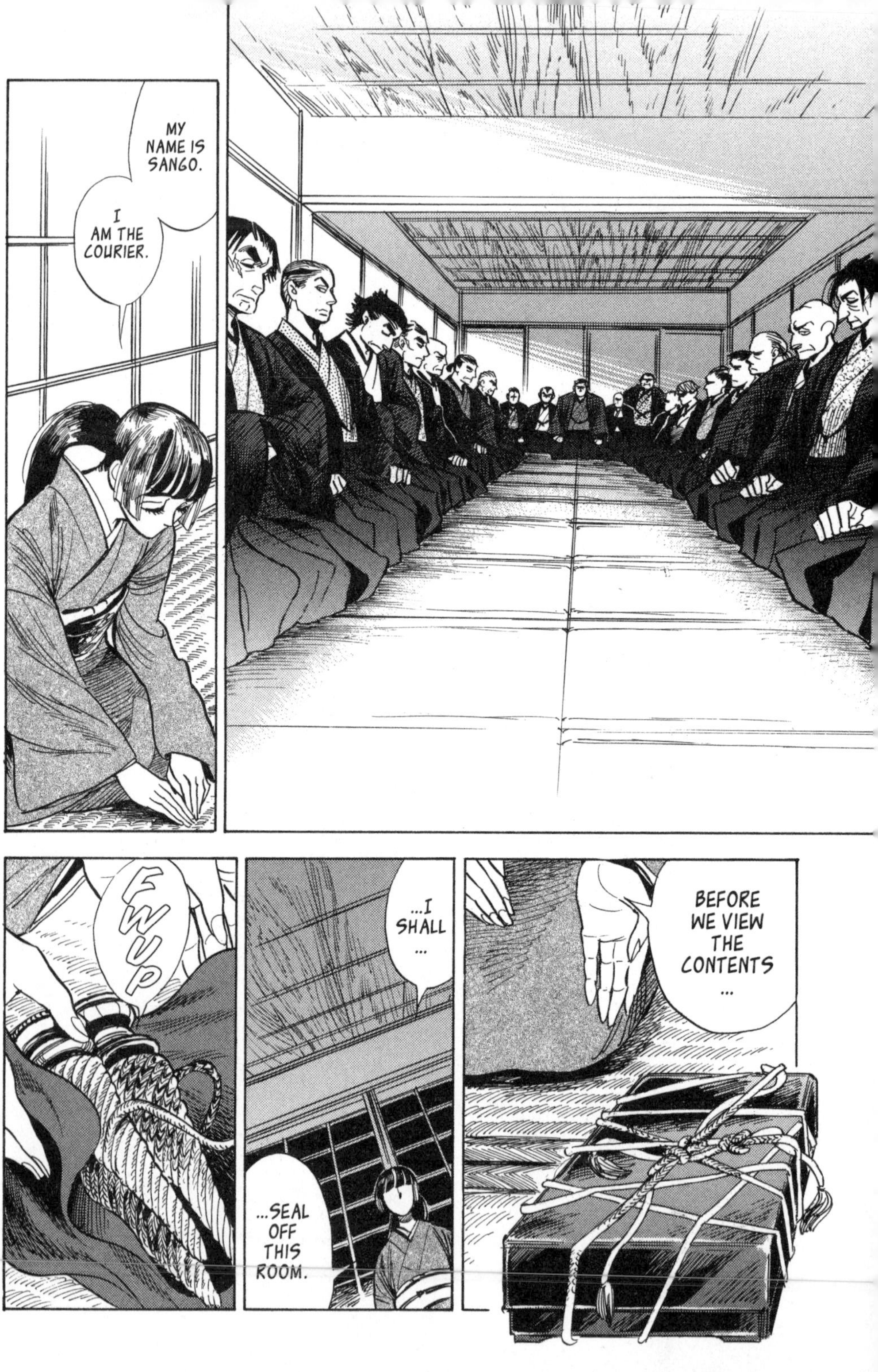
MY NAME IS SANGO.
I AM THE COURIER.
BEFORE WE VIEW THE CONTENTS ...
...I SHALL ...
...SEAL OFF THIS ROOM.
FWUP

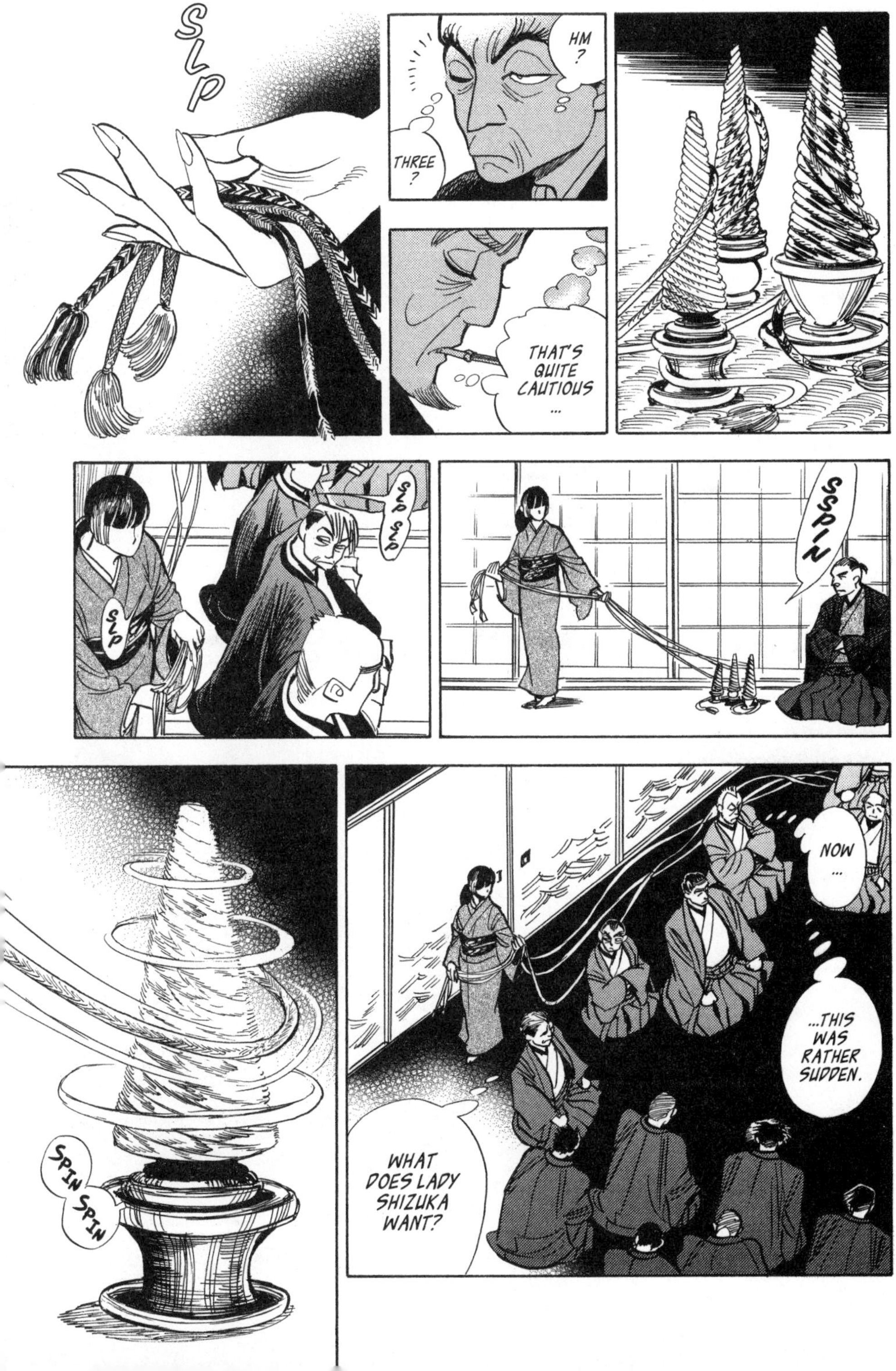
HM?
THREE?
THAT'S QUITE CAUTIOUS...
SLP
SSPIN
SLP SLP
SLP
NOW...
...THIS WAS RATHER SUDDEN.
WHAT DOES LADY SHIZUKA WANT?
SPIN SPIN

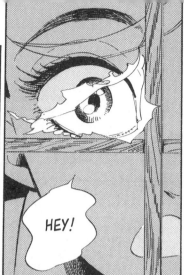

WHY IS IT PITCH-BLACK IN THERE?

What're they doing?

I CAN'T HEAR ANYTHING.

NO FAIR!

DON'T BUTT IN!

DRAG

RTTL

RTTL

AND THE DOOR WON'T OPEN.

HEY!

...HAS REQUESTED THAT LORD ZEN...

...SEE FIRST.

SLP

LADY SHIZUKA...

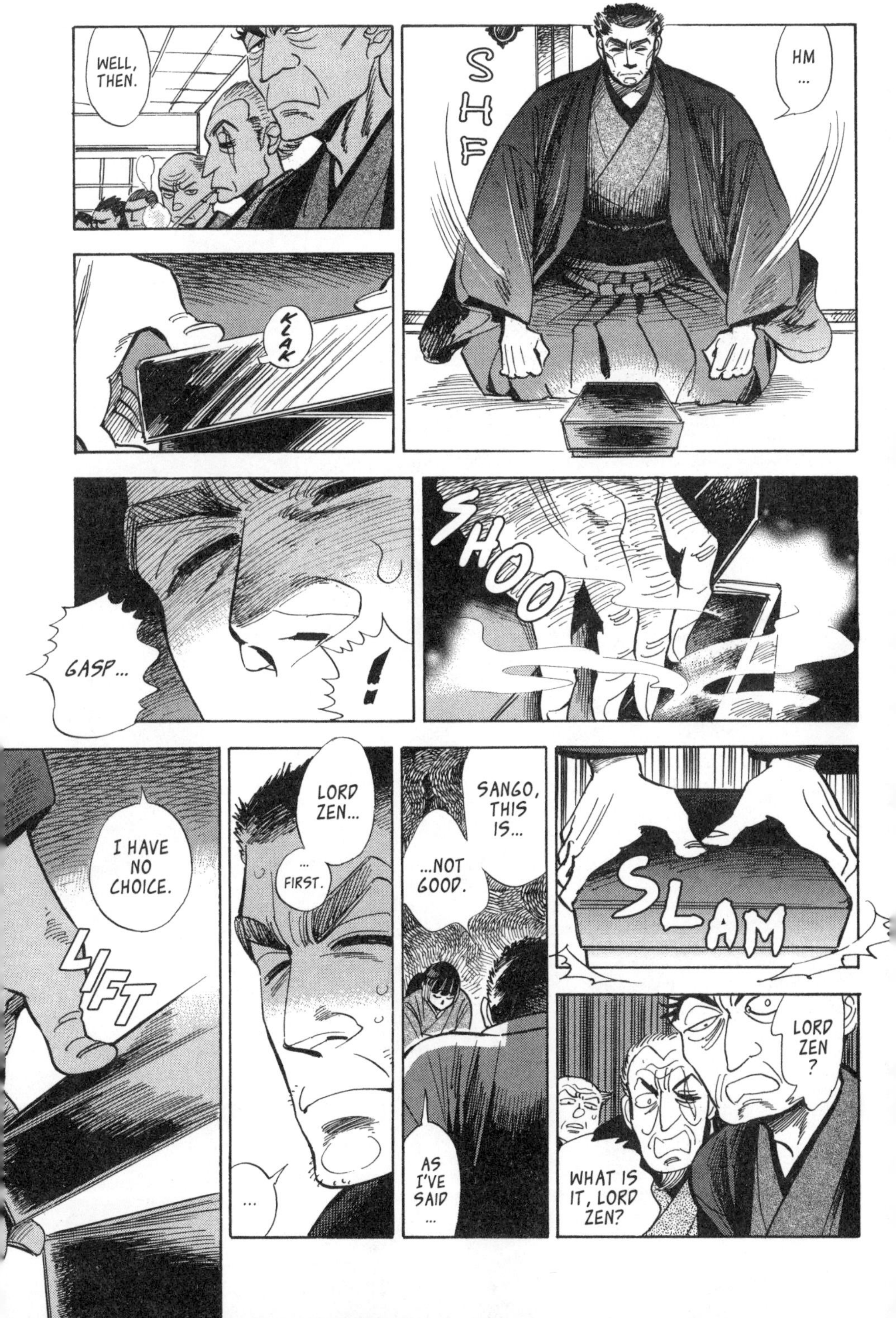
HM ...
SHF
WELL, THEN.
KLAK
SHOO
GASP...
!
SLAM
LORD ZEN ?
WHAT IS IT, LORD ZEN?
SANGO, THIS IS...
...NOT GOOD.
AS I'VE SAID ...
LORD ZEN...
... FIRST.
...
I HAVE NO CHOICE.
LIFT

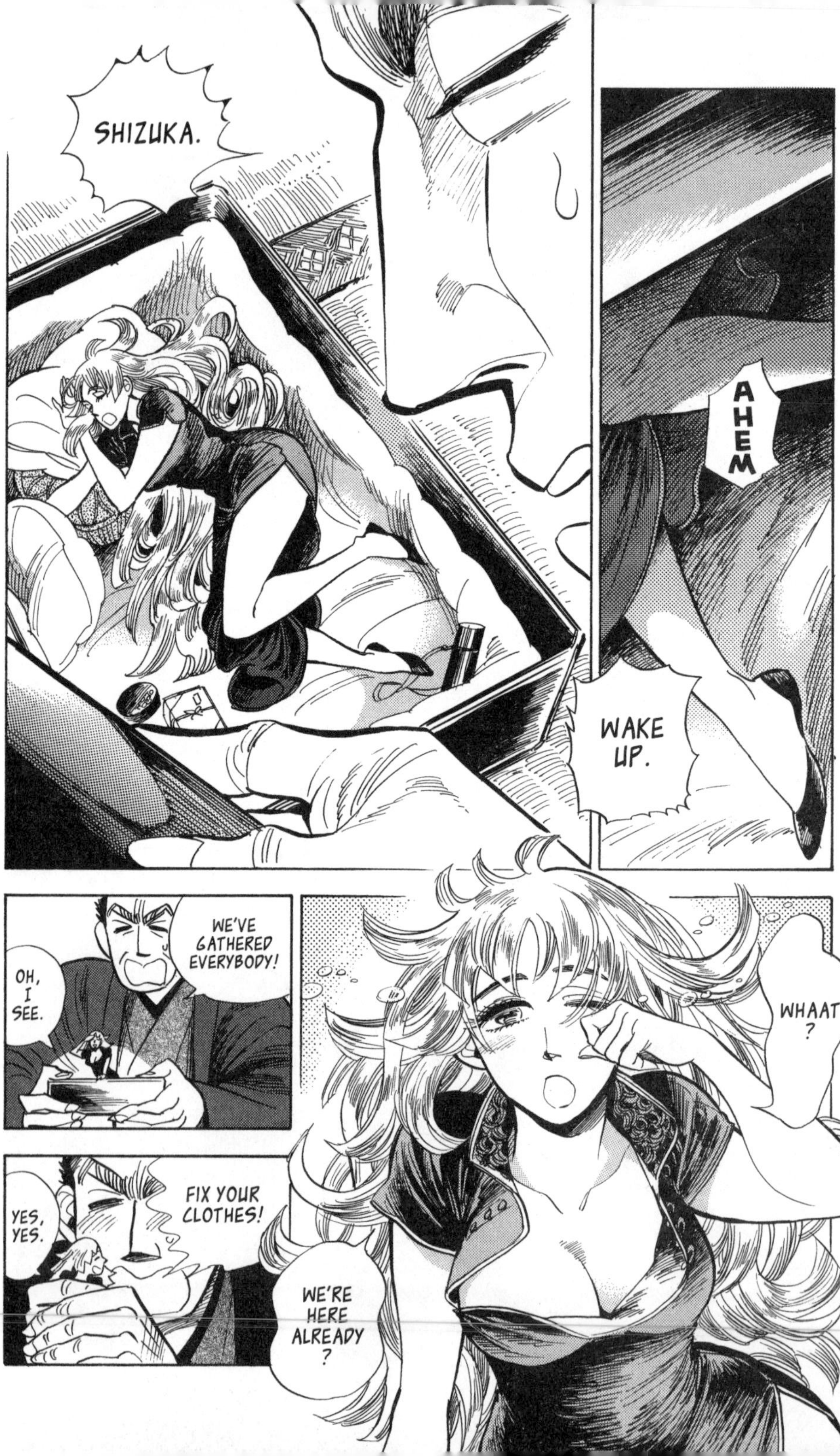
AHEM
SHIZUKA.
WAKE UP.
WHAAT?
WE'RE HERE ALREADY?
WE'VE GATHERED EVERYBODY!
OH, I SEE.
FIX YOUR CLOTHES!
YES, YES.

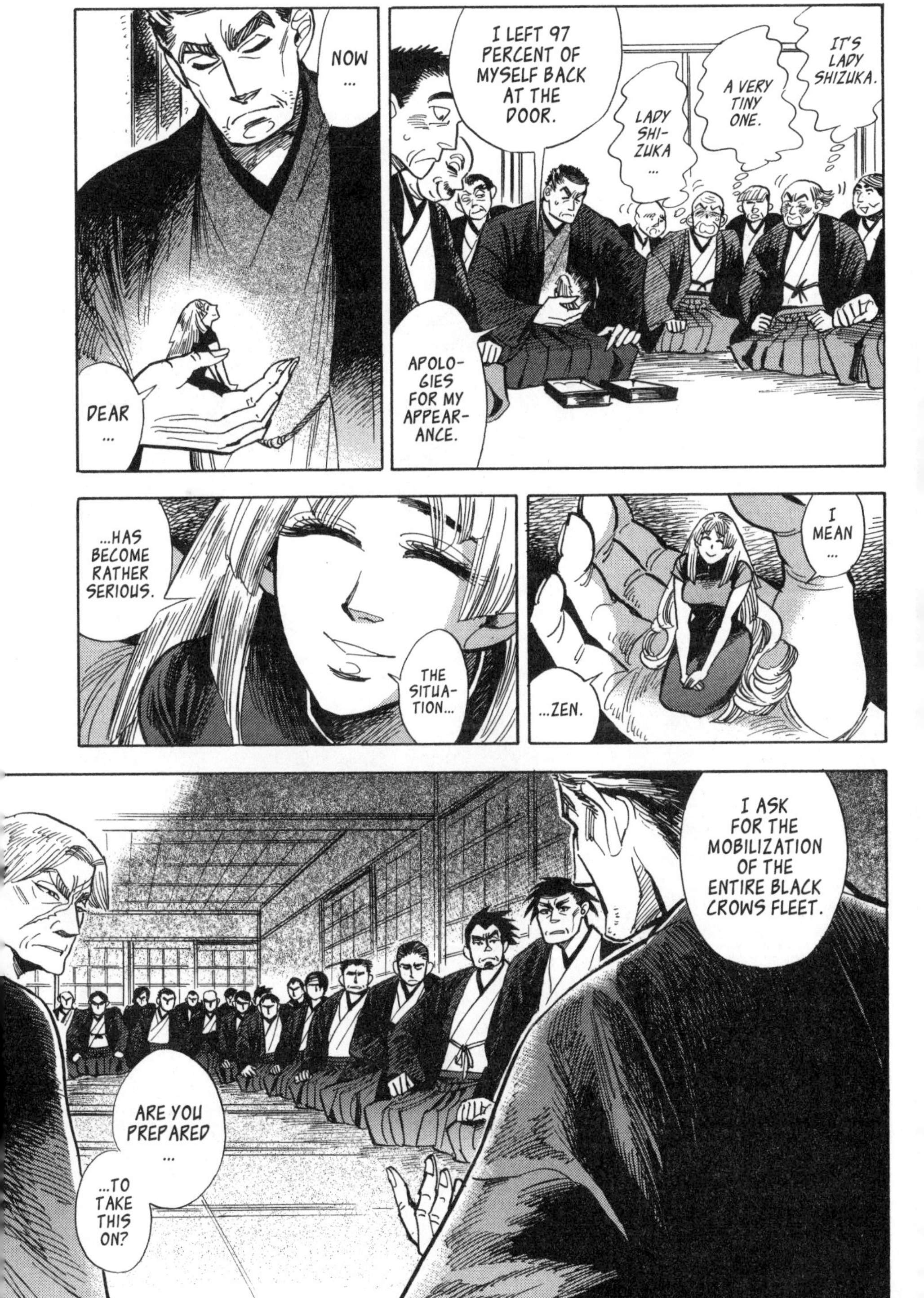
IT'S LADY SHIZUKA.
A VERY TINY ONE.
LADY SHI-ZUKA ...
I LEFT 97 PERCENT OF MYSELF BACK AT THE DOOR.
APOLO-GIES FOR MY APPEAR-ANCE.
NOW ...
DEAR ...
...ZEN.
I MEAN ...
THE SITUA-TION...
...HAS BECOME RATHER SERIOUS.
I ASK FOR THE MOBILIZATION OF THE ENTIRE BLACK CROWS FLEET.
ARE YOU PREPARED ...
...TO TAKE THIS ON?

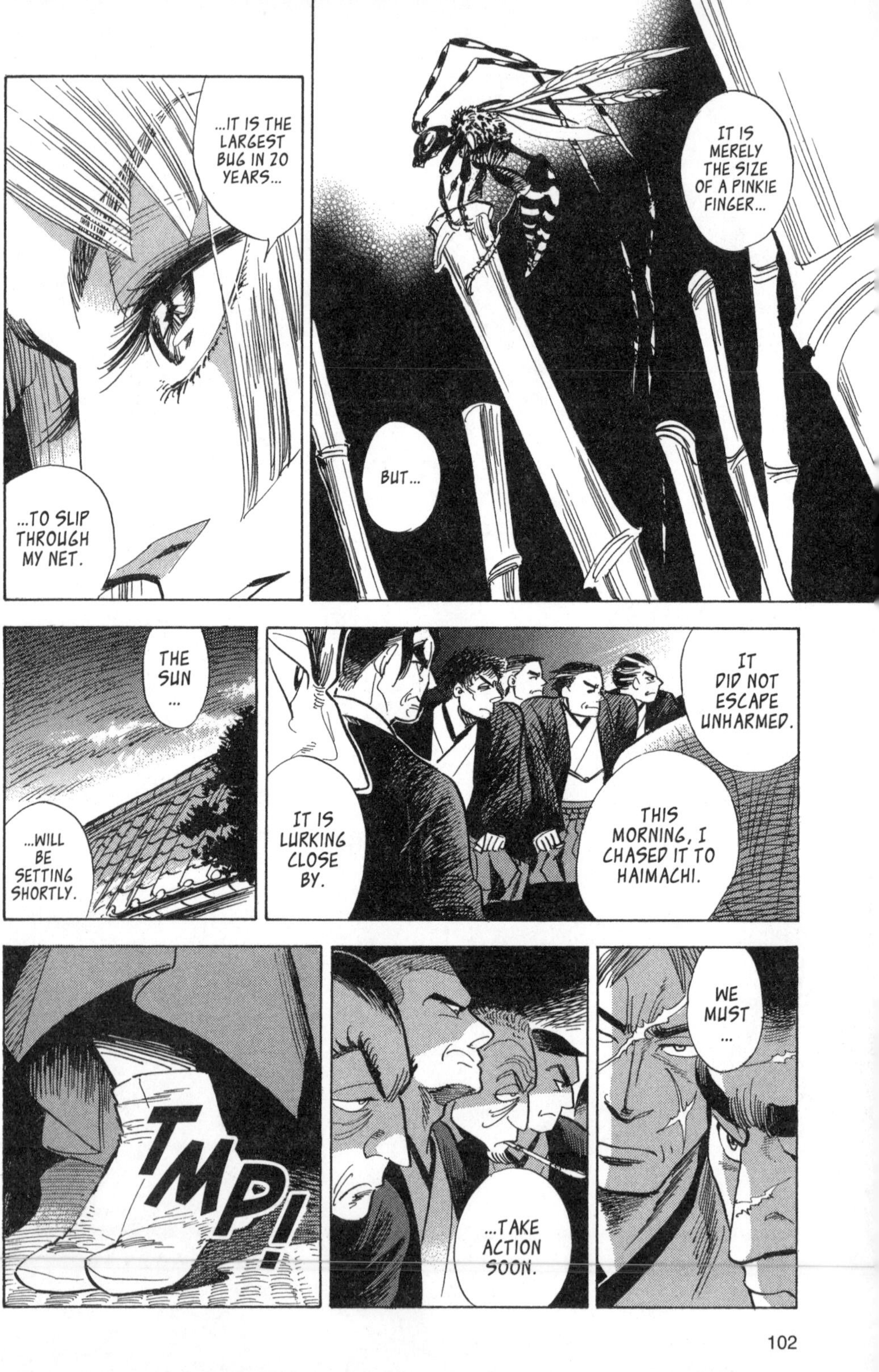
IT IS MERELY THE SIZE OF A PINKIE FINGER...
BUT...
...IT IS THE LARGEST BUG IN 20 YEARS...
...TO SLIP THROUGH MY NET.
IT DID NOT ESCAPE UNHARMED.
THIS MORNING, I CHASED IT TO HAIMACHI.
IT IS LURKING CLOSE BY.
THE SUN ...
...WILL BE SETTING SHORTLY.
WE MUST ...
...TAKE ACTION SOON.
TMP!

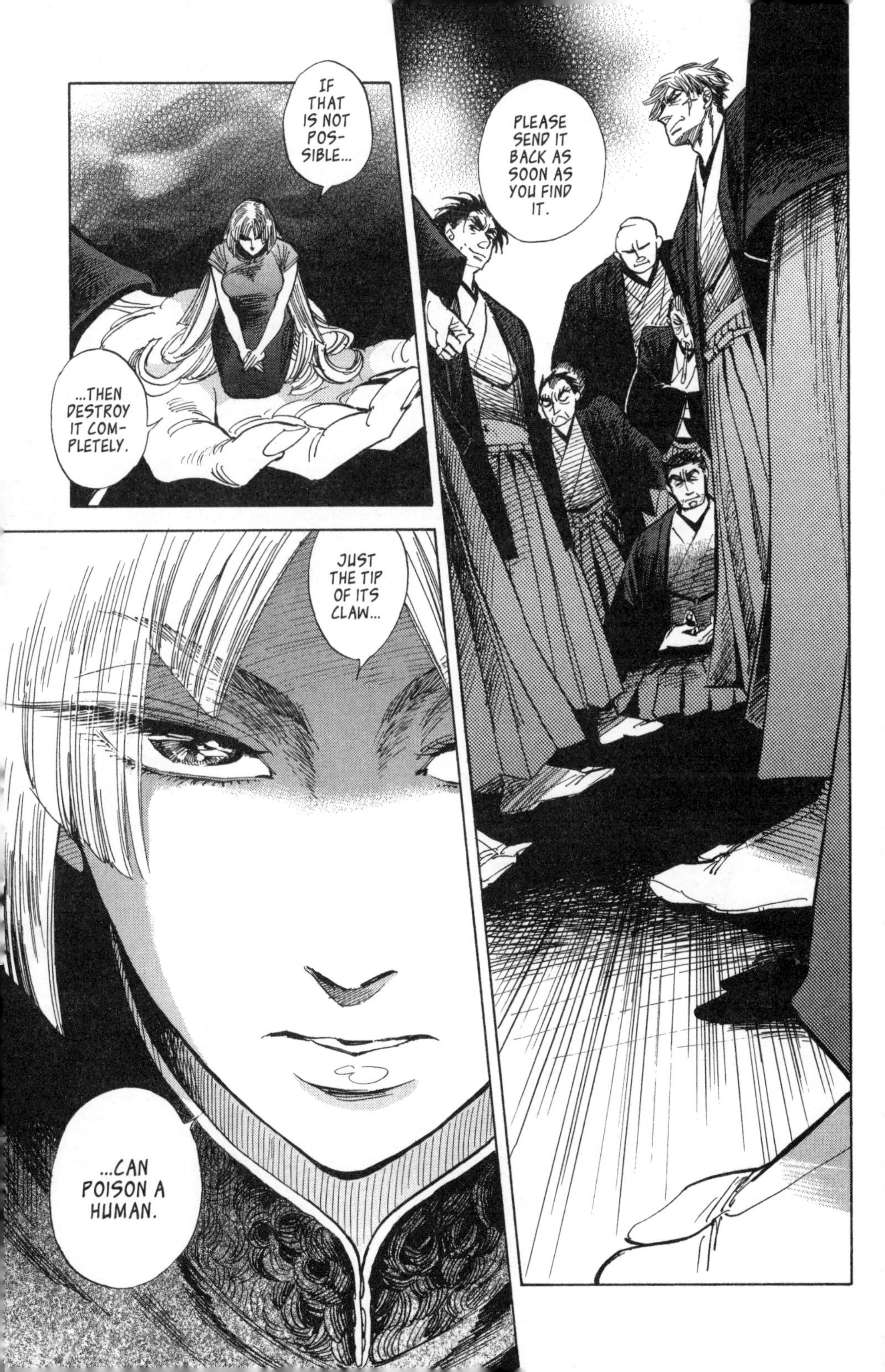
PLEASE SEND IT BACK AS SOON AS YOU FIND IT.
IF THAT IS NOT POS-SIBLE...
...THEN DESTROY IT COM-PLETELY.
JUST THE TIP OF ITS CLAW...
...CAN POISON A HUMAN.

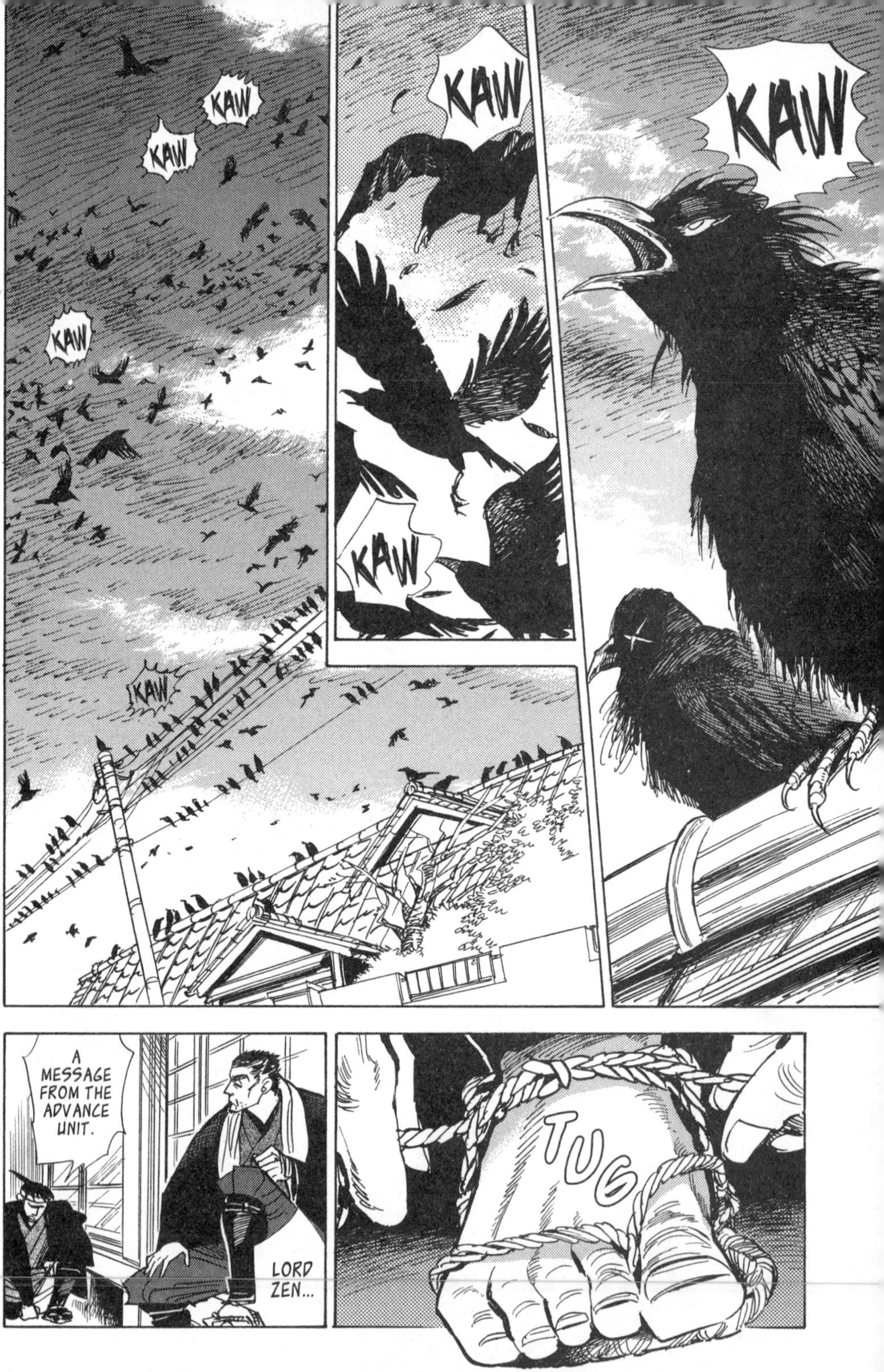
KAW
KAW
KAW
KAW
KAW
KAW
KAW
KAW
TUG
LORD ZEN...
A MESSAGE FROM THE ADVANCE UNIT.

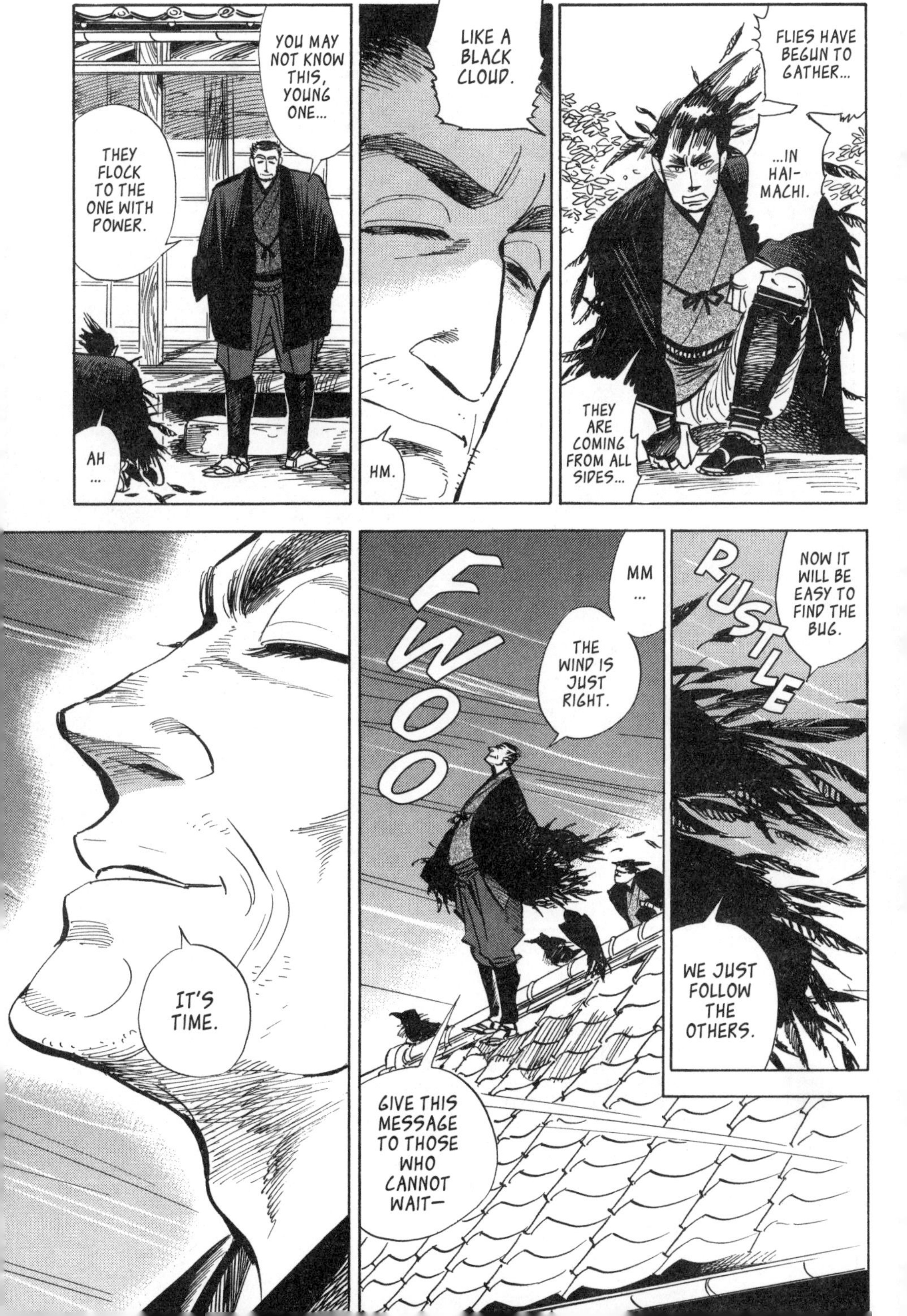
FLIES HAVE BEGUN TO GATHER...
...IN HAI-MACHI.
THEY ARE COMING FROM ALL SIDES...
LIKE A BLACK CLOUD.
HM.
YOU MAY NOT KNOW THIS, YOUNG ONE...
THEY FLOCK TO THE ONE WITH POWER.
AH...
RUSTLE
NOW IT WILL BE EASY TO FIND THE BUG.
WE JUST FOLLOW THE OTHERS.
FWOOO
MM...
THE WIND IS JUST RIGHT.
GIVE THIS MESSAGE TO THOSE WHO CANNOT WAIT—
IT'S TIME.

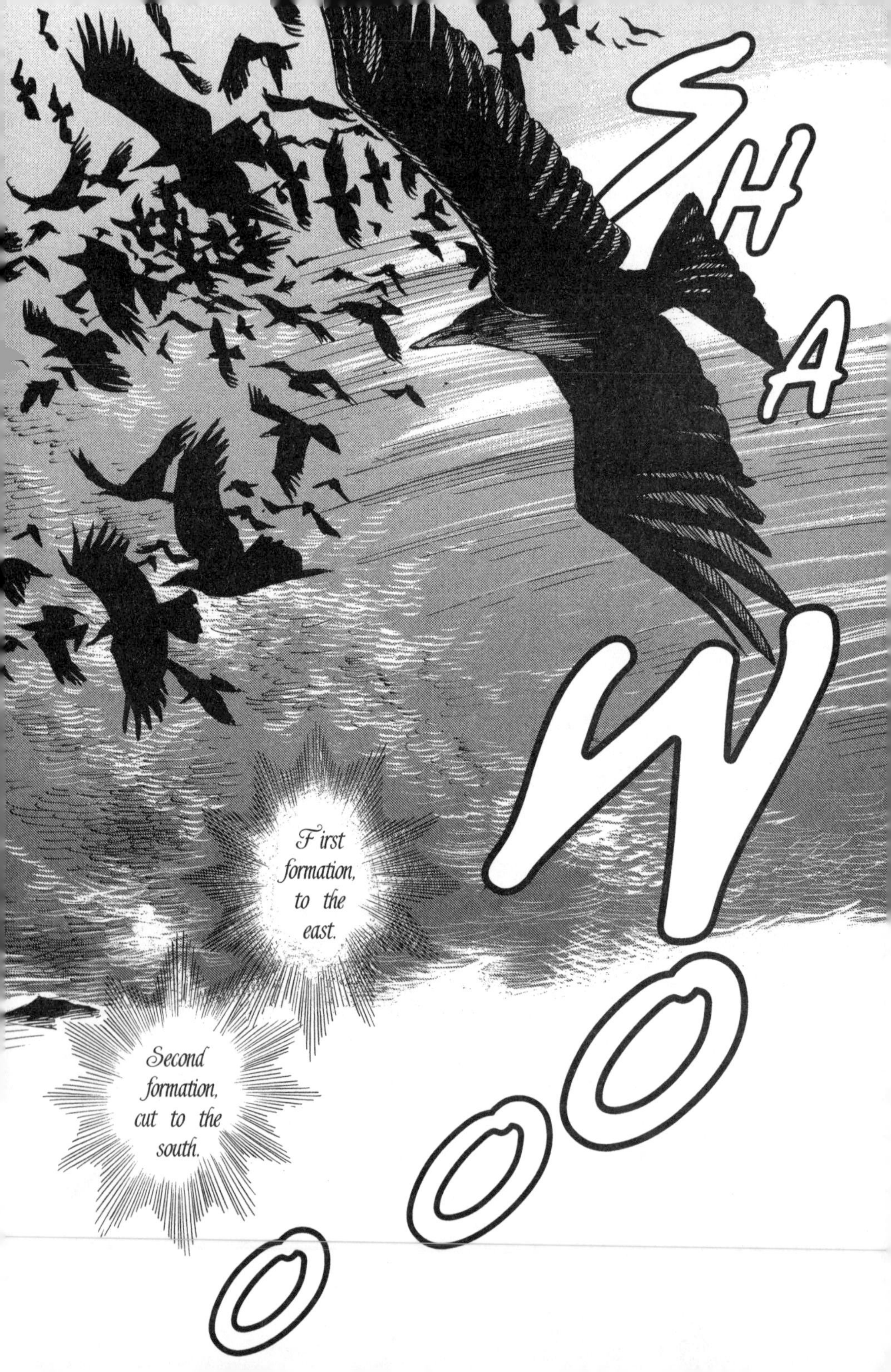
SHAWOOOO
First formation, to the east.
Second formation, cut to the south.

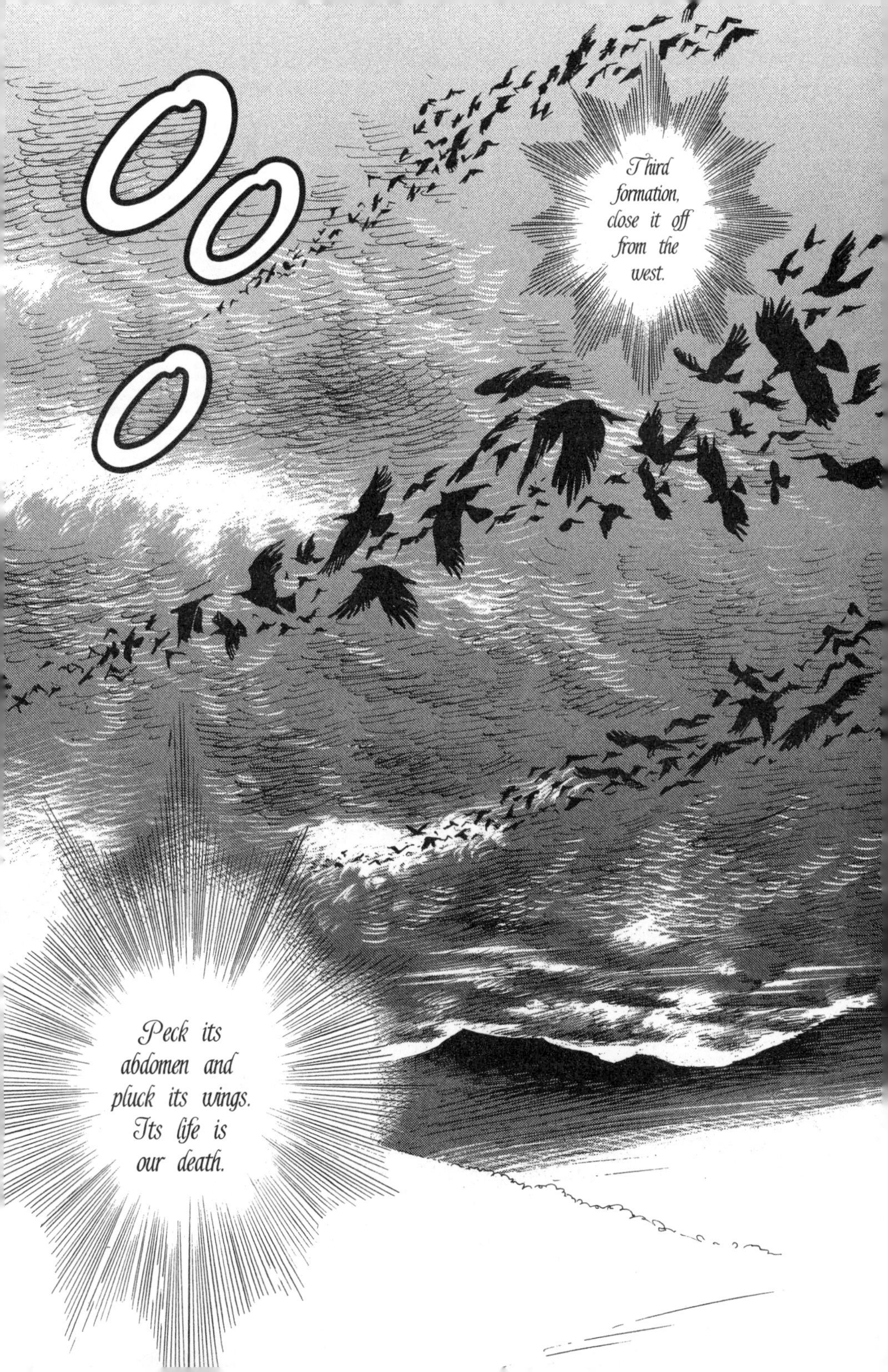
OOO
Third formation, close it off from the west.
Peck its abdomen and pluck its wings. Its life is our death.

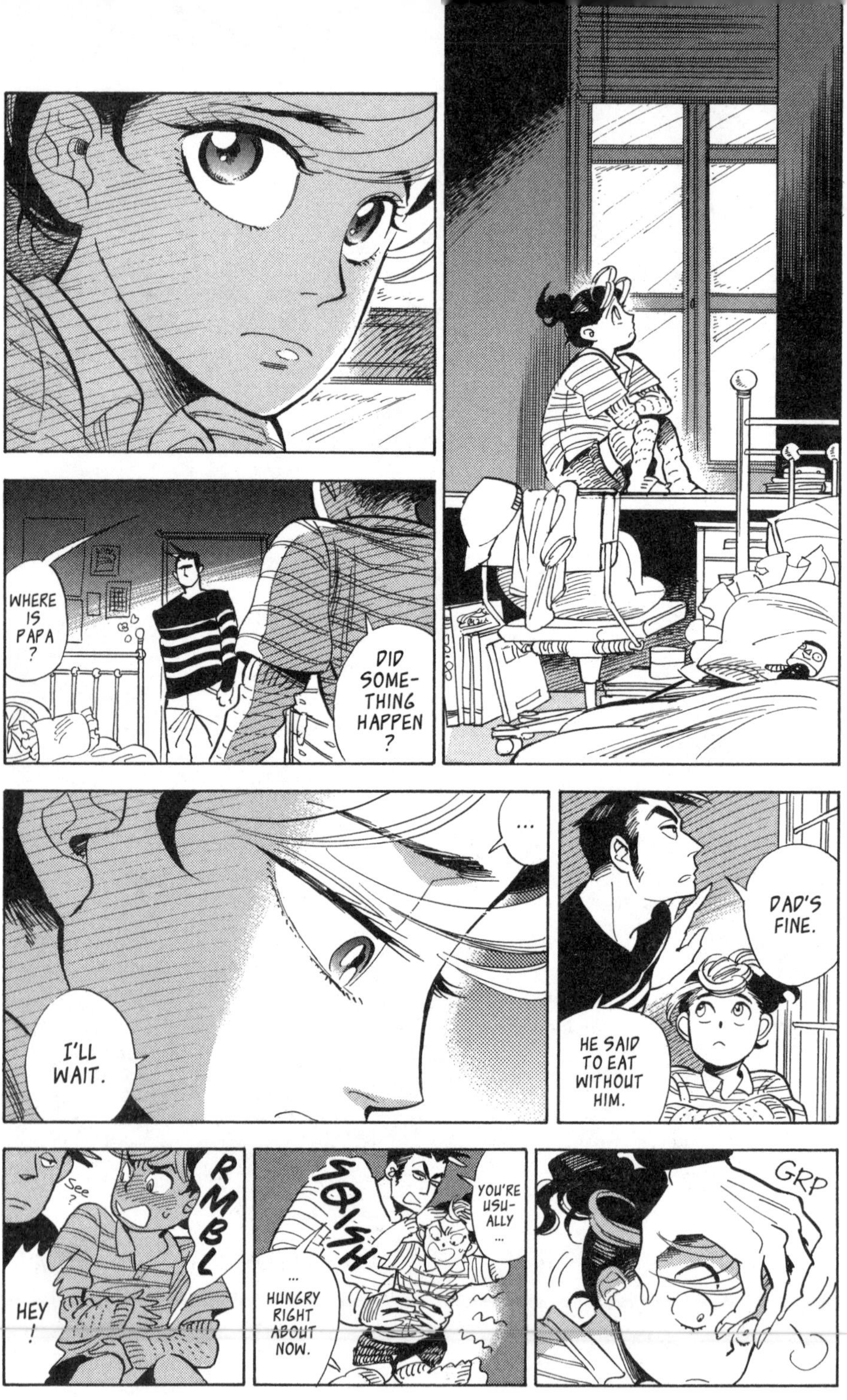
DID SOMETHING HAPPEN?
WHERE IS PAPA?
DAD'S FINE.
HE SAID TO EAT WITHOUT HIM.
...
I'LL WAIT.
GRP
YOU'RE USUALLY...
...HUNGRY RIGHT ABOUT NOW.
RMBL
See?
HEY!

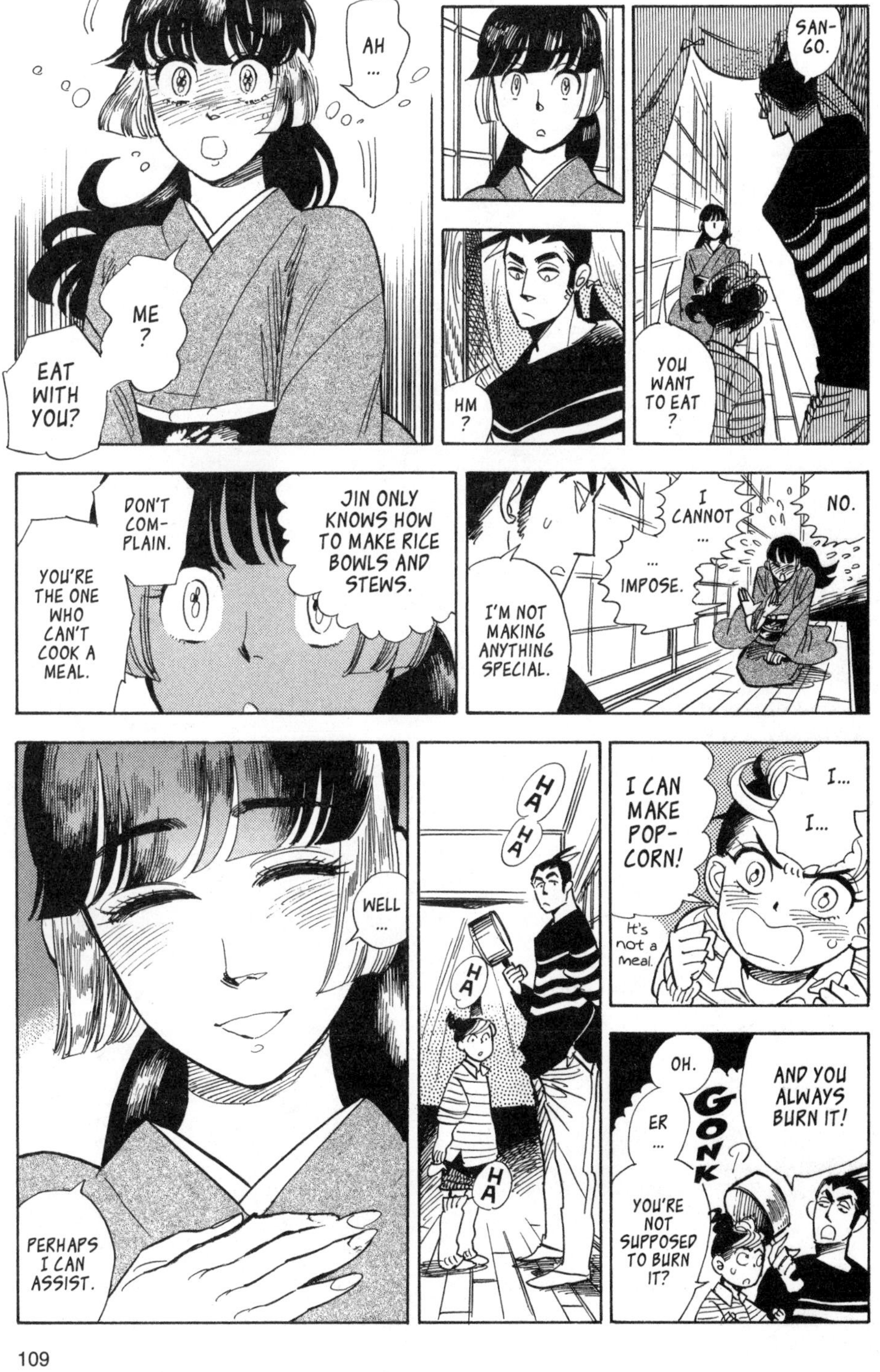
SAN-GO.
YOU WANT TO EAT ?
HM ?
AH ...
ME ?
EAT WITH YOU?
NO.
I CANNOT ...
... IMPOSE.
I'M NOT MAKING ANYTHING SPECIAL.
JIN ONLY KNOWS HOW TO MAKE RICE BOWLS AND STEWS.
DON'T COM-PLAIN.
YOU'RE THE ONE WHO CAN'T COOK A MEAL.
I...
I...
I CAN MAKE POP-CORN!
It's not a meal.
AND YOU ALWAYS BURN IT!
GONK
OH.
ER ...
YOU'RE NOT SUPPOSED TO BURN IT?
HA HA
HA
HA
WELL ...
PERHAPS I CAN ASSIST.

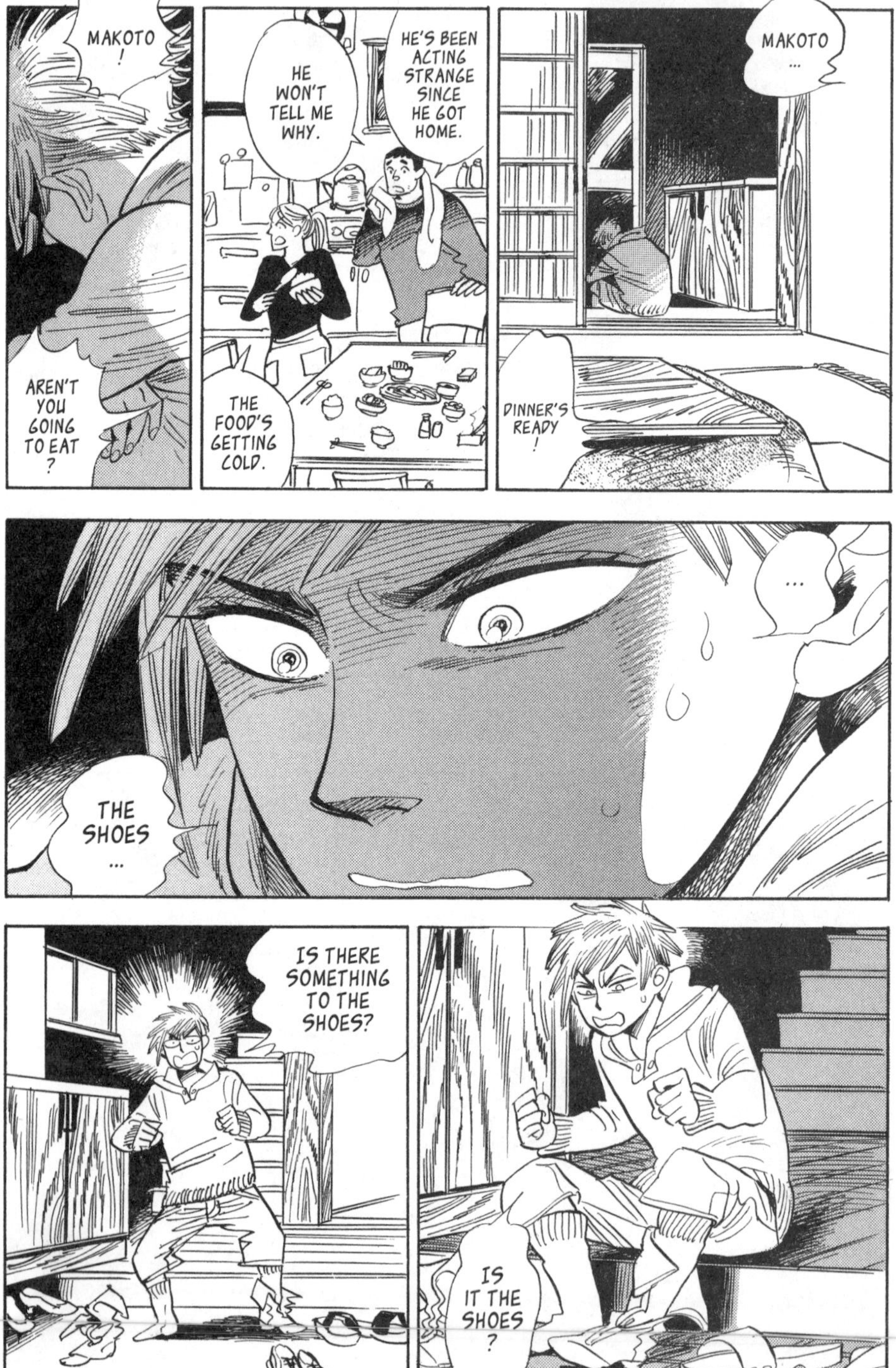
MAKOTO...
DINNER'S READY!
HE'S BEEN ACTING STRANGE SINCE HE GOT HOME.
HE WON'T TELL ME WHY.
THE FOOD'S GETTING COLD.
MAKOTO!
AREN'T YOU GOING TO EAT?
...
THE SHOES...
IS IT THE SHOES?
IS THERE SOMETHING TO THE SHOES?

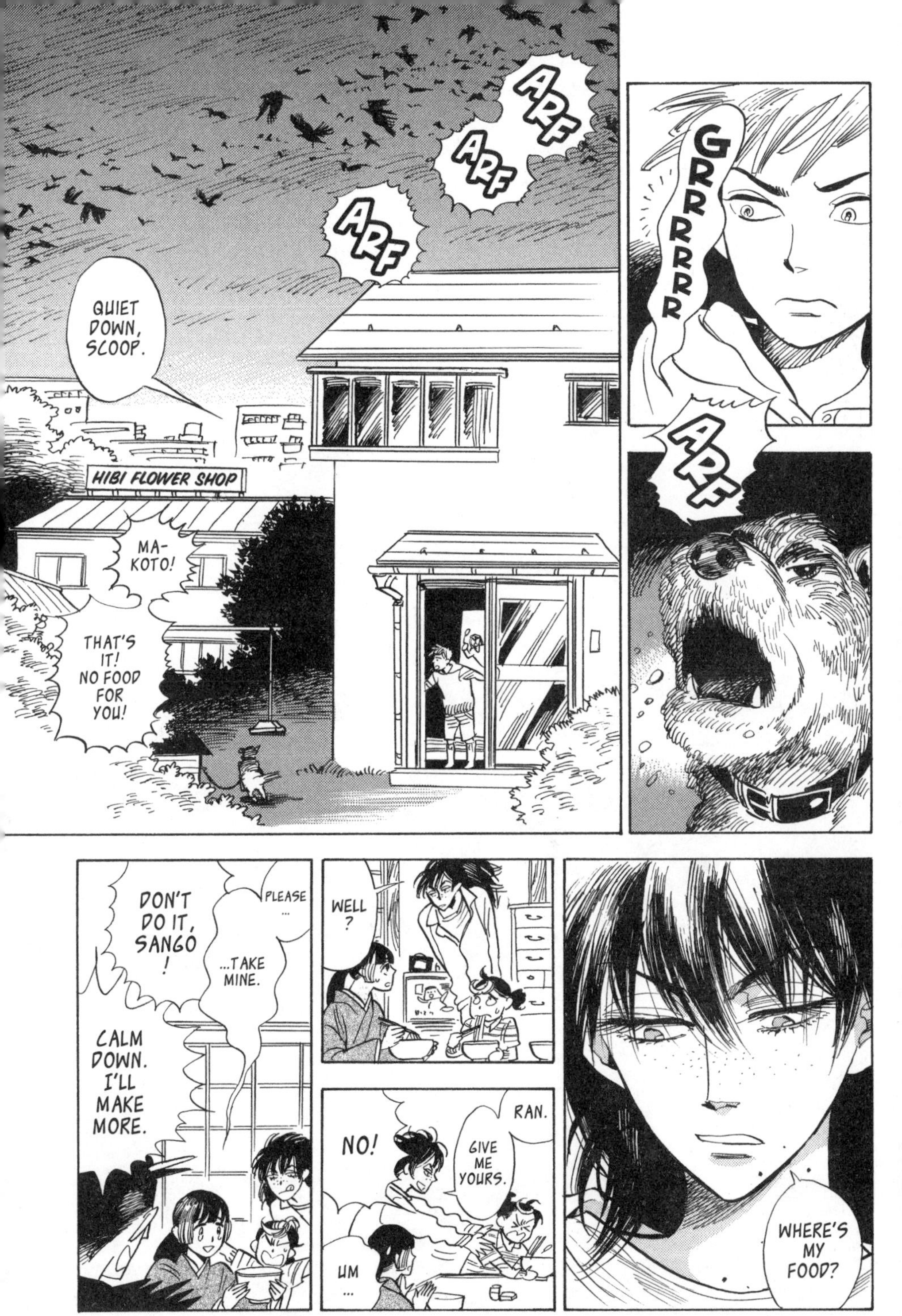
GRRRRRR
ARF
ARF
ARF
ARF
QUIET DOWN, SCOOP.
HIBI FLOWER SHOP
MA-KOTO!
THAT'S IT! NO FOOD FOR YOU!
WHERE'S MY FOOD?
WELL?
RAN.
GIVE ME YOURS.
NO!
UM...
PLEASE...
...TAKE MINE.
DON'T DO IT, SANGO!
CALM DOWN. I'LL MAKE MORE.

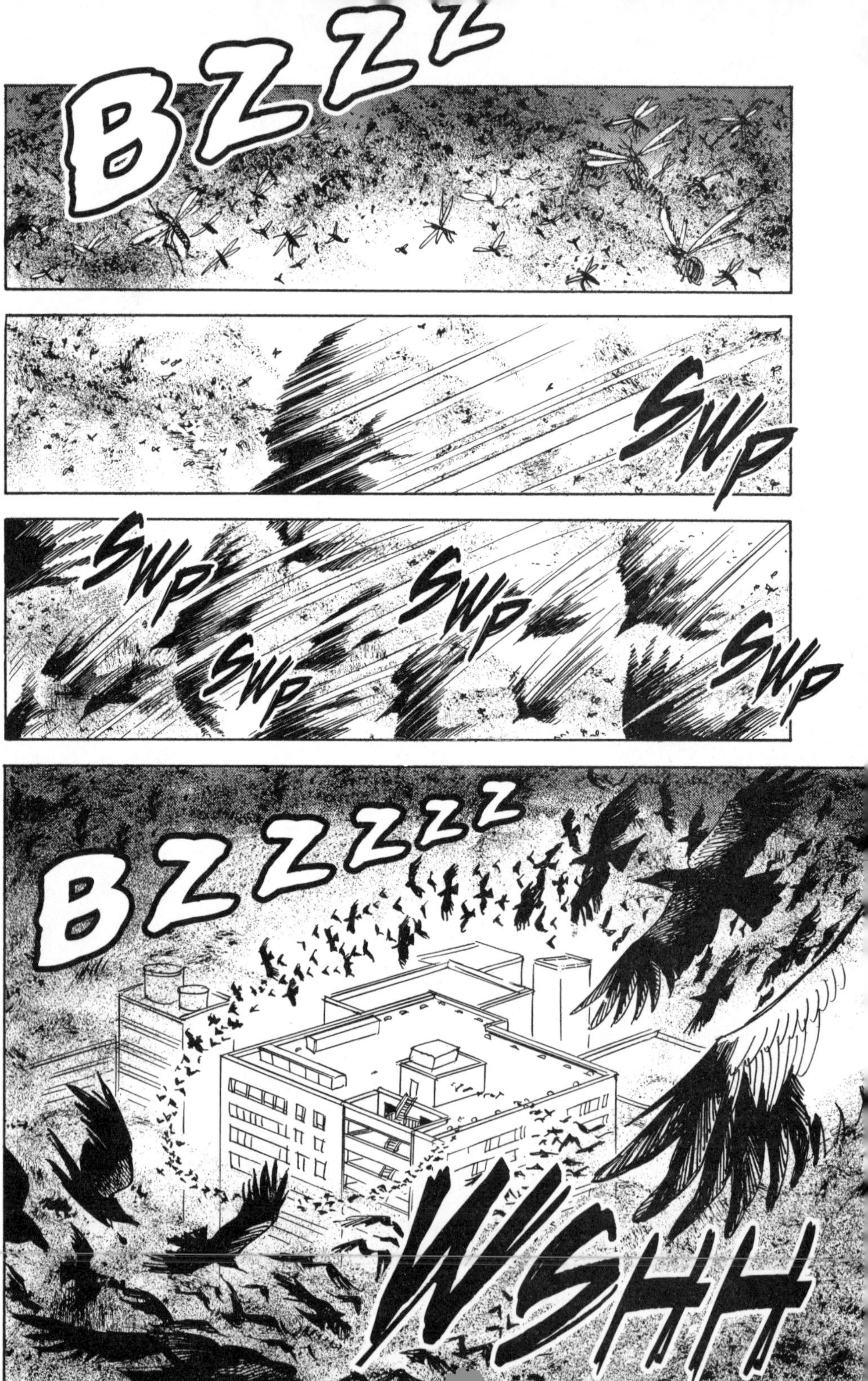
BZZZZ
SWP
SWP
SWP
SWP
SWP
BZZZZZZ
WSHH

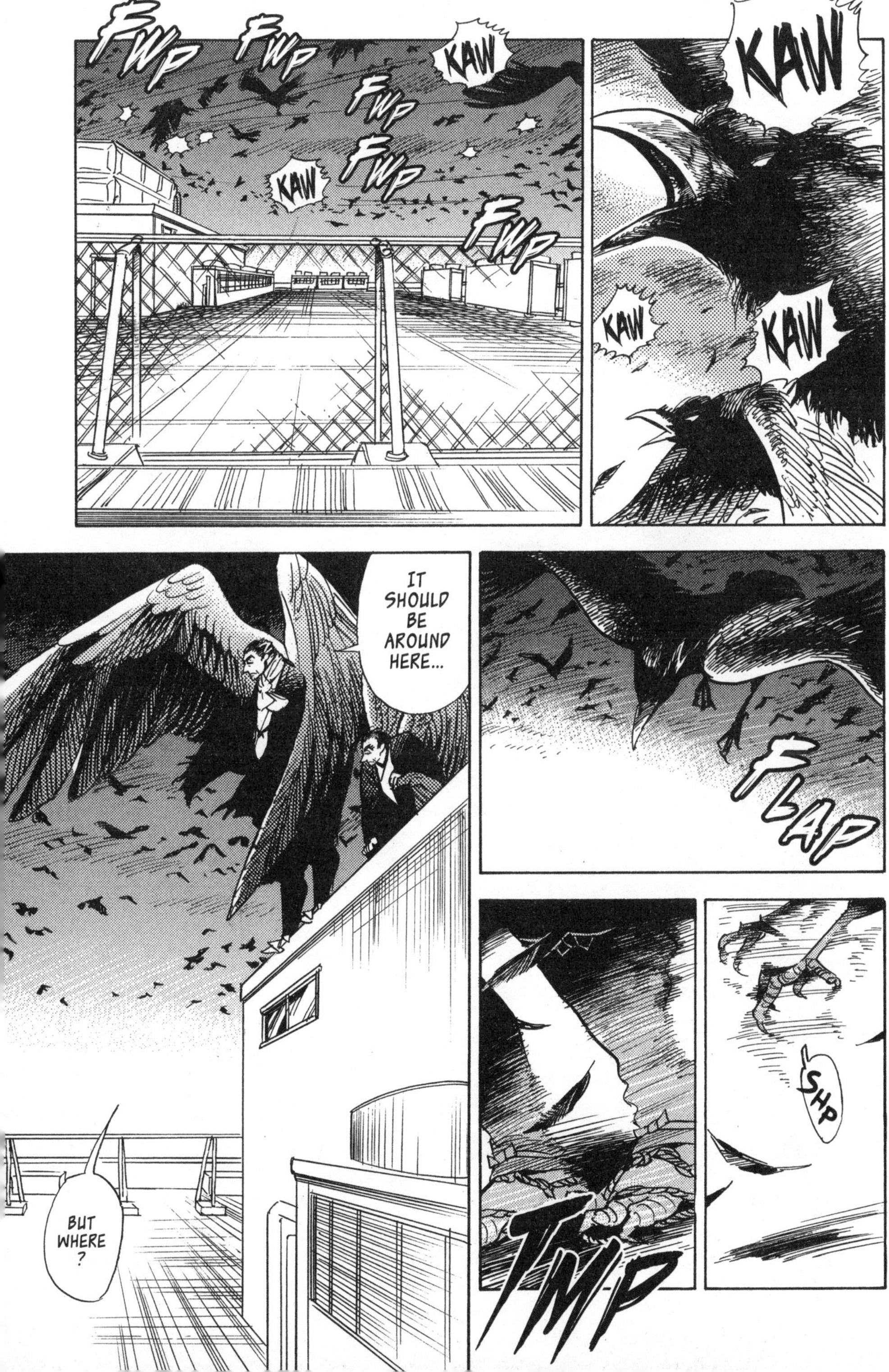
KAW
KAW
KAW
KAW
FWP
FWP
FWP
FWP
KAW
FWP
FLAP
SHP
TMP
IT SHOULD BE AROUND HERE...
BUT WHERE?

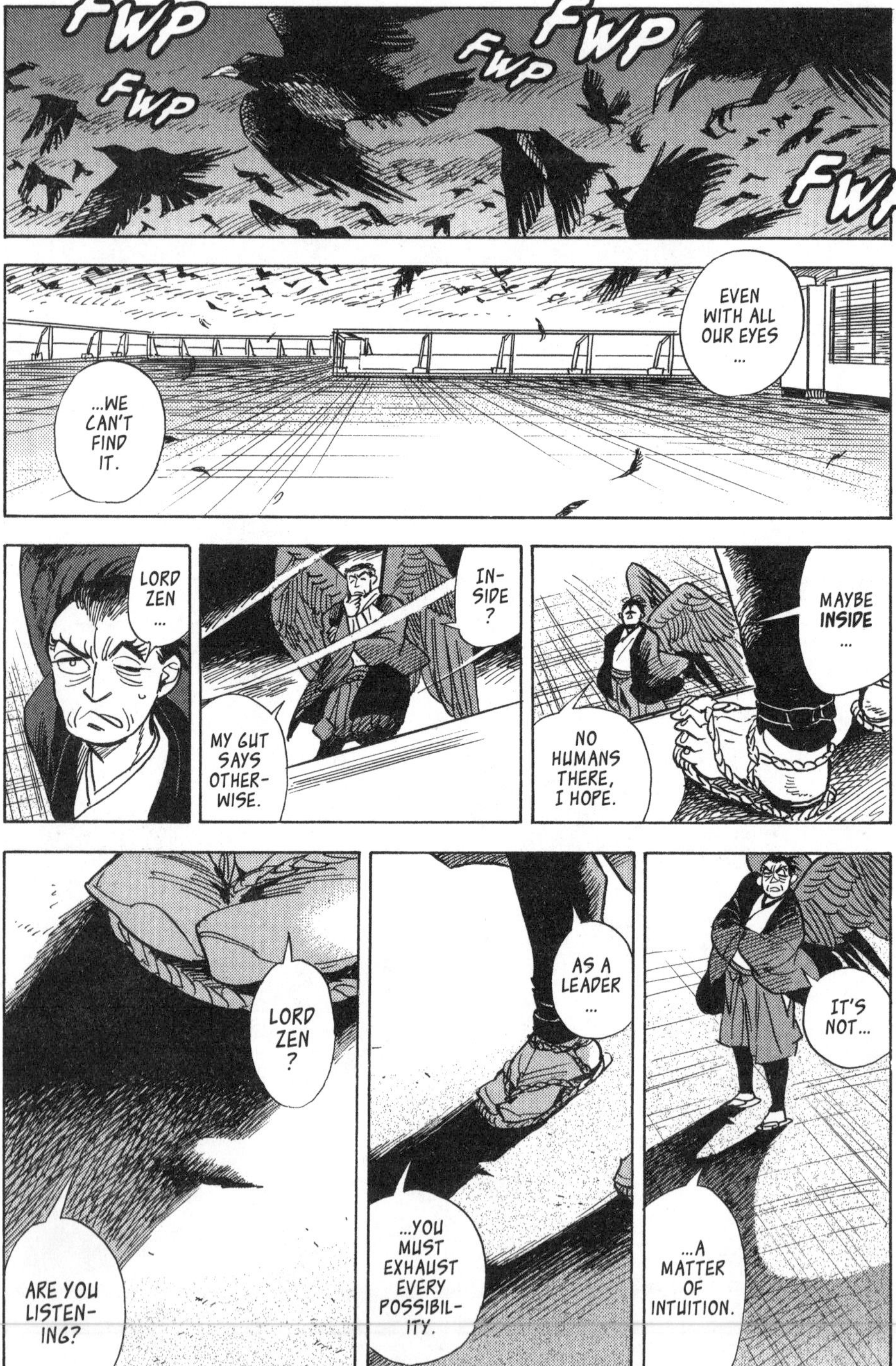
FWP
FWP
FWP
FWP
FWP
EVEN WITH ALL OUR EYES ...
...WE CAN'T FIND IT.
MAYBE **INSIDE** ...
NO HUMANS THERE, I HOPE.
IN-SIDE?
MY GUT SAYS OTHER-WISE.
LORD ZEN ...
IT'S NOT...
...A MATTER OF INTUITION.
AS A LEADER ...
...YOU MUST EXHAUST EVERY POSSIBIL-ITY.
LORD ZEN?
ARE YOU LISTEN-ING?

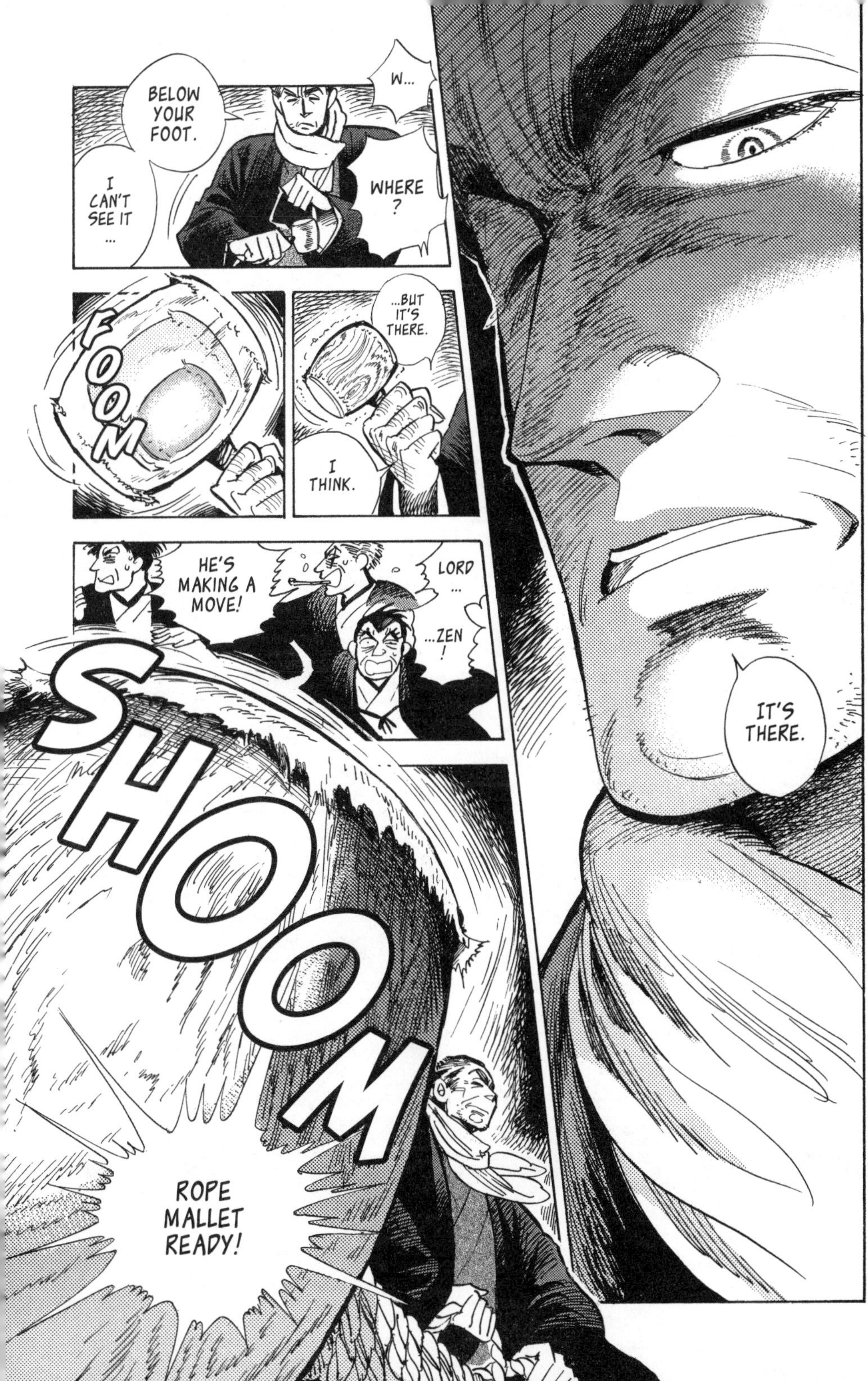
IT'S THERE.
W...
WHERE ?
BELOW YOUR FOOT.
I CAN'T SEE IT ...
...BUT IT'S THERE.
I THINK.
FOOOM
LORD ...
...ZEN !
HE'S MAKING A MOVE!
SHOOOM
ROPE MALLET READY!

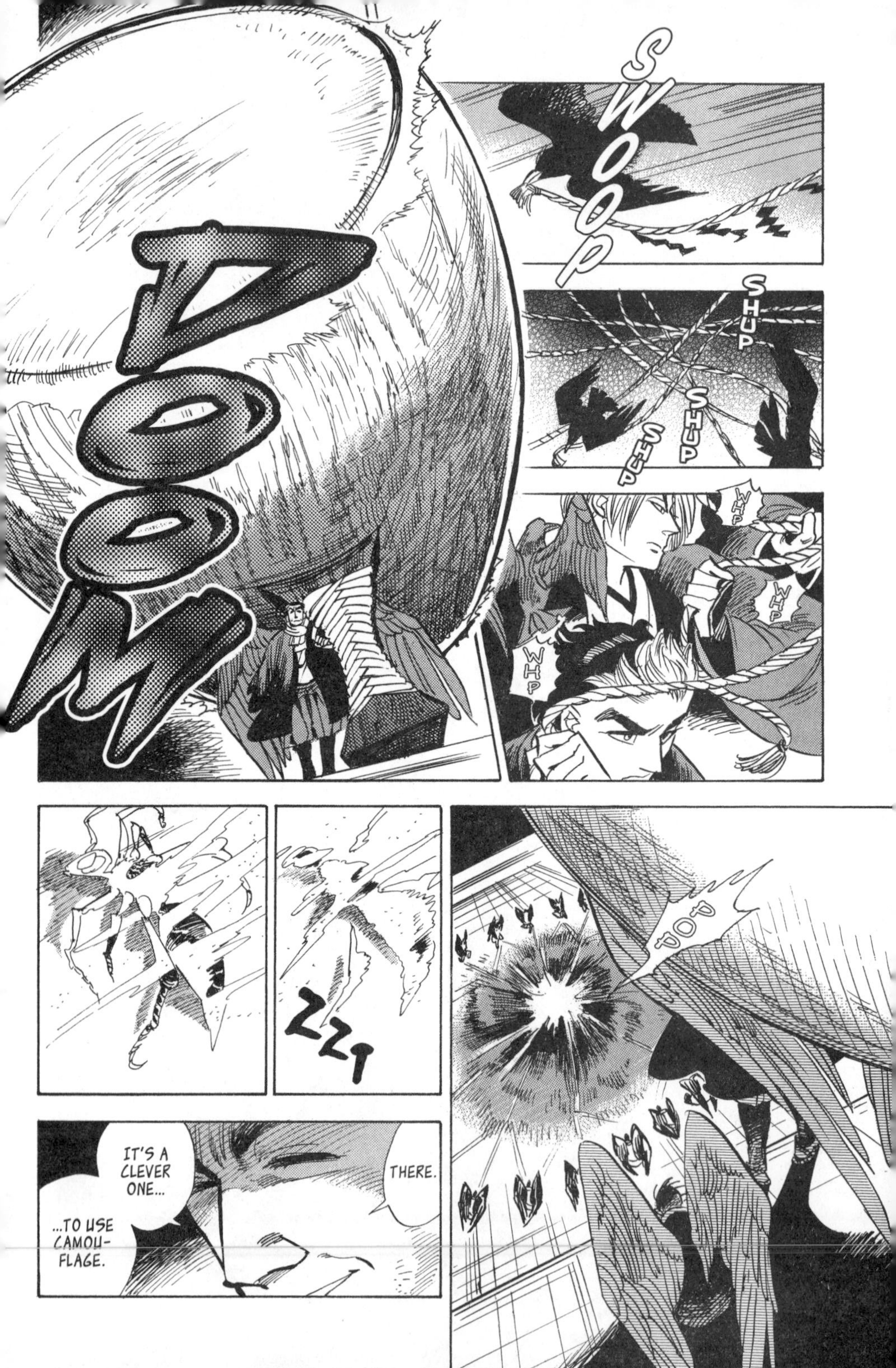
SWOOP
SHUP
SHUP
SHUP
WHP
WHP
WHP
DOOM
POP
THERE.
IT'S A CLEVER ONE...
...TO USE CAMOUFLAGE.

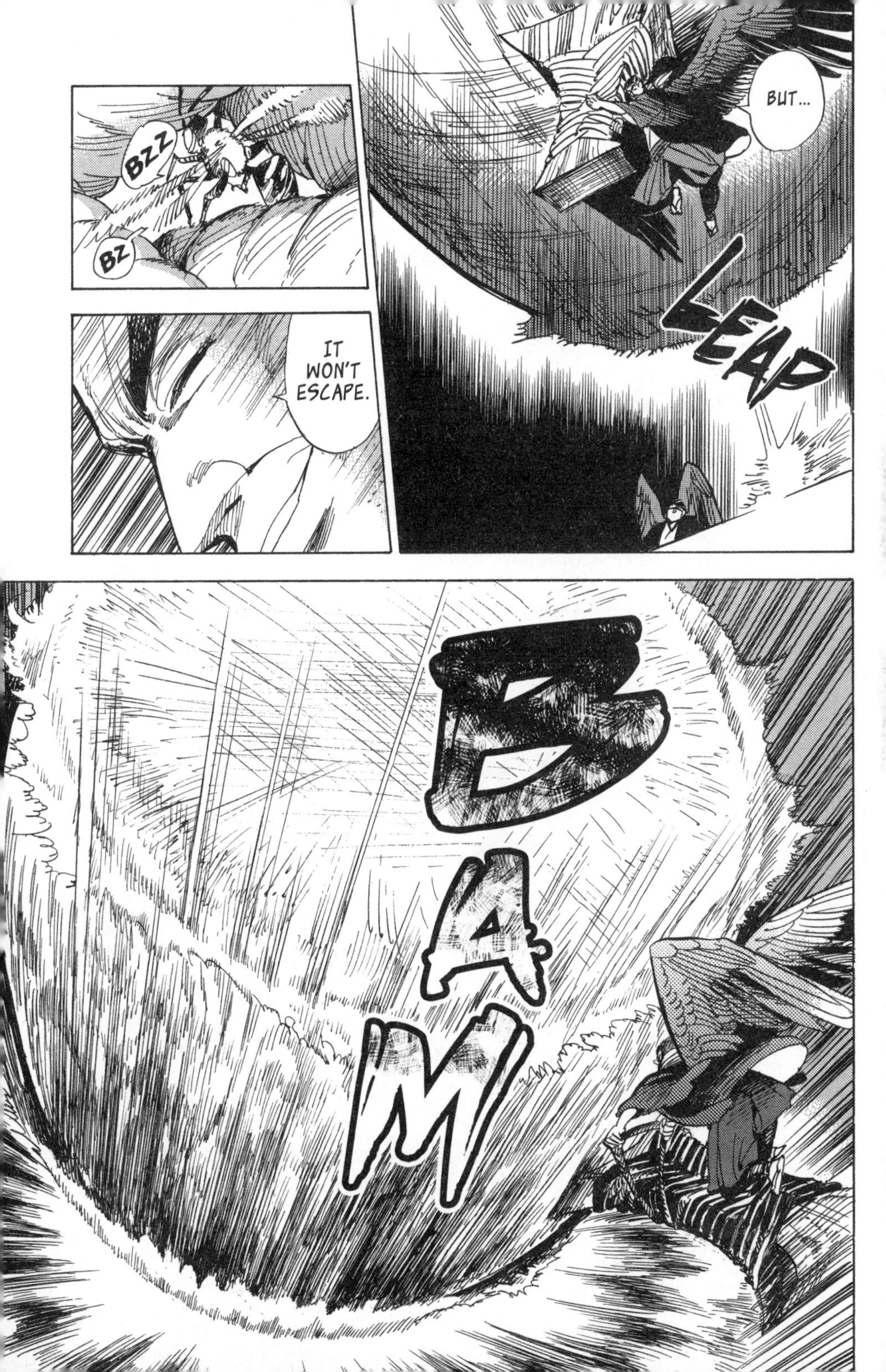
BUT...
LEAP
BZZ
BZ
IT WON'T ESCAPE.
BAM

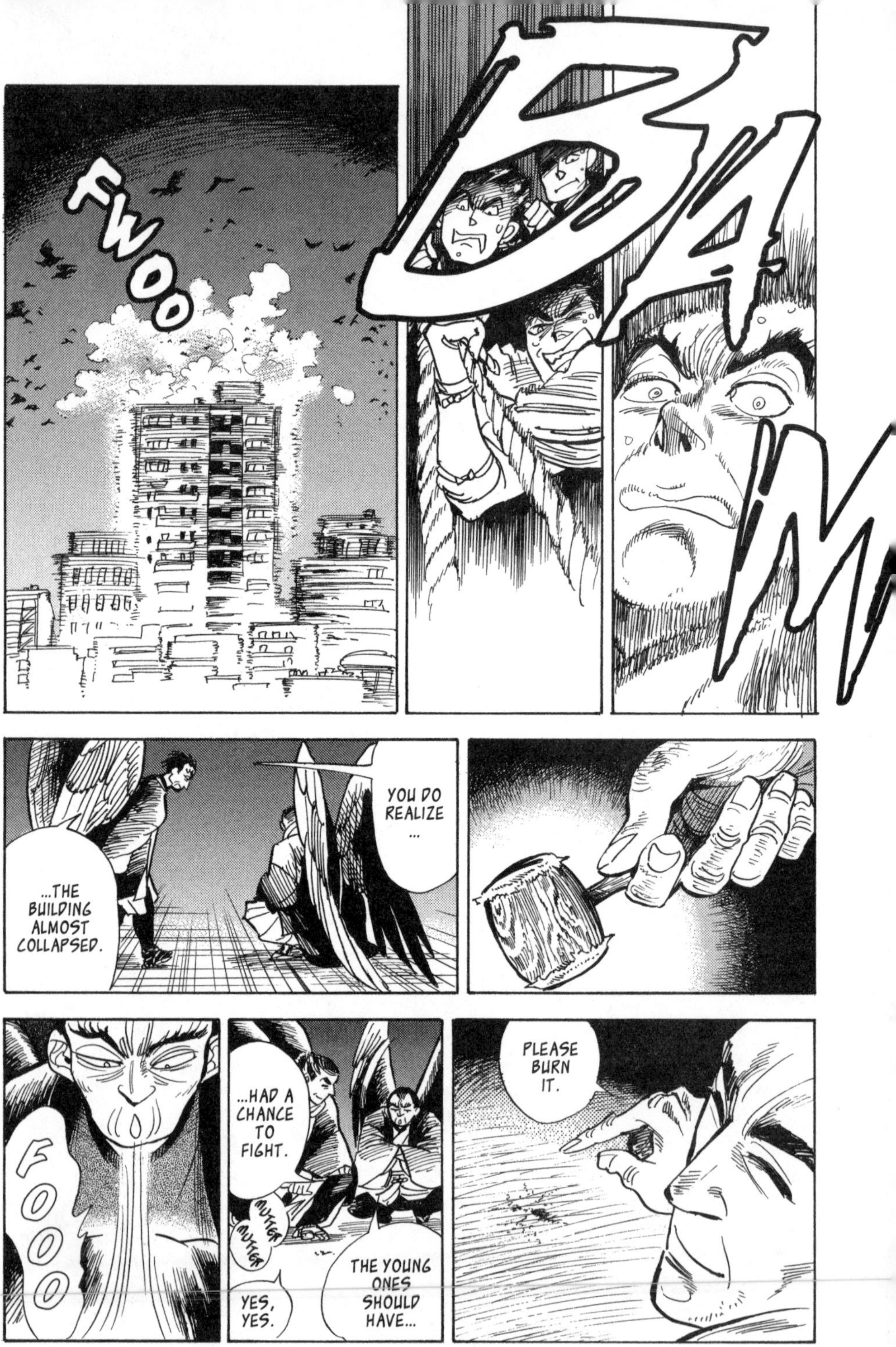
BAM
FWOO
YOU DO REALIZE ...
...THE BUILDING ALMOST COLLAPSED.
PLEASE BURN IT.
THE YOUNG ONES SHOULD HAVE...
...HAD A CHANCE TO FIGHT.
MUTTER MUTTER
YES, YES.
FOOOO

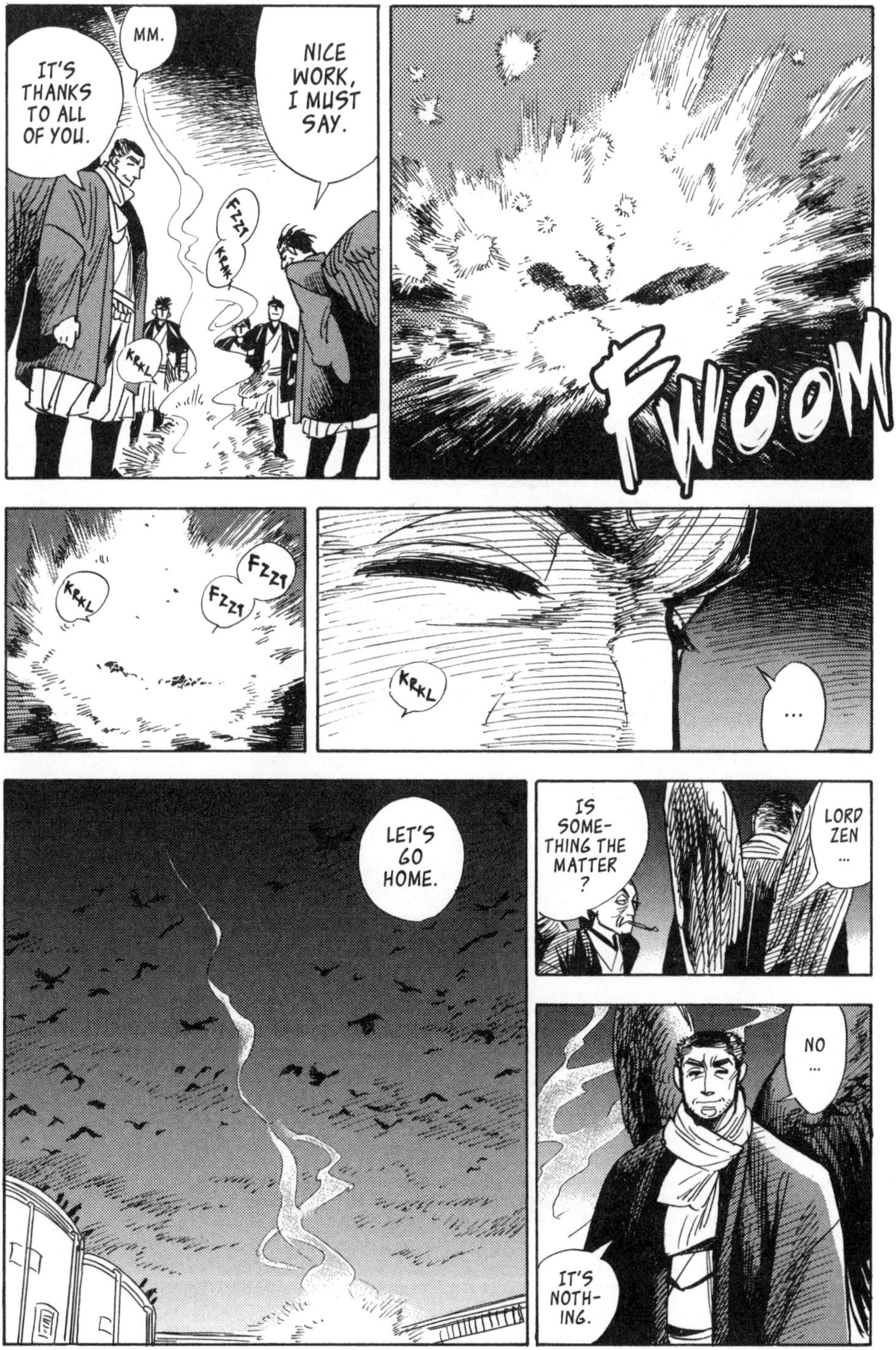
FWOOM
NICE WORK, I MUST SAY.
MM.
IT'S THANKS TO ALL OF YOU.
FZZT
KRKL
KRKL
...
KRKL
FZZT
FZZT
KRKL
LORD ZEN ...
IS SOME-THING THE MATTER ?
NO ...
IT'S NOTH-ING.
LET'S GO HOME.

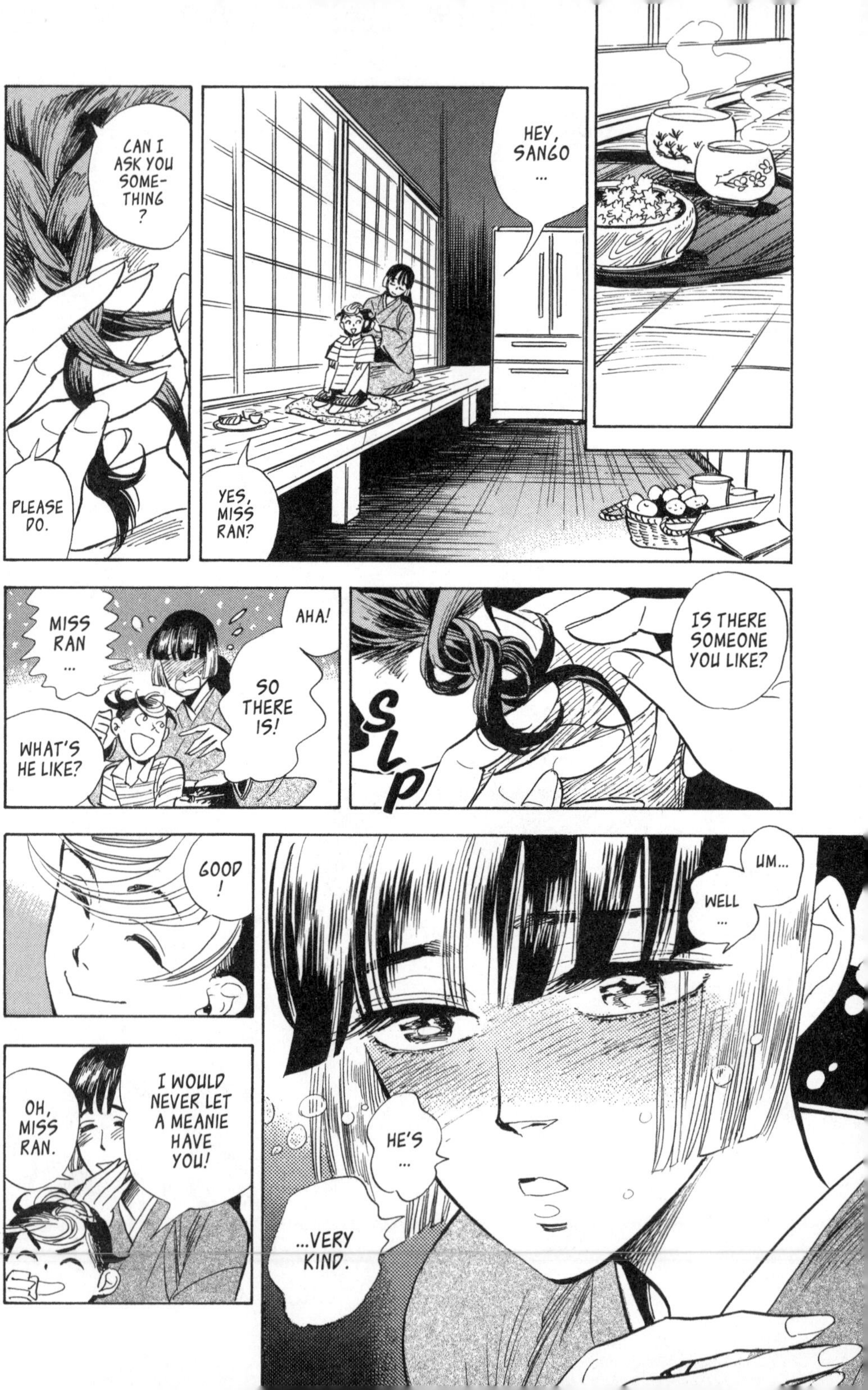
HEY, SANGO ...
YES, MISS RAN?
CAN I ASK YOU SOME-THING?
PLEASE DO.
IS THERE SOMEONE YOU LIKE?
SLP
AHA!
SO THERE IS!
MISS RAN ...
WHAT'S HE LIKE?
UM...
WELL ...
HE'S ...
...VERY KIND.
GOOD!
I WOULD NEVER LET A MEANIE HAVE YOU!
OH, MISS RAN.

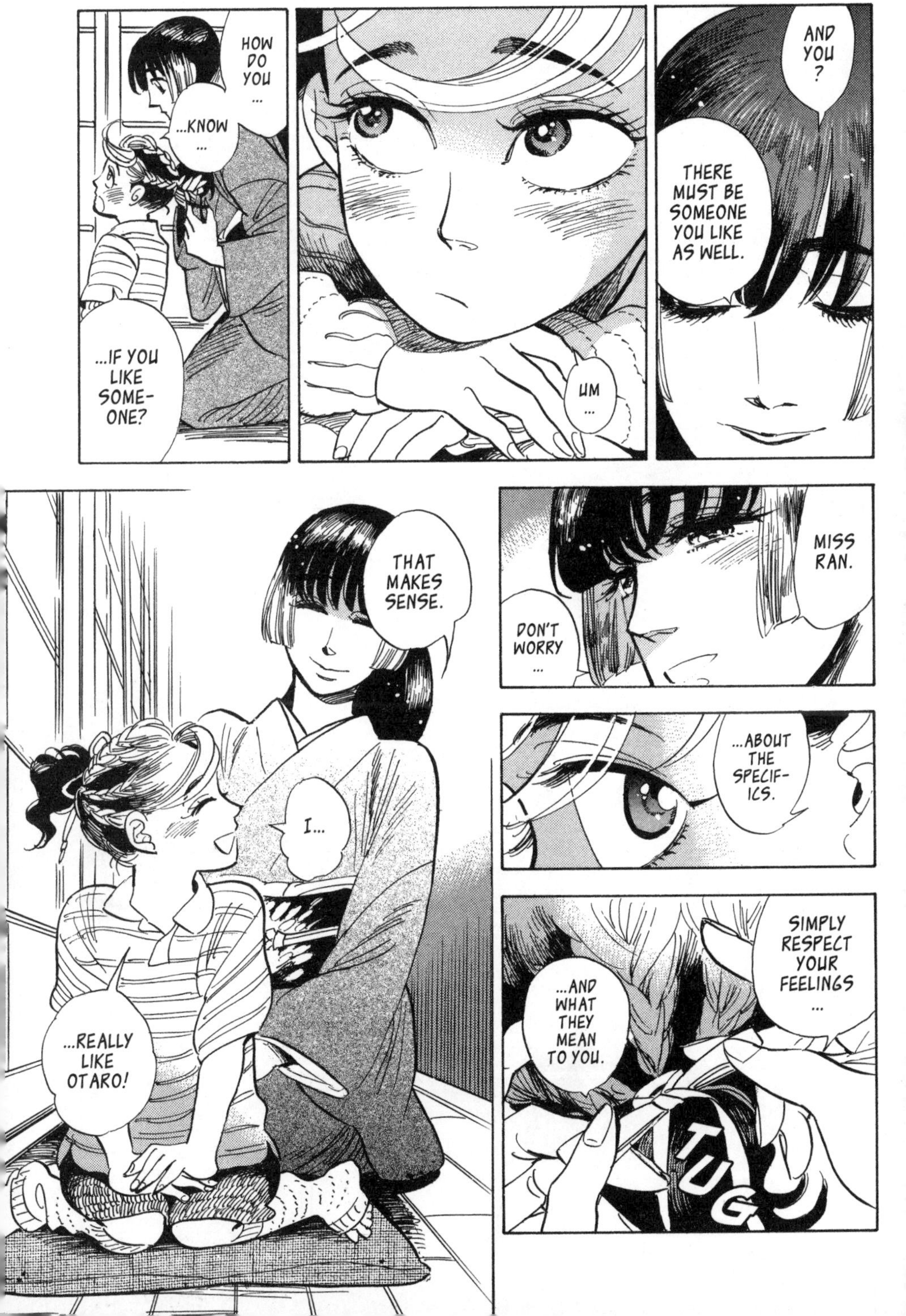
AND YOU?
THERE MUST BE SOMEONE YOU LIKE AS WELL.
UM...
HOW DO YOU...
...KNOW...
...IF YOU LIKE SOME-ONE?
MISS RAN.
DON'T WORRY...
...ABOUT THE SPECIF-ICS.
SIMPLY RESPECT YOUR FEELINGS...
...AND WHAT THEY MEAN TO YOU.
TUG.
THAT MAKES SENSE.
I...
...REALLY LIKE OTARO!

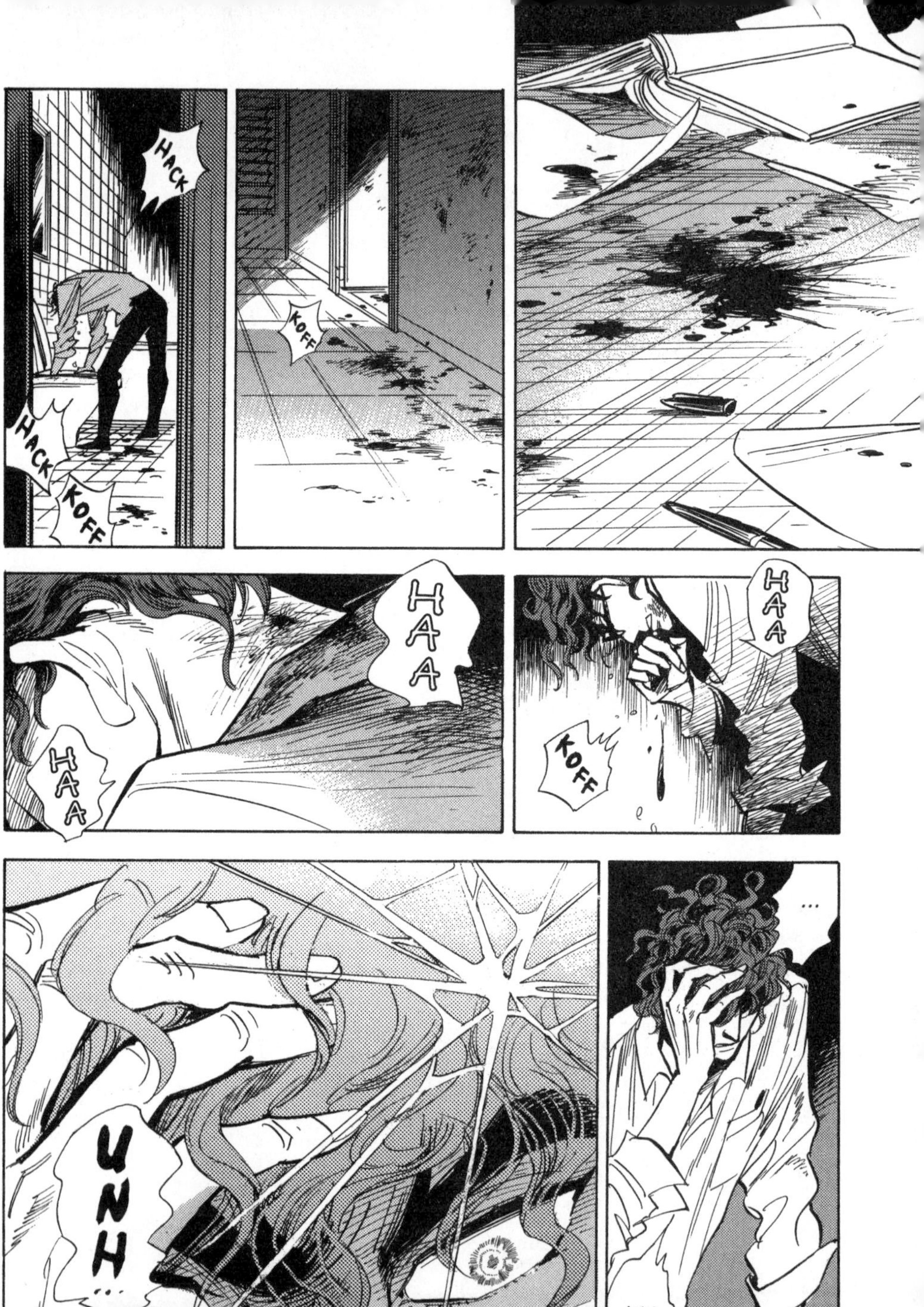
KOFF
HACK
HACK
KOFF
HAA
KOFF
HAA
HAA
...
AHH ...
UNH!...

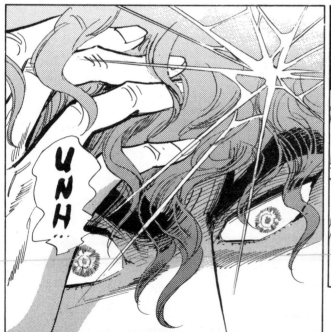

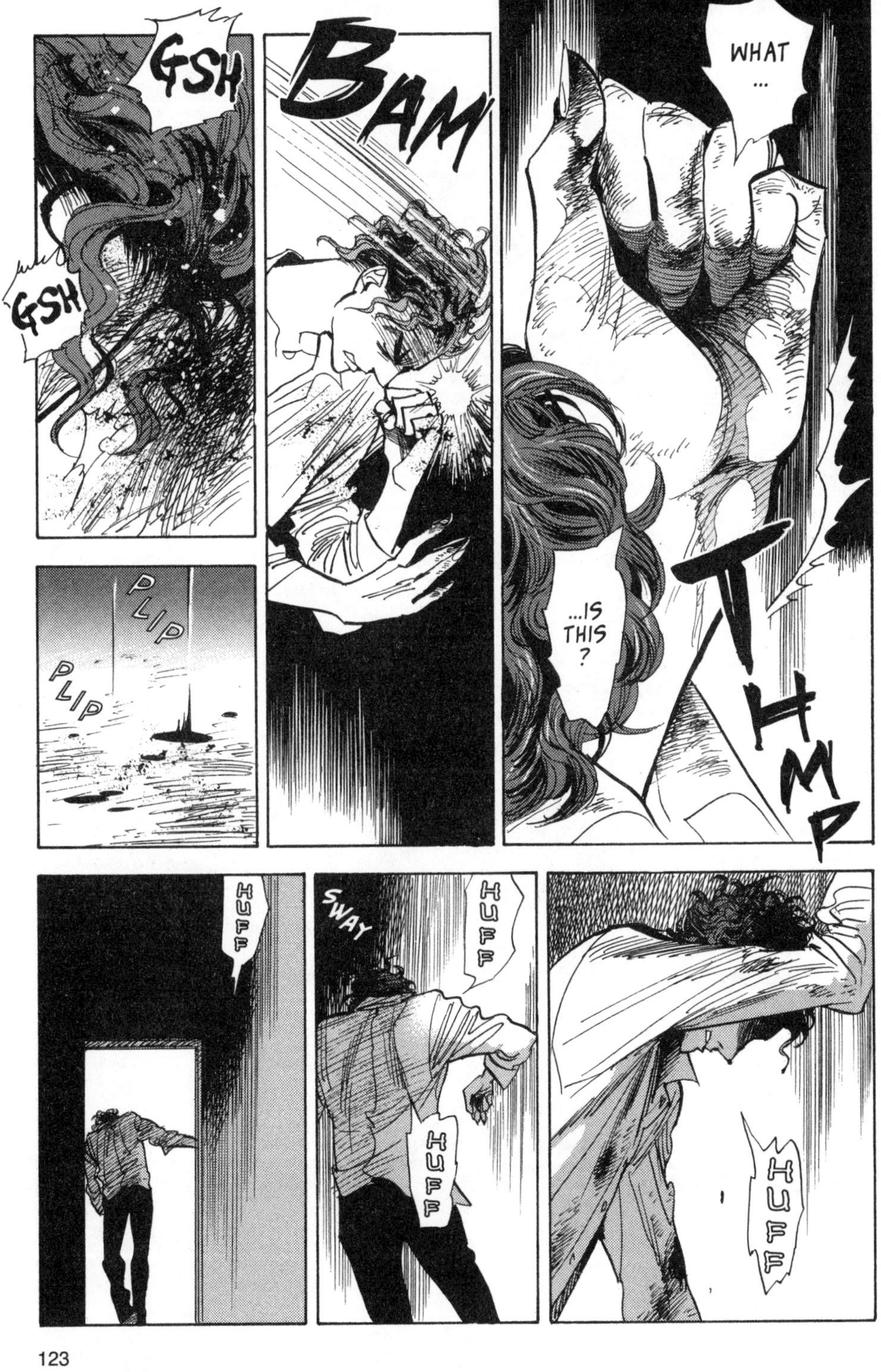
WHAT ...
THMP
...IS THIS?
BAM
GSH
GSH
PLIP
PLIP
HUFF
SWAY
HUFF
HUFF
HUFF

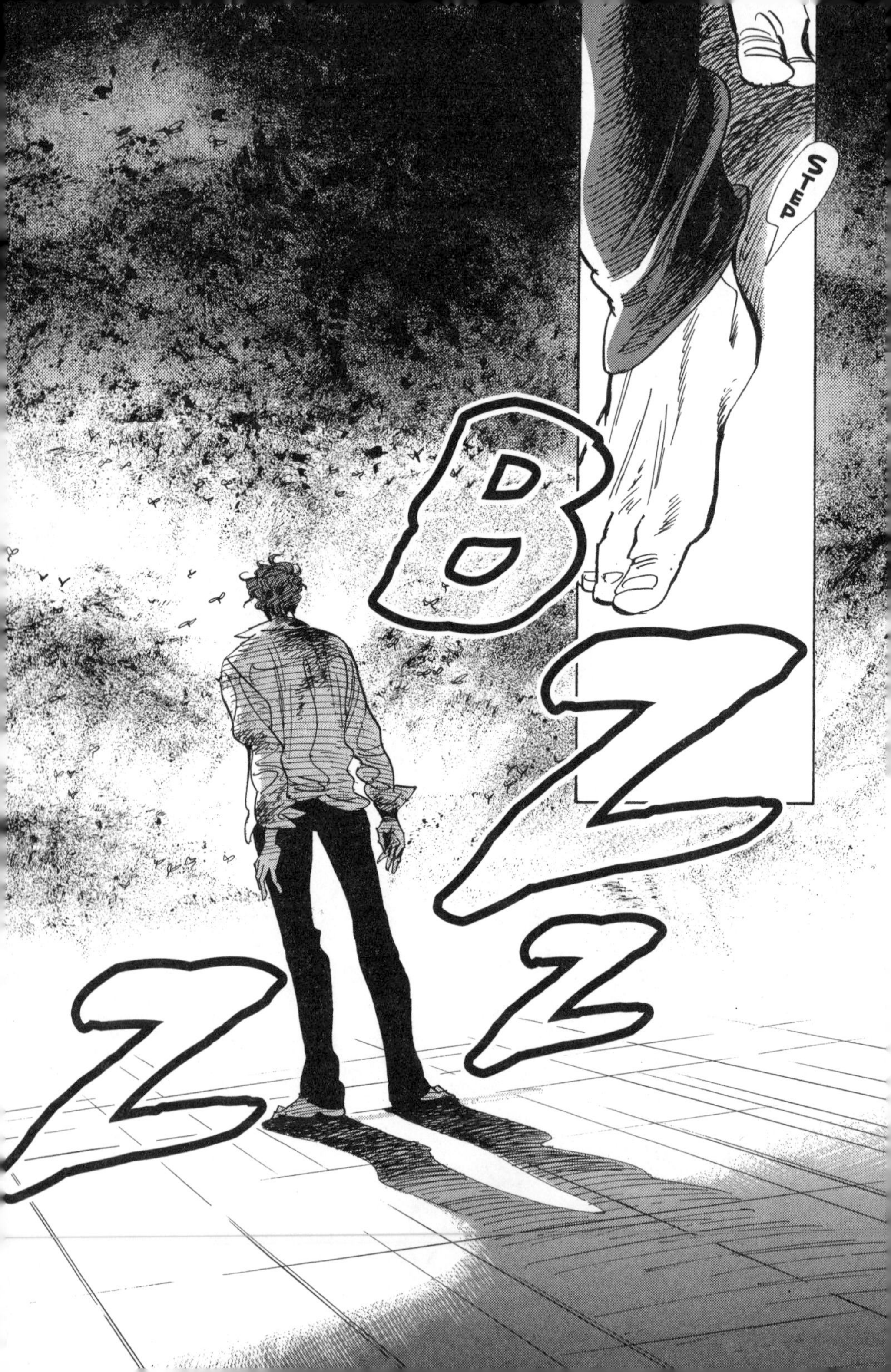
STEP
BZZZZ

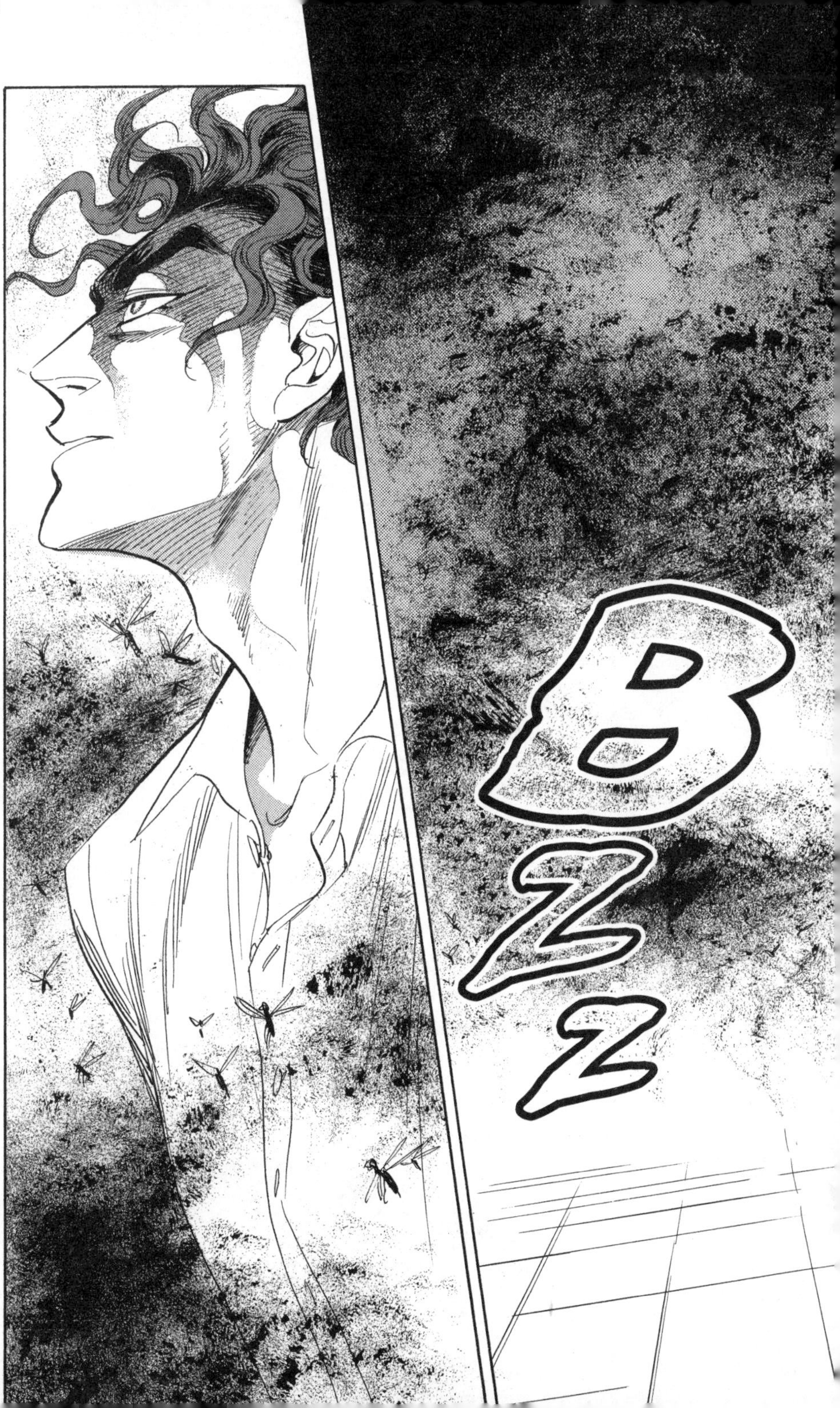
BZZ

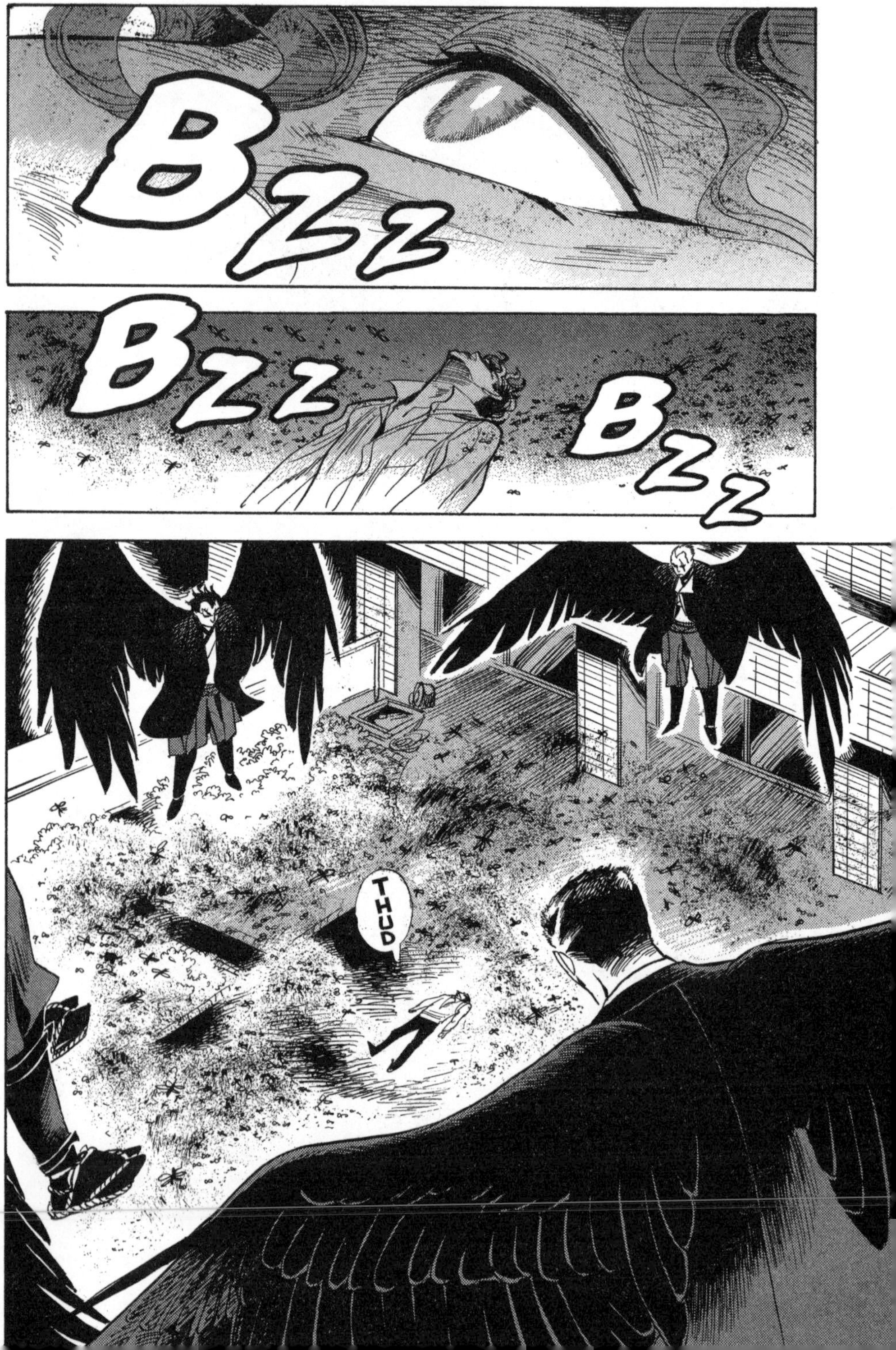
BZZ
BZZ
BZZ
THUD

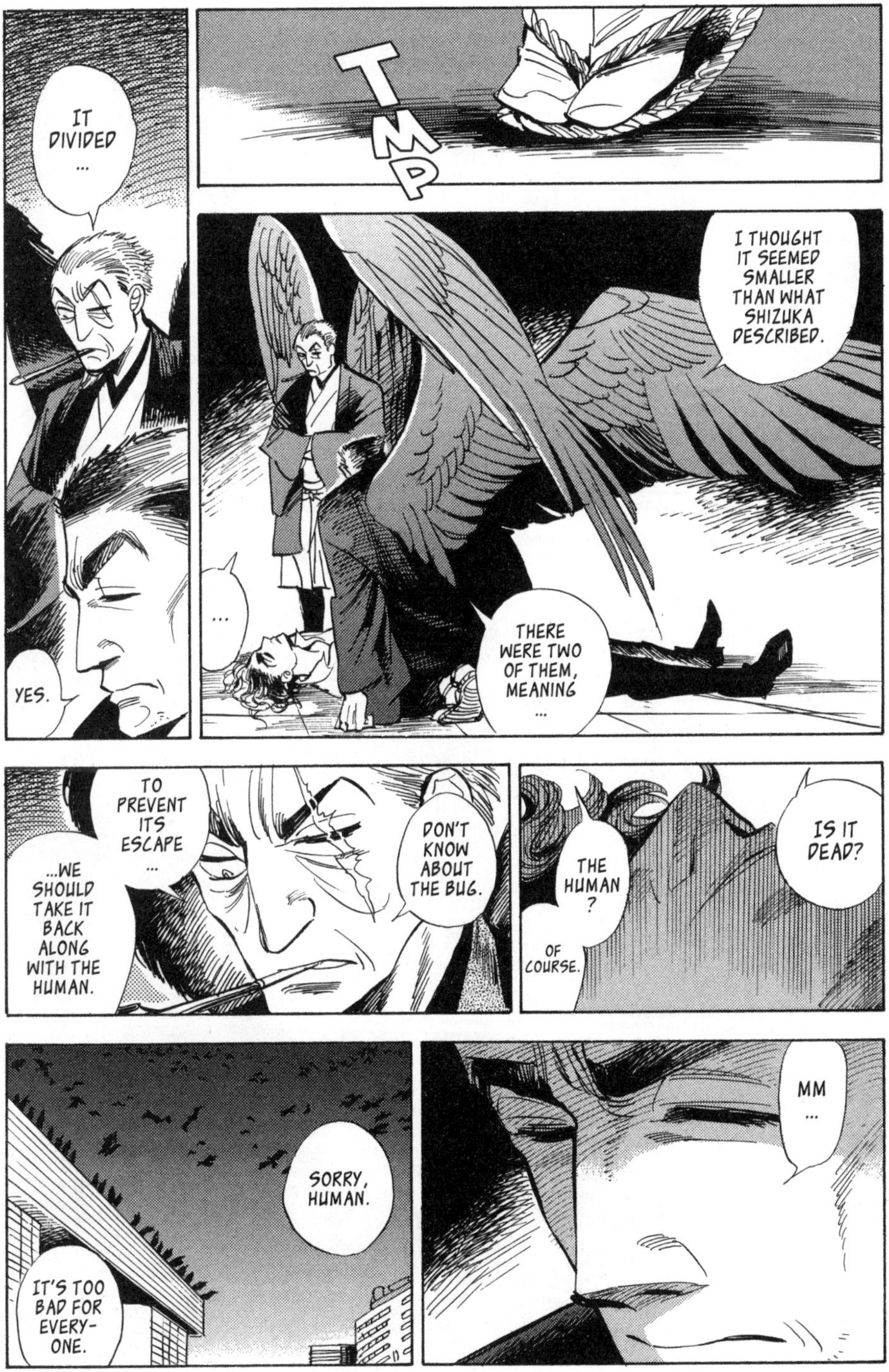
TMP
I THOUGHT IT SEEMED SMALLER THAN WHAT SHIZUKA DESCRIBED.
THERE WERE TWO OF THEM, MEANING ...
...
IT DIVIDED ...
YES.
IS IT DEAD?
THE HUMAN?
OF COURSE.
DON'T KNOW ABOUT THE BUG.
TO PREVENT ITS ESCAPE ...
...WE SHOULD TAKE IT BACK ALONG WITH THE HUMAN.
MM ...
SORRY, HUMAN.
IT'S TOO BAD FOR EVERY-ONE.

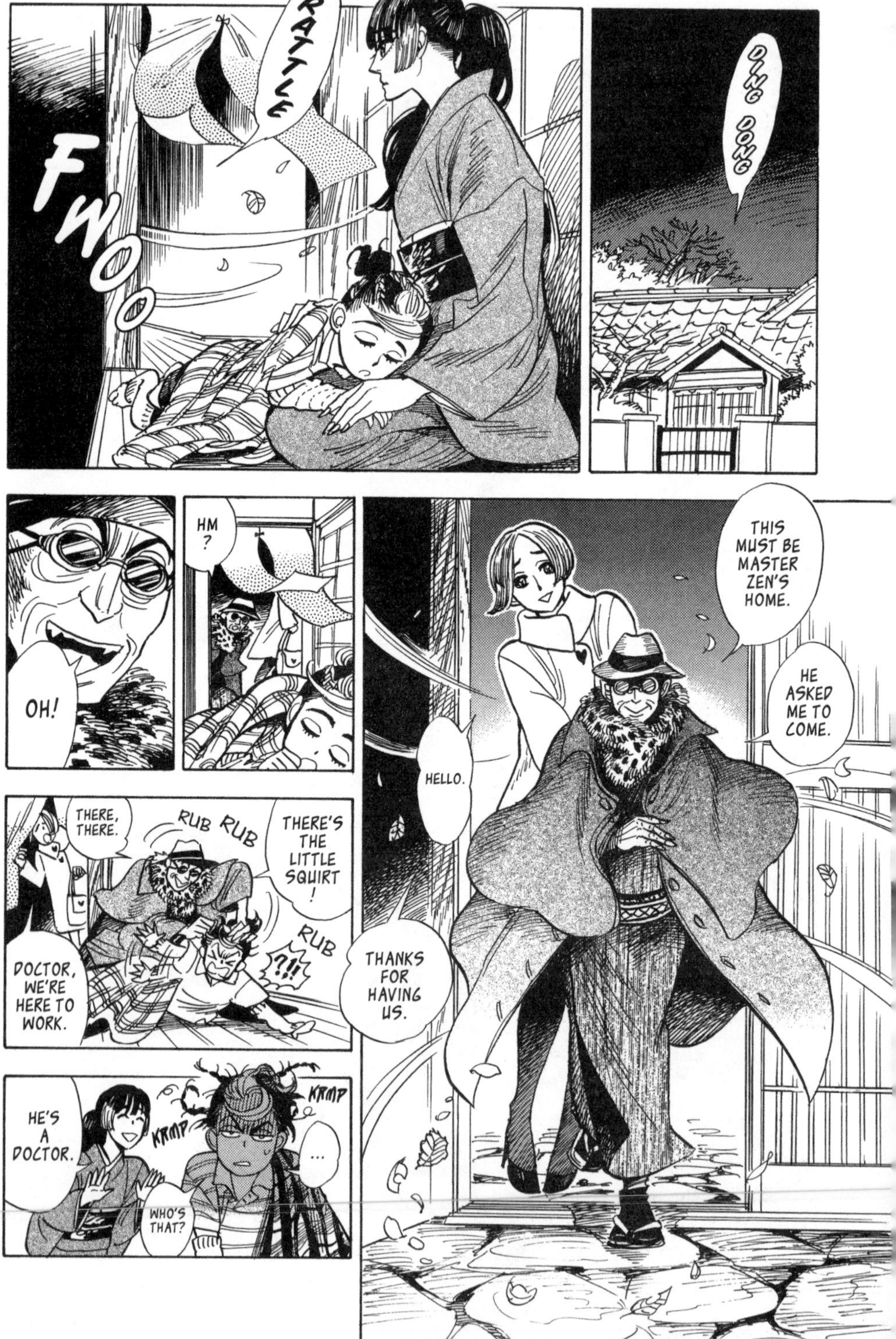
DING DONG
RATTLE
FWOOO
THIS MUST BE MASTER ZEN'S HOME.
HE ASKED ME TO COME.
HELLO.
THANKS FOR HAVING US.
HM?
OH!
THERE'S THE LITTLE SQUIRT!
RUB RUB
RUB
?!!
THERE, THERE.
DOCTOR, WE'RE HERE TO WORK.
KRMP
...
KRMP
HE'S A DOCTOR.
WHO'S THAT?

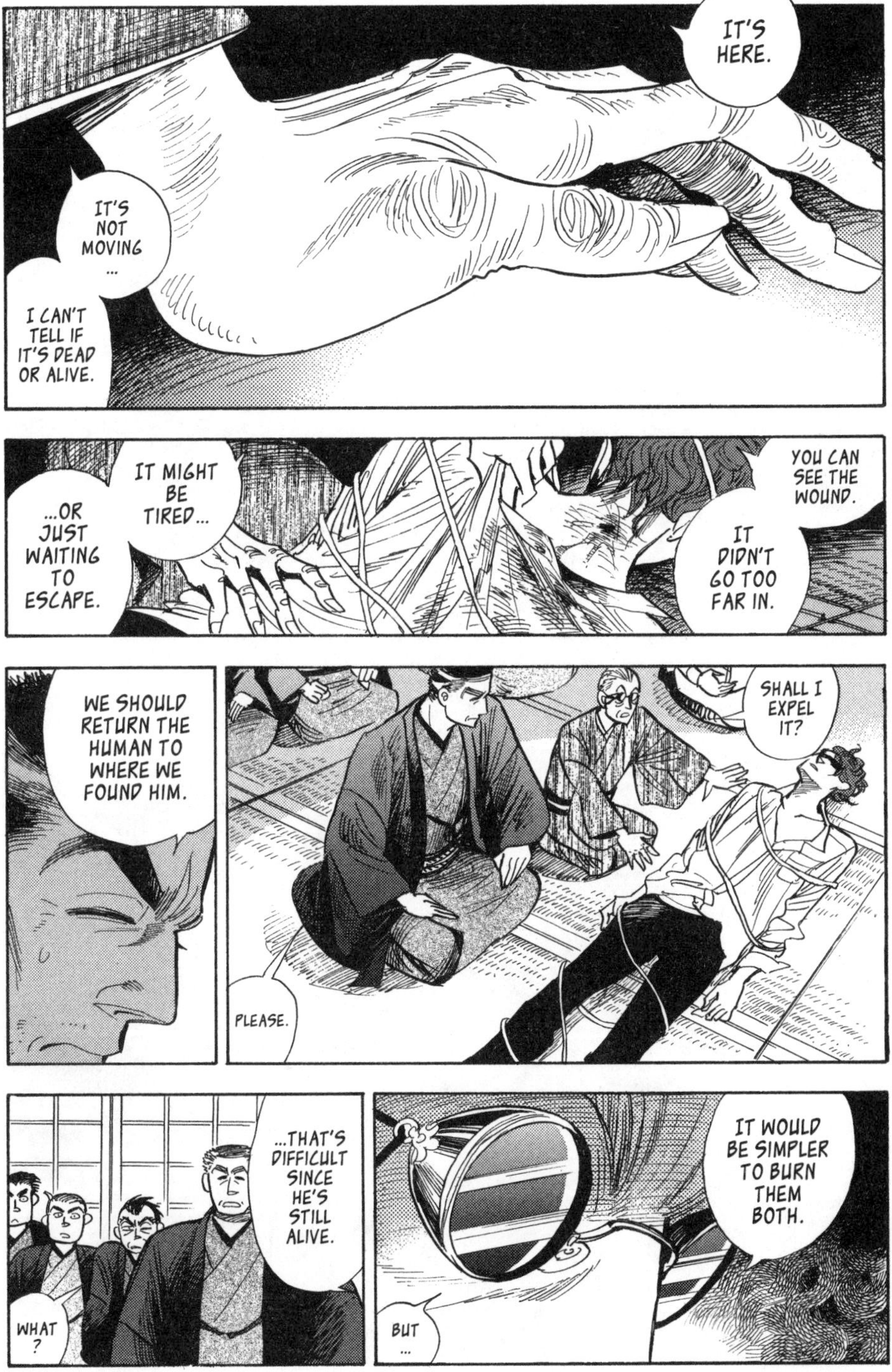
IT'S HERE.
IT'S NOT MOVING ...
I CAN'T TELL IF IT'S DEAD OR ALIVE.
YOU CAN SEE THE WOUND.
IT DIDN'T GO TOO FAR IN.
IT MIGHT BE TIRED...
...OR JUST WAITING TO ESCAPE.
SHALL I EXPEL IT?
PLEASE.
WE SHOULD RETURN THE HUMAN TO WHERE WE FOUND HIM.
IT WOULD BE SIMPLER TO BURN THEM BOTH.
BUT ...
...THAT'S DIFFICULT SINCE HE'S STILL ALIVE.
WHAT ?

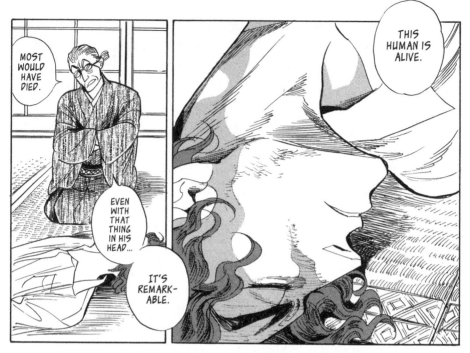

THIS HUMAN IS ALIVE.
MOST WOULD HAVE DIED.
EVEN WITH THAT THING IN HIS HEAD...
IT'S REMARKABLE.
NOT QUITE A COMPLIMENT, BUT THIS HUMAN...
...HAS IMMENSE RESISTANCE...
...AND A POISONOUS QUALITY ABOUT HIM.
Don't like it either way...
TOO BAD... HE'S SO HANDSOME...
THUP
TIME TO GET STARTED.
ZIP
PLEASE BE CAREFUL.
IF THE BUG IS ALIVE...
...THERE'S A CHANCE IT WILL BURROW INTO SOMEONE ELSE'S HEAD.

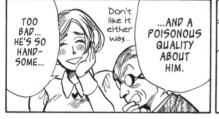

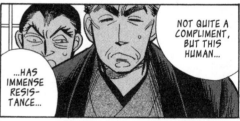

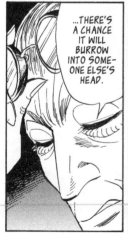

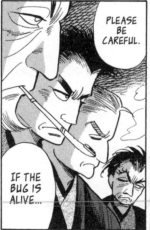

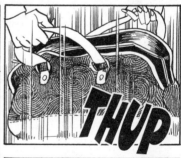

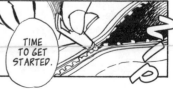

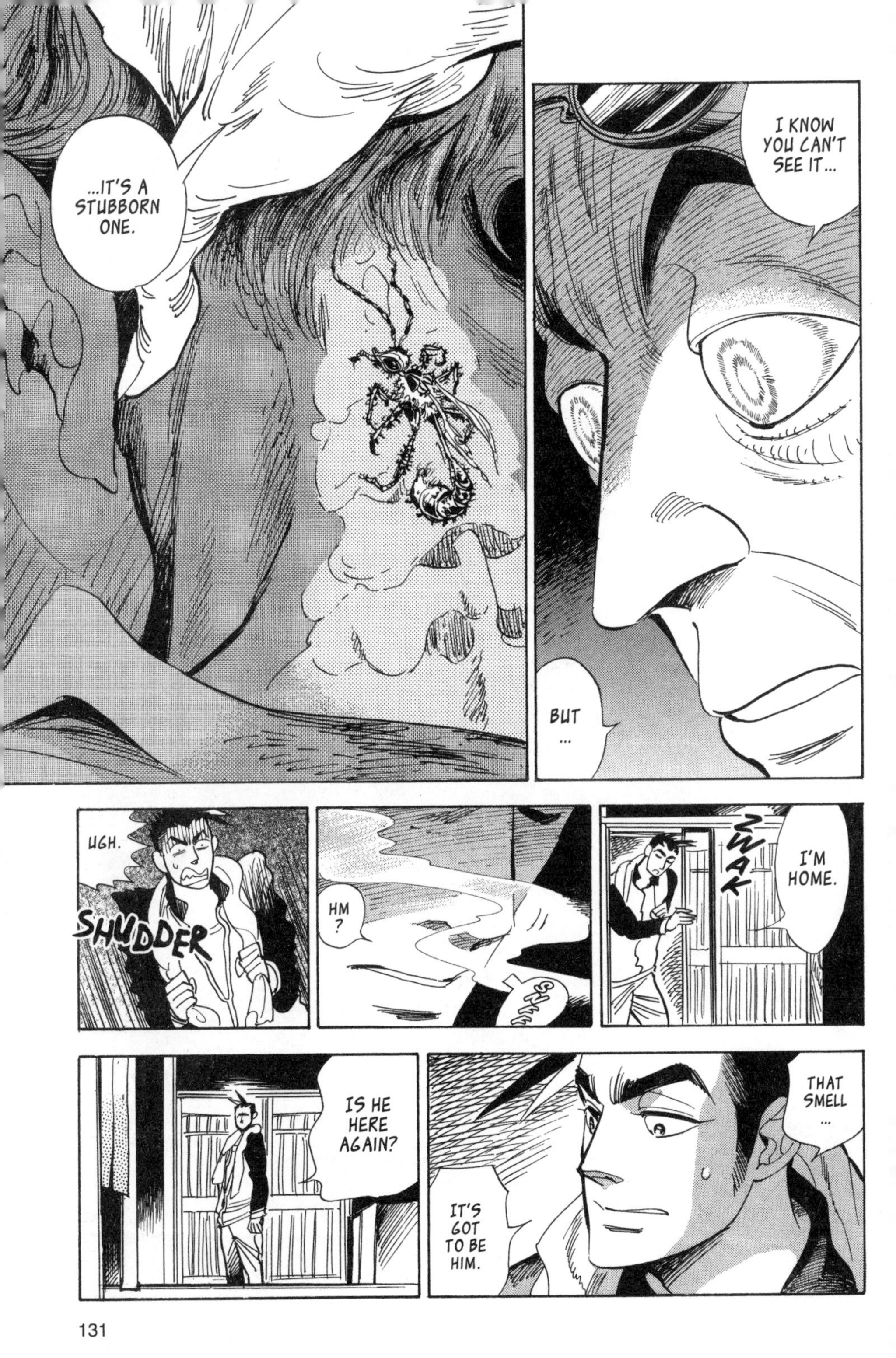
I KNOW YOU CAN'T SEE IT...
BUT ...
...IT'S A STUBBORN ONE.
I'M HOME.
ZWAK
HM ?
UGH.
SHUDDER
THAT SMELL ...
IT'S GOT TO BE HIM.
IS HE HERE AGAIN?

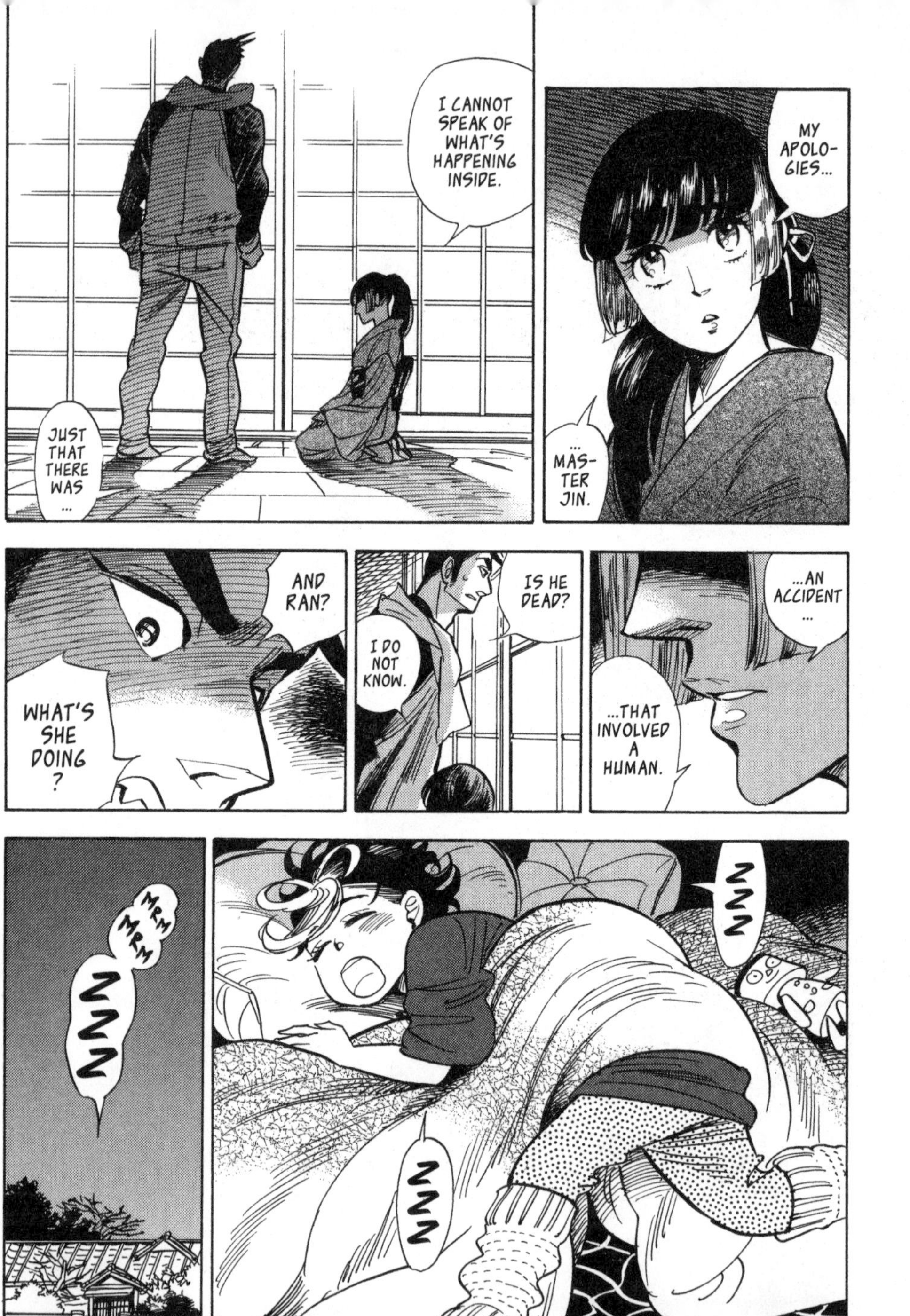
MY APOLOGIES...
...MASTER JIN.
I CANNOT SPEAK OF WHAT'S HAPPENING INSIDE.
JUST THAT THERE WAS...
...AN ACCIDENT...
...THAT INVOLVED A HUMAN.
IS HE DEAD?
I DO NOT KNOW.
AND RAN?
WHAT'S SHE DOING?
ZZZ
ZZZ
MRM MRM
ZZZ

Chapter 9 / The End

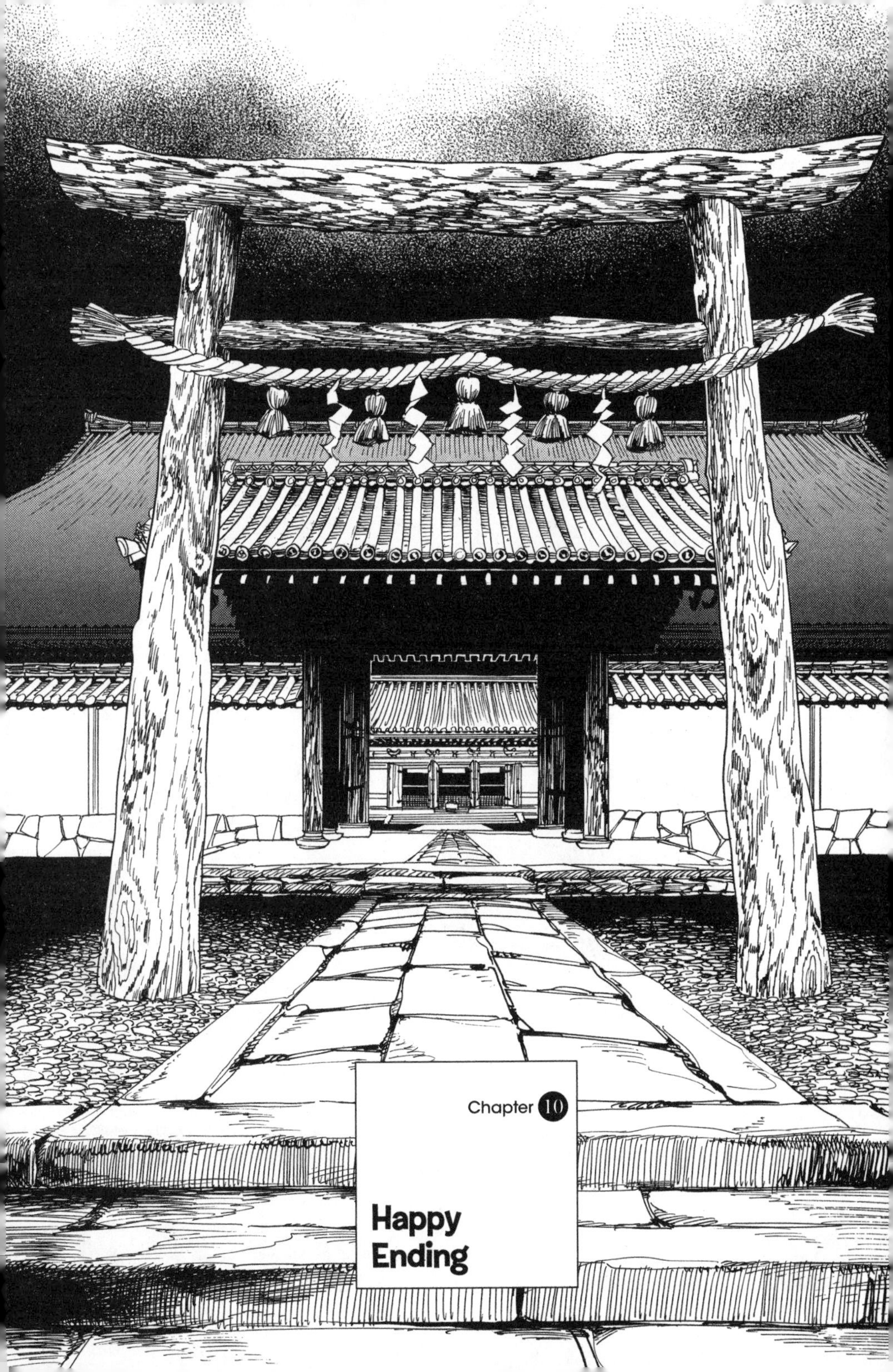

Chapter 10

Happy Ending

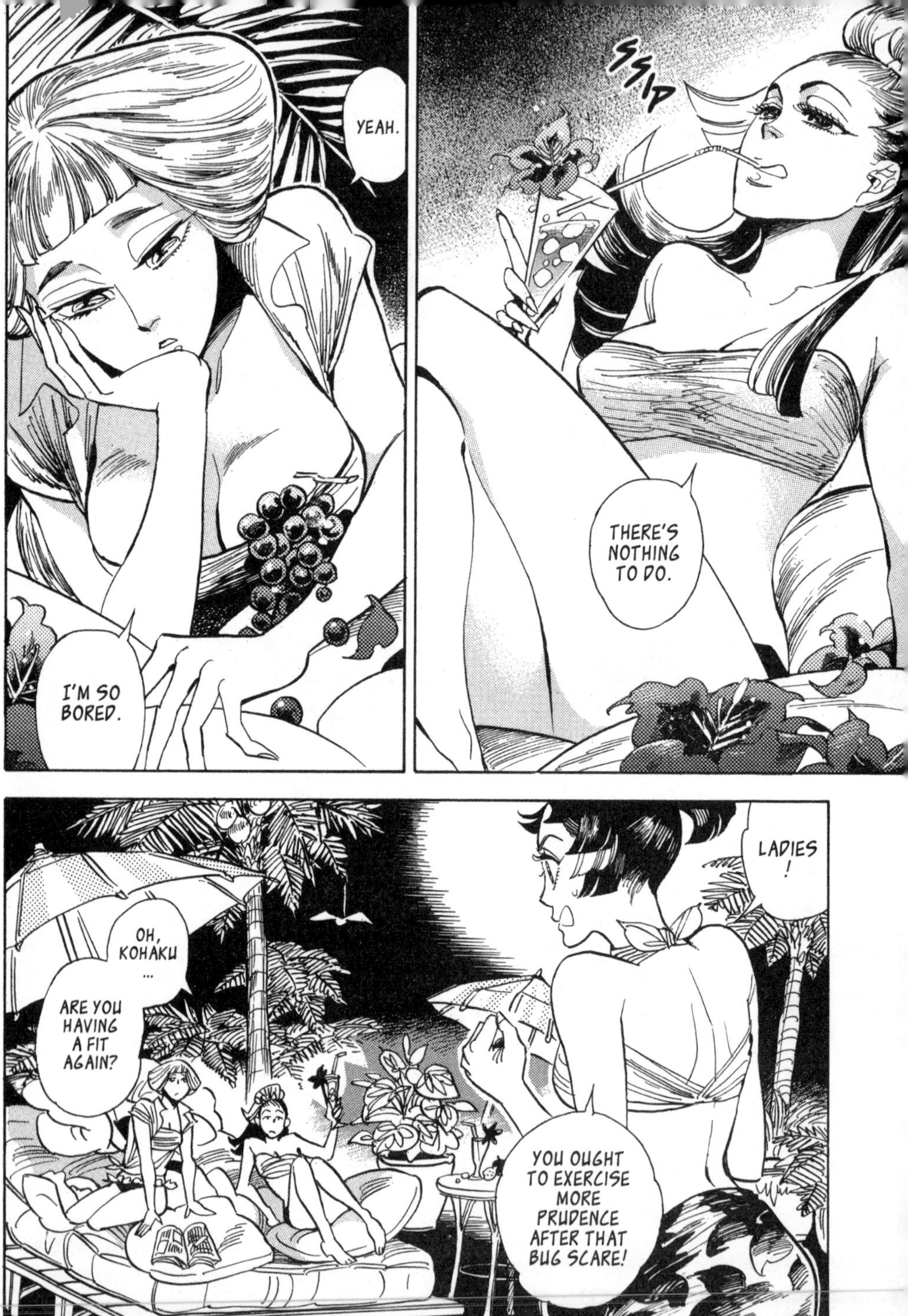
SSIP
THERE'S NOTHING TO DO.
YEAH.
I'M SO BORED.
LADIES!
OH, KOHAKU...
ARE YOU HAVING A FIT AGAIN?
YOU OUGHT TO EXERCISE MORE PRUDENCE AFTER THAT BUG SCARE!

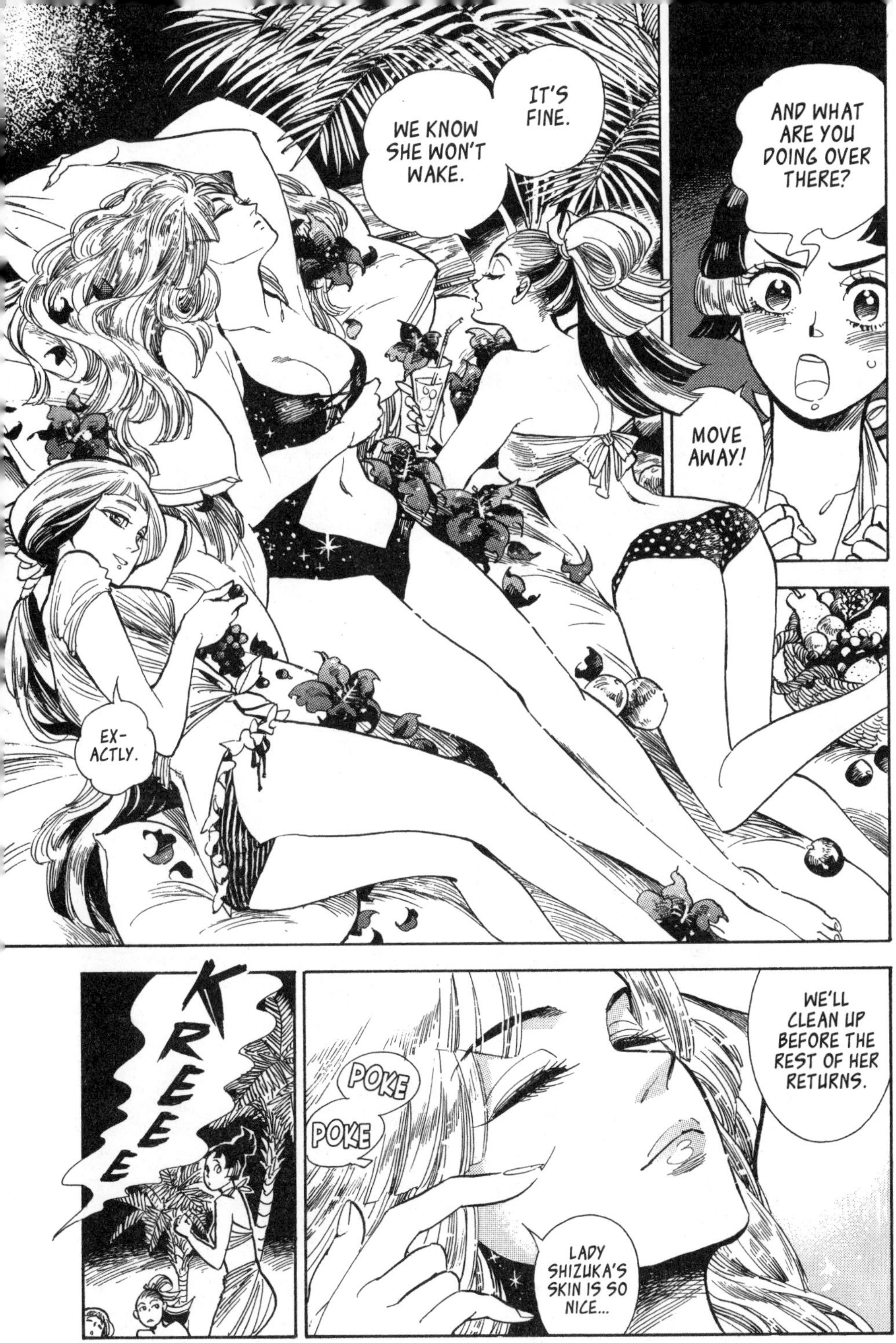
AND WHAT ARE YOU DOING OVER THERE?
MOVE AWAY!
IT'S FINE.
WE KNOW SHE WON'T WAKE.
EX-ACTLY.
WE'LL CLEAN UP BEFORE THE REST OF HER RETURNS.
POKE
POKE
LADY SHIZUKA'S SKIN IS SO NICE...
KREEEE

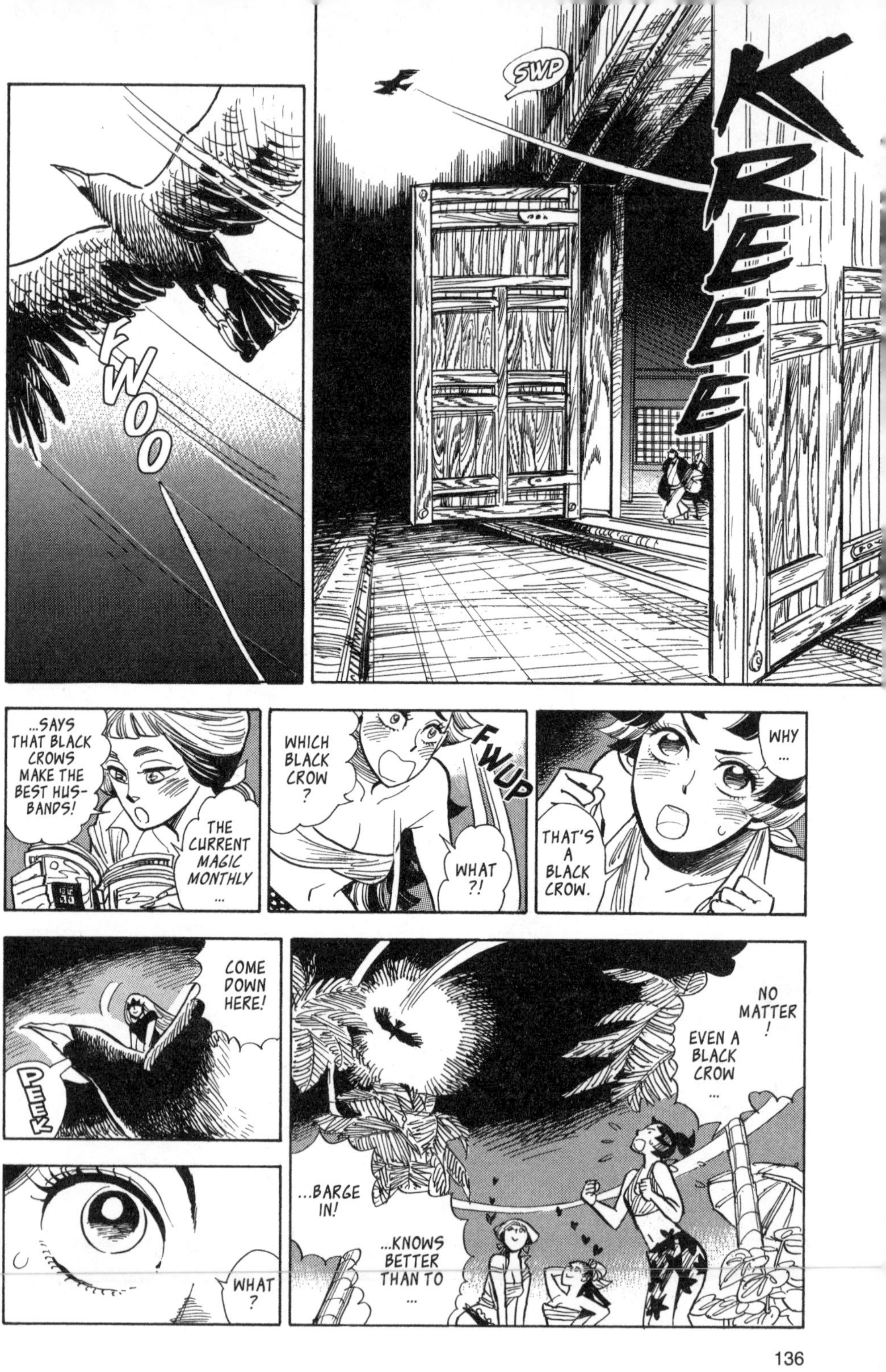
SWP
KREEEE
FWOO
WHY ...
THAT'S A BLACK CROW.
WHICH BLACK CROW ?
FWUP
WHAT ?!
THE CURRENT MAGIC MONTHLY ...
...SAYS THAT BLACK CROWS MAKE THE BEST HUS-BANDS!
NO MATTER !
EVEN A BLACK CROW ...
...KNOWS BETTER THAN TO ...
...BARGE IN!
COME DOWN HERE!
PEEK
WHAT ?

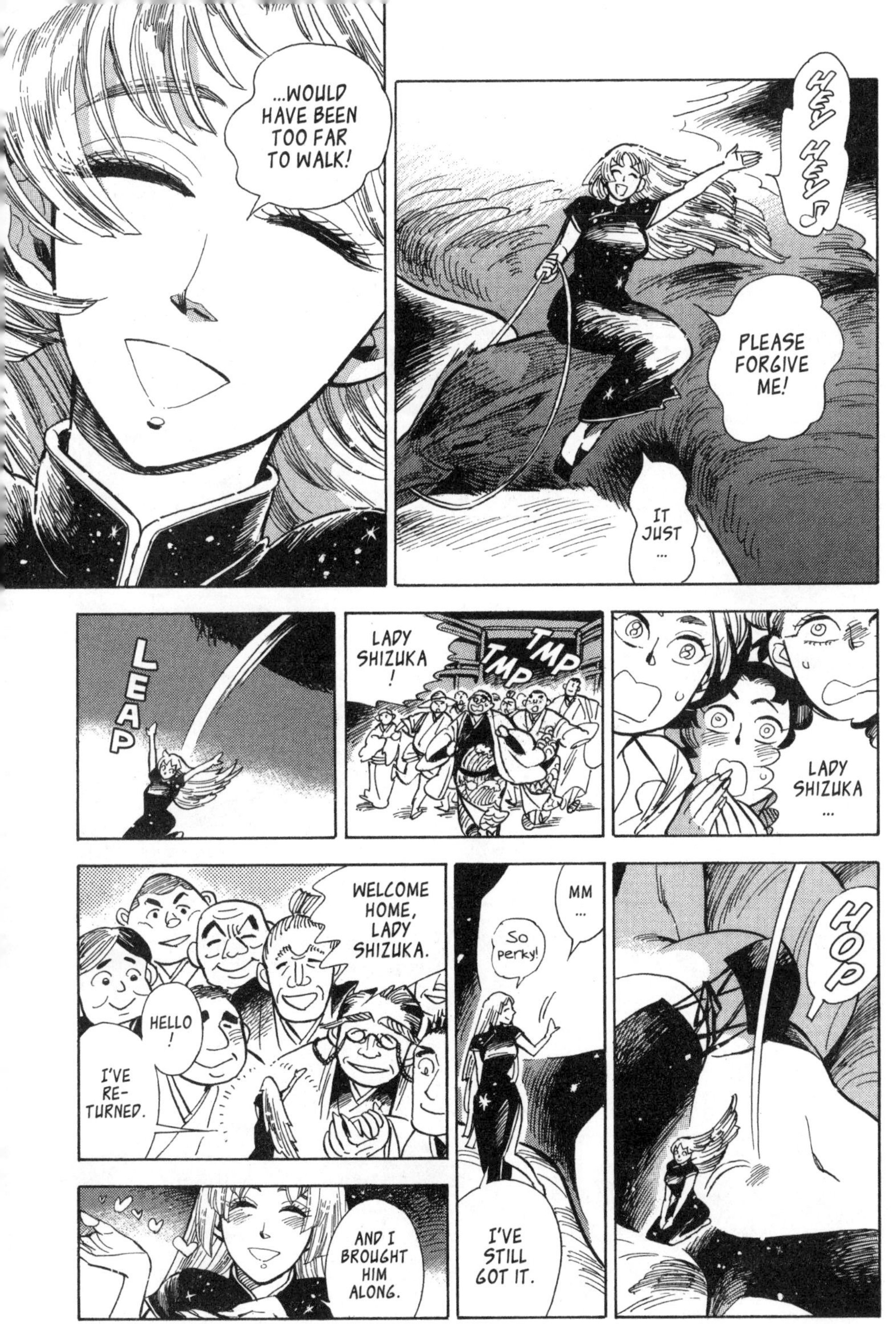
HEY HEY♪
PLEASE FORGIVE ME!
IT JUST...
...WOULD HAVE BEEN TOO FAR TO WALK!
LADY SHIZUKA...
LADY SHIZUKA!
TMP TMP
LEAP
HOP
MM...
So perky!
I'VE STILL GOT IT.
WELCOME HOME, LADY SHIZUKA.
HELLO!
I'VE RE-TURNED.
AND I BROUGHT HIM ALONG.

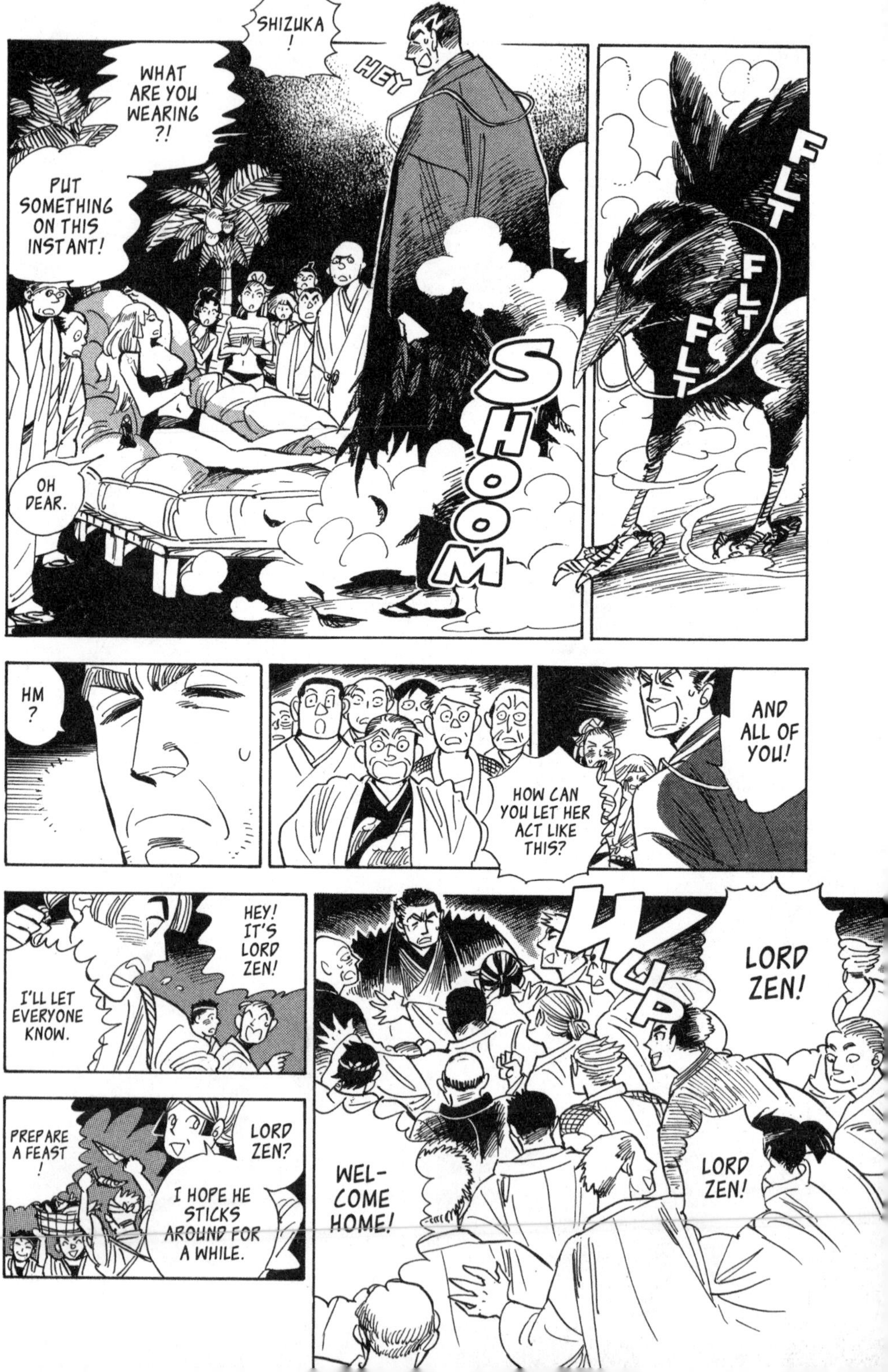
FLT FLT FLT
SHIZUKA!
HEY
WHAT ARE YOU WEARING?!
PUT SOMETHING ON THIS INSTANT!
SHOOOM
OH DEAR.
AND ALL OF YOU!
HOW CAN YOU LET HER ACT LIKE THIS?
HM?
LORD ZEN!
WUP
LORD ZEN!
WEL-COME HOME!
HEY! IT'S LORD ZEN!
I'LL LET EVERYONE KNOW.
LORD ZEN?
I HOPE HE STICKS AROUND FOR A WHILE.
PREPARE A FEAST!

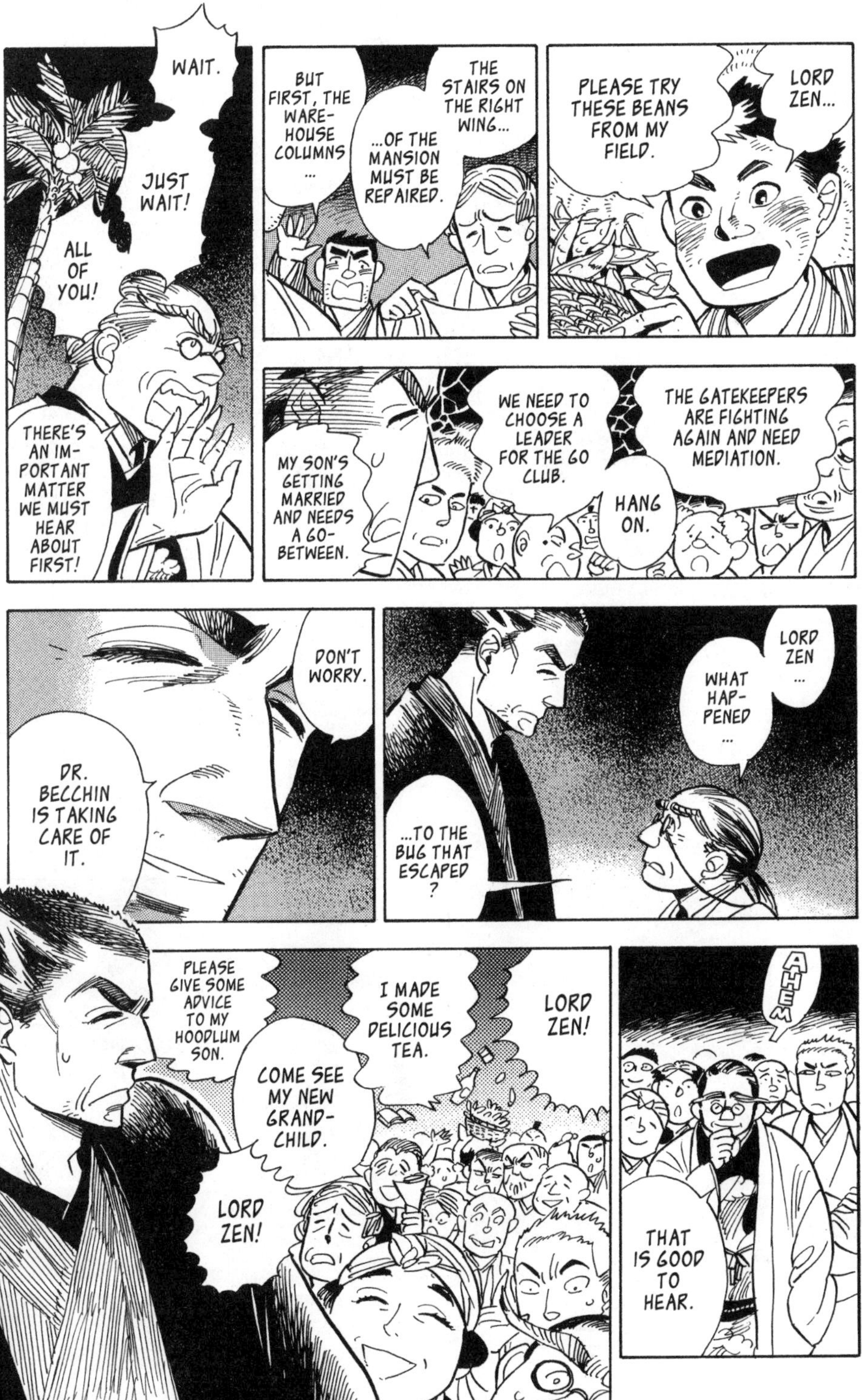
LORD ZEN...
PLEASE TRY THESE BEANS FROM MY FIELD.
THE STAIRS ON THE RIGHT WING...
...OF THE MANSION MUST BE REPAIRED.
BUT FIRST, THE WARE-HOUSE COLUMNS...
THE GATEKEEPERS ARE FIGHTING AGAIN AND NEED MEDIATION.
HANG ON.
WE NEED TO CHOOSE A LEADER FOR THE GO CLUB.
MY SON'S GETTING MARRIED AND NEEDS A GO-BETWEEN.
WAIT.
JUST WAIT!
ALL OF YOU!
THERE'S AN IM-PORTANT MATTER WE MUST HEAR ABOUT FIRST!
LORD ZEN...
WHAT HAP-PENED...
...TO THE BUG THAT ESCAPED?
DON'T WORRY.
DR. BECCHIN IS TAKING CARE OF IT.
AHEM
THAT IS GOOD TO HEAR.
LORD ZEN!
I MADE SOME DELICIOUS TEA.
PLEASE GIVE SOME ADVICE TO MY HOODLUM SON.
COME SEE MY NEW GRAND-CHILD.
LORD ZEN!

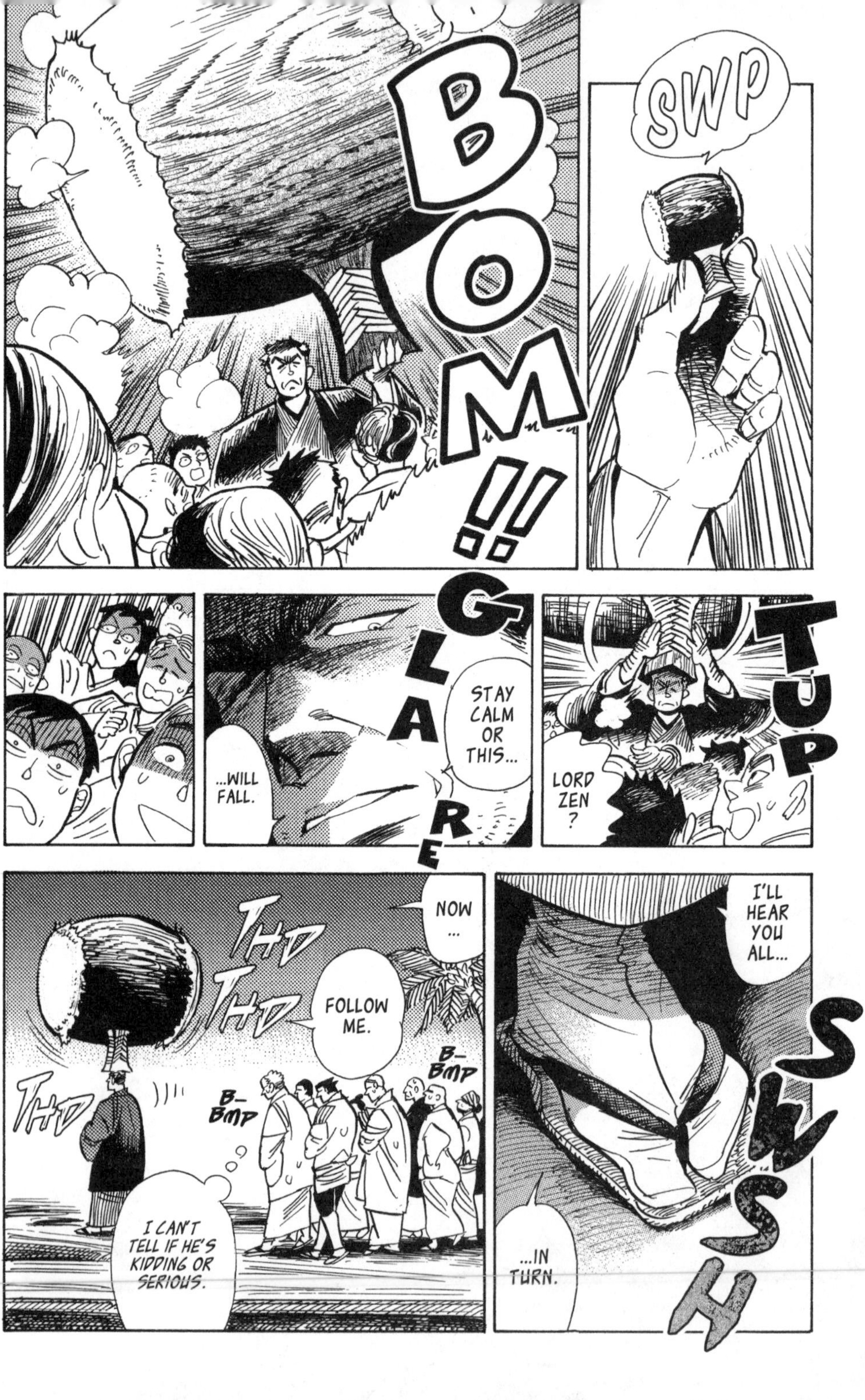
SWP
BOMM!!
TUP
LORD ZEN?
GLARE
STAY CALM OR THIS...
...WILL FALL.
I'LL HEAR YOU ALL...
...IN TURN.
SWSSH
NOW...
THD THD
FOLLOW ME.
B-BMP
B-BMP
THD
I CAN'T TELL IF HE'S KIDDING OR SERIOUS.

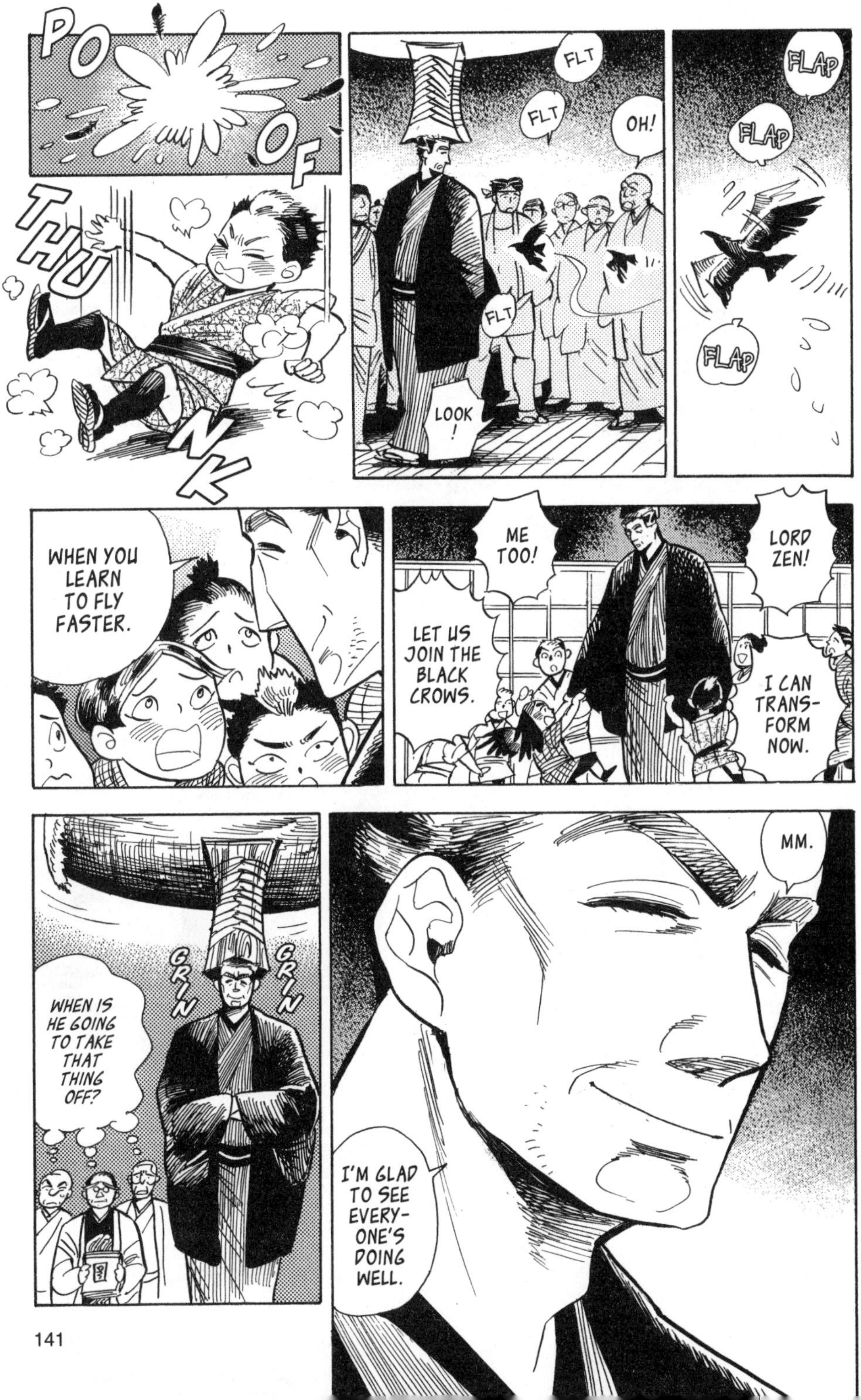
FLAP
FLAP
FLAP
FLT
OH!
FLT
FLT
LOOK!
POOF
THUNK
LORD ZEN!
ME TOO!
I CAN TRANSFORM NOW.
LET US JOIN THE BLACK CROWS.
WHEN YOU LEARN TO FLY FASTER.
MM.
I'M GLAD TO SEE EVERYONE'S DOING WELL.
GRIN
GRIN
WHEN IS HE GOING TO TAKE THAT THING OFF?

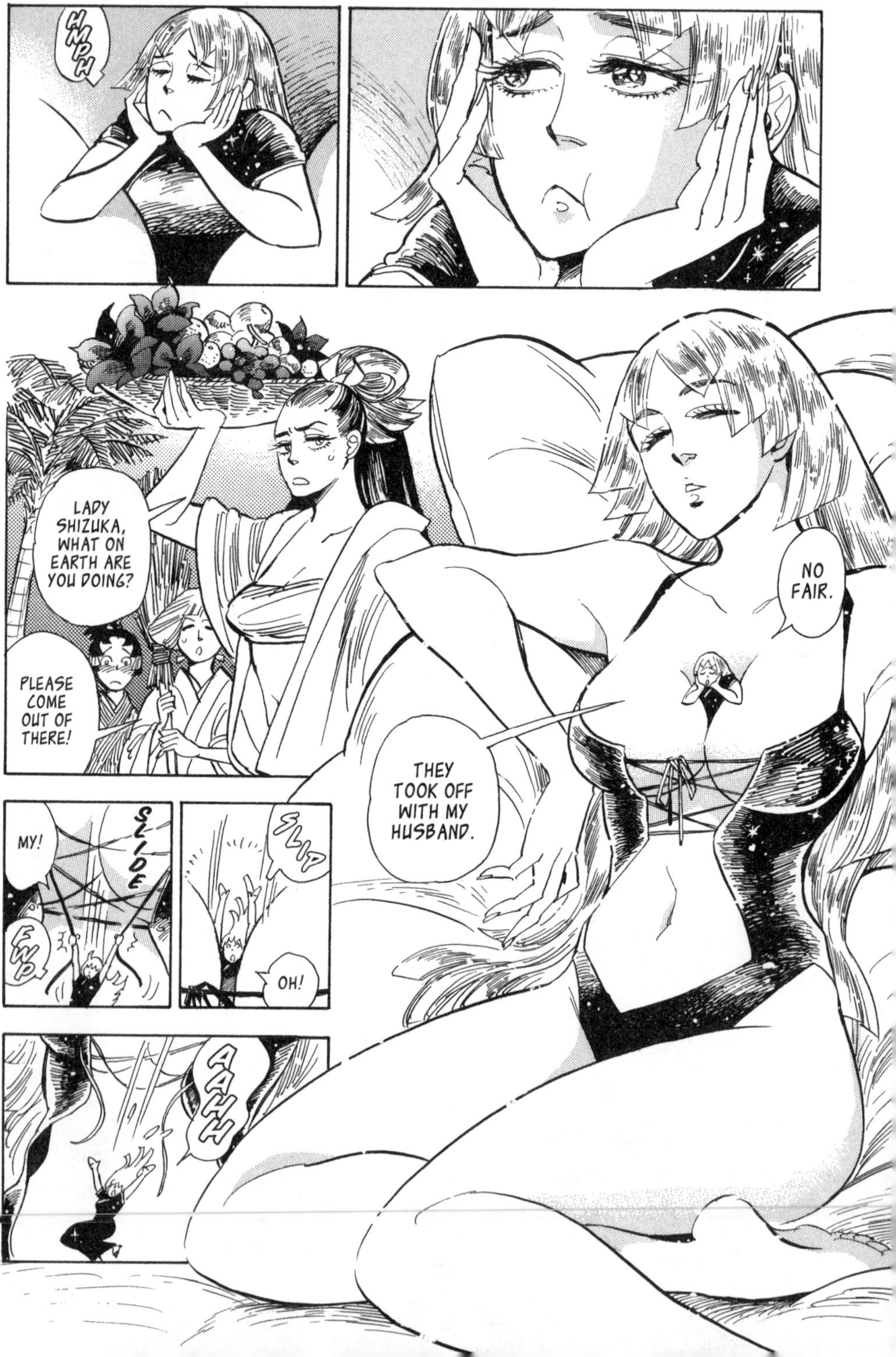
HMPH
LADY SHIZUKA, WHAT ON EARTH ARE YOU DOING?
PLEASE COME OUT OF THERE!
NO FAIR.
THEY TOOK OFF WITH MY HUSBAND.
SLIP
OH!
MY!
SLIDE
FWP
AAHH

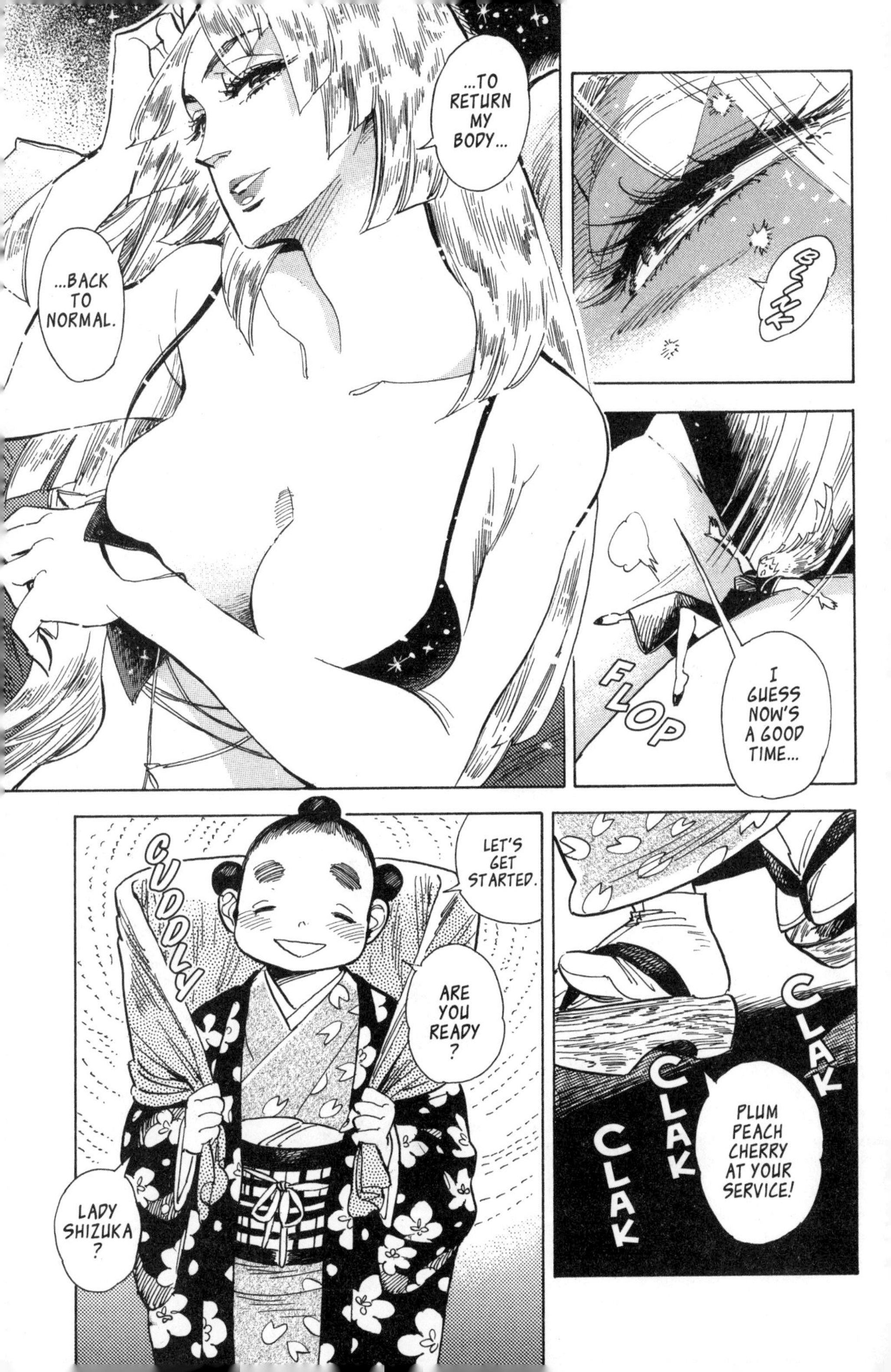
BLINK
FLOP
I GUESS NOW'S A GOOD TIME...
...TO RETURN MY BODY...
...BACK TO NORMAL.
CLAK
CLAK
CLAK
PLUM PEACH CHERRY AT YOUR SERVICE!
CUDDLY
LET'S GET STARTED.
ARE YOU READY?
LADY SHIZUKA?

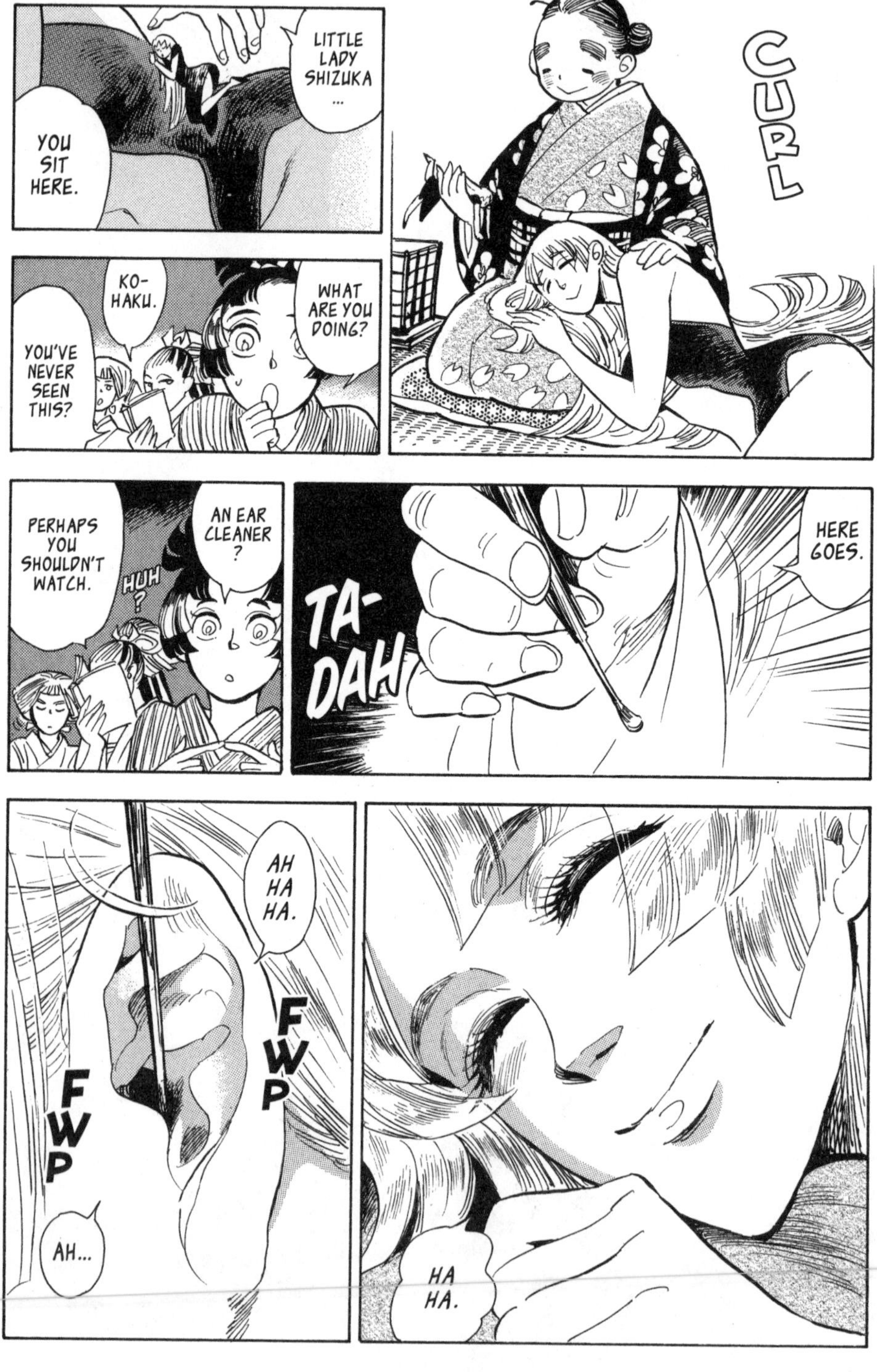
CURL
LITTLE LADY SHIZUKA...
YOU SIT HERE.
WHAT ARE YOU DOING?
KO-HAKU.
YOU'VE NEVER SEEN THIS?
HERE GOES.
TA-DAH
AN EAR CLEANER?
HUH?
PERHAPS YOU SHOULDN'T WATCH.
HA HA.
AH HA HA.
FWP
FWP
AH...

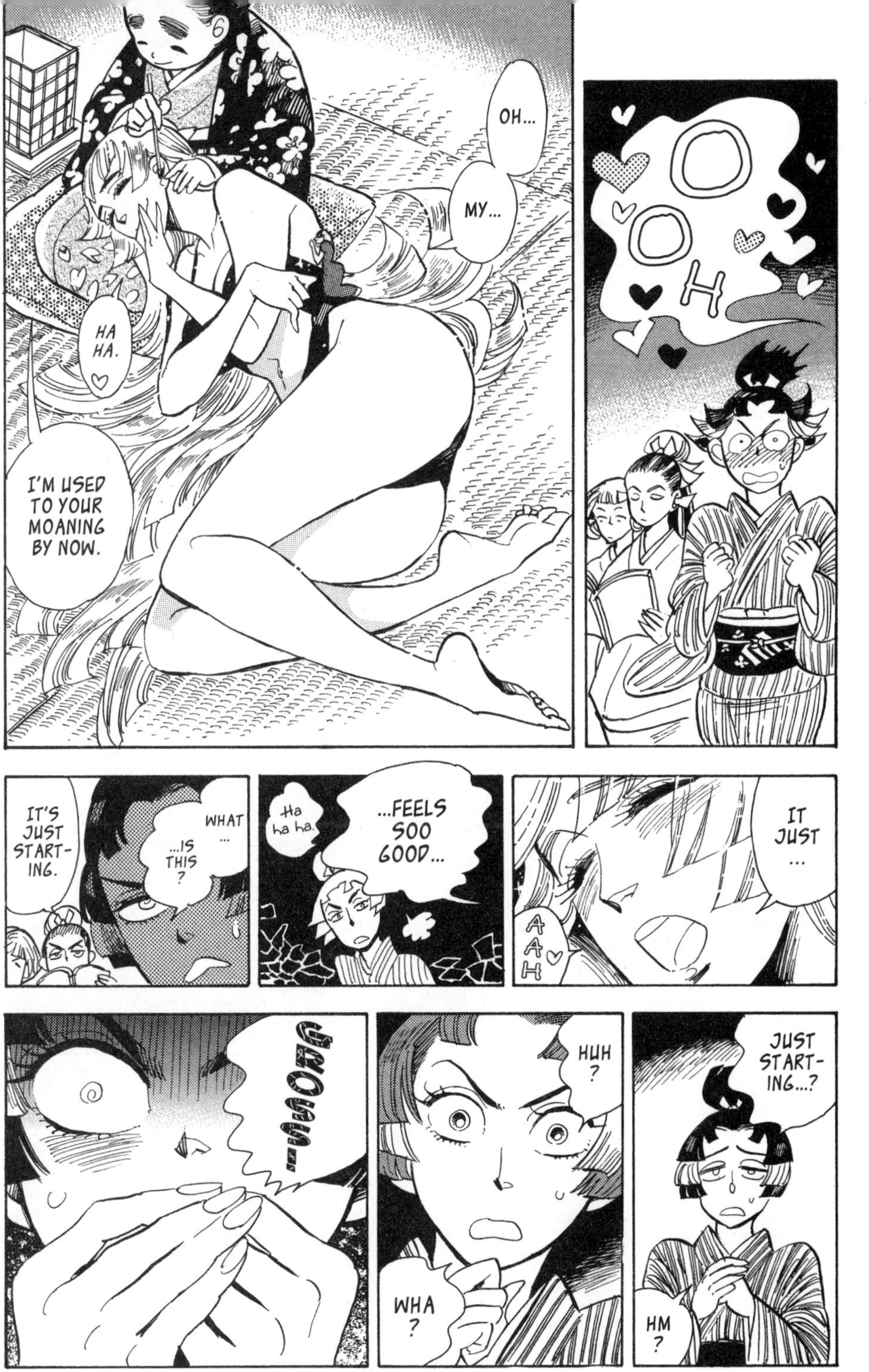
OOOH
OH...
MY...
HA HA. ♥
I'M USED TO YOUR MOANING BY NOW.
IT JUST ...
AAH ♥
...FEELS SOO GOOD...
Ha ha ha.
WHAT ...
...IS THIS?
IT'S JUST STARTING.
JUST STARTING...?
HM?
HUH?
WHA?
GROSS-!

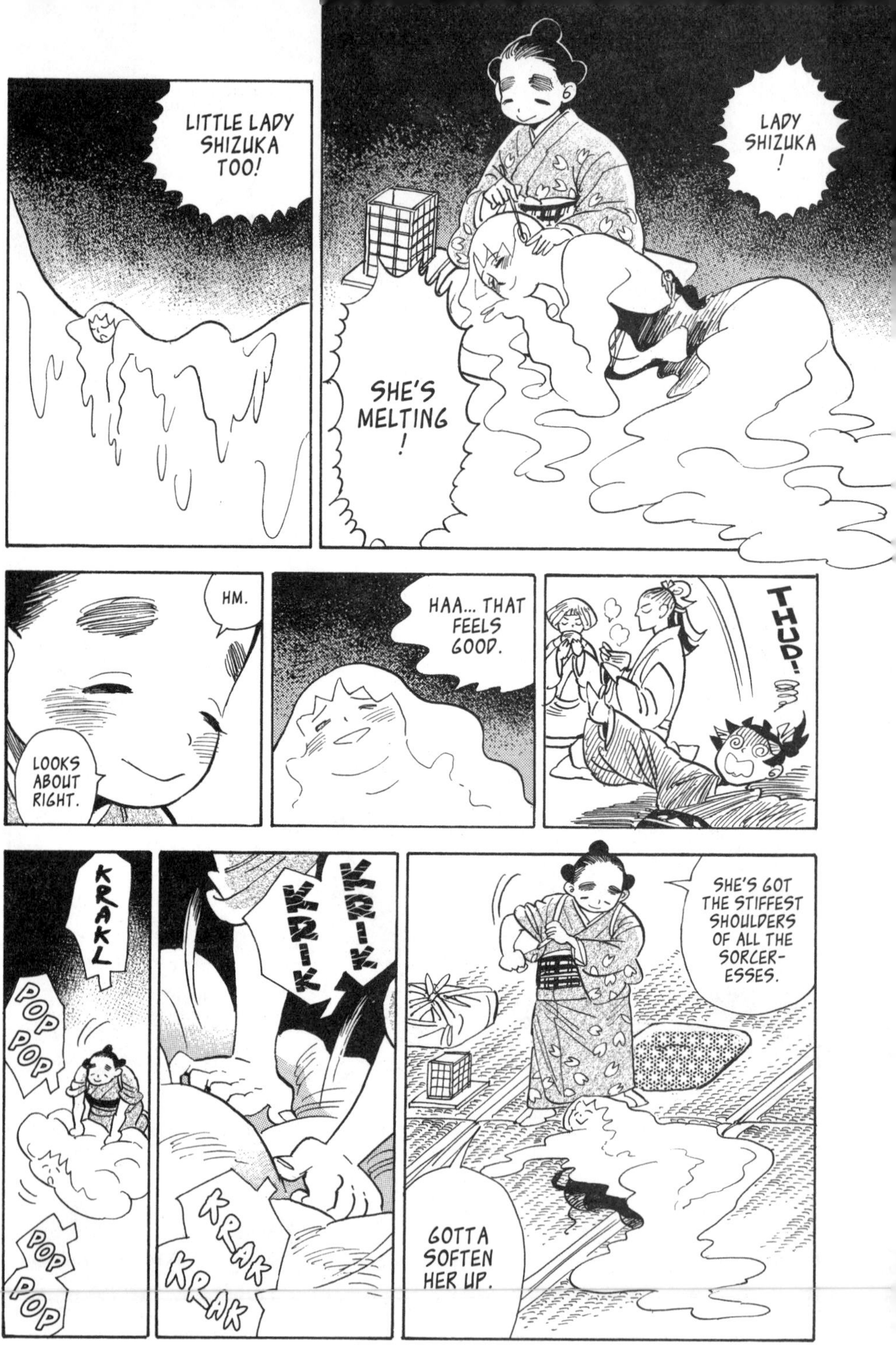
LADY SHIZUKA!
SHE'S MELTING!
LITTLE LADY SHIZUKA TOO!
THUD!
HAA... THAT FEELS GOOD.
HM.
LOOKS ABOUT RIGHT.
SHE'S GOT THE STIFFEST SHOULDERS OF ALL THE SORCER-ESSES.
GOTTA SOFTEN HER UP.
KRIK
KRIK
KRAK
KRAK
KRAKL
POP POP
POP POP

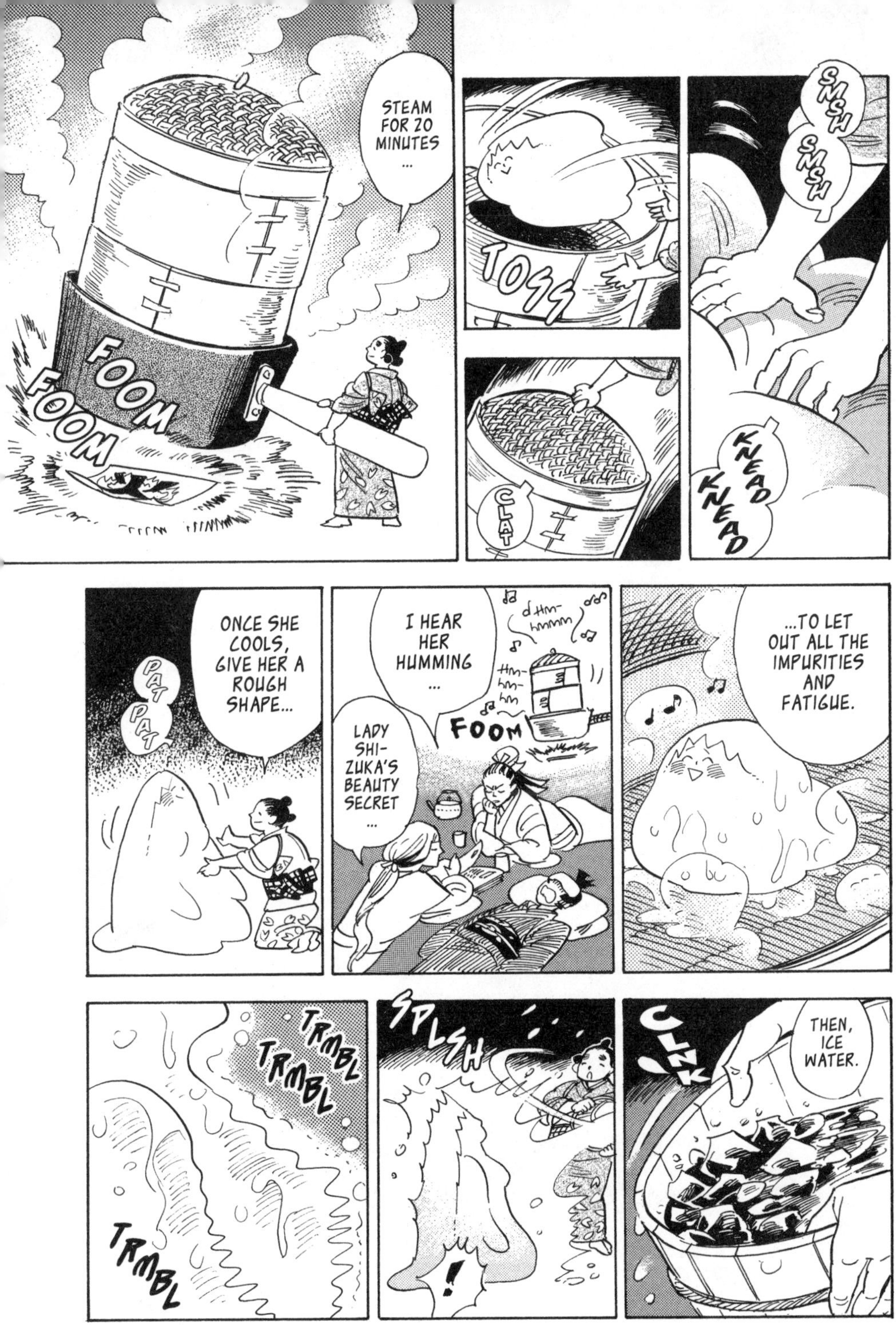
SMSH
SMSH
KNEAD
KNEAD
TOSS
CLAT
STEAM FOR 20 MINUTES ...
FOOM
FOOM
...TO LET OUT ALL THE IMPURITIES AND FATIGUE.
I HEAR HER HUMMING ...
Hm-hmmm
Hm-hm-hm
FOOM
LADY SHI-ZUKA'S BEAUTY SECRET ...
ONCE SHE COOLS, GIVE HER A ROUGH SHAPE...
PAT
PAT
CLNK
THEN, ICE WATER.
SPLSH
!
TRMBL
TRMBL
TRMBL

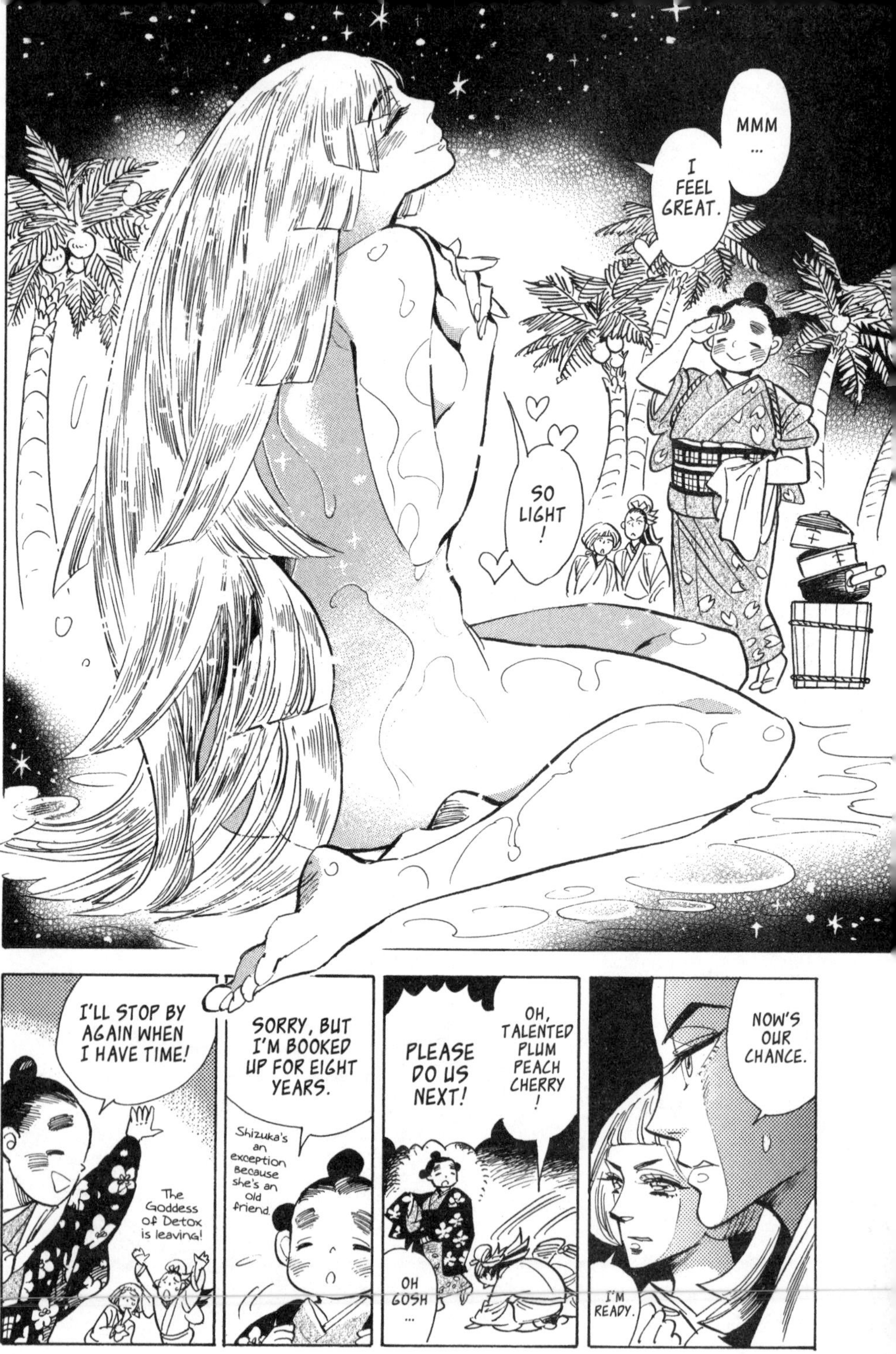
MMM ...
I FEEL GREAT.
SO LIGHT!
NOW'S OUR CHANCE.
I'M READY.
OH, TALENTED PLUM PEACH CHERRY!
PLEASE DO US NEXT!
OH GOSH ...
SORRY, BUT I'M BOOKED UP FOR EIGHT YEARS.
Shizuka's an exception because she's an old friend.
I'LL STOP BY AGAIN WHEN I HAVE TIME!
The Goddess of Detox is leaving!

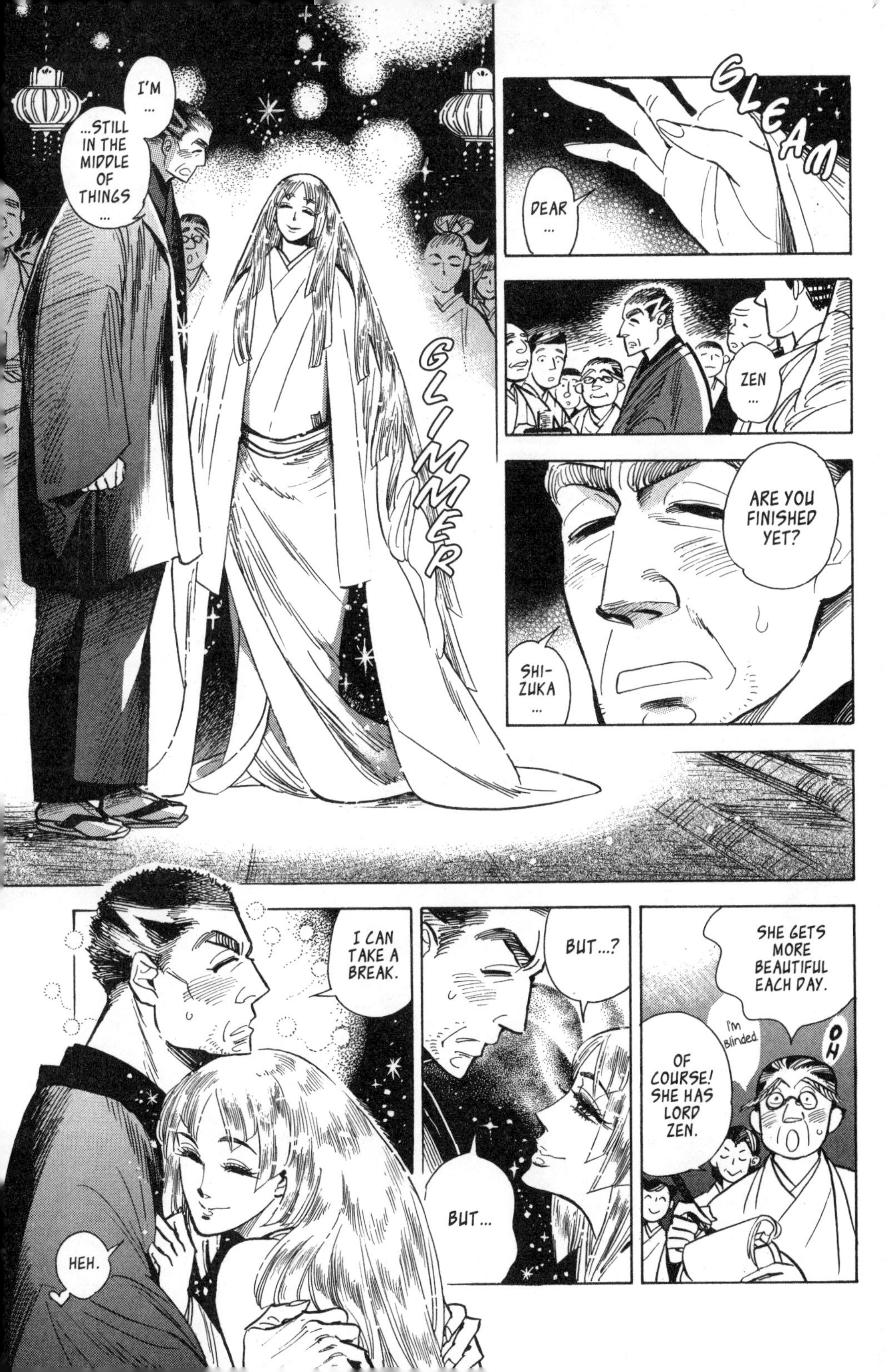
GLEAM
DEAR ...
ZEN ...
ARE YOU FINISHED YET?
SHI-ZUKA ...
I'M ...
...STILL IN THE MIDDLE OF THINGS ...
GLIMMER
OH
SHE GETS MORE BEAUTIFUL EACH DAY.
I'm blinded.
OF COURSE! SHE HAS LORD ZEN.
BUT...?
BUT...
I CAN TAKE A BREAK.
HEH.

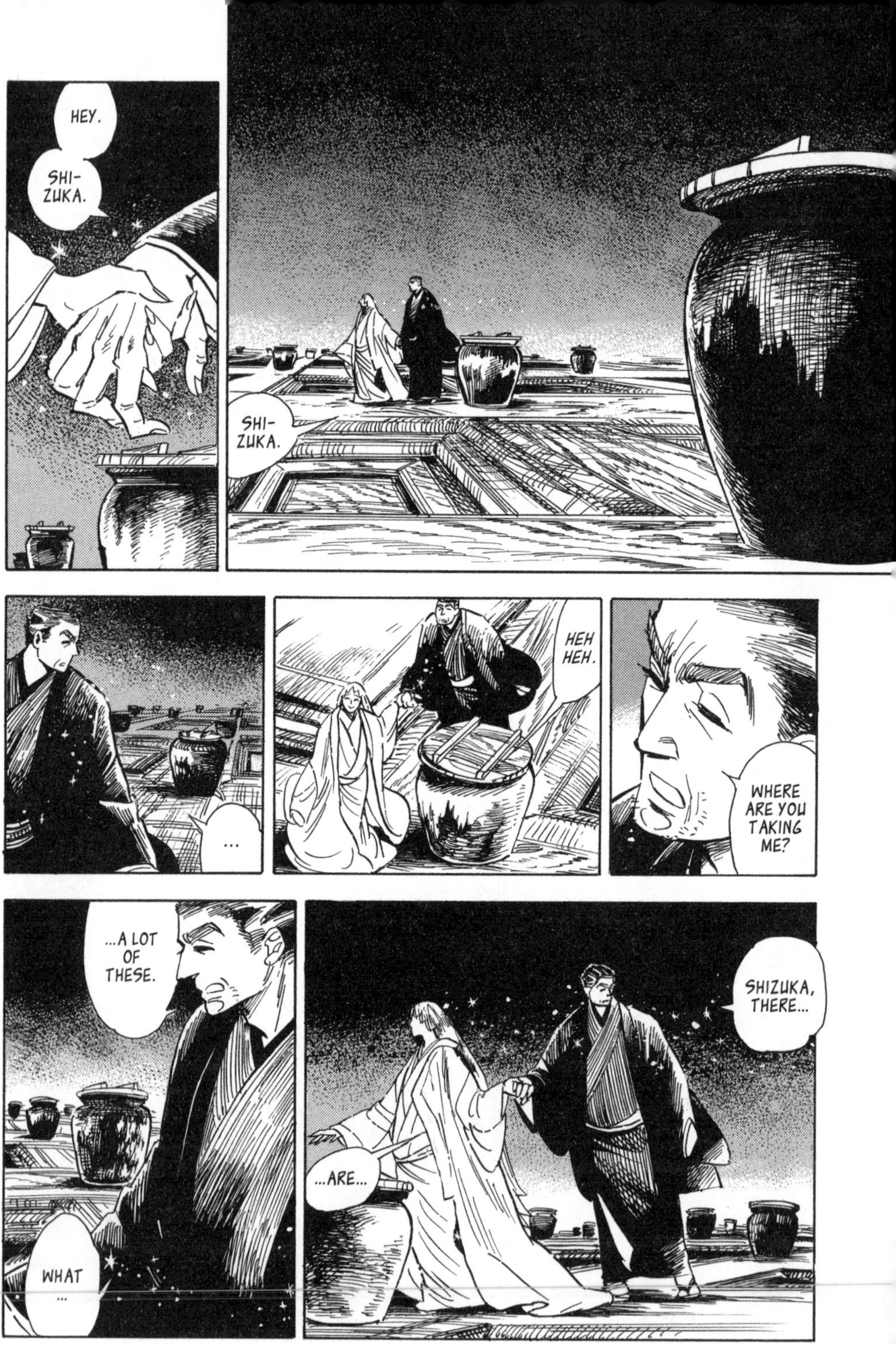
SHI-ZUKA.
HEY.
SHI-ZUKA.
WHERE ARE YOU TAKING ME?
HEH HEH.
...
SHIZUKA, THERE...
...ARE...
...A LOT OF THESE.
WHAT ...

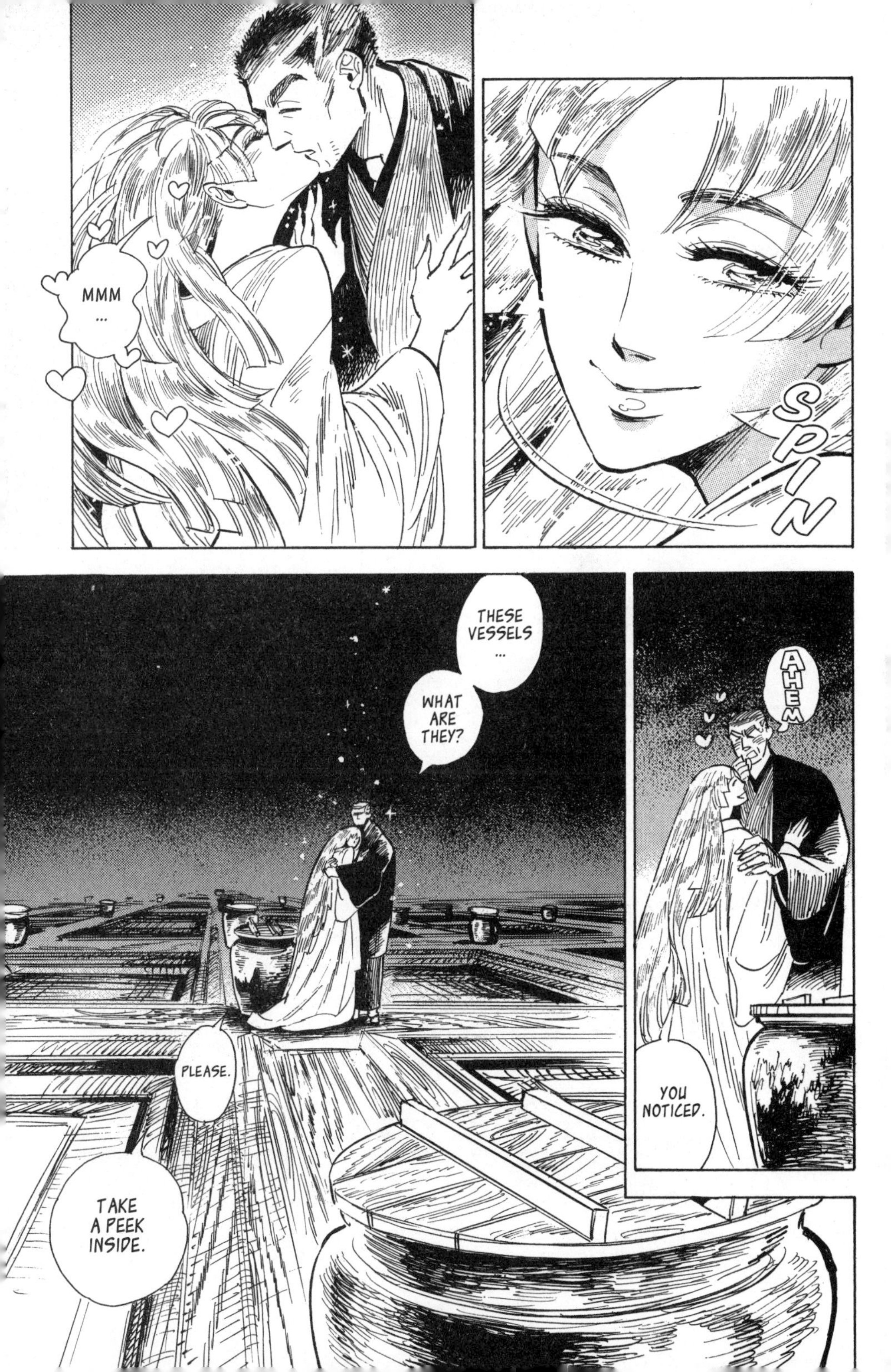
SPIN
MMM ...
AHEM
YOU NOTICED.
THESE VESSELS ...
WHAT ARE THEY?
PLEASE.
TAKE A PEEK INSIDE.

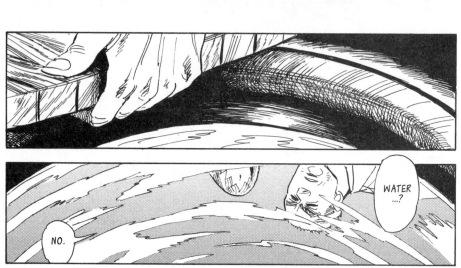

WATER
...?

NO.

THIS
IS NOT
ORDINARY
WATER.

THERE'S
POWERFUL
MAGIC IN
IT.

GRM

ARE
...

...ALL
OF THE
VESSELS
FILLED
WITH
MAGIC?

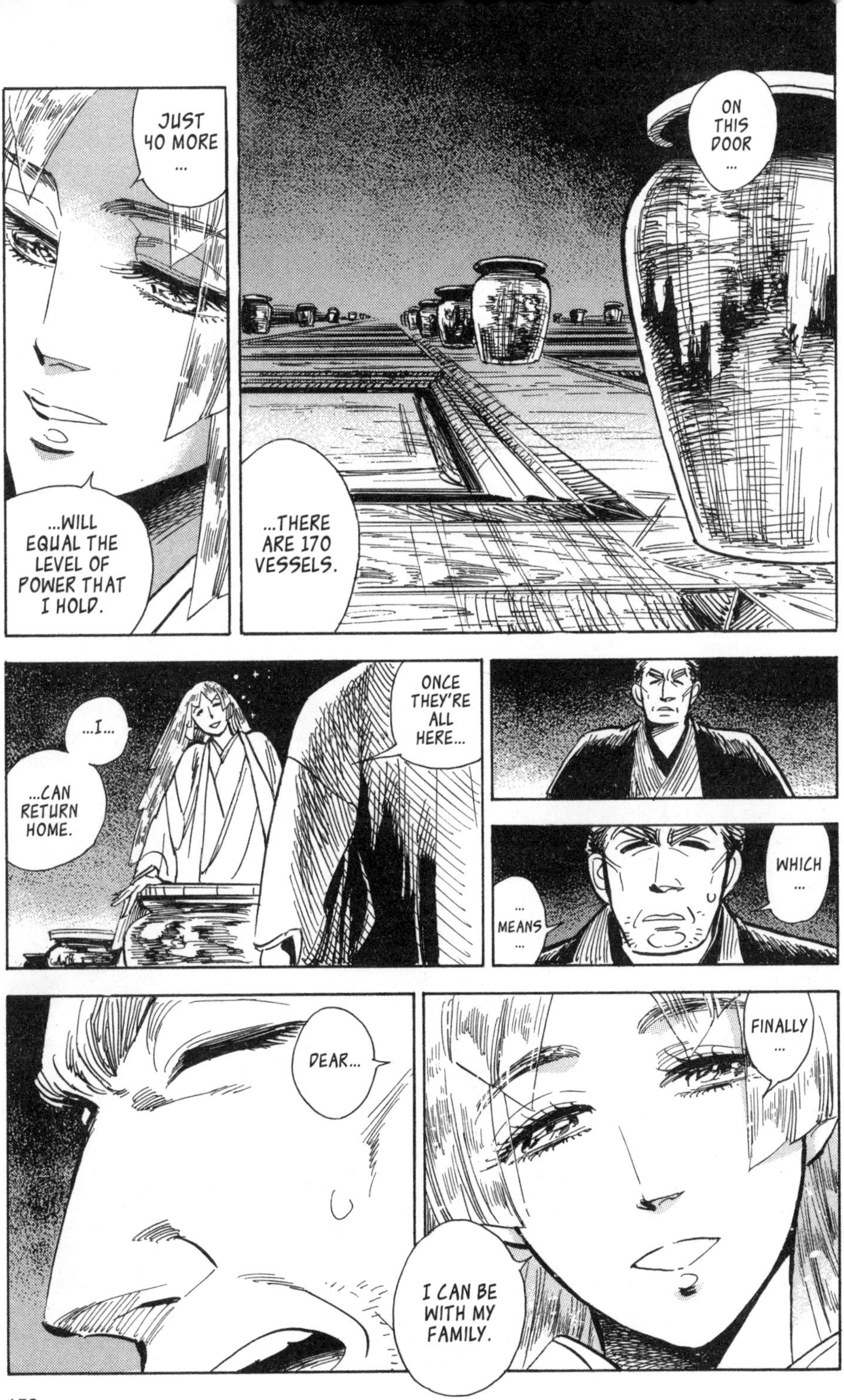
ON THIS DOOR ...
...THERE ARE 170 VESSELS.
JUST 40 MORE ...
...WILL EQUAL THE LEVEL OF POWER THAT I HOLD.
WHICH ...
... MEANS ...
ONCE THEY'RE ALL HERE...
...I...
...CAN RETURN HOME.
FINALLY ...
I CAN BE WITH MY FAMILY.
DEAR...

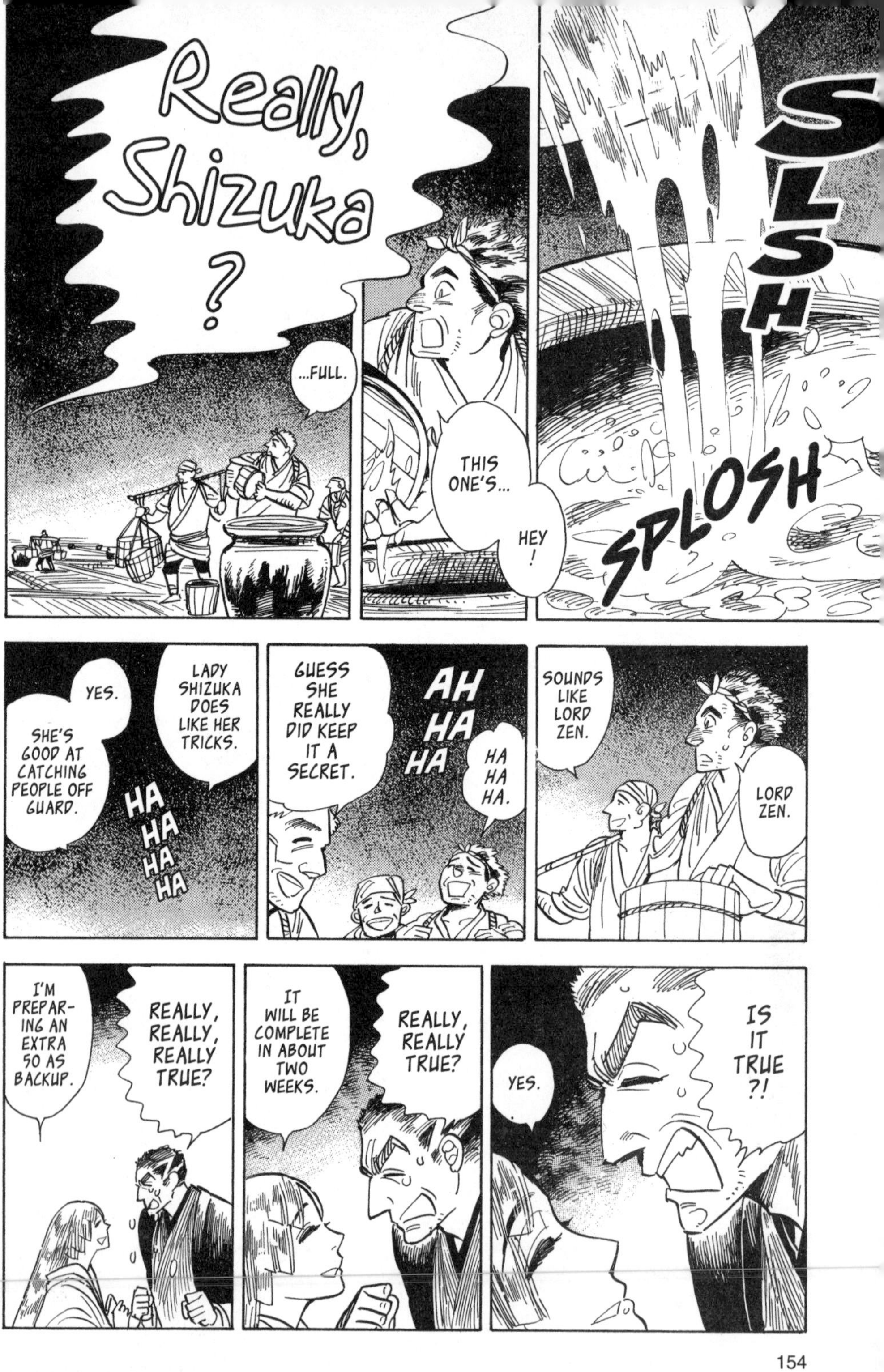
SLSH
SPLOSH
THIS ONE'S...
HEY!
Really, Shizuka?
...FULL.
SOUNDS LIKE LORD ZEN.
LORD ZEN.
AH HA HA
HA HA HA.
GUESS SHE REALLY DID KEEP IT A SECRET.
LADY SHIZUKA DOES LIKE HER TRICKS.
YES.
SHE'S GOOD AT CATCHING PEOPLE OFF GUARD.
HA HA HA HA HA
IS IT TRUE?!
YES.
REALLY, REALLY TRUE?
IT WILL BE COMPLETE IN ABOUT TWO WEEKS.
REALLY, REALLY, REALLY TRUE?
I'M PREPAR-ING AN EXTRA 50 AS BACKUP.

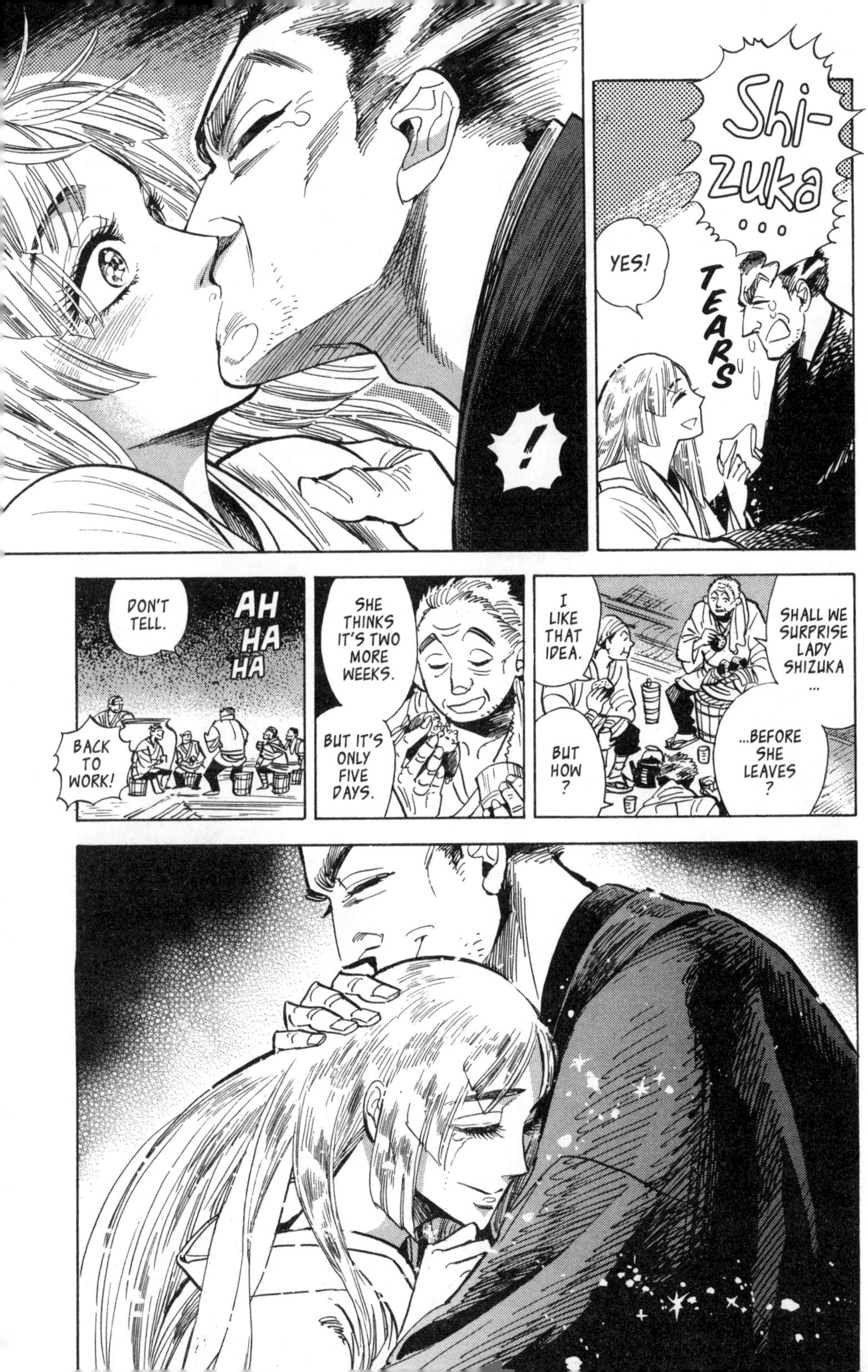
Shi-zuka...
YES!
TEARS
!
SHALL WE SURPRISE LADY SHIZUKA ...
...BEFORE SHE LEAVES?
I LIKE THAT IDEA.
BUT HOW?
SHE THINKS IT'S TWO MORE WEEKS.
BUT IT'S ONLY FIVE DAYS.
DON'T TELL.
AH HA HA
BACK TO WORK!

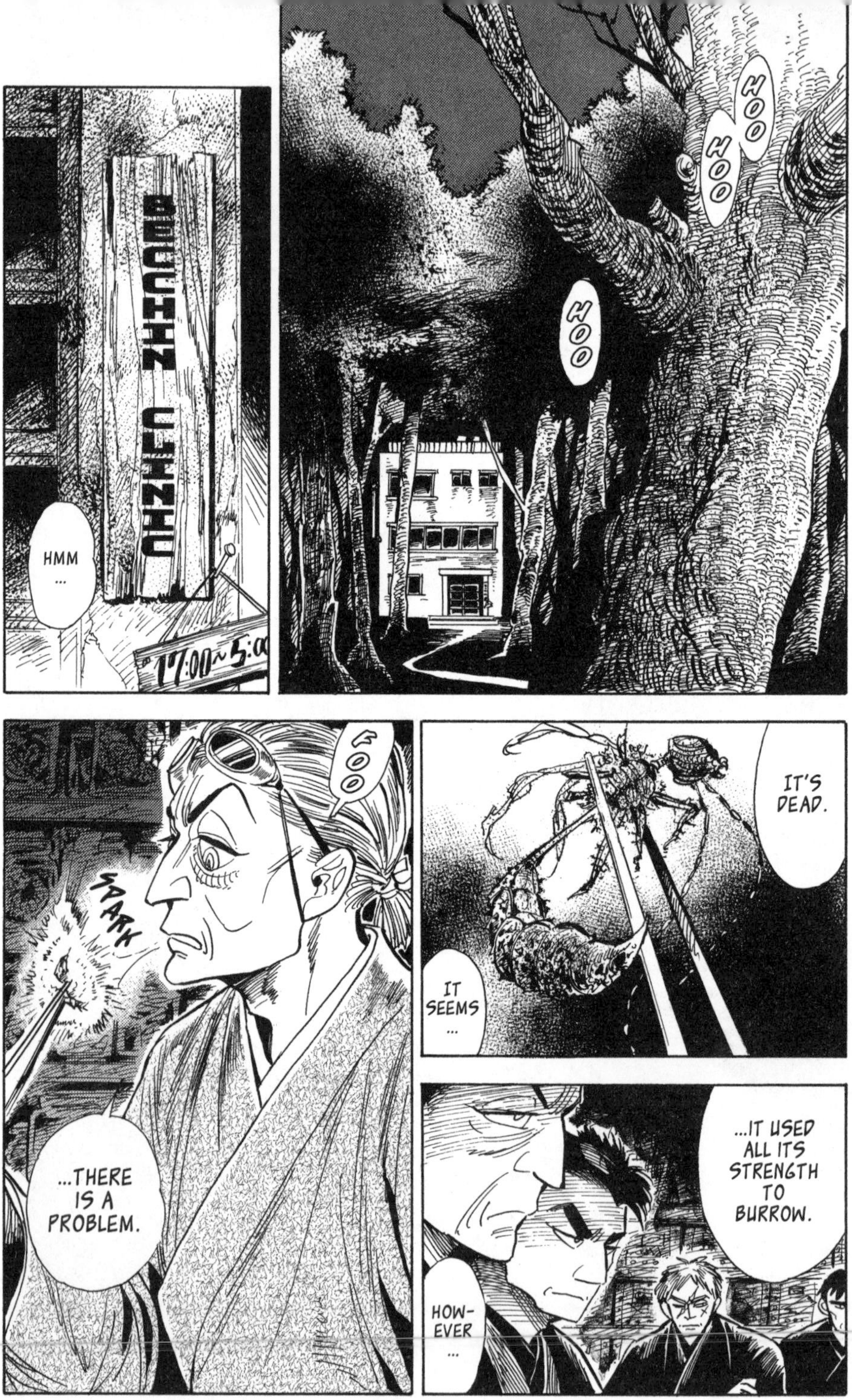
HOO
HOO
HOO
HOO
BECCHIN CLINIC
17:00~5:00
HMM ...
IT'S DEAD.
IT SEEMS ...
...IT USED ALL ITS STRENGTH TO BURROW.
HOW-EVER ...
FOO
SPARK
...THERE IS A PROBLEM.

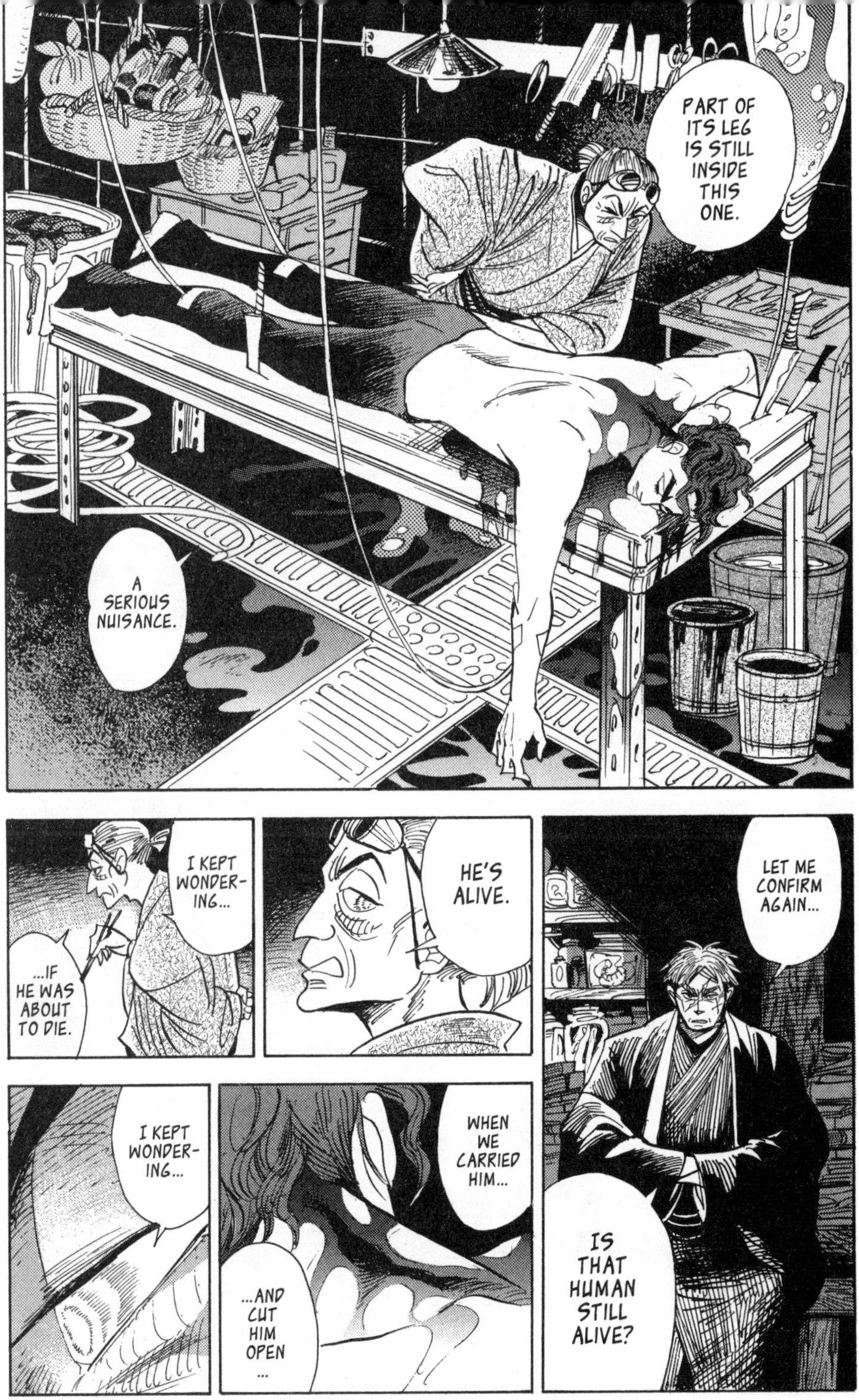
PART OF ITS LEG IS STILL INSIDE THIS ONE.
A SERIOUS NUISANCE.
LET ME CONFIRM AGAIN...
IS THAT HUMAN STILL ALIVE?
HE'S ALIVE.
I KEPT WONDERING...
...IF HE WAS ABOUT TO DIE.
WHEN WE CARRIED HIM...
...AND CUT HIM OPEN...
I KEPT WONDERING...

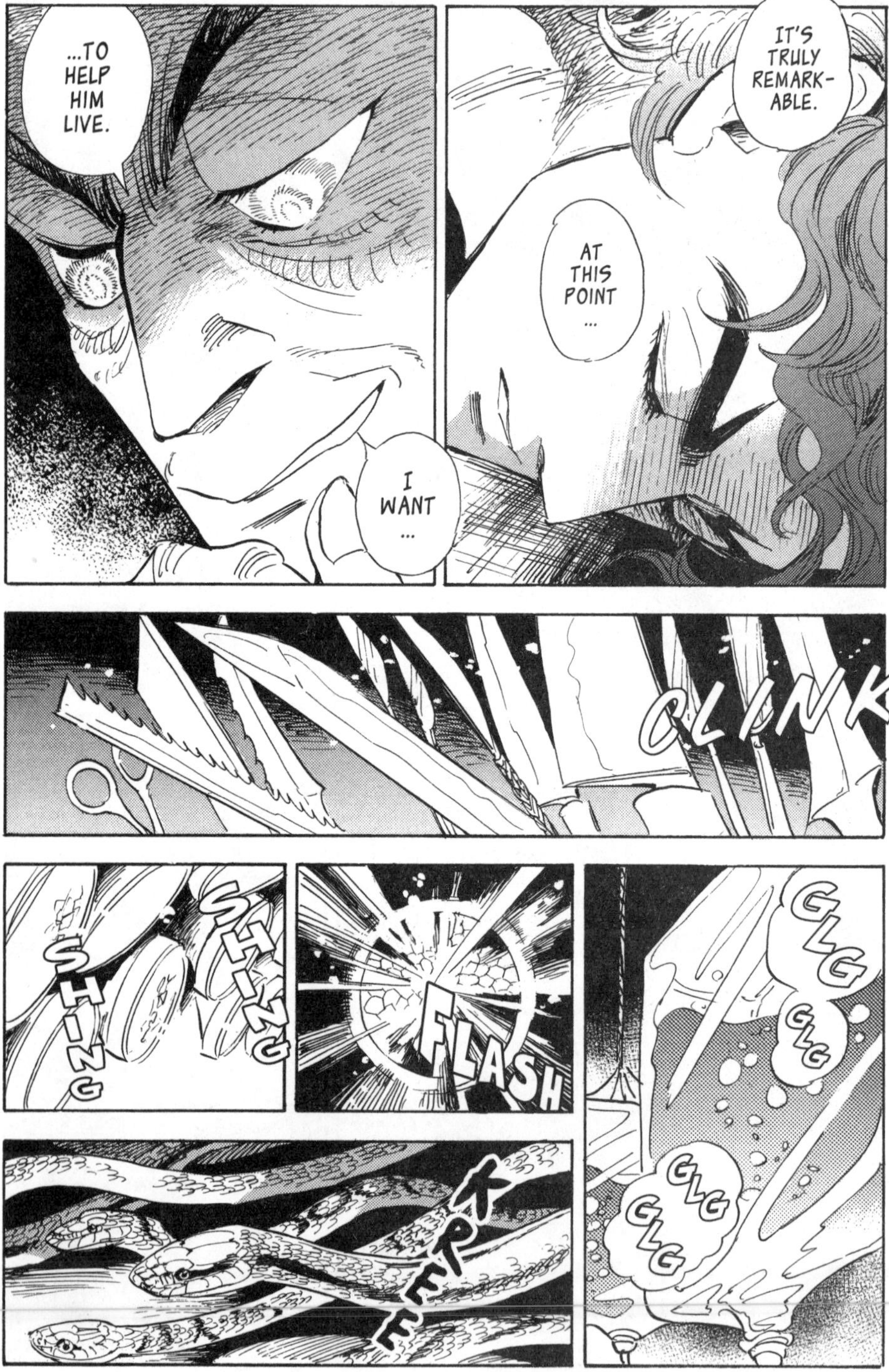
IT'S TRULY REMARK-ABLE.
AT THIS POINT ...
I WANT ...
...TO HELP HIM LIVE.
CLINK
GLG GLG
GLG GLG
FLASH
SHING
SHING
KREEE

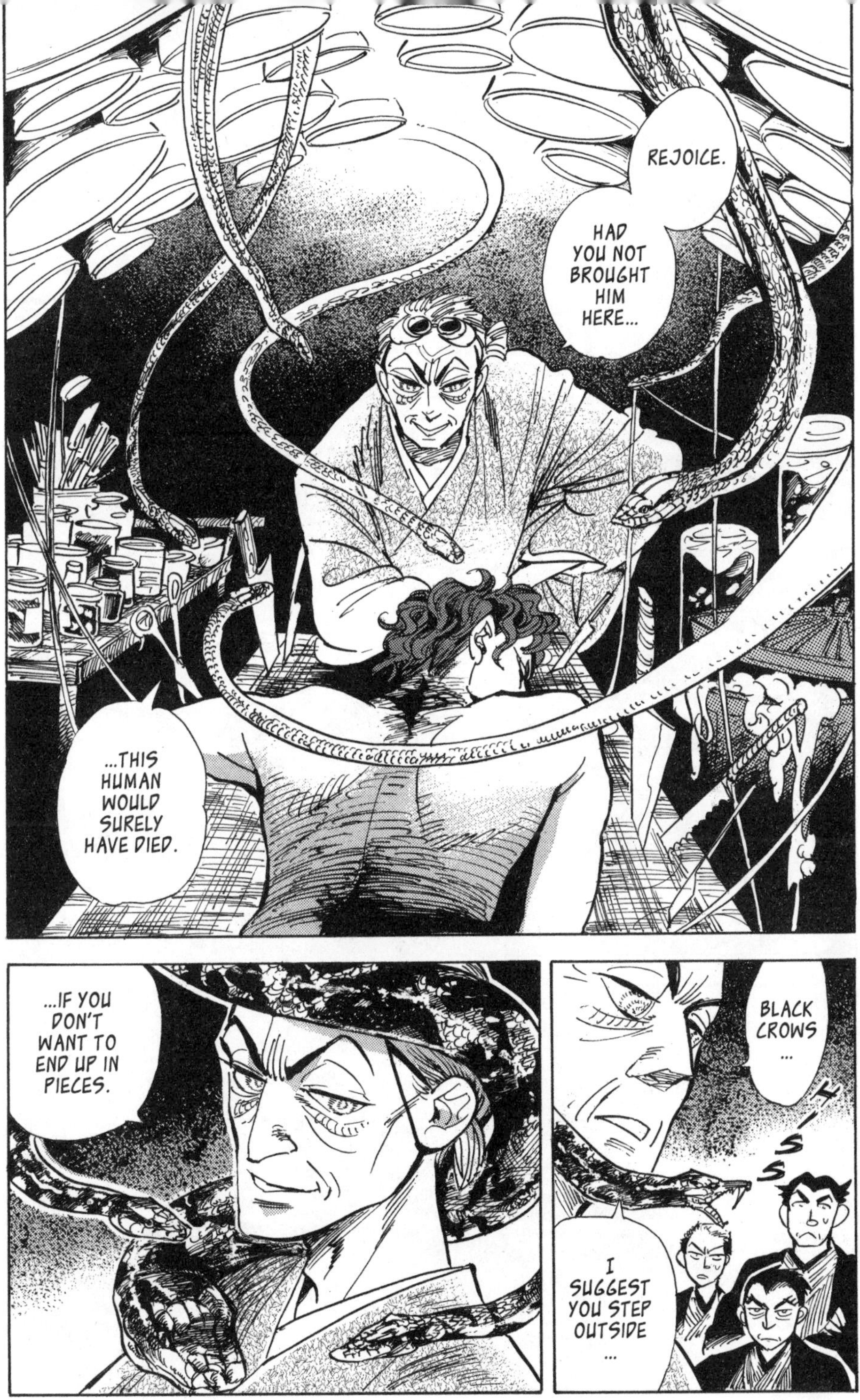

REJOICE.
HAD YOU NOT BROUGHT HIM HERE...
...THIS HUMAN WOULD SURELY HAVE DIED.
BLACK CROWS ...
HISSS
I SUGGEST YOU STEP OUTSIDE ...
...IF YOU DON'T WANT TO END UP IN PIECES.

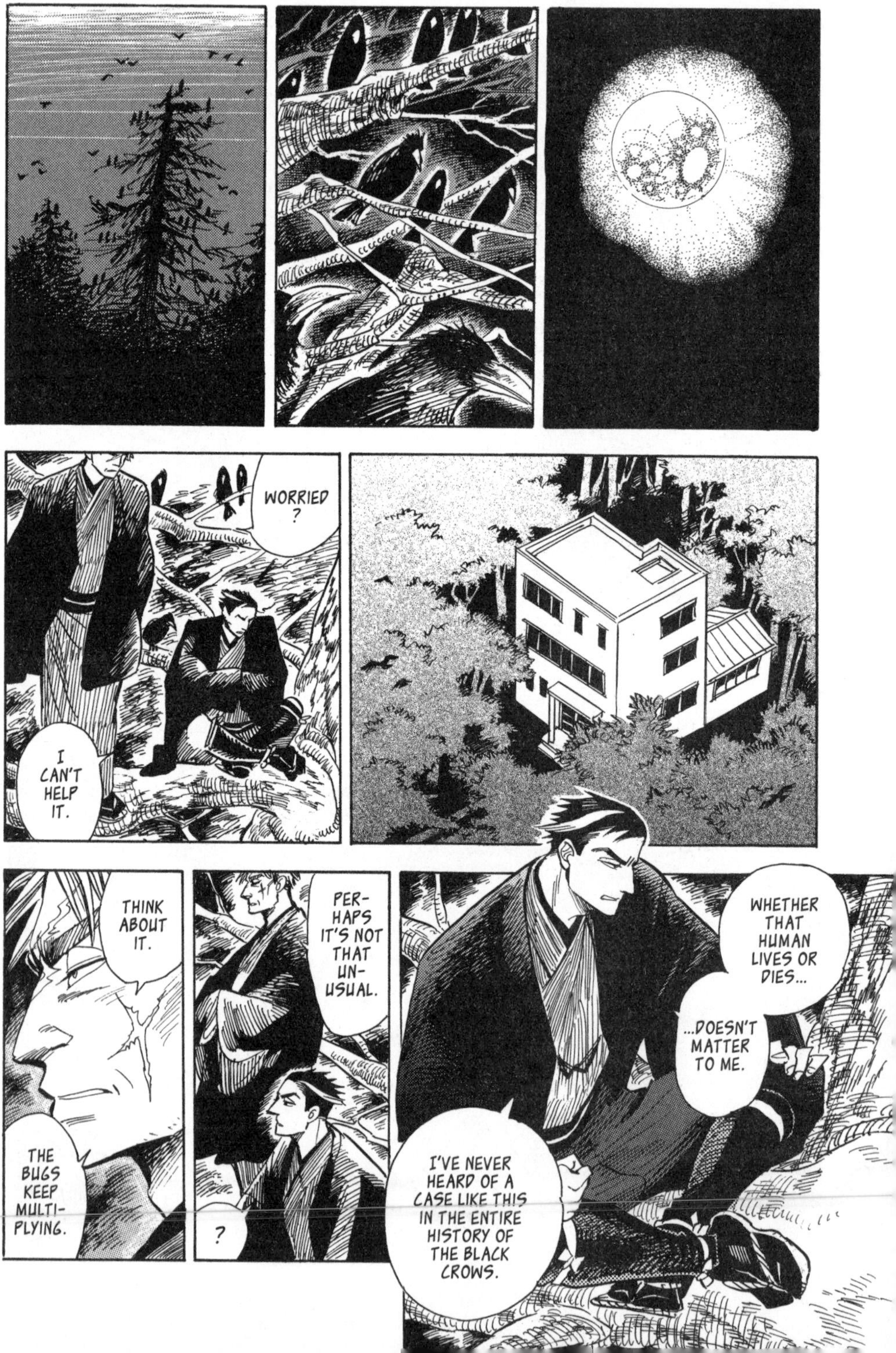
WORRIED?
I CAN'T HELP IT.
WHETHER THAT HUMAN LIVES OR DIES...
...DOESN'T MATTER TO ME.
I'VE NEVER HEARD OF A CASE LIKE THIS IN THE ENTIRE HISTORY OF THE BLACK CROWS.
PER-HAPS IT'S NOT THAT UN-USUAL.
?
THINK ABOUT IT.
THE BUGS KEEP MULTI-PLYING.

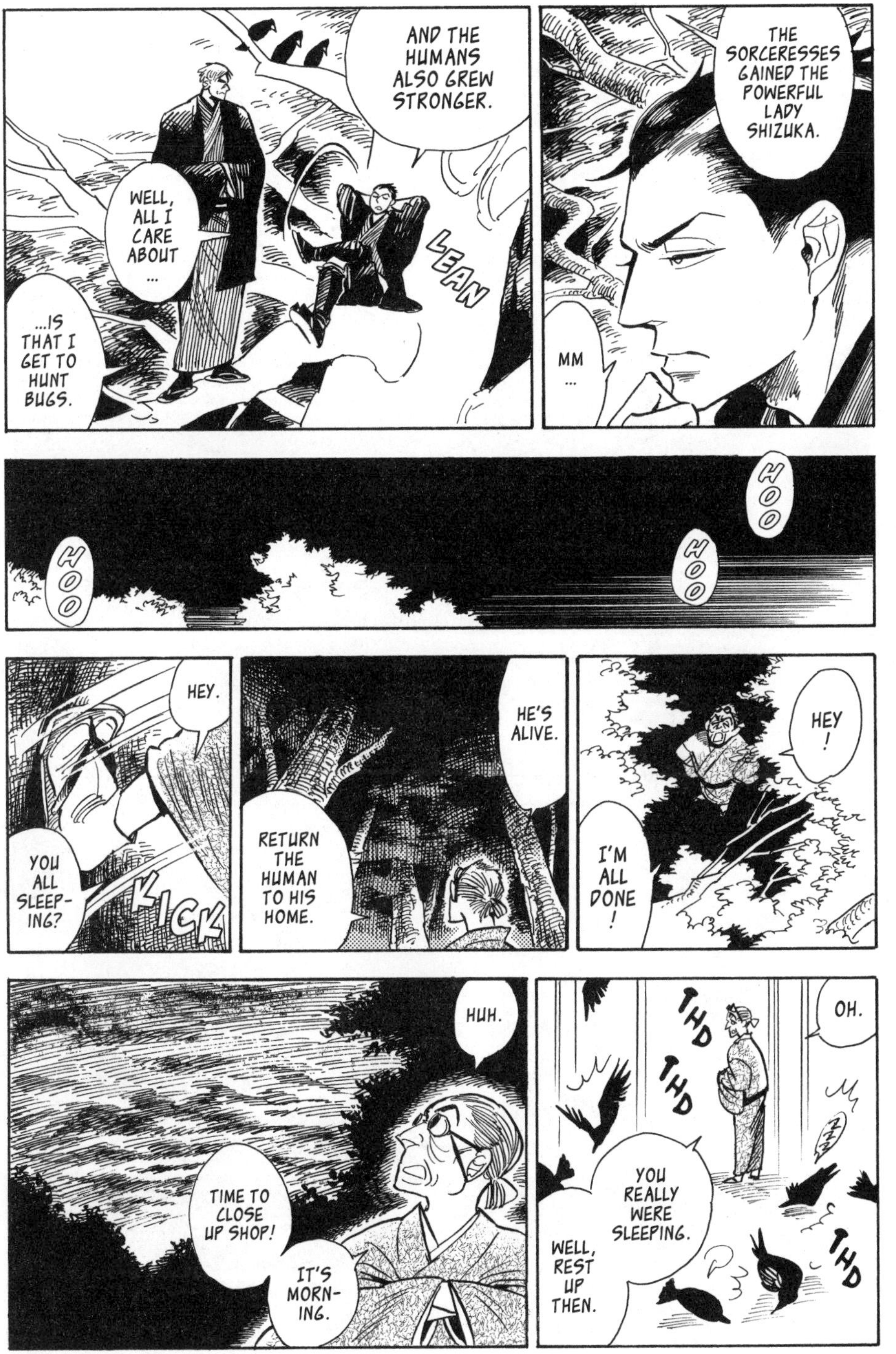
THE SORCERESSES GAINED THE POWERFUL LADY SHIZUKA.
MM ...
AND THE HUMANS ALSO GREW STRONGER.
LEAN
WELL, ALL I CARE ABOUT ...
...IS THAT I GET TO HUNT BUGS.
HOO
HOO
HOO
HEY!
I'M ALL DONE!
HE'S ALIVE.
RETURN THE HUMAN TO HIS HOME.
HEY.
YOU ALL SLEEPING?
KICK
OH.
THD
THD
YOU REALLY WERE SLEEPING.
WELL, REST UP THEN.
THD
HUH.
TIME TO CLOSE UP SHOP!
IT'S MORNING.

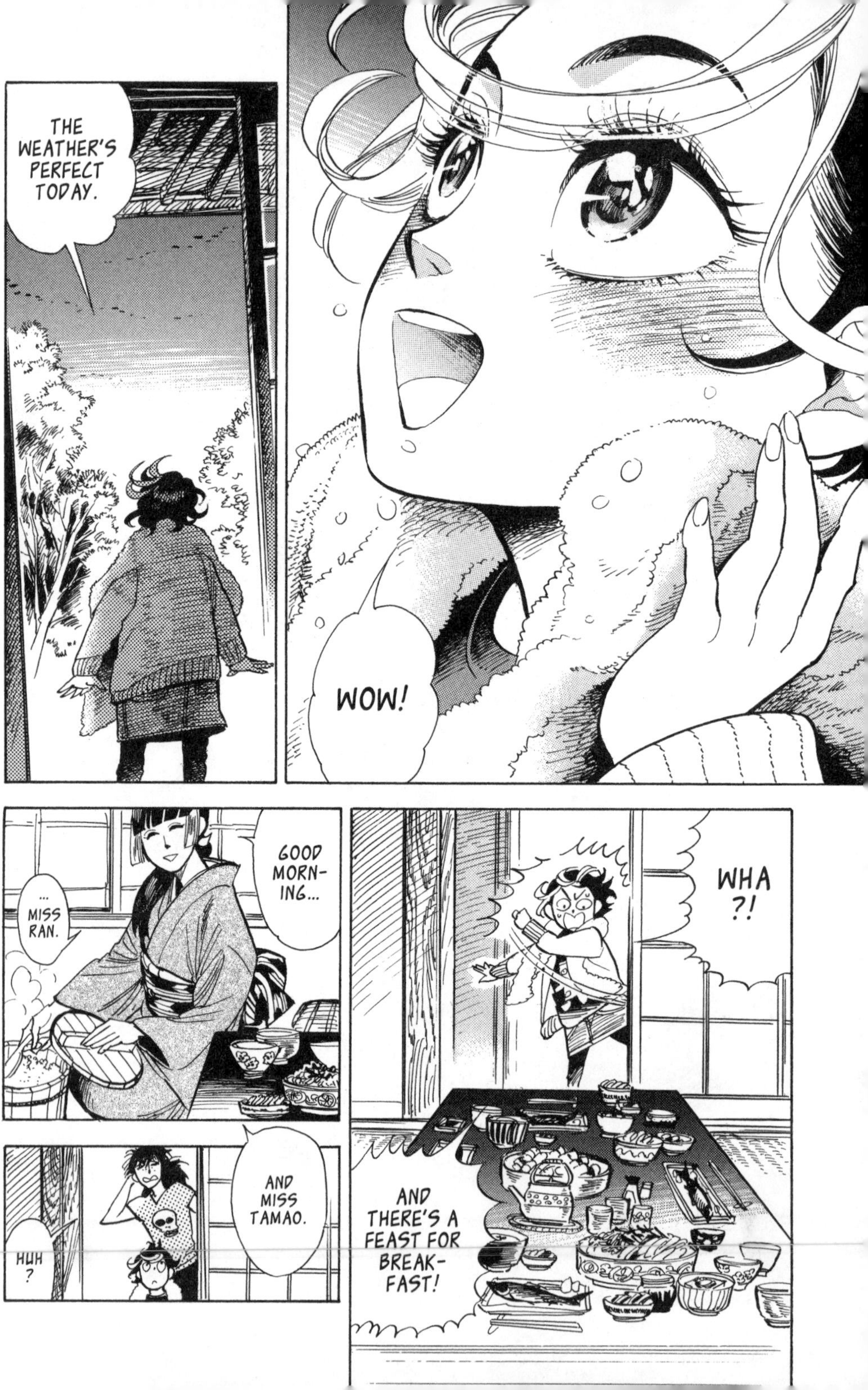
WOW!
THE WEATHER'S PERFECT TODAY.
WHA ?!
AND THERE'S A FEAST FOR BREAK-FAST!
GOOD MORN-ING...
... MISS RAN.
AND MISS TAMAO.
HUH ?

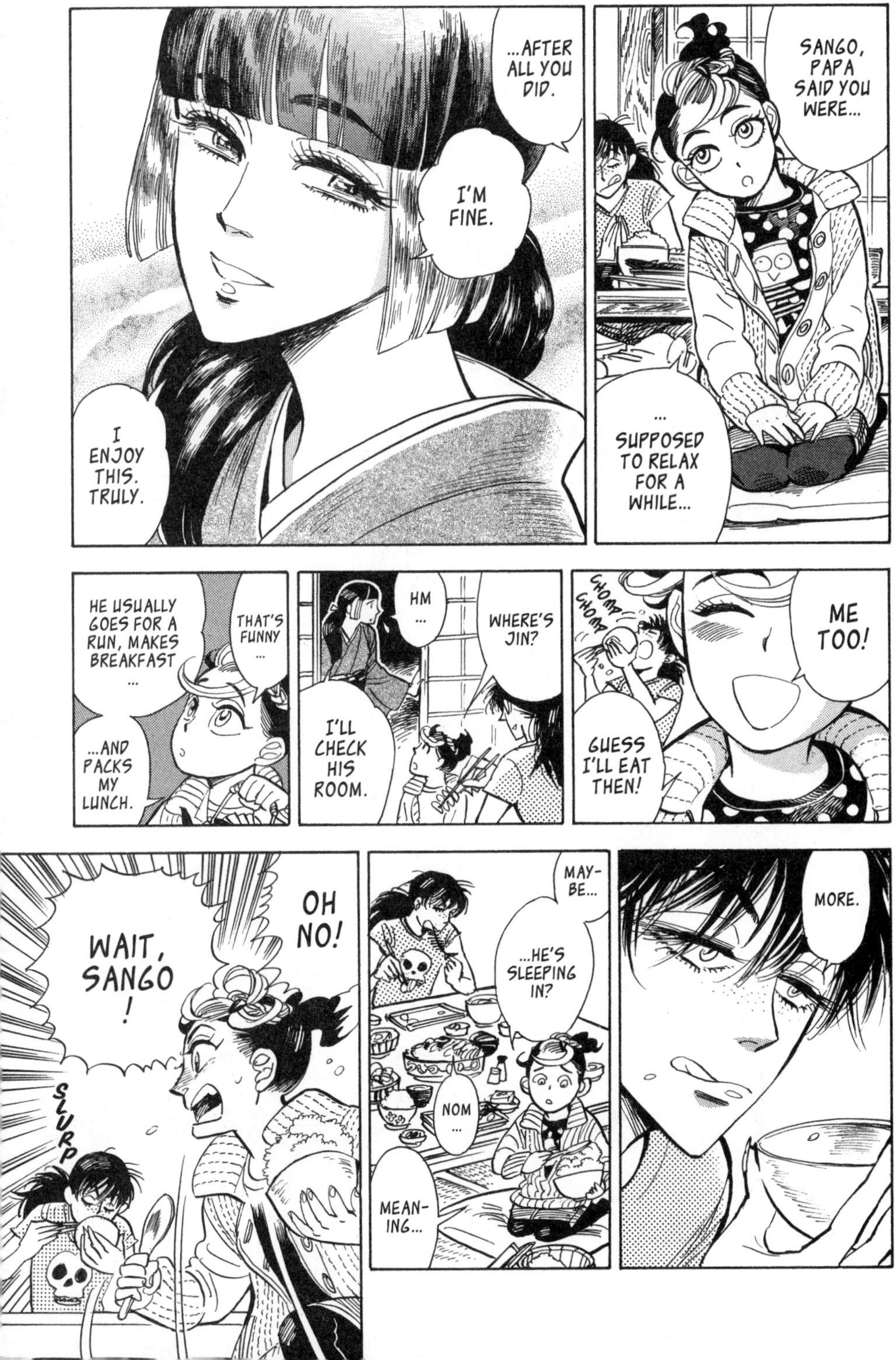
SANGO, PAPA SAID YOU WERE...
...SUPPOSED TO RELAX FOR A WHILE...
...AFTER ALL YOU DID.
I'M FINE.
I ENJOY THIS. TRULY.
ME TOO!
CHOMP CHOMP
GUESS I'LL EAT THEN!
WHERE'S JIN?
HM ...
I'LL CHECK HIS ROOM.
THAT'S FUNNY ...
HE USUALLY GOES FOR A RUN, MAKES BREAKFAST ...
...AND PACKS MY LUNCH.
MORE.
MAY-BE...
...HE'S SLEEPING IN?
NOM ...
MEAN-ING...
OH NO!
WAIT, SANGO !
SLURP

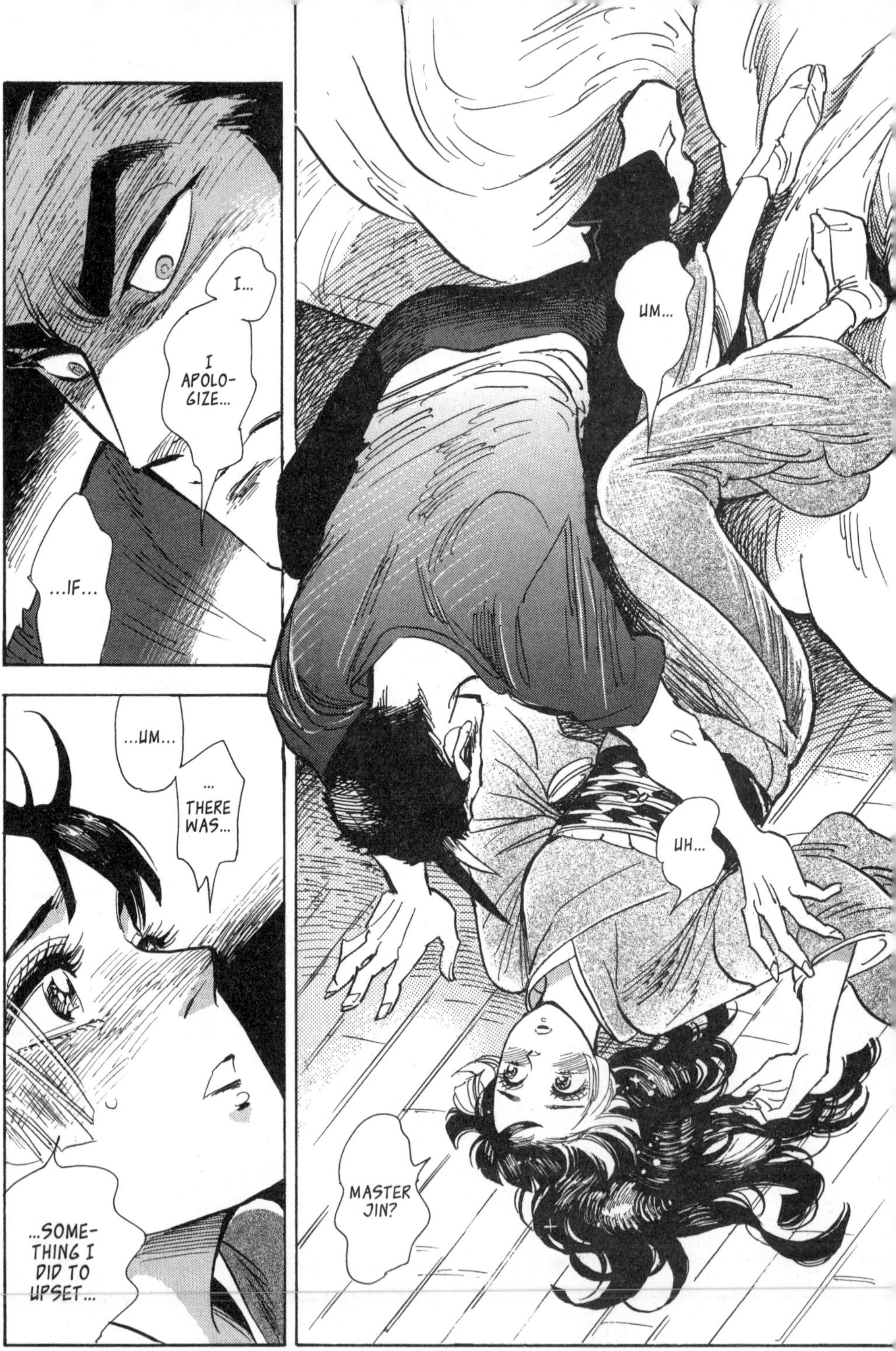
UM...
UH...
MASTER JIN?
I...
I APOLOGIZE...
...IF...
...UM...
... THERE WAS...
...SOMETHING I DID TO UPSET...

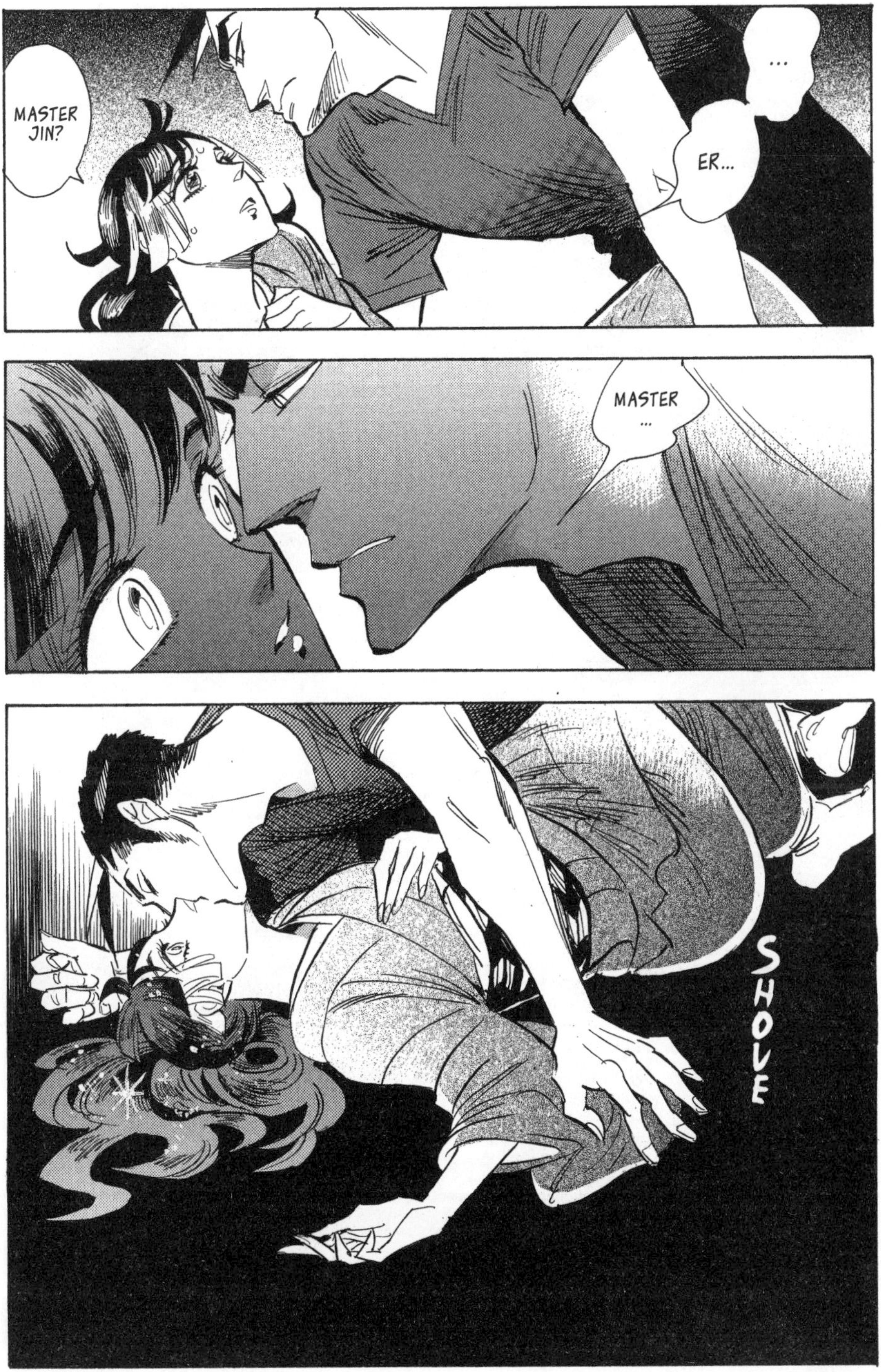
...
ER...
MASTER JIN?
MASTER ...
SHOVE

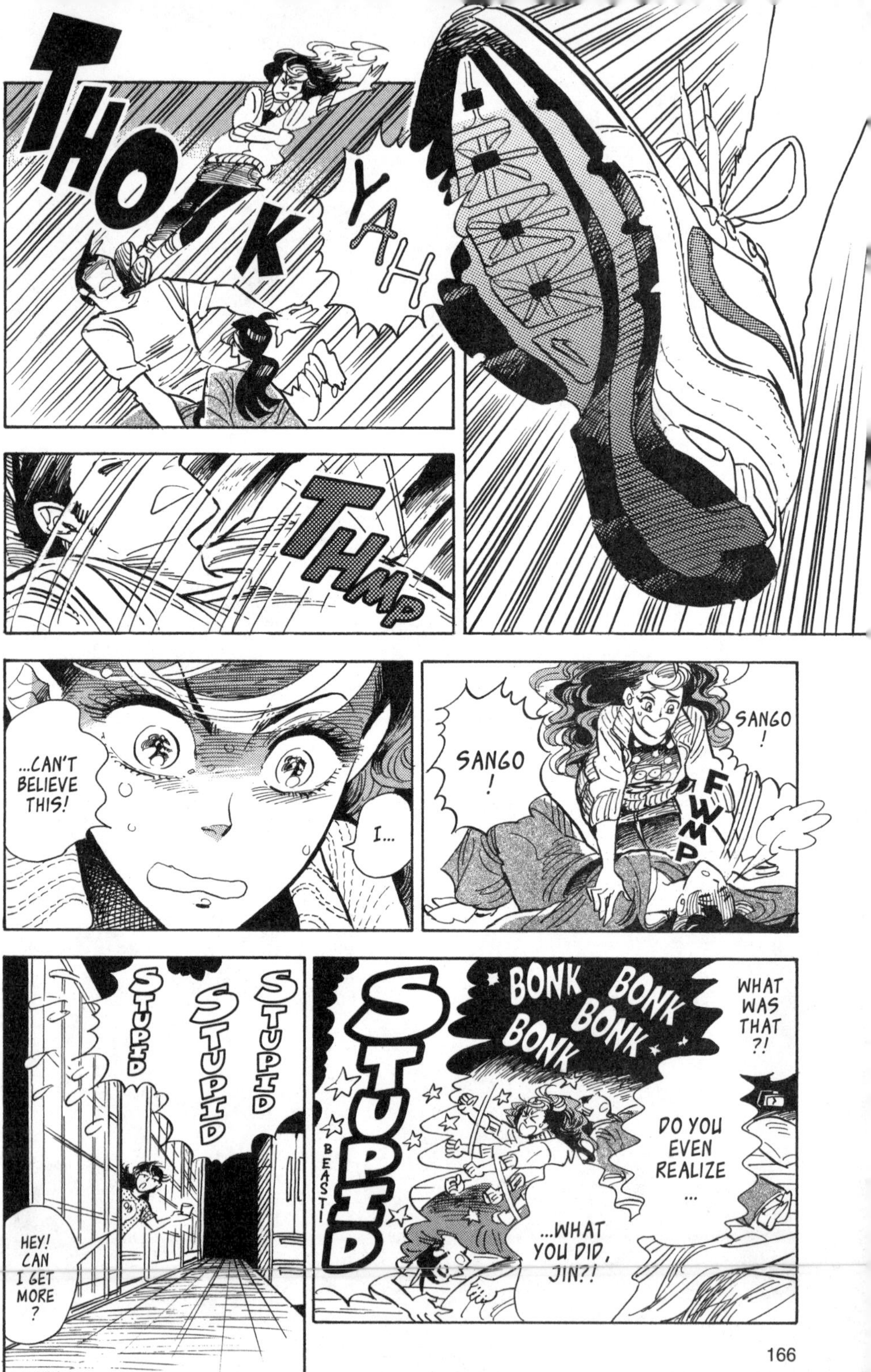
YAH
THOK
THMP
SANGO!
SANGO!
FWMP
I...
...CAN'T BELIEVE THIS!
WHAT WAS THAT?!
BONK BONK BONK BONK
DO YOU EVEN REALIZE...
...WHAT YOU DID, JIN?!
STUPID
BEAST!
STUPID
STUPID
STUPID
HEY! CAN I GET MORE?

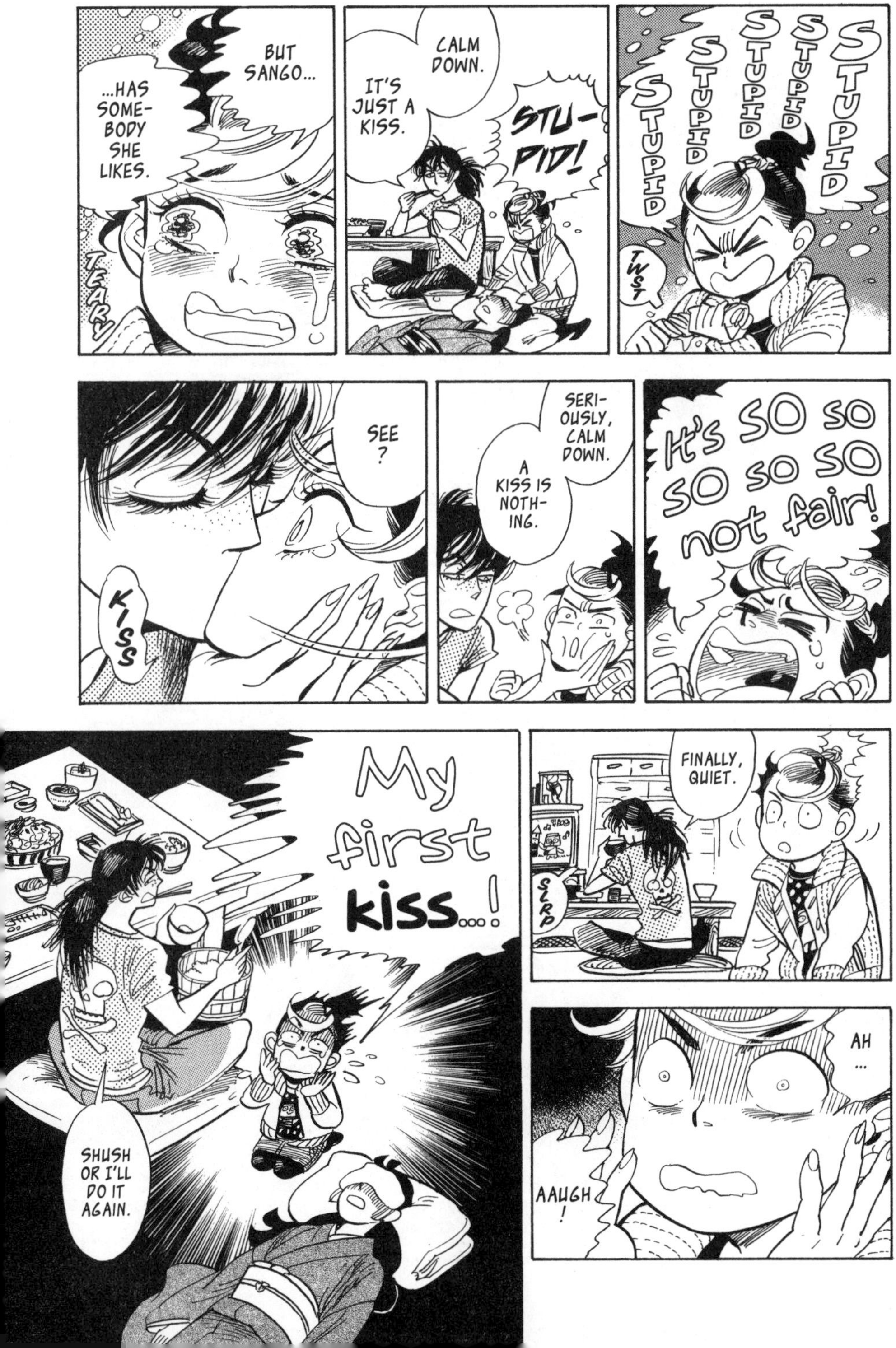
STUPID
STUPID
STUPID
STUPID
STUPID
TWST
CALM DOWN.
IT'S JUST A KISS.
STU-PID!
BUT SANGO...
...HAS SOME-BODY SHE LIKES.
TEARY
It's SO so SO so so SO not fair!
SERI-OUSLY, CALM DOWN.
A KISS IS NOTH-ING.
SEE?
KISS
FINALLY, QUIET.
SLRP
AH...
AAUGH!
My first kiss...!
SHUSH OR I'LL DO IT AGAIN.

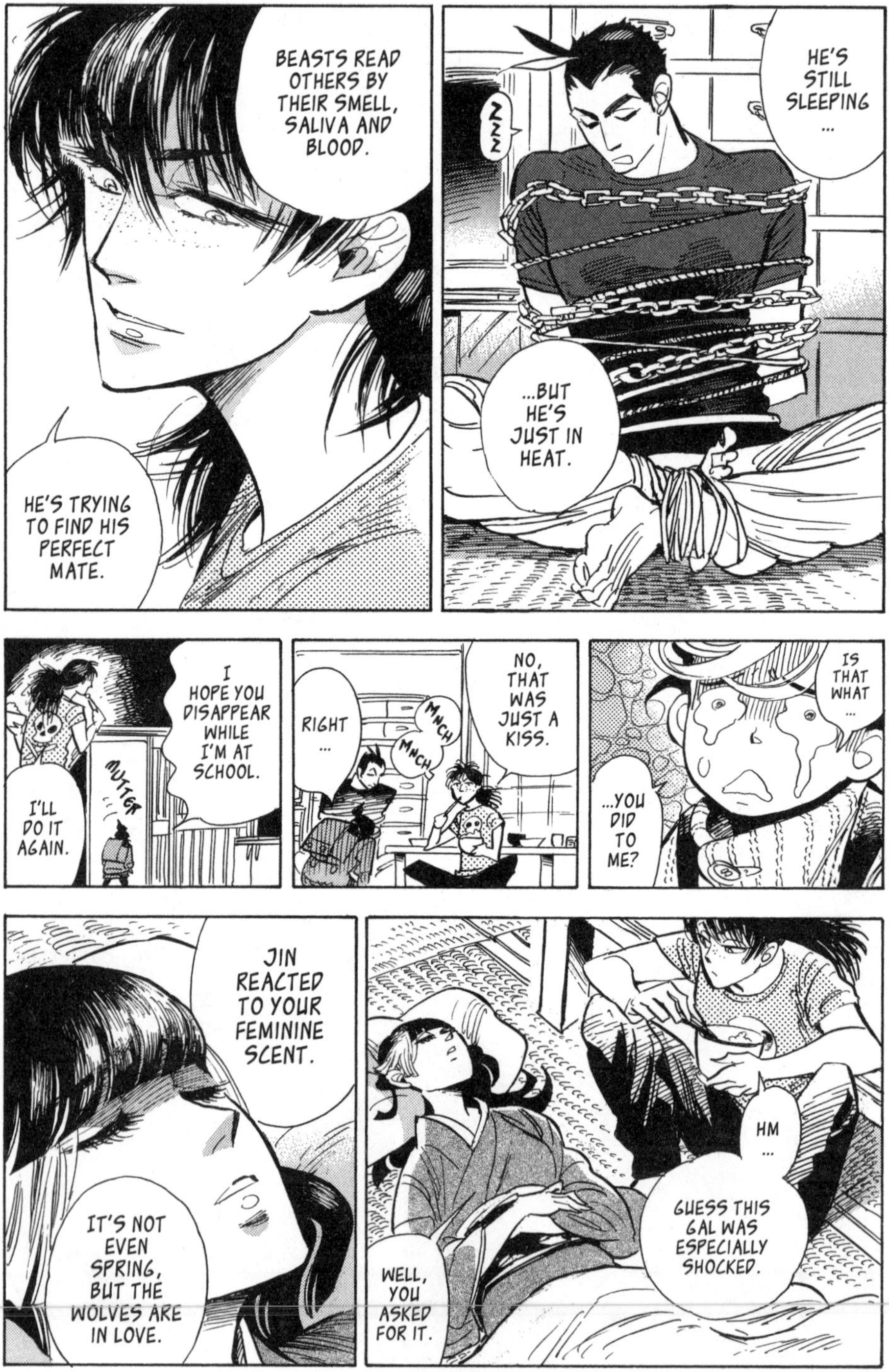
HE'S STILL SLEEPING ...
ZZZ
...BUT HE'S JUST IN HEAT.
BEASTS READ OTHERS BY THEIR SMELL, SALIVA AND BLOOD.
HE'S TRYING TO FIND HIS PERFECT MATE.
IS THAT WHAT ...
...YOU DID TO ME?
NO, THAT WAS JUST A KISS.
MNCH
MNCH
RIGHT ...
I HOPE YOU DISAPPEAR WHILE I'M AT SCHOOL.
MUTTER
I'LL DO IT AGAIN.
HM ...
GUESS THIS GAL WAS ESPECIALLY SHOCKED.
WELL, YOU ASKED FOR IT.
JIN REACTED TO YOUR FEMININE SCENT.
IT'S NOT EVEN SPRING, BUT THE WOLVES ARE IN LOVE.

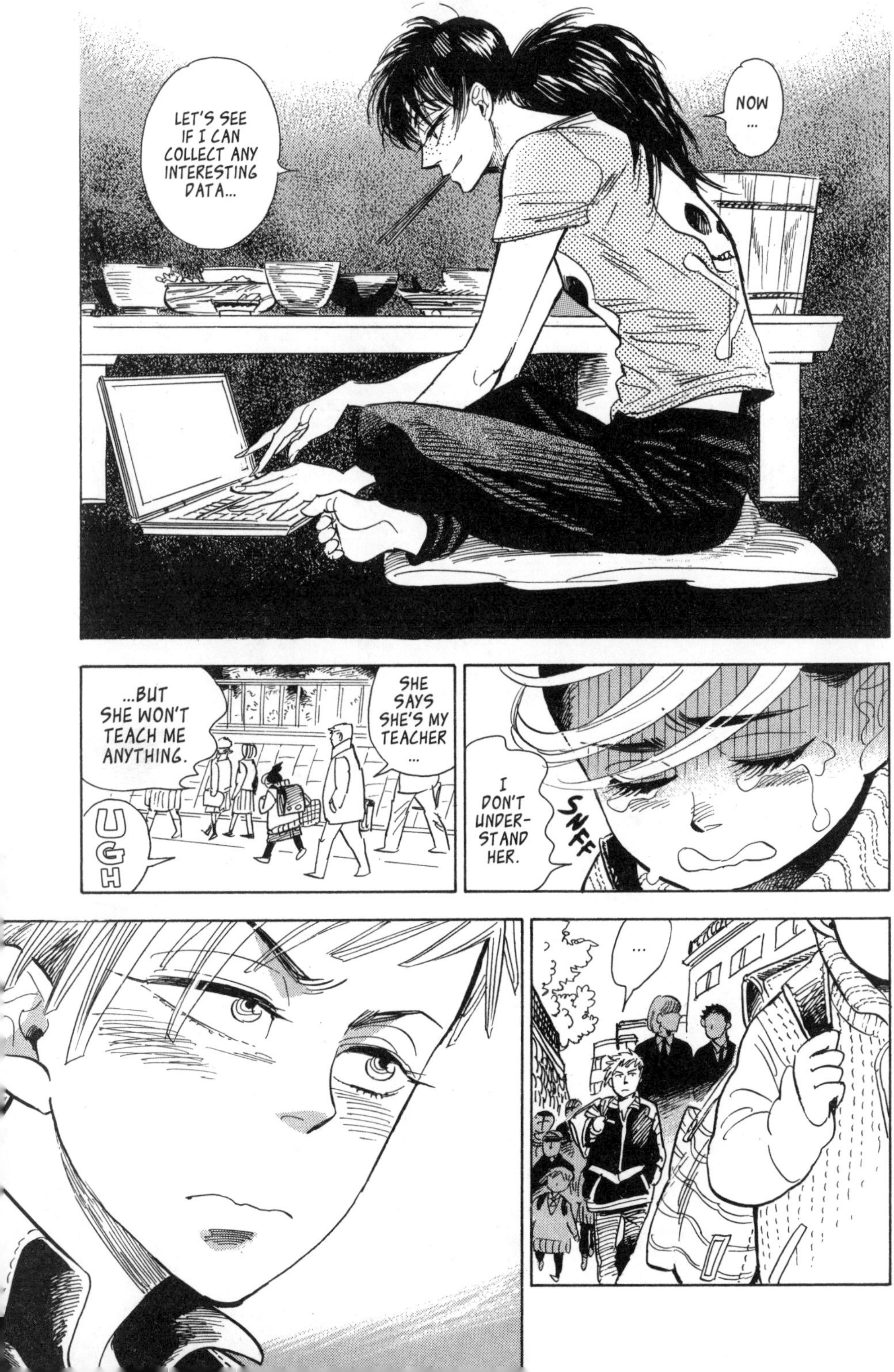
NOW ...
LET'S SEE IF I CAN COLLECT ANY INTERESTING DATA...
I DON'T UNDER-STAND HER.
SNFF
SHE SAYS SHE'S MY TEACHER ...
...BUT SHE WON'T TEACH ME ANYTHING.
UGH
...

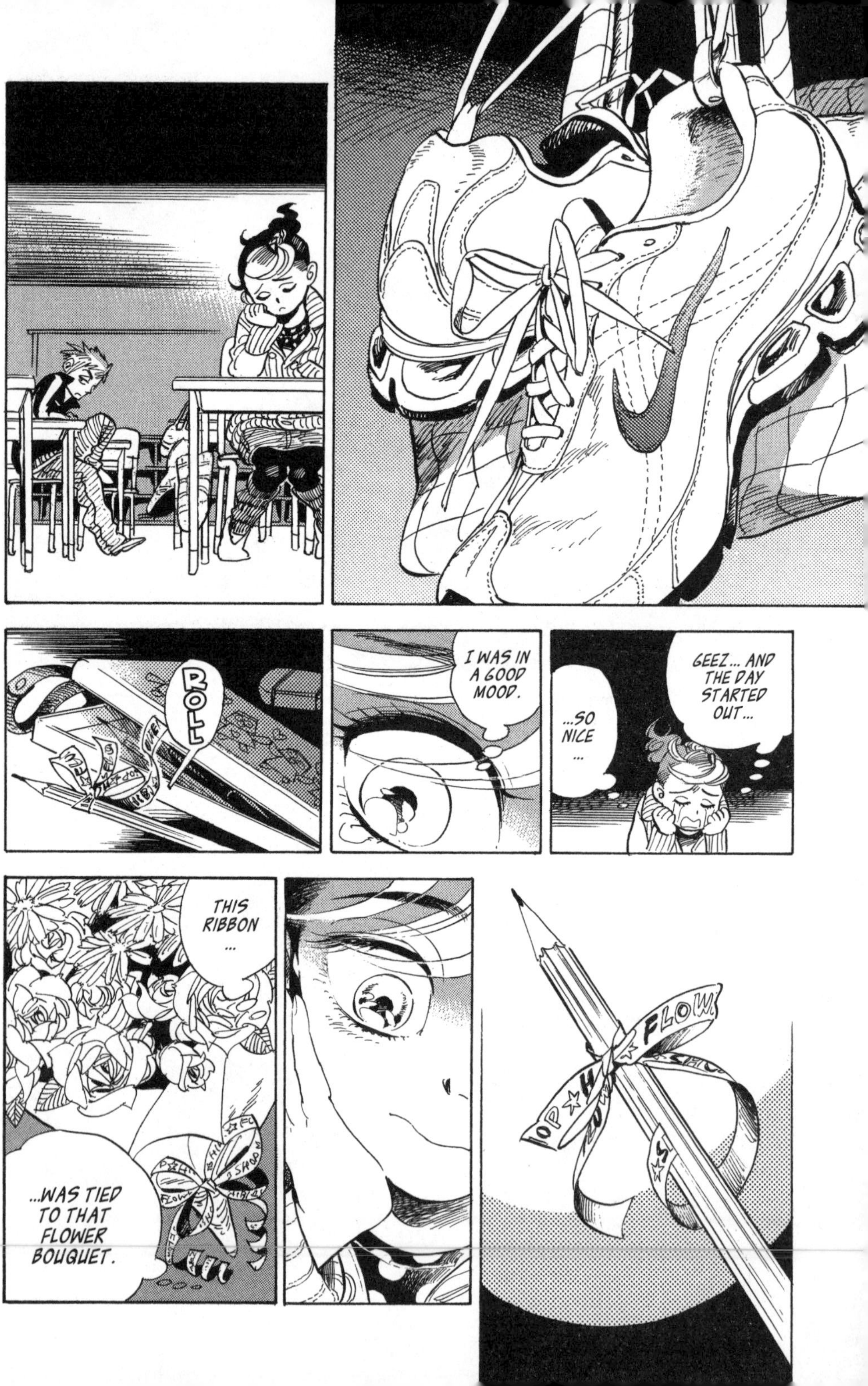
GEEZ... AND THE DAY STARTED OUT...
...SO NICE...
I WAS IN A GOOD MOOD.
ROLL
THIS RIBBON...
...WAS TIED TO THAT FLOWER BOUQUET.

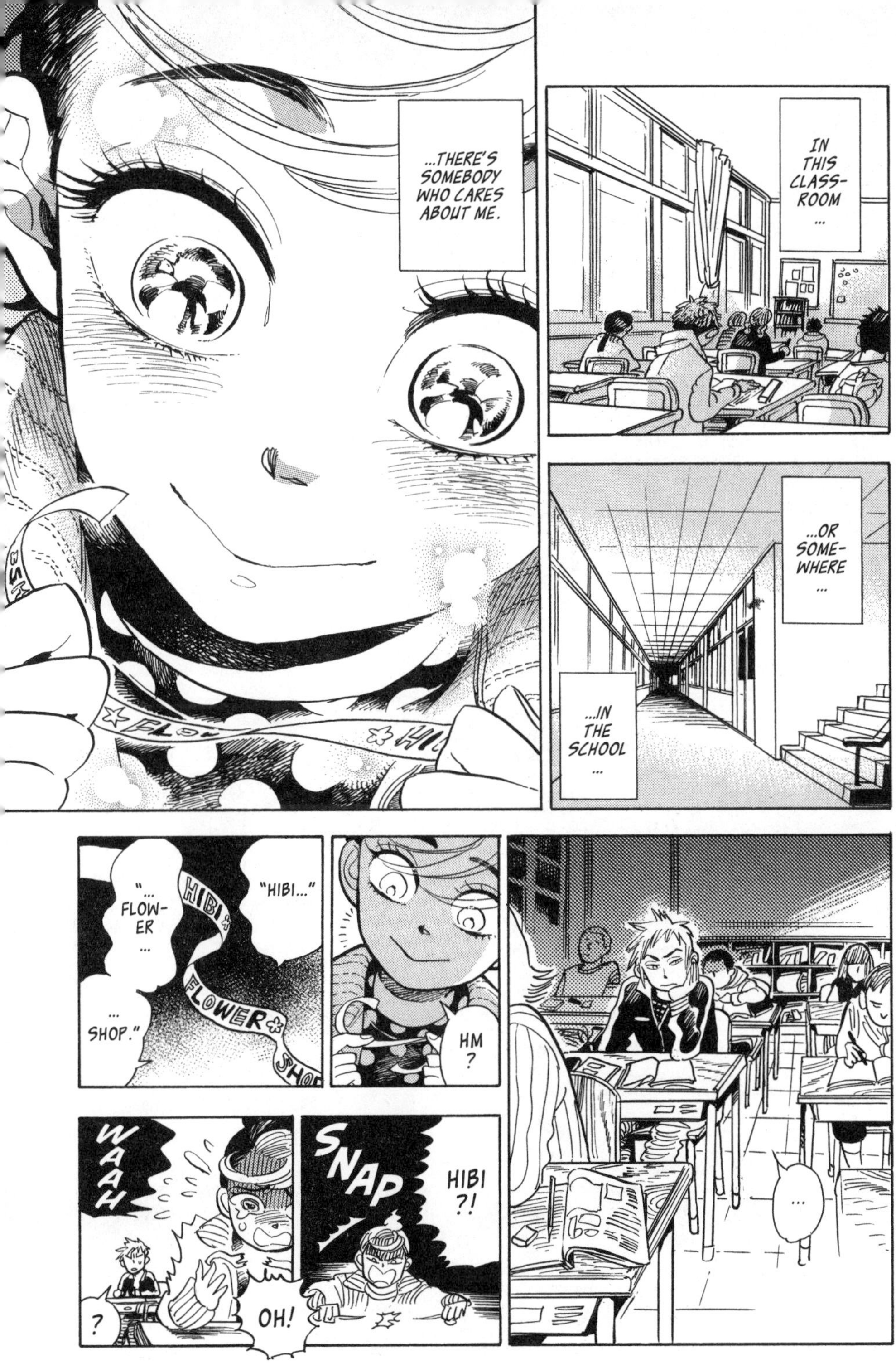
IN THIS CLASS-ROOM...
...OR SOME-WHERE...
...IN THE SCHOOL...
...THERE'S SOMEBODY WHO CARES ABOUT ME.
...
HM?
"HIBI..."
HIBI FLOWER SHOP
"...FLOWER...
...SHOP."
SNAP
HIBI?!
OH!
WAAH
?

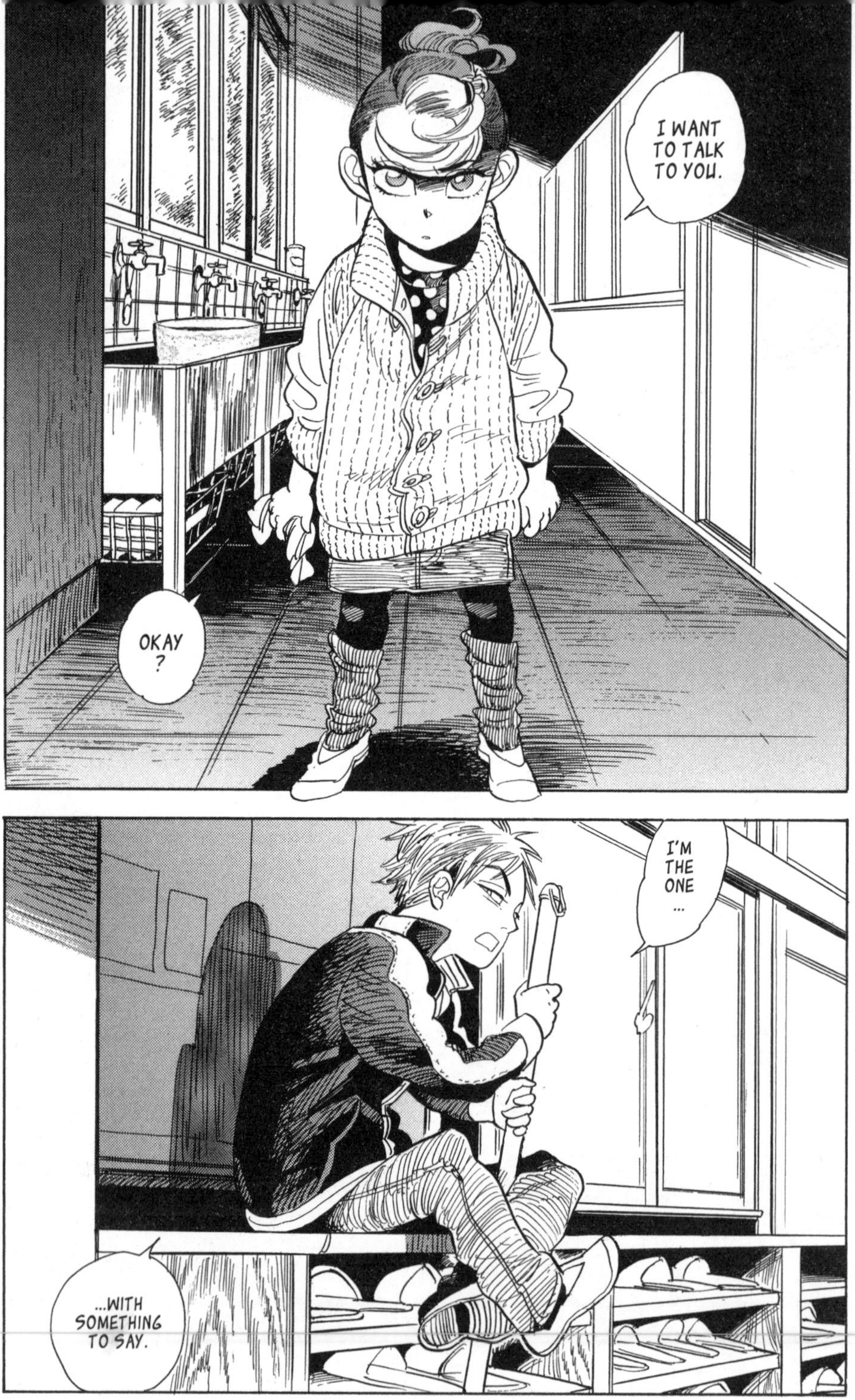
I WANT TO TALK TO YOU.
OKAY?
I'M THE ONE...
...WITH SOMETHING TO SAY.

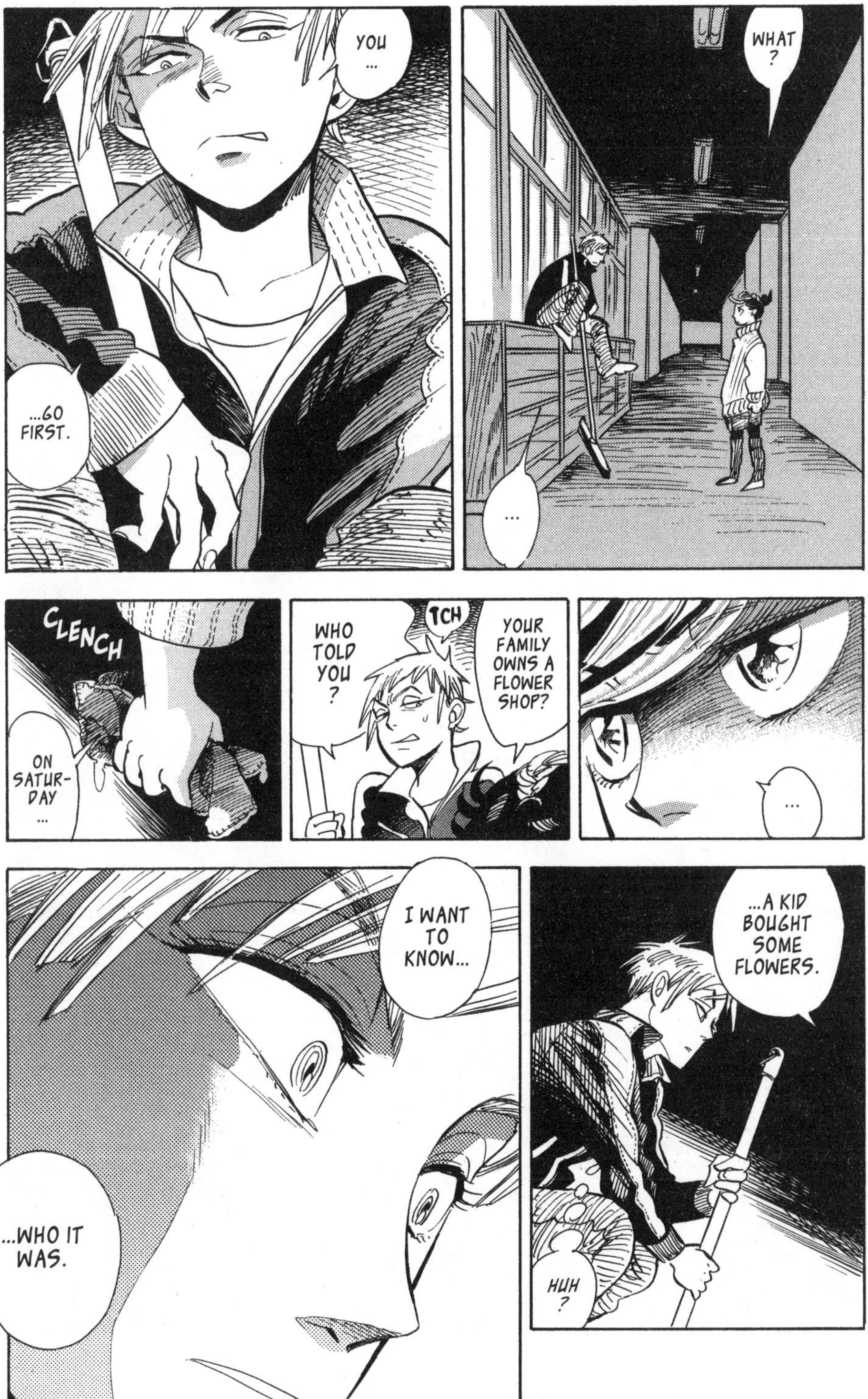
WHAT?
...
YOU...
...GO FIRST.
...
YOUR FAMILY OWNS A FLOWER SHOP?
TCH
WHO TOLD YOU?
CLENCH
ON SATURDAY...
...A KID BOUGHT SOME FLOWERS.
HUH?
I WANT TO KNOW...
...WHO IT WAS.

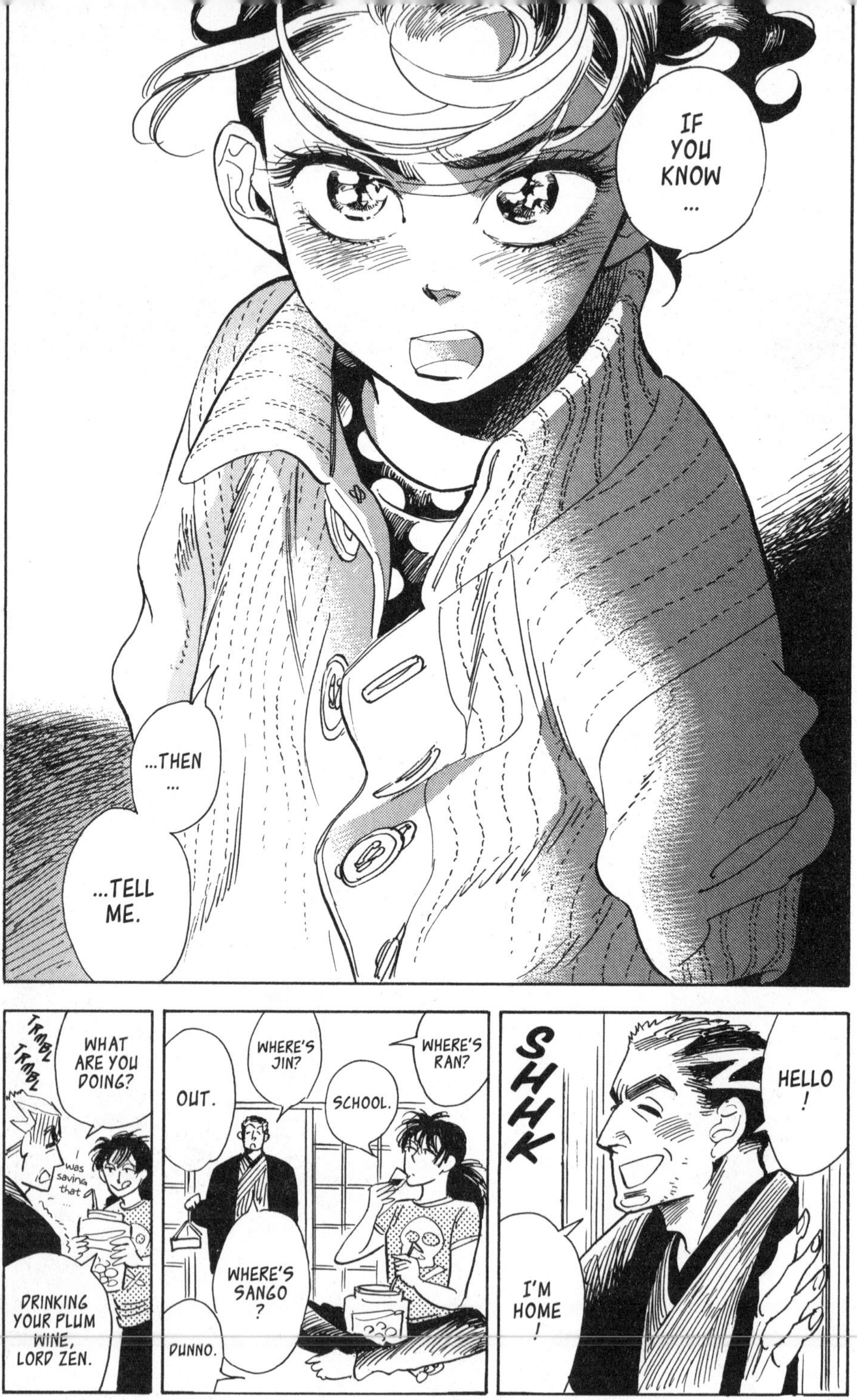
IF YOU KNOW ...
...THEN ...
...TELL ME.
SHHK
HELLO!
I'M HOME!
WHERE'S RAN?
SCHOOL.
WHERE'S JIN?
OUT.
WHERE'S SANGO?
DUNNO.
TRMBL TRMBL
WHAT ARE YOU DOING?
DRINKING YOUR PLUM WINE, LORD ZEN.
I was saving that ...

Chapter 10 / The End

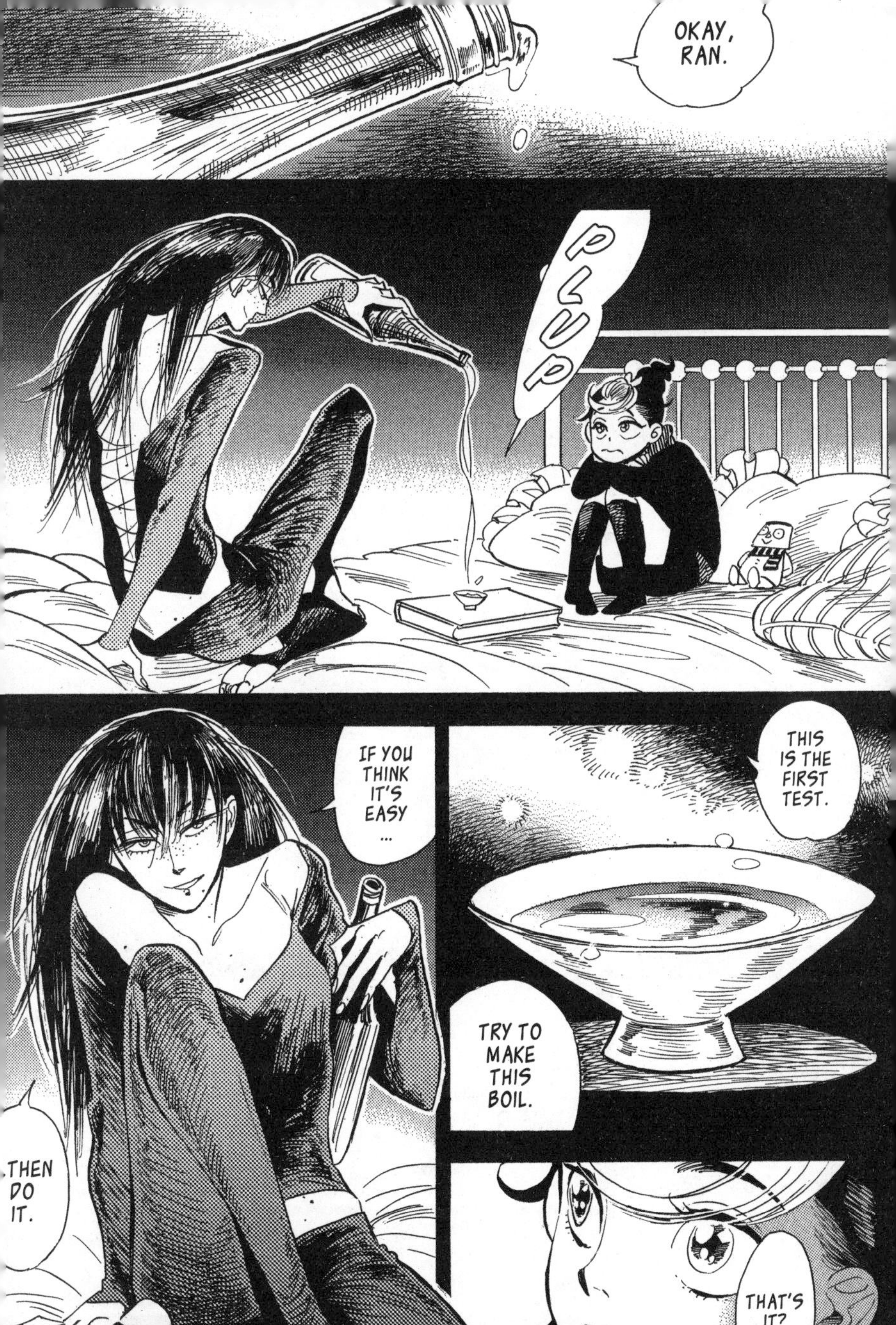
OKAY, RAN.
PLUP
THIS IS THE FIRST TEST.
TRY TO MAKE THIS BOIL.
THAT'S IT?
IF YOU THINK IT'S EASY ...
THEN DO IT.

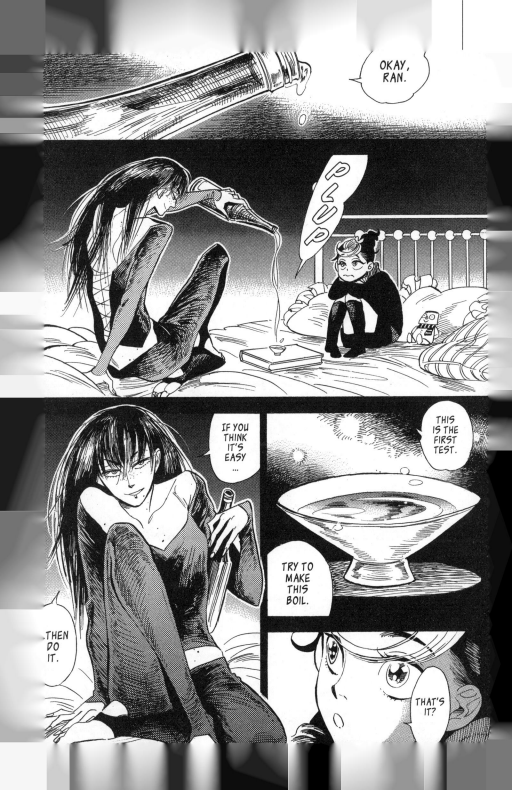

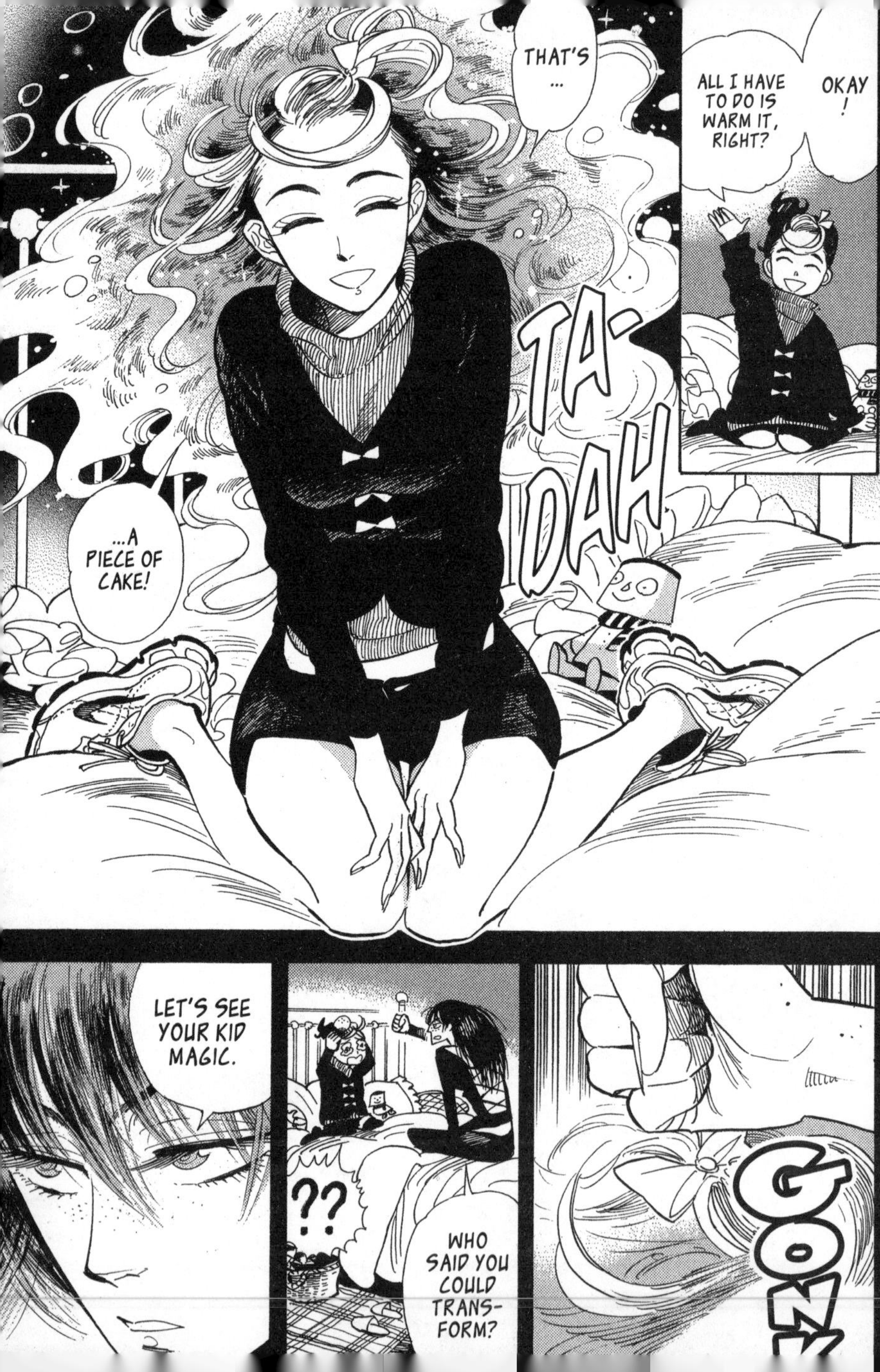
OKAY!
ALL I HAVE TO DO IS WARM IT, RIGHT?
THAT'S ...
TA-DAH
...A PIECE OF CAKE!
GON
WHO SAID YOU COULD TRANS-FORM?
??
LET'S SEE YOUR KID MAGIC.

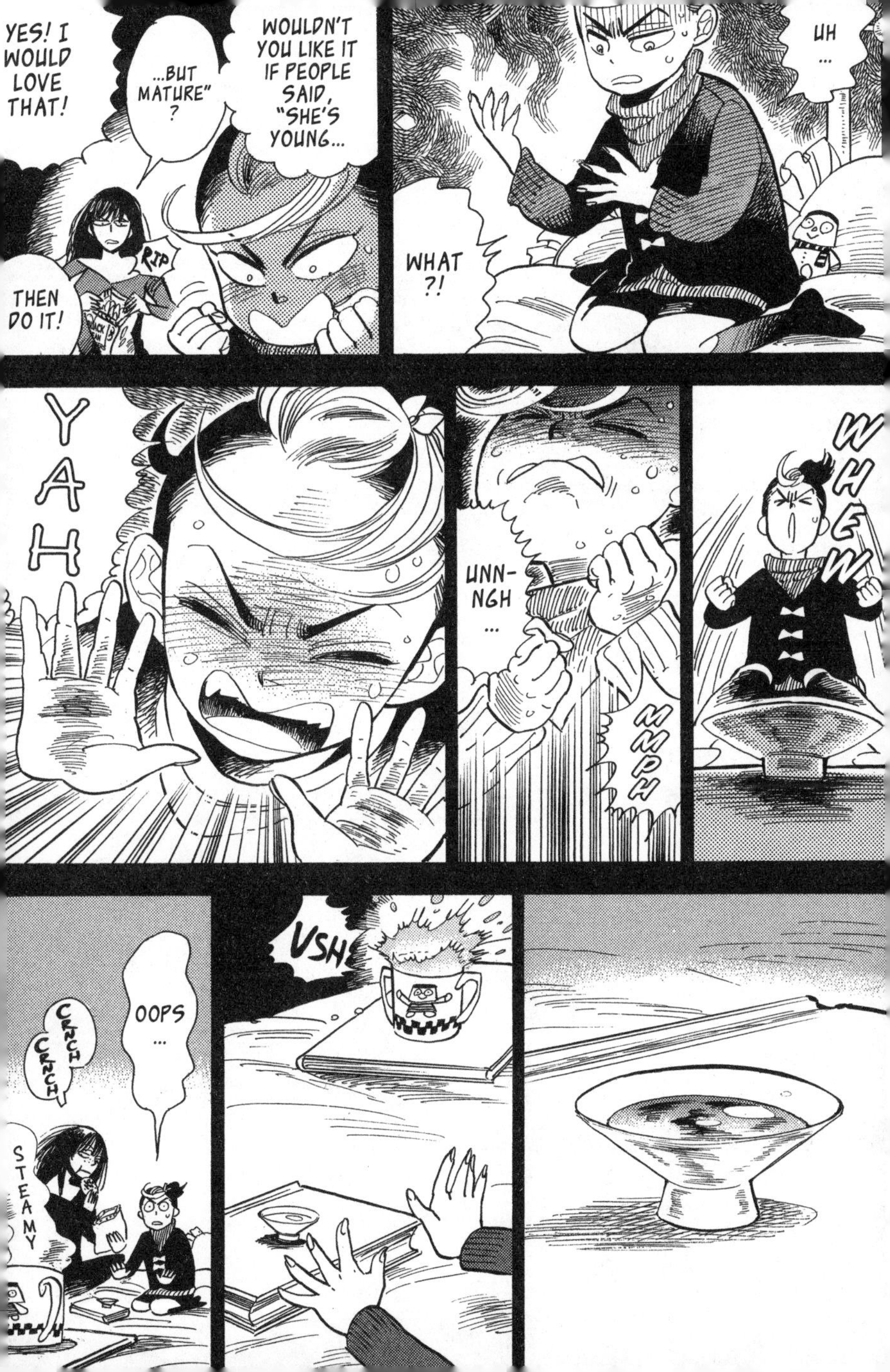
UH ...
WHAT ?!
WOULDN'T YOU LIKE IT IF PEOPLE SAID, "SHE'S YOUNG...
...BUT MATURE" ?
YES! I WOULD LOVE THAT!
RIP
THEN DO IT!
WHEW
UNN-NGH ...
MMPH
YAH
VSH
OOPS ...
CRNCH
CRNCH
STEAMY

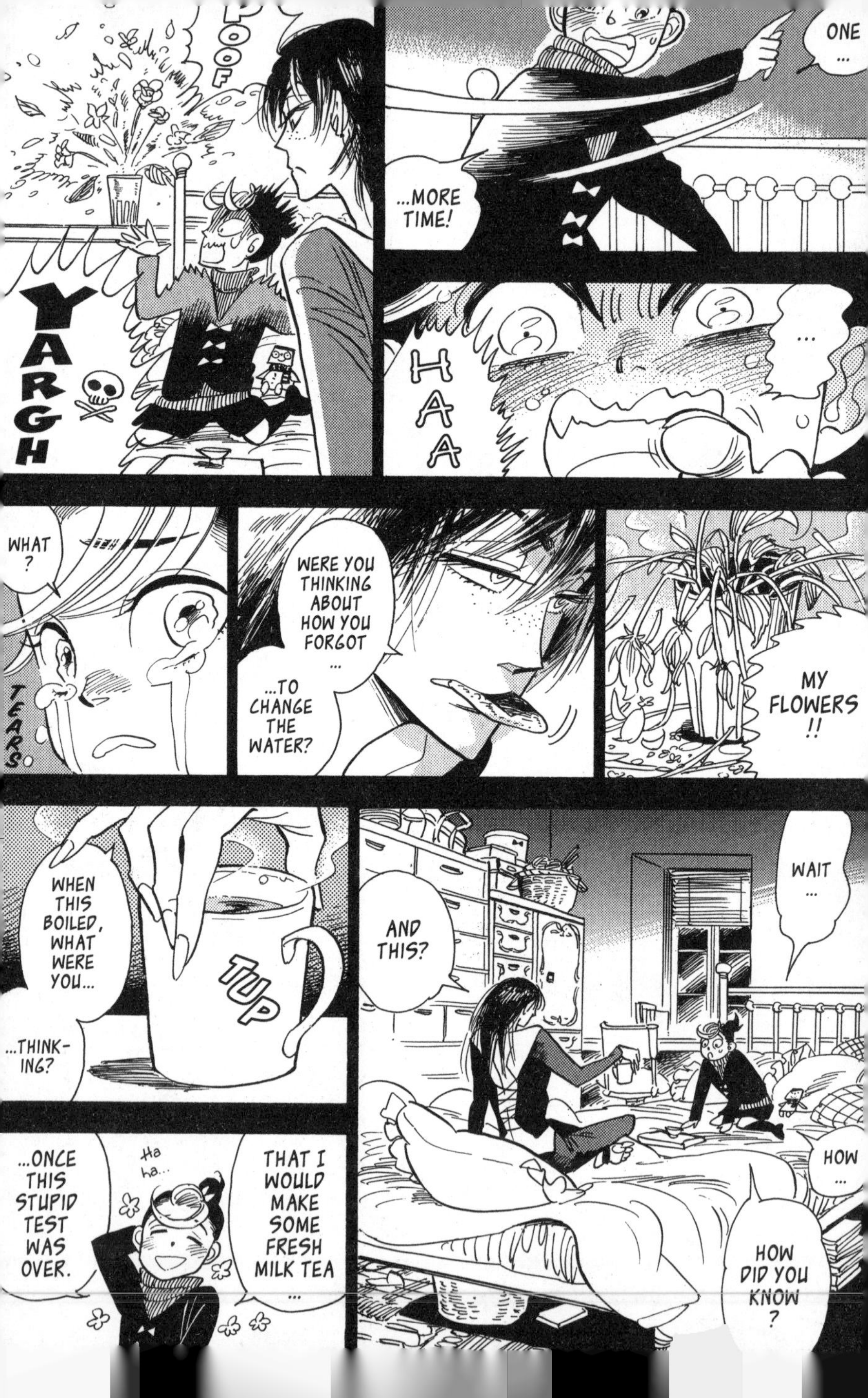
ONE ...
...MORE TIME!
...
HAA
POOF
YARGH
MY FLOWERS !!
WERE YOU THINKING ABOUT HOW YOU FORGOT ...
...TO CHANGE THE WATER?
WHAT ?
TEARS
WAIT ...
AND THIS?
HOW ...
HOW DID YOU KNOW ?
WHEN THIS BOILED, WHAT WERE YOU...
...THINKING?
TUP
THAT I WOULD MAKE SOME FRESH MILK TEA ...
Ha ha...
...ONCE THIS STUPID TEST WAS OVER.

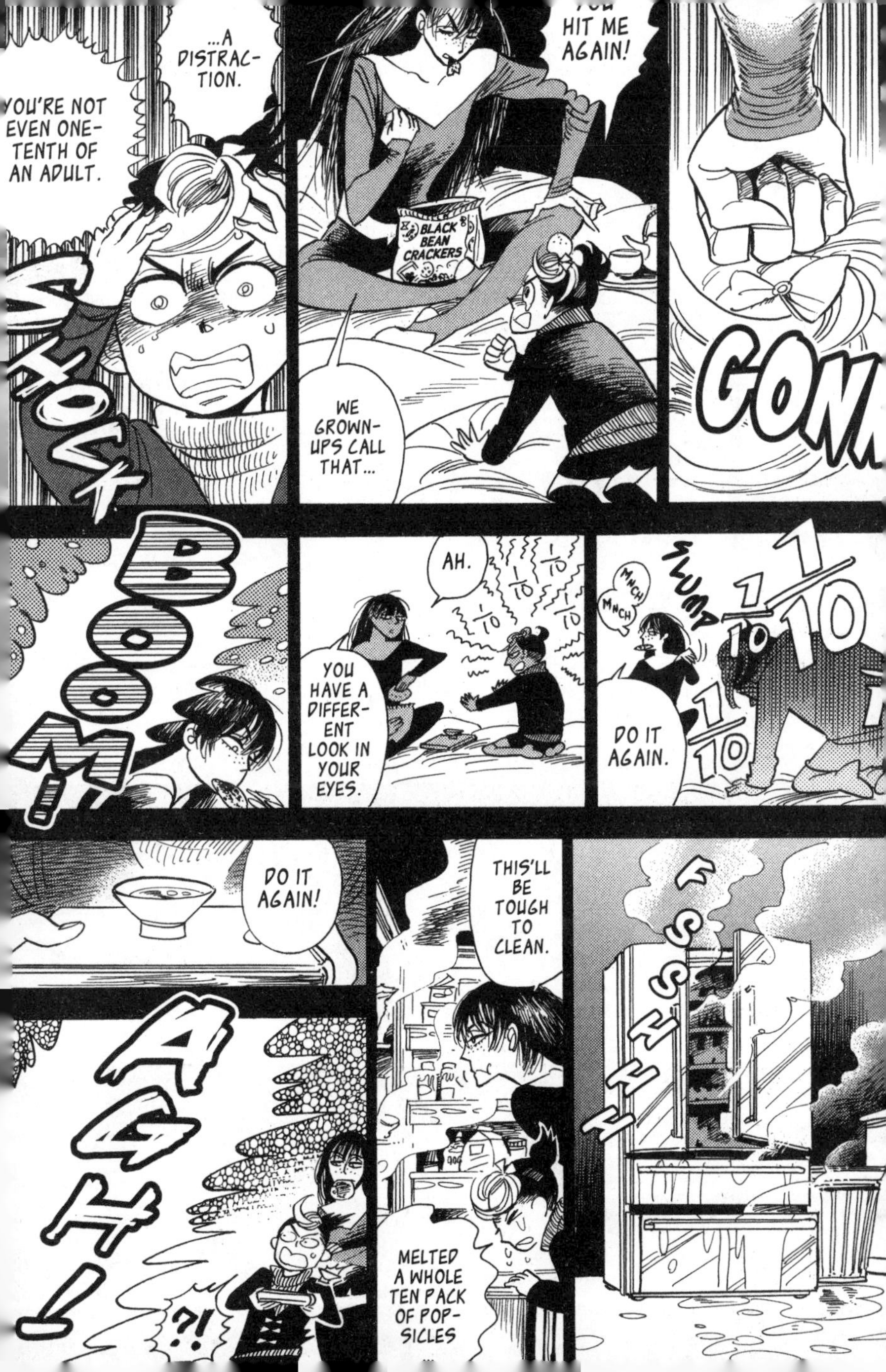
GON
HIT ME AGAIN!
WE GROWN-UPS CALL THAT...
...A DISTRACTION.
YOU'RE NOT EVEN ONE-TENTH OF AN ADULT.
SHOCK
SLUMP
MNCH MNCH
1/10
DO IT AGAIN.
AH.
1/10
YOU HAVE A DIFFERENT LOOK IN YOUR EYES.
BOOOM!
FSSHHH
THIS'LL BE TOUGH TO CLEAN.
MELTED A WHOLE TEN PACK OF POPSICLES
DO IT AGAIN!
AGH!
?!

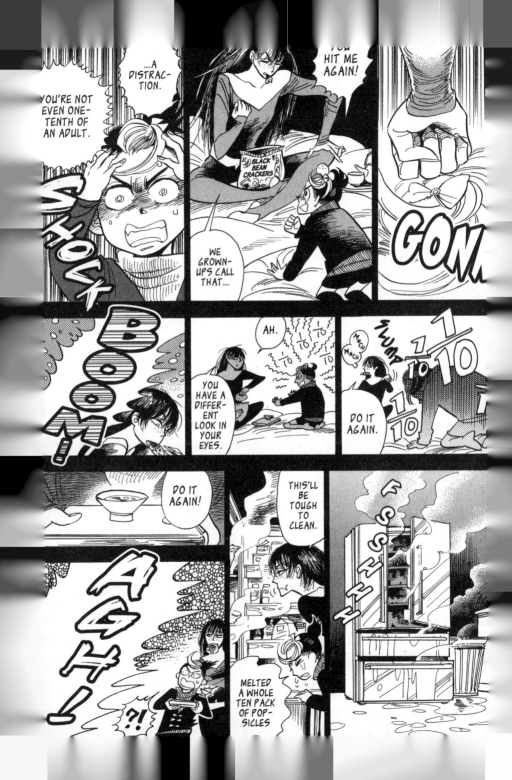

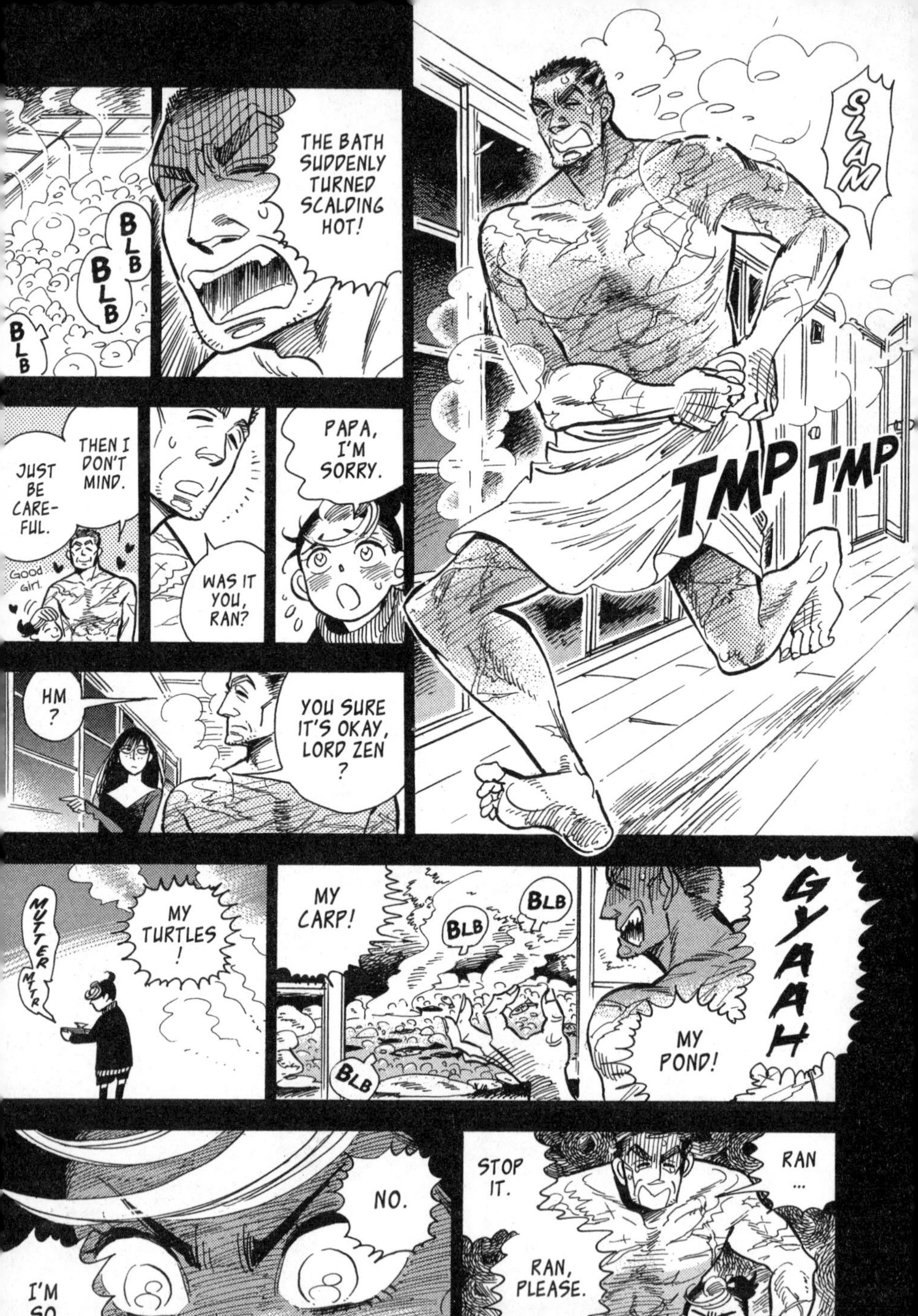
SLAM
TMP TMP
THE BATH SUDDENLY TURNED SCALDING HOT!
BLB BLB
BLB
PAPA, I'M SORRY.
WAS IT YOU, RAN?
THEN I DON'T MIND.
JUST BE CARE-FUL.
Good girl.
YOU SURE IT'S OKAY, LORD ZEN?
HM?
GYAAAH
MY POND!
BLB
BLB
MY CARP!
BLB
MY TURTLES!
MUTTER MTTR
RAN...
STOP IT.
RAN, PLEASE.
NO.
I'M SO CLOSE!

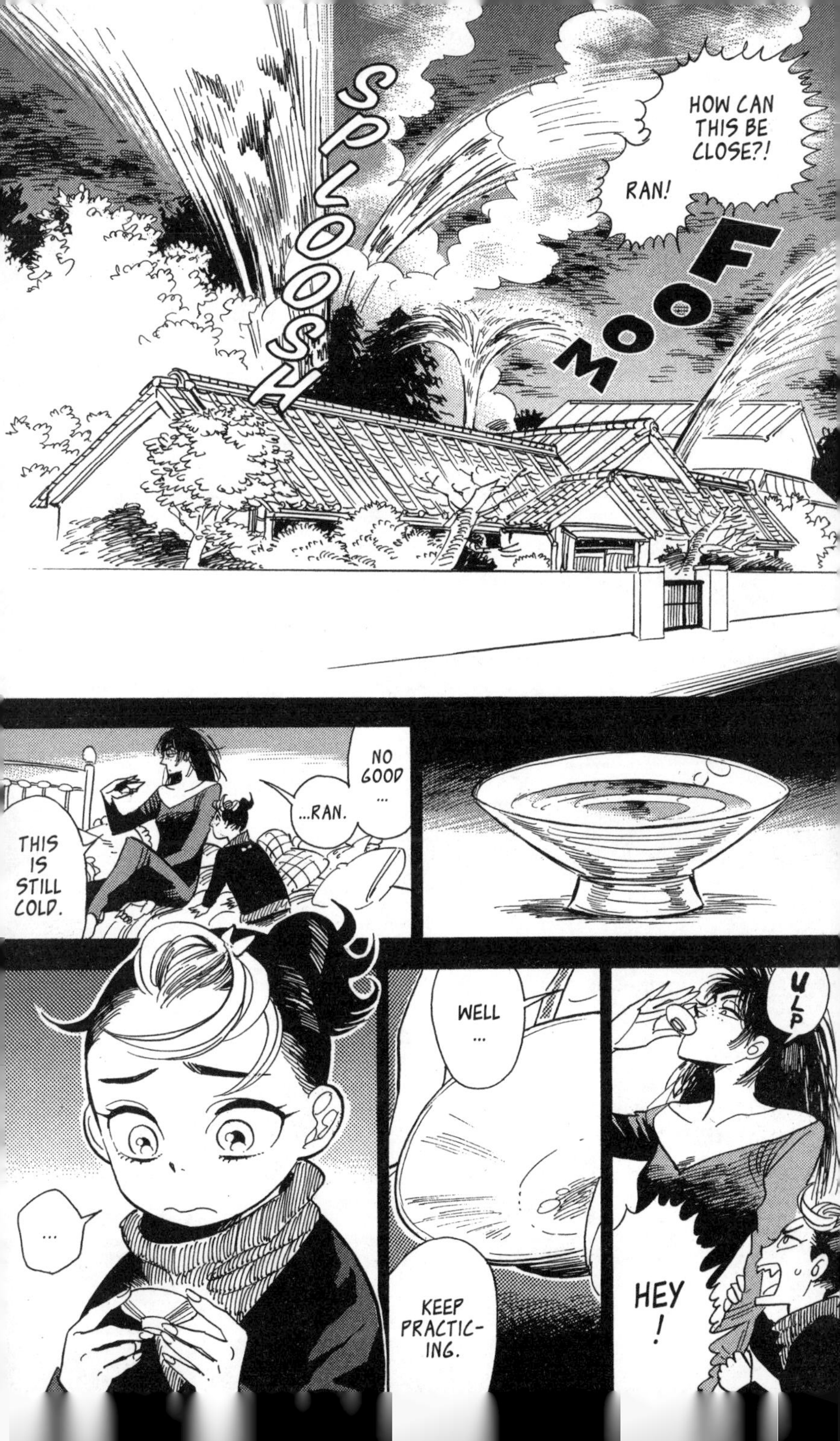
HOW CAN THIS BE CLOSE?!
RAN!
FOOM
SPLOOSH
NO GOOD ...
...RAN.
THIS IS STILL COLD.
ULP
HEY!
WELL ...
KEEP PRACTIC-ING.
...

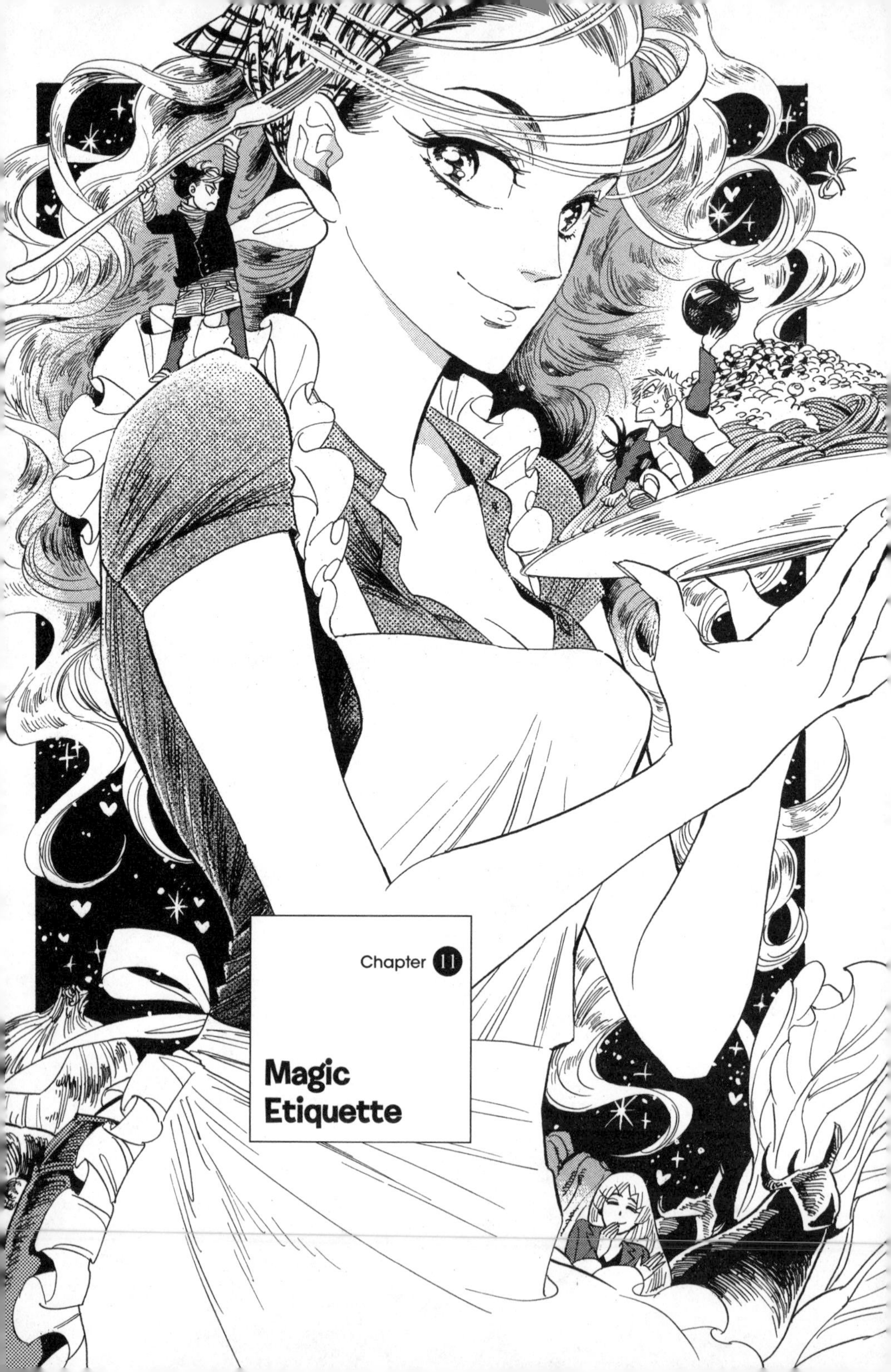

Chapter 11 Magic Etiquette

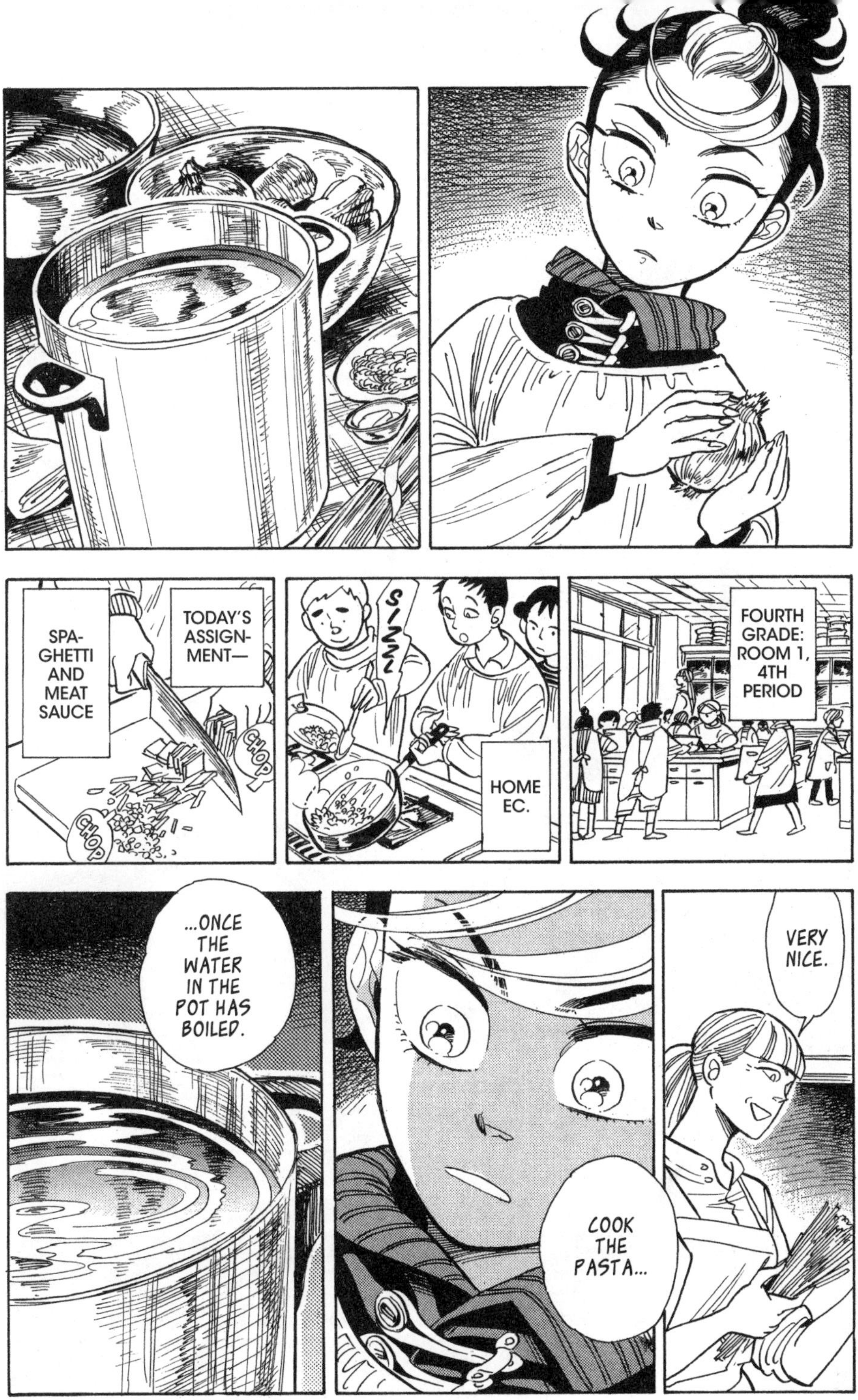
FOURTH GRADE: ROOM 1, 4TH PERIOD
SIZZZ
HOME EC.
TODAY'S ASSIGNMENT—
SPAGHETTI AND MEAT SAUCE
CHOP
CHOP
VERY NICE.
COOK THE PASTA...
...ONCE THE WATER IN THE POT HAS BOILED.

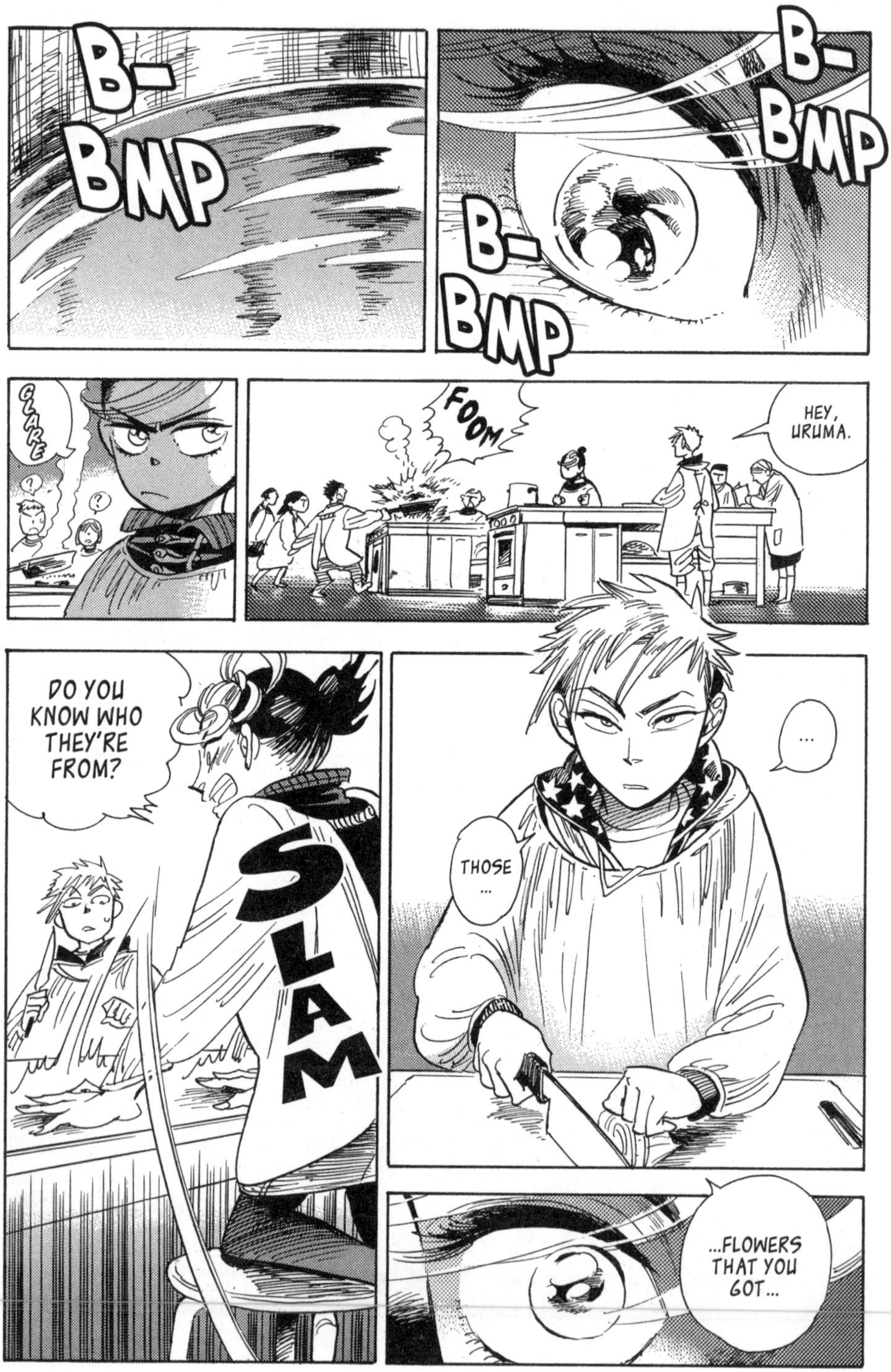
B-BMP
B-BMP
B-BMP
HEY, URUMA.
FOOM
GLARE
?
?
...
THOSE ...
DO YOU KNOW WHO THEY'RE FROM?
SLAM
...FLOWERS THAT YOU GOT...

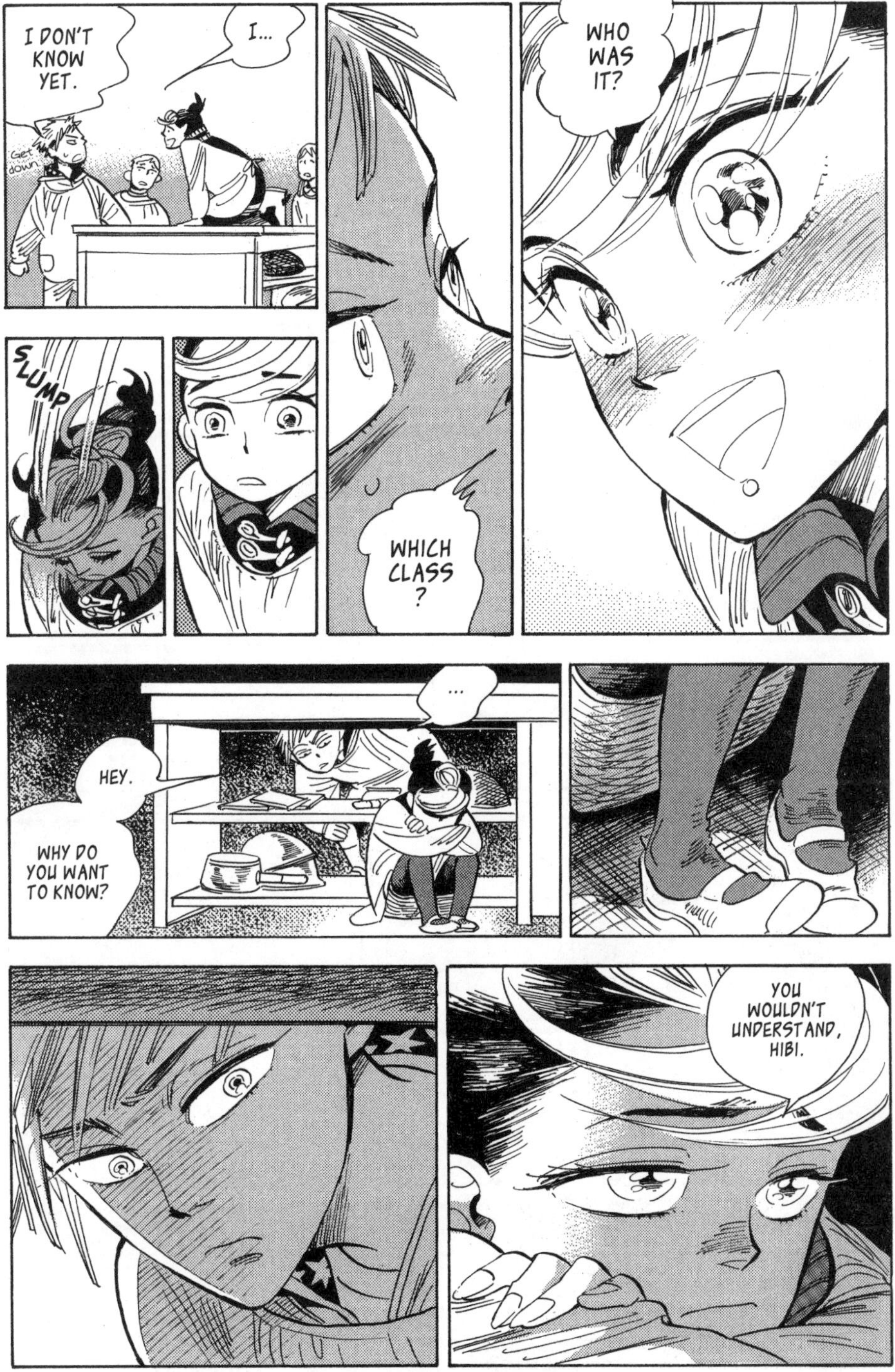
WHO WAS IT?
WHICH CLASS?
I...
I DON'T KNOW YET.
Get down.
SLUMP
...
HEY.
WHY DO YOU WANT TO KNOW?
YOU WOULDN'T UNDERSTAND, HIBI.

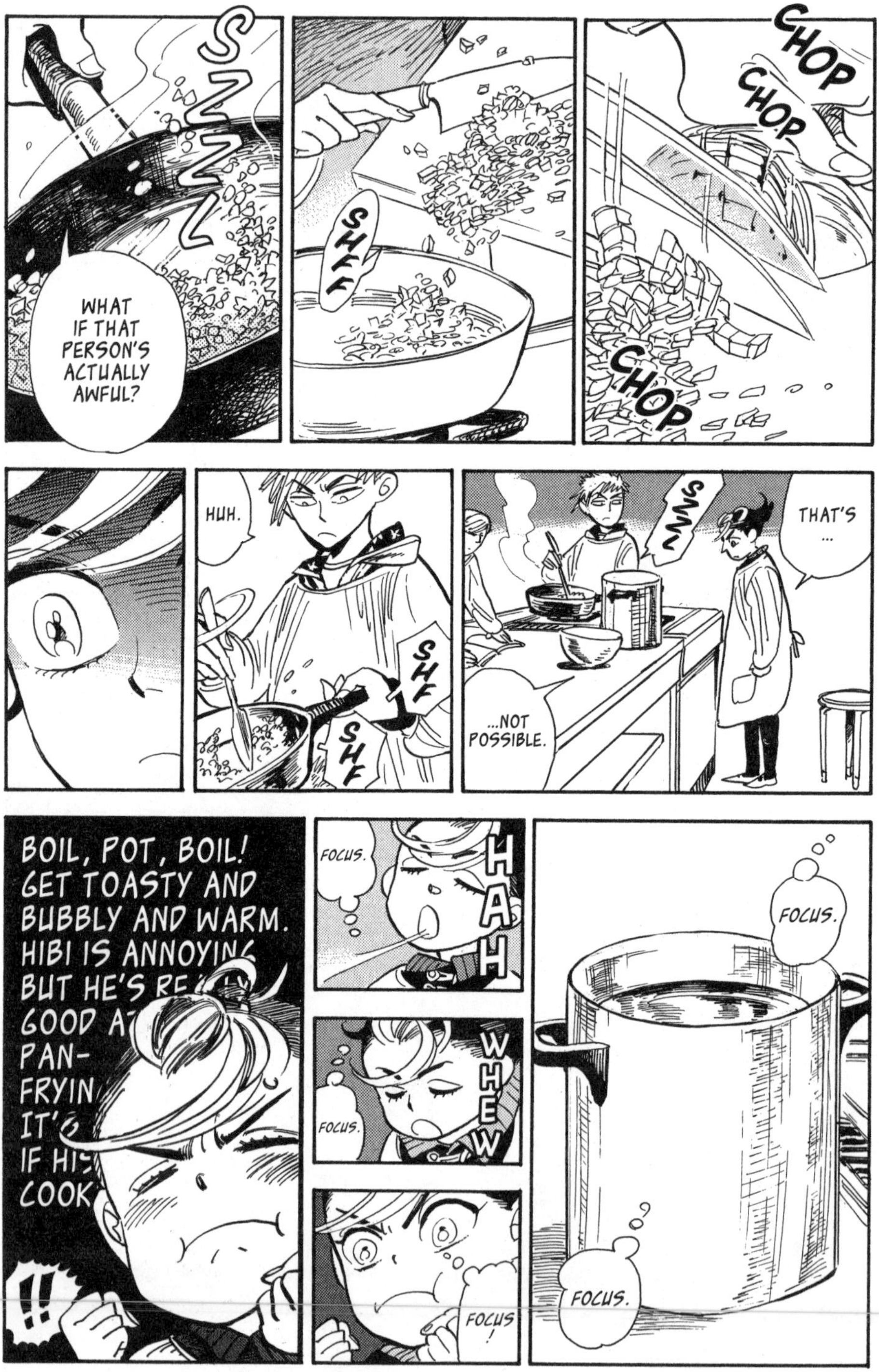
CHOP
CHOP
CHOP
SHFF
SZZZ
WHAT IF THAT PERSON'S ACTUALLY AWFUL?
THAT'S ...
SNNN
...NOT POSSIBLE.
HUH.
SHF
SHF
FOCUS.
FOCUS.
FOCUS.
HAH
FOCUS.
WHEW
FOCUS!
BOIL, POT, BOIL! GET TOASTY AND BUBBLY AND WARM. HIBI IS ANNOYIN BUT HE'S RE GOOD A PAN- FRYIN IT'S IF HIS COOK
!!

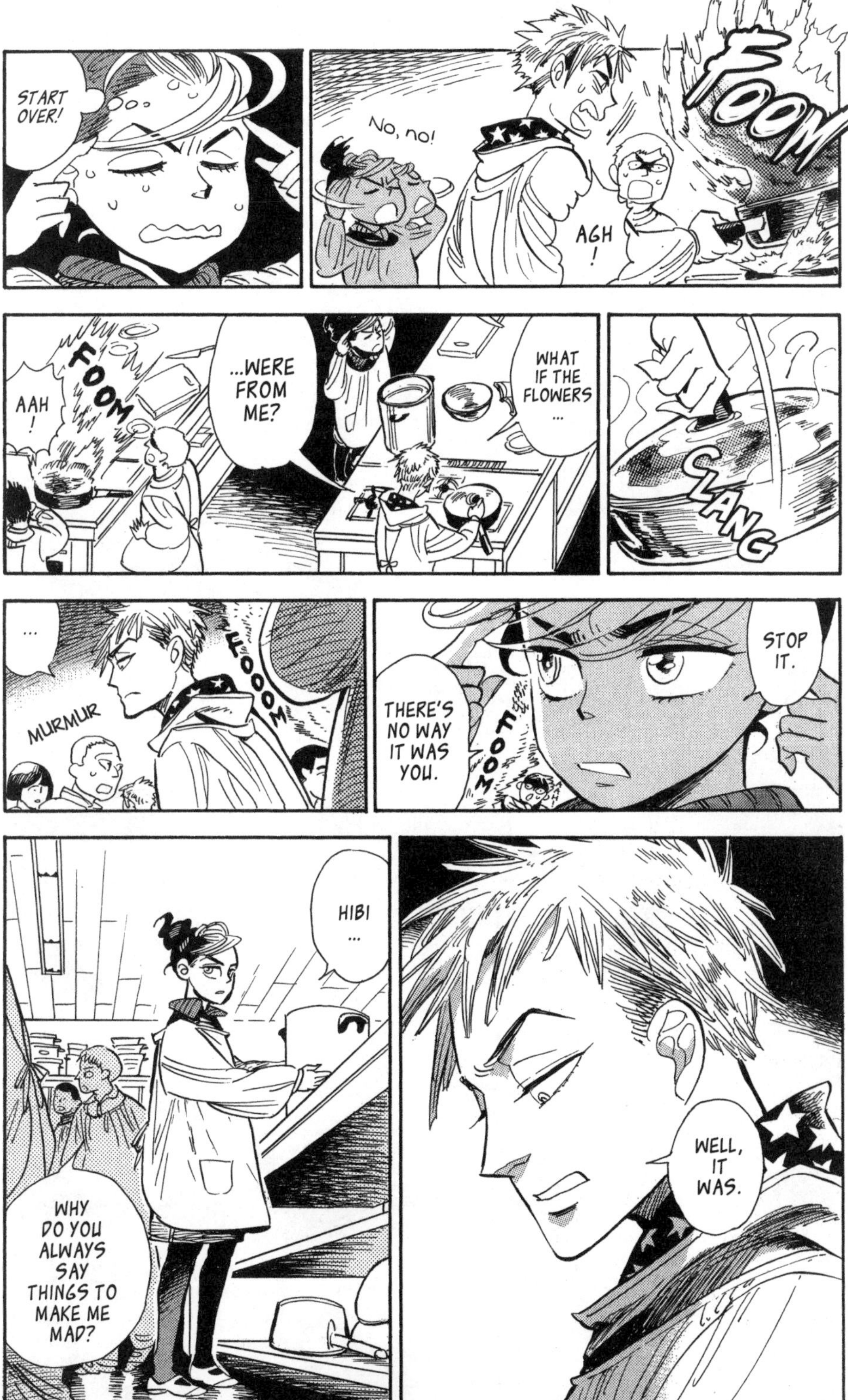
FOOM
No, no!
AGH!
START OVER!
CLANG
WHAT IF THE FLOWERS...
...WERE FROM ME?
FOOM
AAH!
STOP IT.
THERE'S NO WAY IT WAS YOU.
FOOM
FOOOOM
...
MURMUR
WELL, IT WAS.
HIBI...
WHY DO YOU ALWAYS SAY THINGS TO MAKE ME MAD?

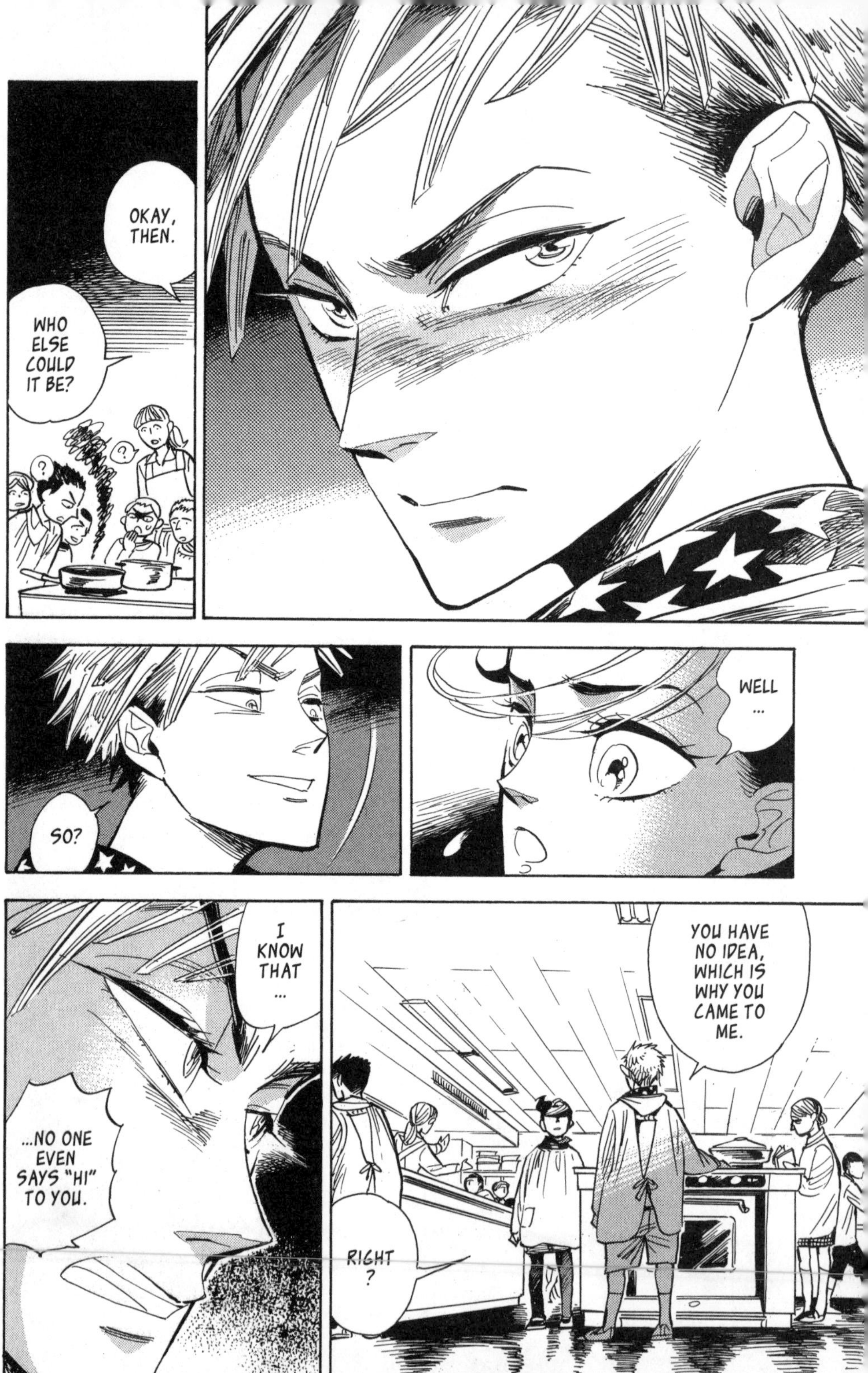
OKAY, THEN.
WHO ELSE COULD IT BE?
WELL ...
SO?
YOU HAVE NO IDEA, WHICH IS WHY YOU CAME TO ME.
RIGHT?
I KNOW THAT ...
...NO ONE EVEN SAYS "HI" TO YOU.

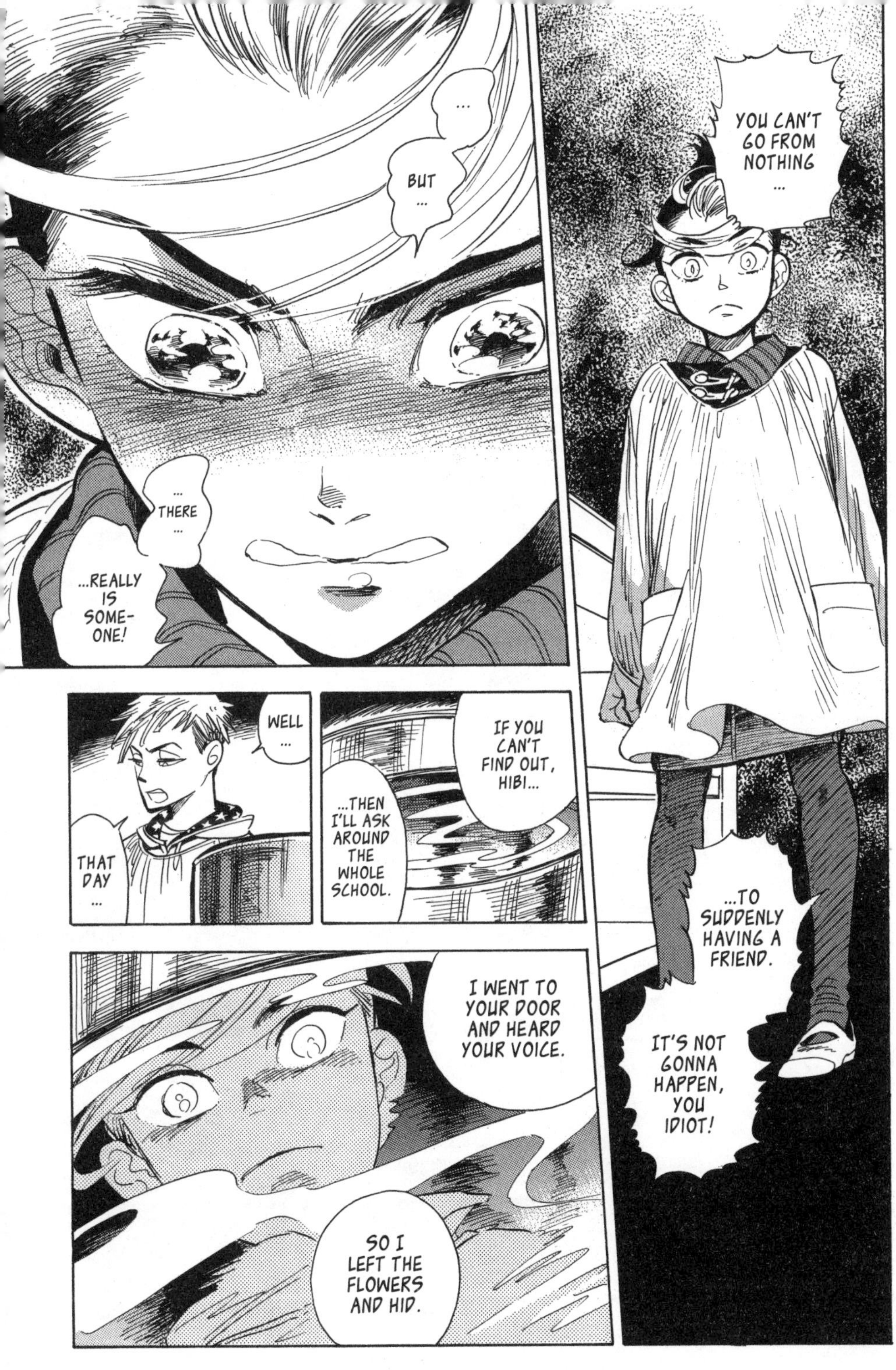
YOU CAN'T GO FROM NOTHING ...
...TO SUDDENLY HAVING A FRIEND.
IT'S NOT GONNA HAPPEN, YOU IDIOT!
...
BUT ...
... THERE ...
...REALLY IS SOME-ONE!
IF YOU CAN'T FIND OUT, HIBI...
...THEN I'LL ASK AROUND THE WHOLE SCHOOL.
WELL ...
THAT DAY ...
I WENT TO YOUR DOOR AND HEARD YOUR VOICE.
SO I LEFT THE FLOWERS AND HID.

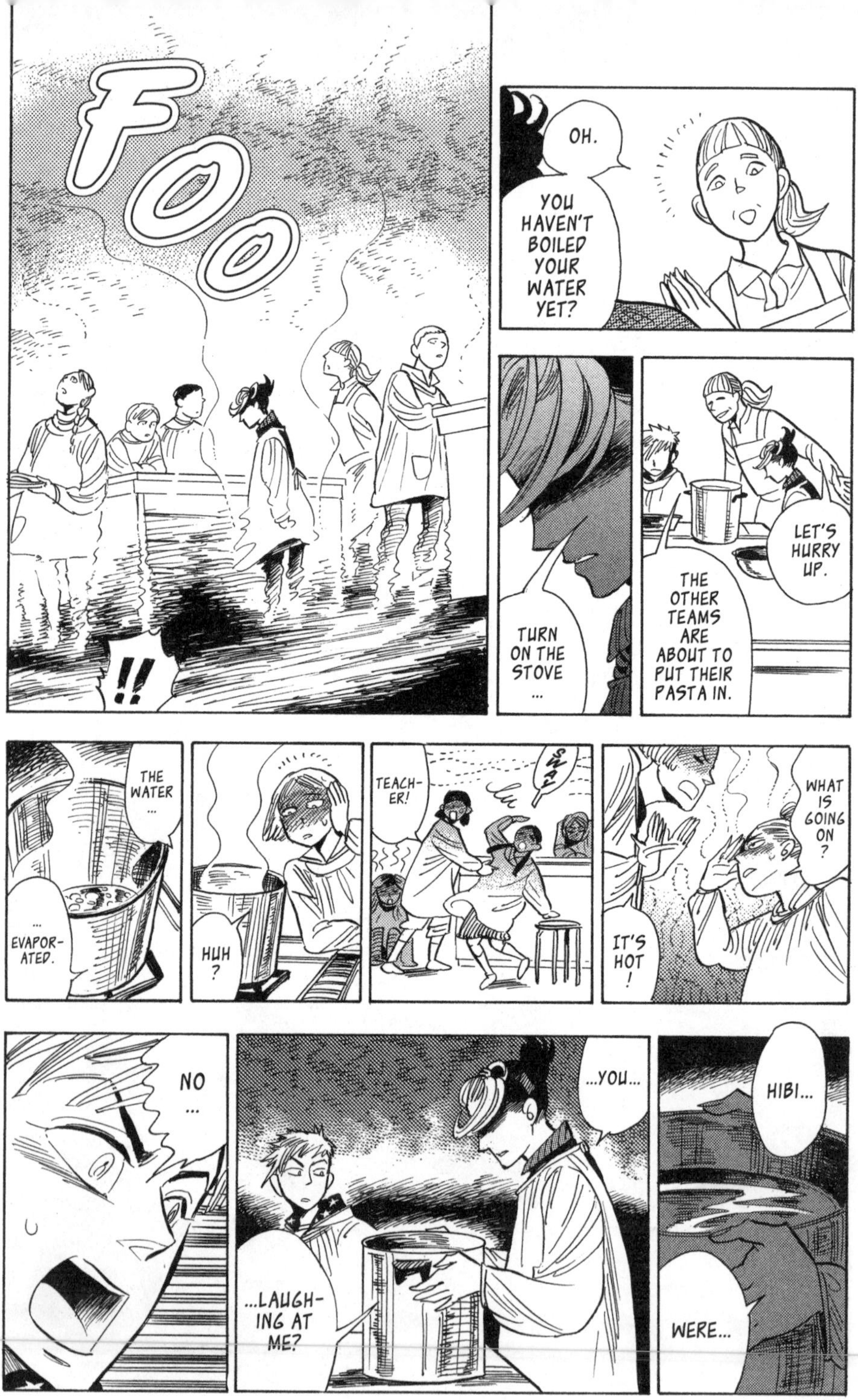
OH.
YOU HAVEN'T BOILED YOUR WATER YET?
LET'S HURRY UP.
THE OTHER TEAMS ARE ABOUT TO PUT THEIR PASTA IN.
TURN ON THE STOVE ...
FOO
!!
WHAT IS GOING ON?
IT'S HOT!
SWAY
TEACHER!
HUH?
THE WATER ...
... EVAPORATED.
HIBI...
WERE...
...YOU...
...LAUGHING AT ME?
NO ...

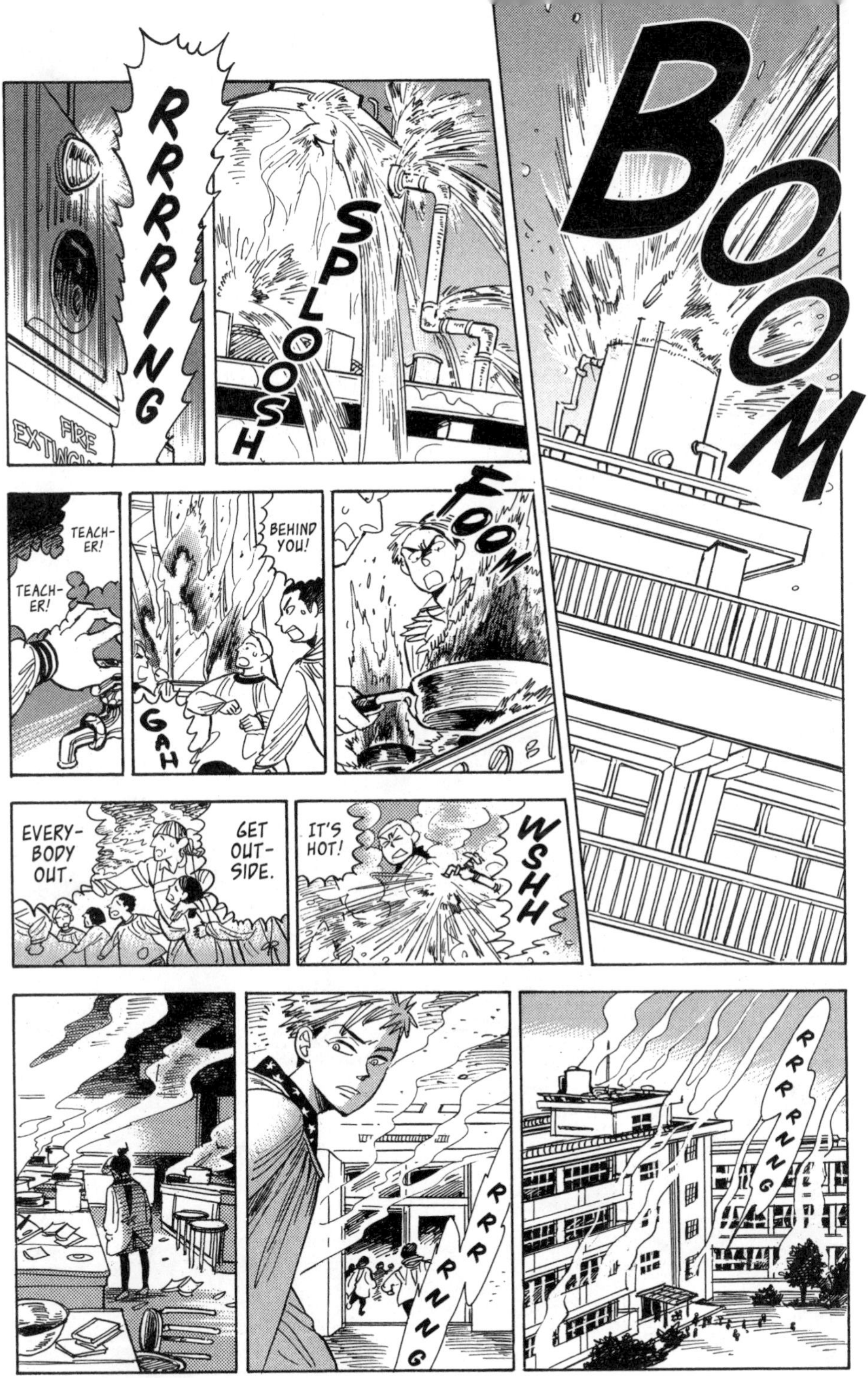
BOOOM
SPLOOOSH
RRRRRING
FIRE
FOOOM
BEHIND YOU!
GAH
TEACHER!
TEACHER!
WSHH
IT'S HOT!
GET OUTSIDE.
EVERYBODY OUT.
RRRRNNG
RRRRNNG

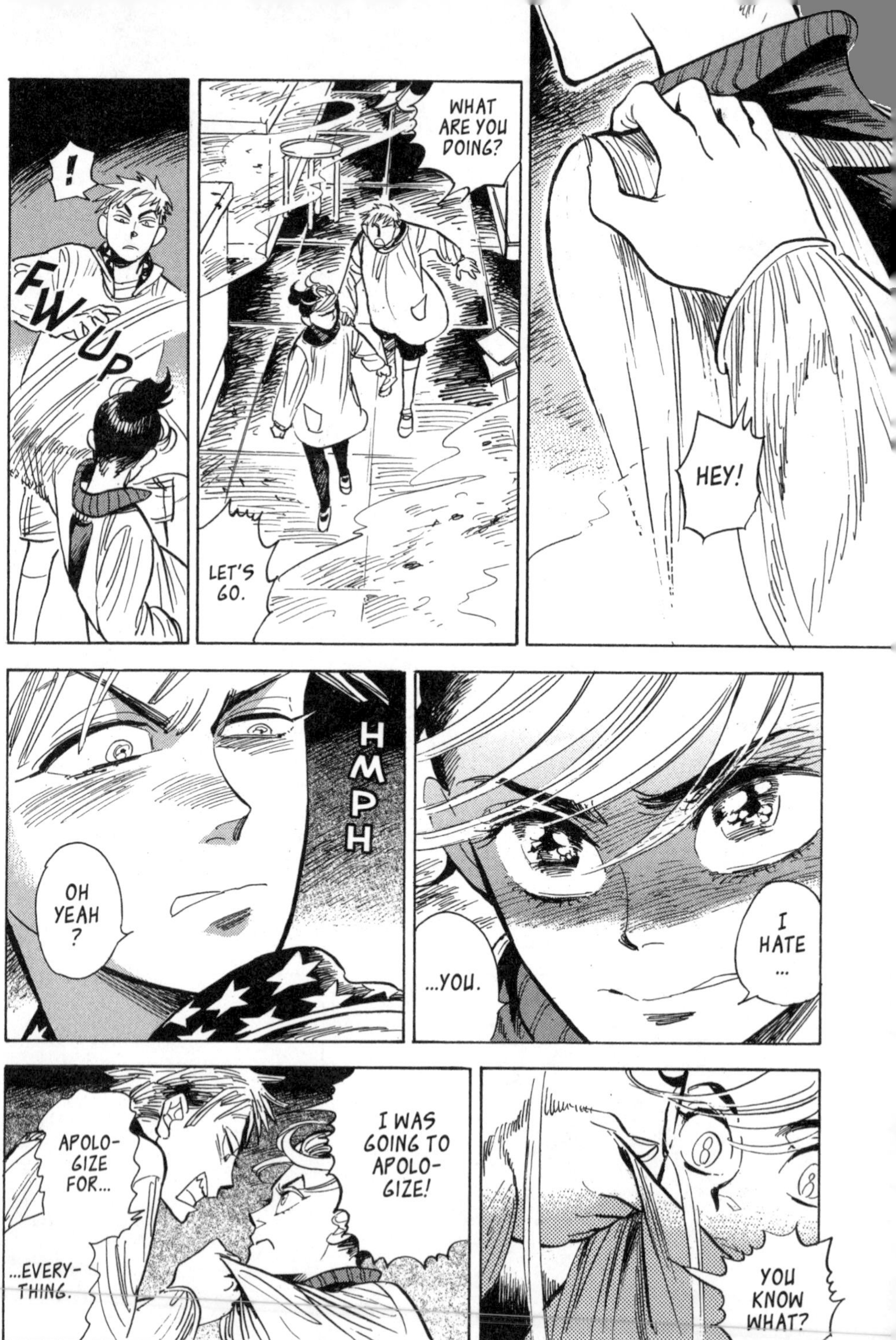
HEY!
WHAT ARE YOU DOING?
LET'S GO.
!
FWUP
I HATE...
...YOU.
HMPH
OH YEAH?
YOU KNOW WHAT?
I WAS GOING TO APOLOGIZE!
APOLOGIZE FOR...
...EVERYTHING.

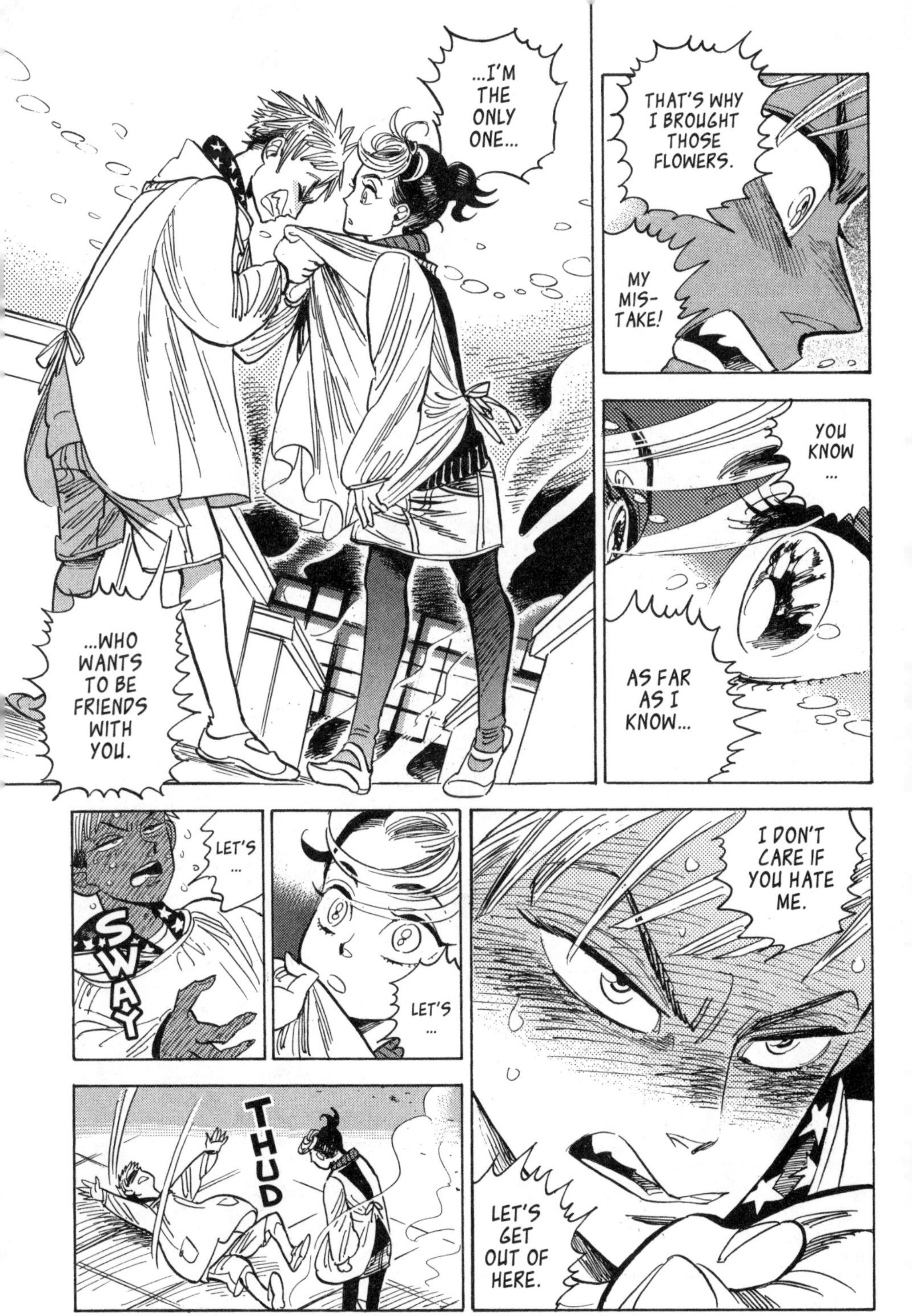
THAT'S WHY I BROUGHT THOSE FLOWERS.
MY MISTAKE!
YOU KNOW ...
AS FAR AS I KNOW...
...I'M THE ONLY ONE...
...WHO WANTS TO BE FRIENDS WITH YOU.
I DON'T CARE IF YOU HATE ME.
LET'S GET OUT OF HERE.
LET'S ...
LET'S ...
SWAY
THUD

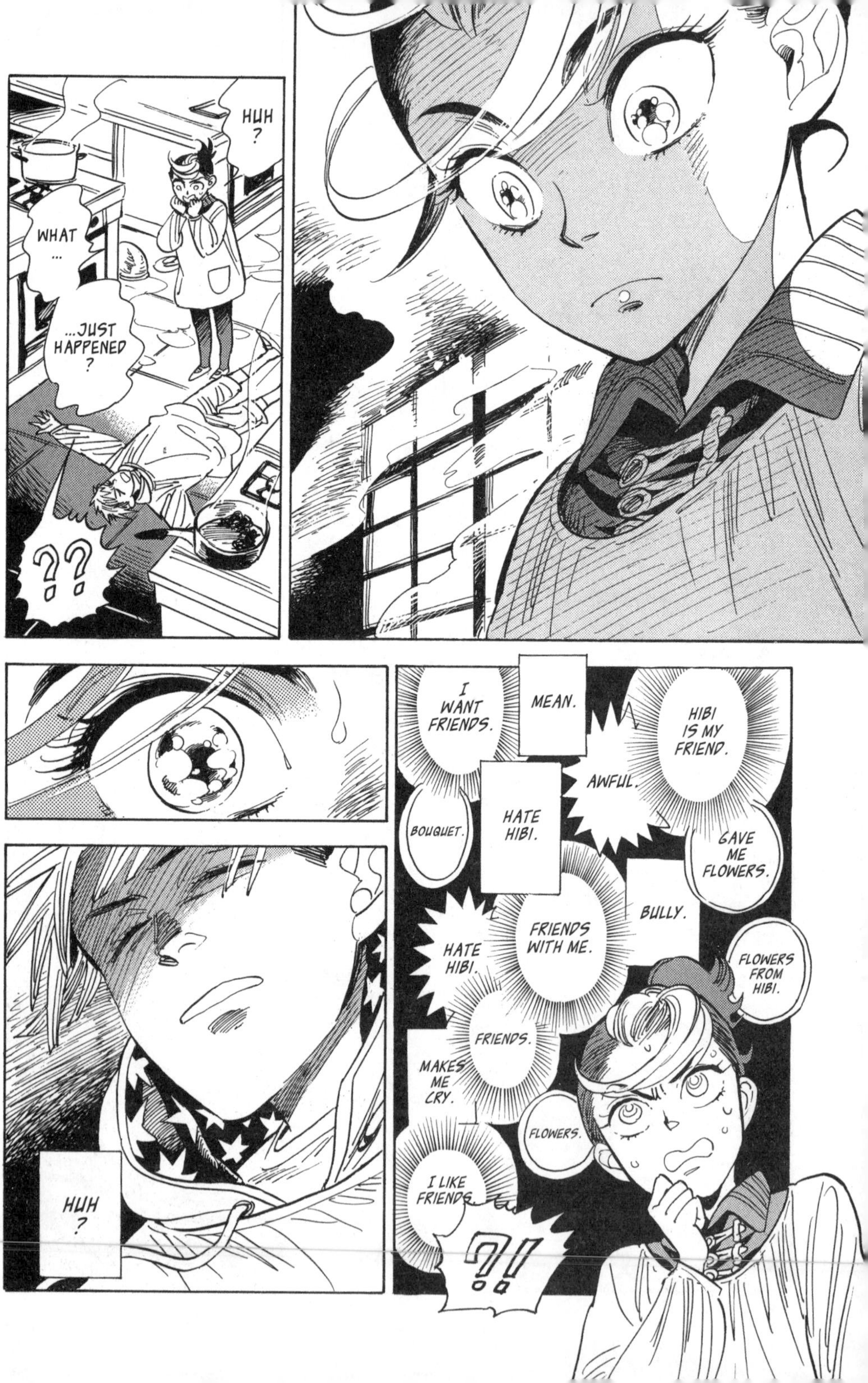
HUH ?
WHAT ...
...JUST HAPPENED ?
??
HIBI IS MY FRIEND.
MEAN.
I WANT FRIENDS.
AWFUL.
GAVE ME FLOWERS.
HATE HIBI.
BOUQUET.
BULLY.
FLOWERS FROM HIBI.
FRIENDS WITH ME.
HATE HIBI.
FRIENDS.
MAKES ME CRY.
FLOWERS.
I LIKE FRIENDS.
?!
HUH ?

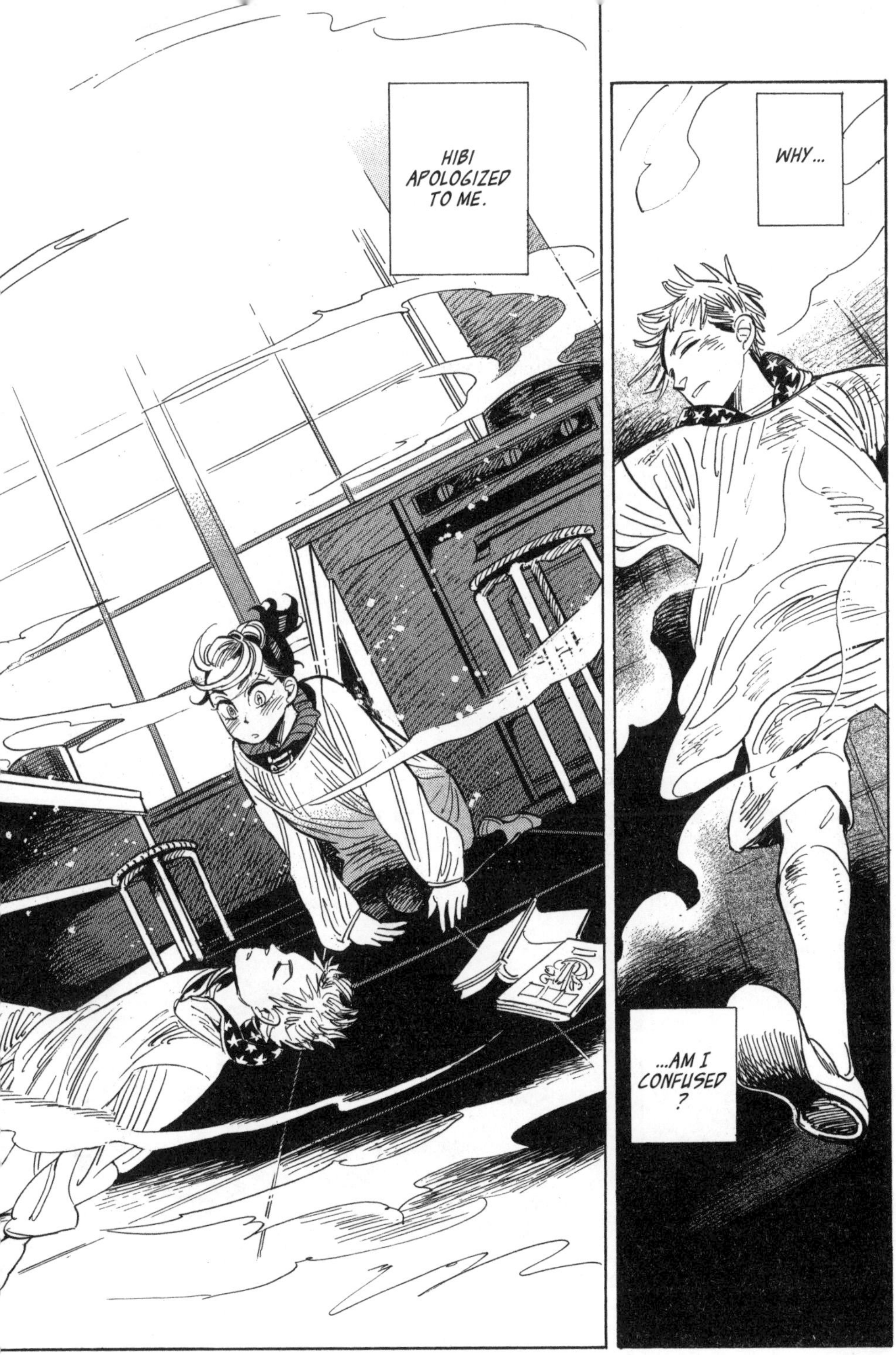
WHY...
...AM I CONFUSED ?
HIBI APOLOGIZED TO ME.

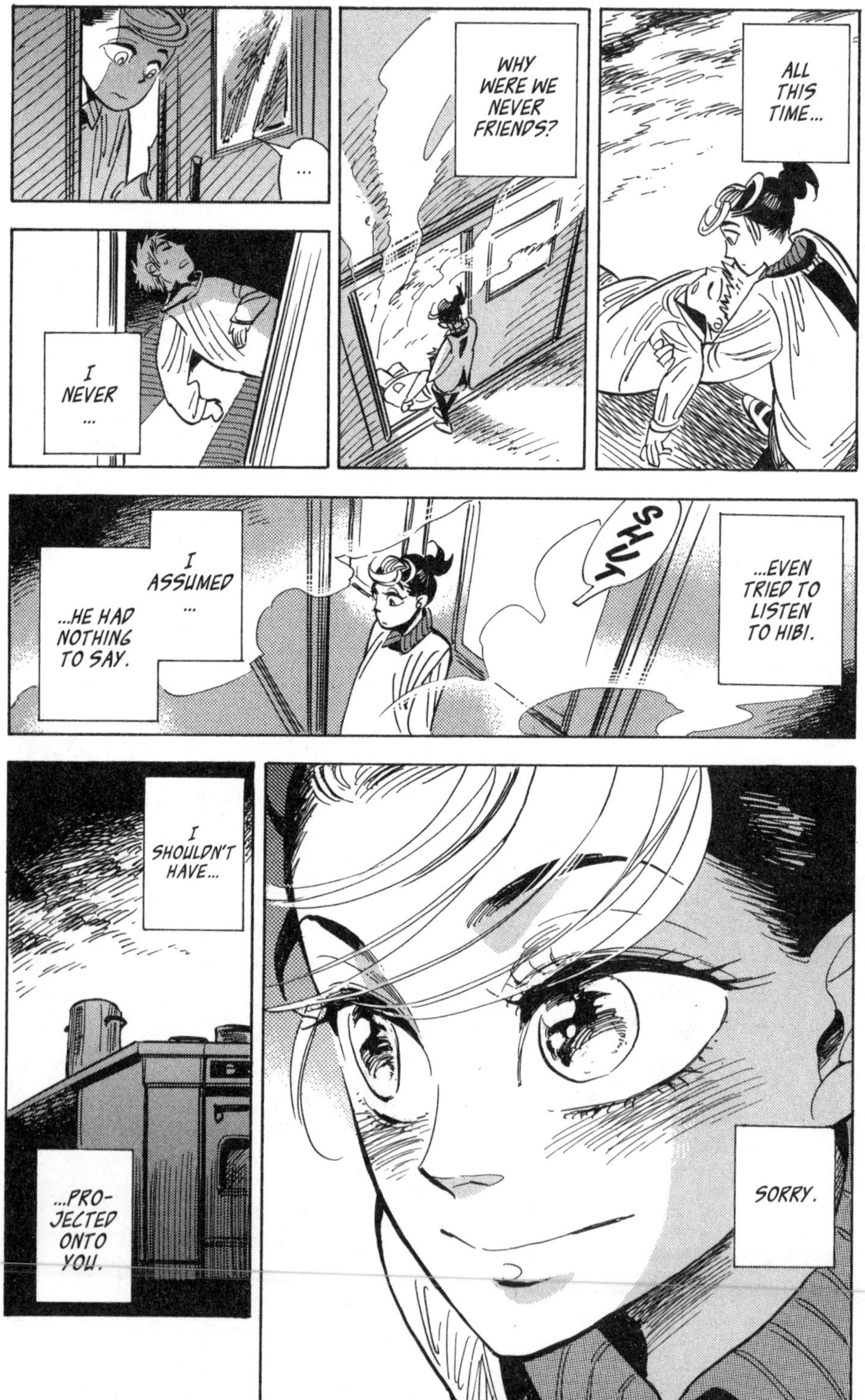
ALL THIS TIME...
WHY WERE WE NEVER FRIENDS?
...
I NEVER ...
...EVEN TRIED TO LISTEN TO HIBI.
SHUT
I ASSUMED ...
...HE HAD NOTHING TO SAY.
SORRY.
I SHOULDN'T HAVE...
...PRO-JECTED ONTO YOU.

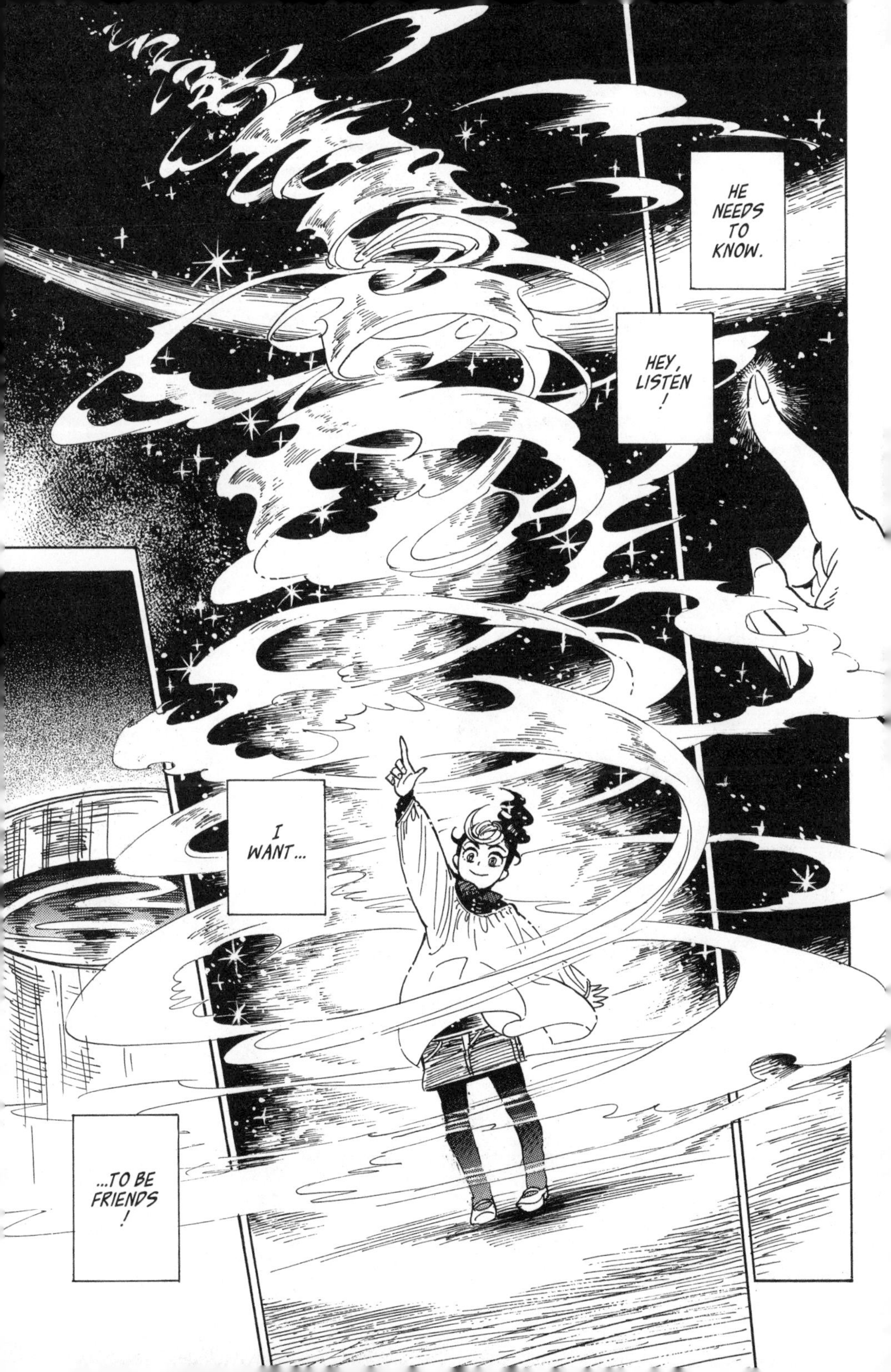
HE NEEDS TO KNOW.
HEY, LISTEN!
I WANT...
...TO BE FRIENDS!

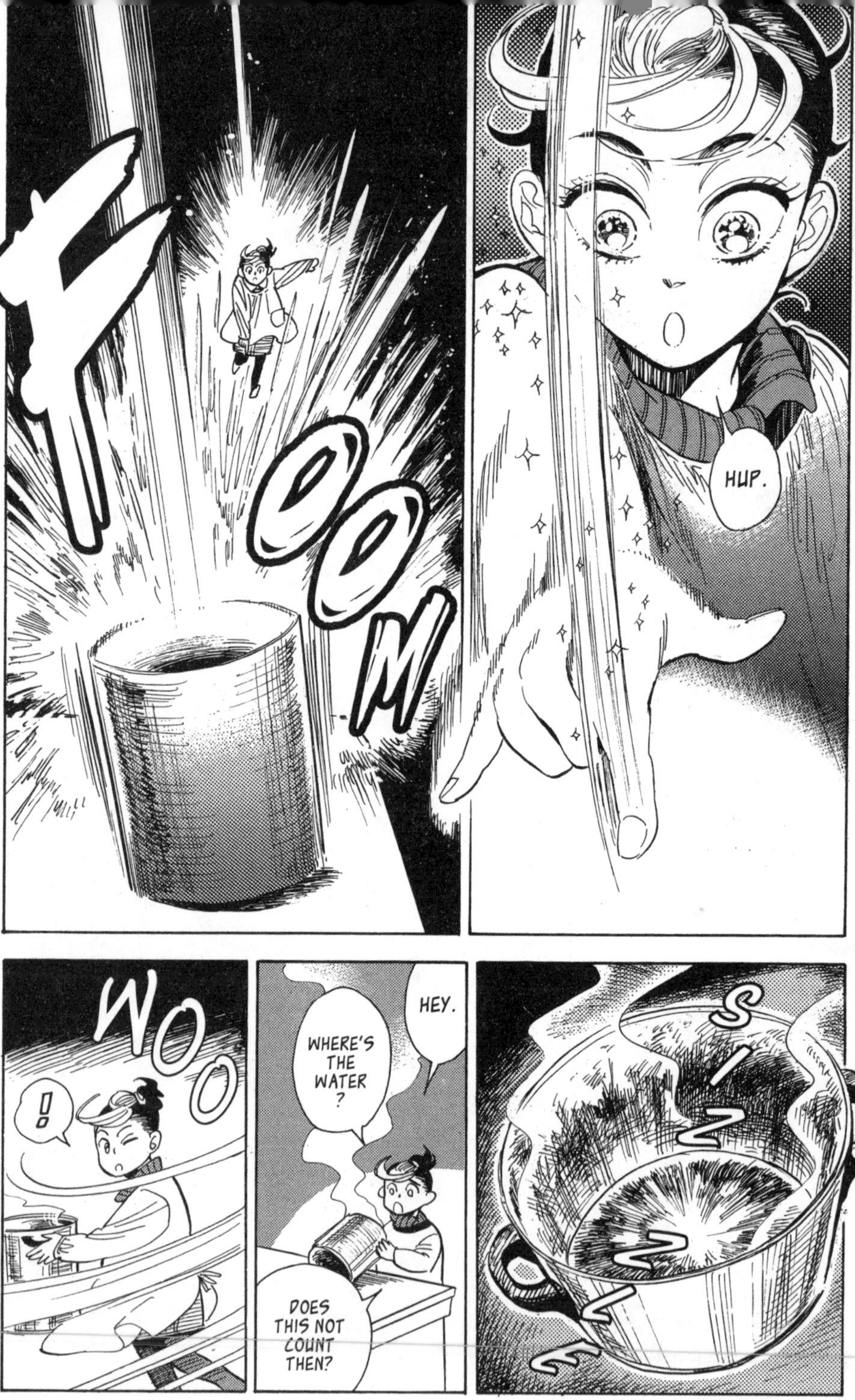
HUP.
FOOOM
SIZZLE
HEY.
WHERE'S THE WATER?
DOES THIS NOT COUNT THEN?
WOOO
!

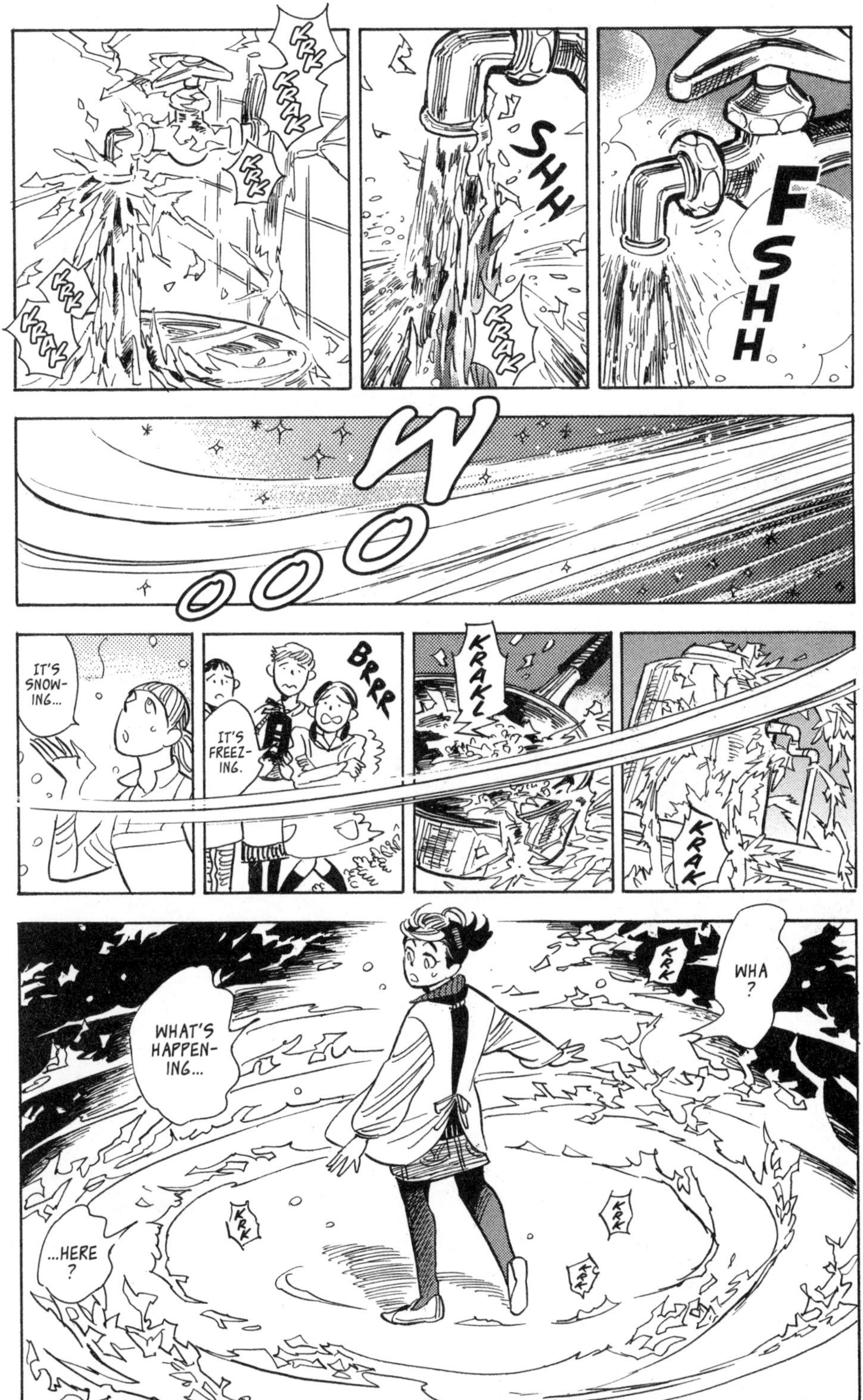
FSHH
SHH
KRAK
KRK KRAK
KRK
KRK KRAK
WOOOO
KRAK
KRAK!
BRRR
IT'S FREEZ-ING.
IT'S SNOW-ING...
KRK
WHA?
WHAT'S HAPPEN-ING...
KRK
KRK
KRK
...HERE?

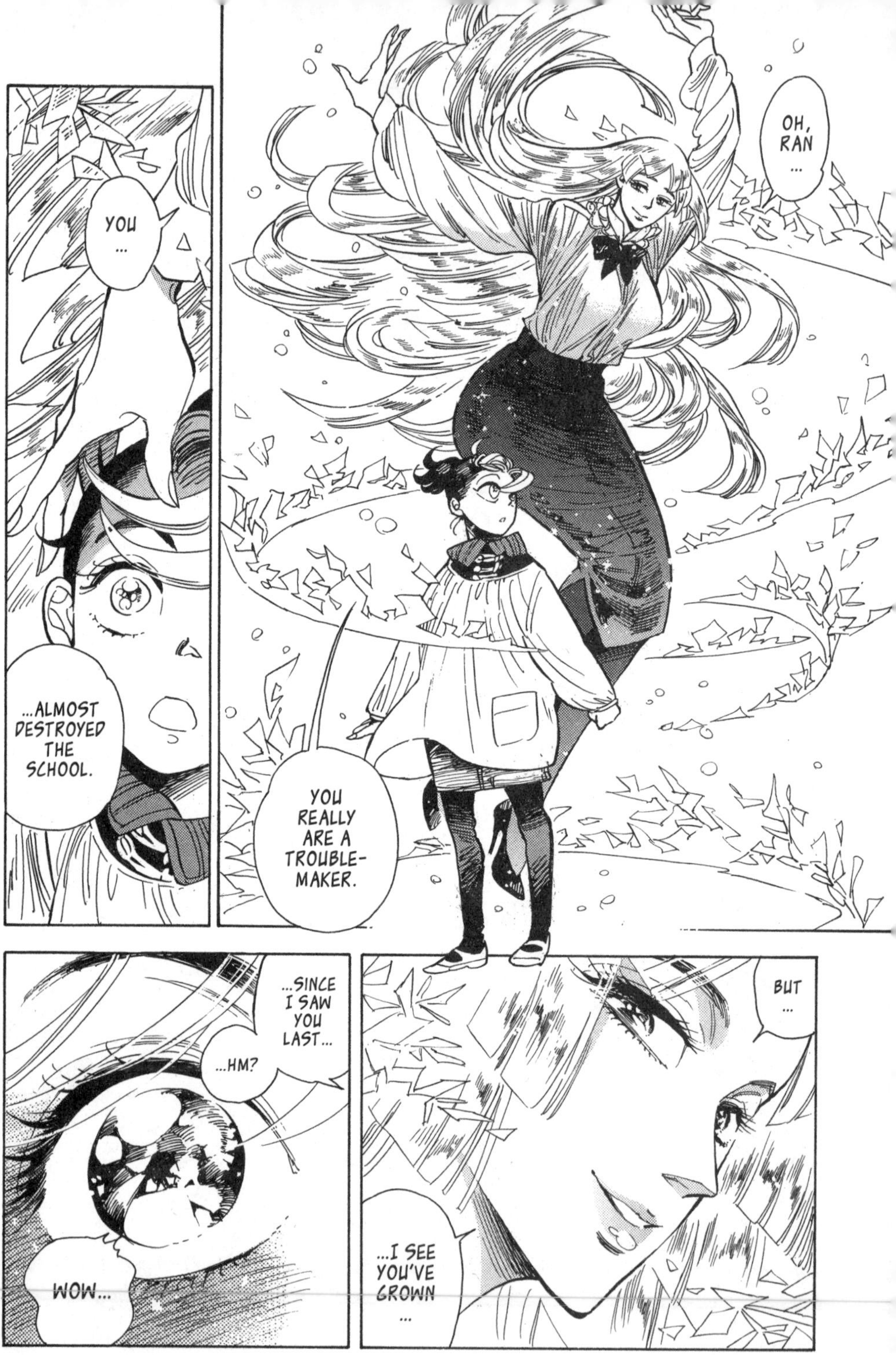
OH, RAN ...
YOU REALLY ARE A TROUBLE-MAKER.
YOU ...
...ALMOST DESTROYED THE SCHOOL.
BUT ...
...I SEE YOU'VE GROWN ...
...SINCE I SAW YOU LAST...
...HM?
WOW...

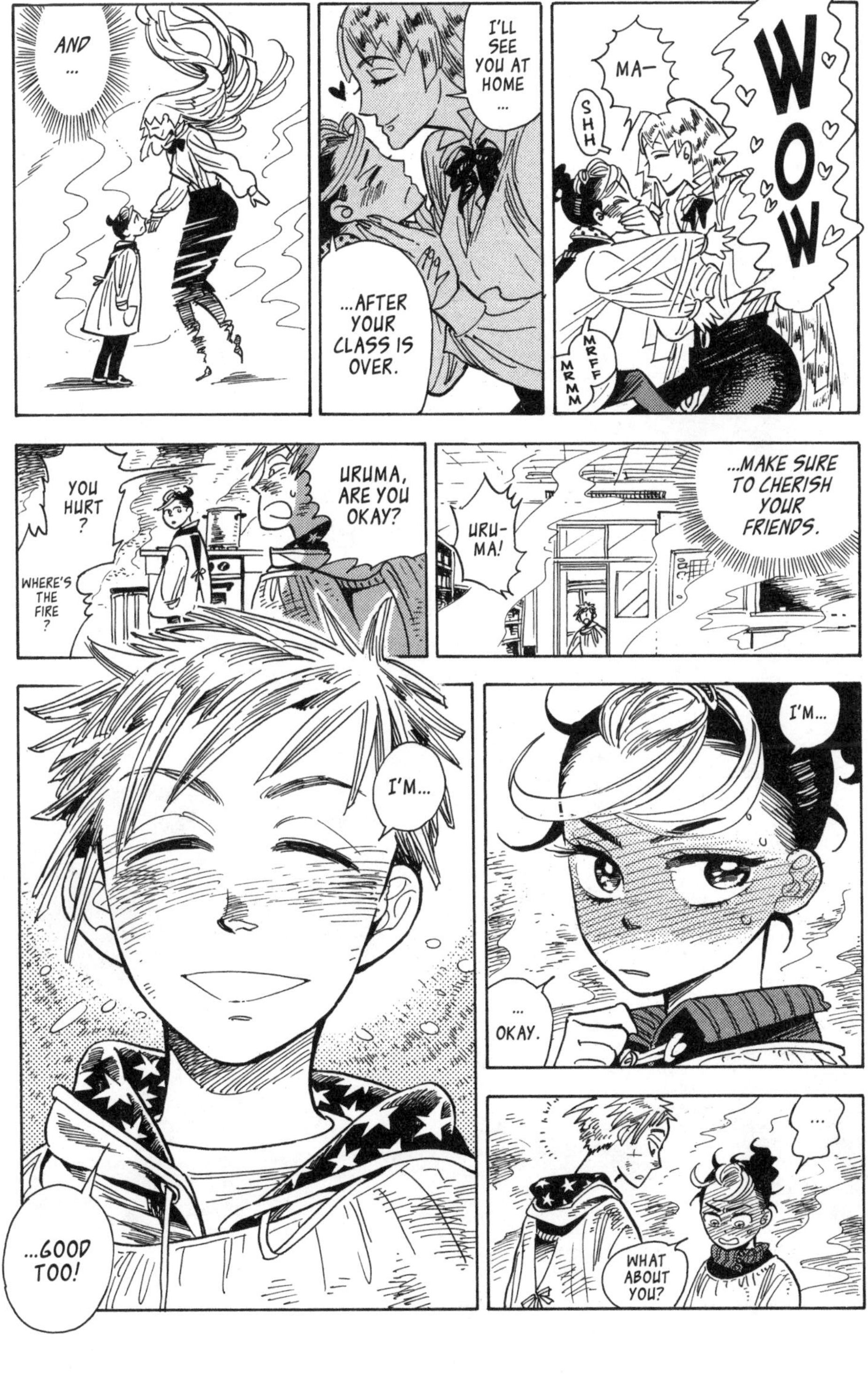
MA—
SHH
WOW
MRFF
MRMM
I'LL SEE YOU AT HOME ...
...AFTER YOUR CLASS IS OVER.
AND ...
...MAKE SURE TO CHERISH YOUR FRIENDS.
URU-MA!
URUMA, ARE YOU OKAY?
YOU HURT?
WHERE'S THE FIRE?
I'M...
... OKAY.
...
WHAT ABOUT YOU?
I'M...
...GOOD TOO!

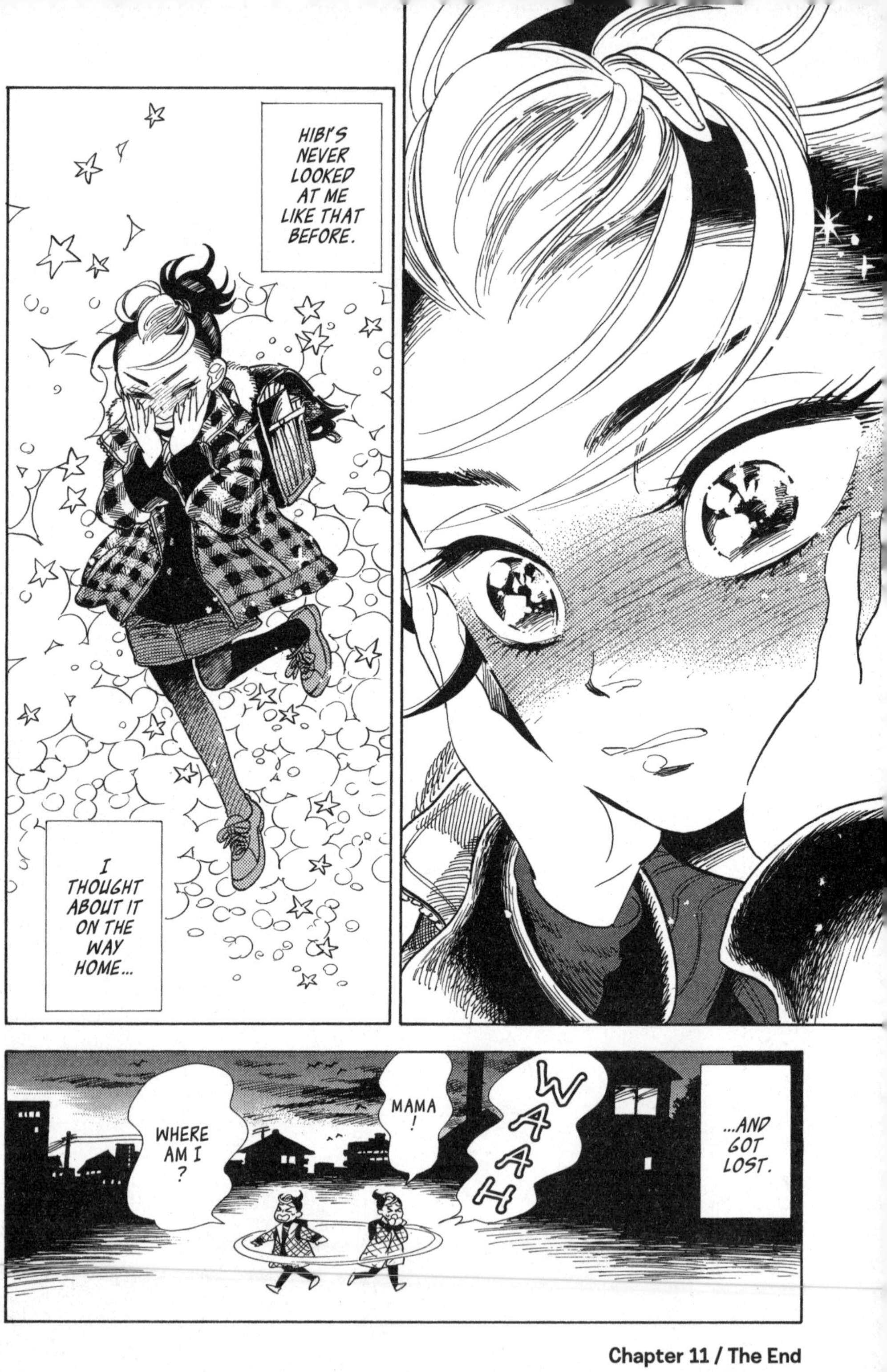
HIBI'S NEVER LOOKED AT ME LIKE THAT BEFORE.
I THOUGHT ABOUT IT ON THE WAY HOME...
...AND GOT LOST.
WAAH
MAMA!
WHERE AM I?

Chapter 11 / The End

Ran and the Gray World

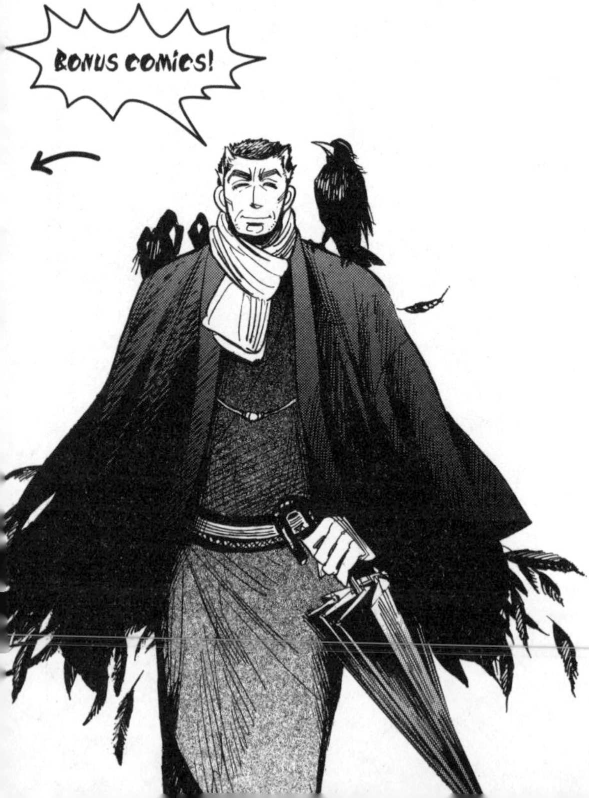
BONUS COMICS!

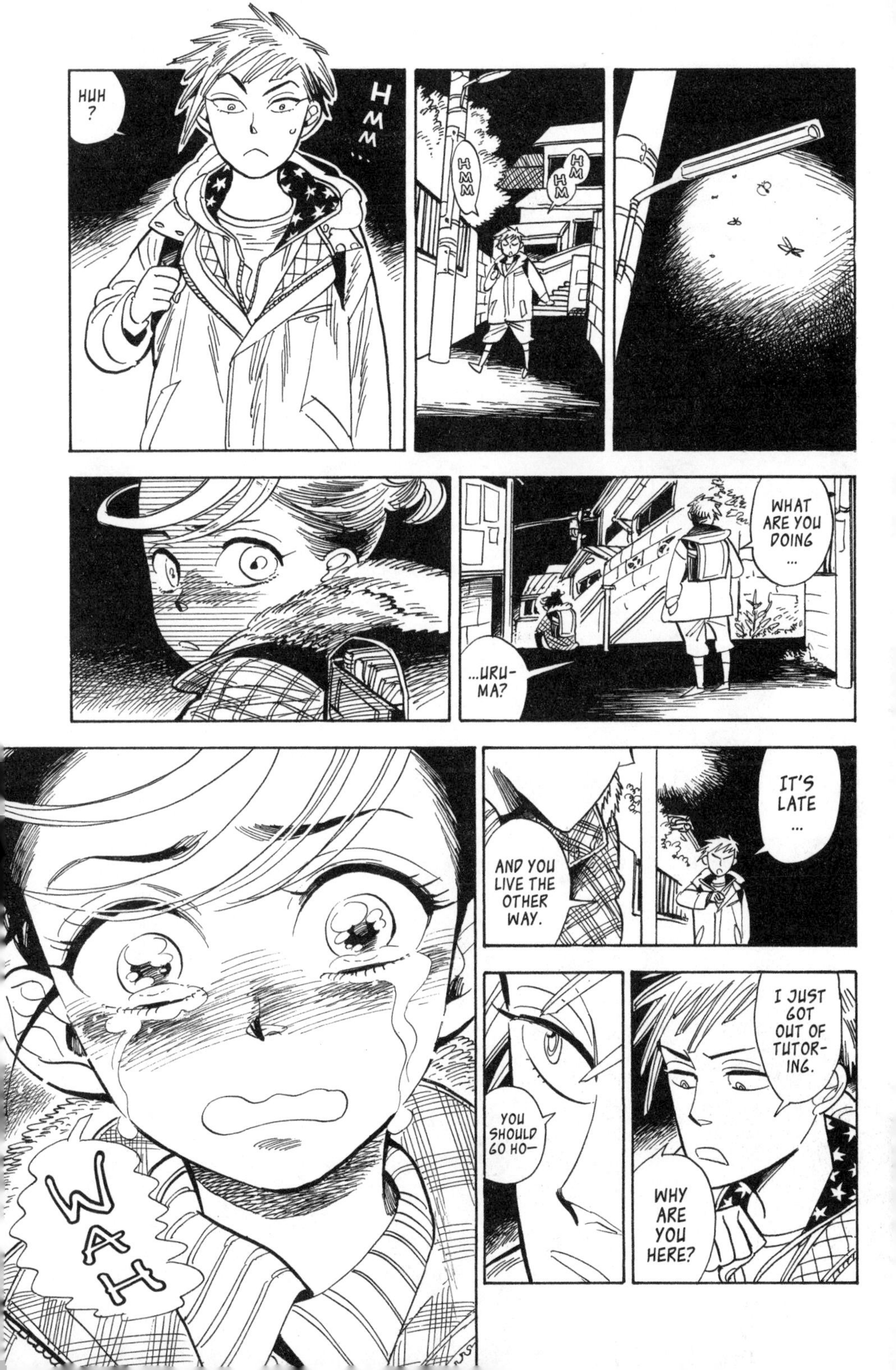
HMM...
HUH?
HM HM
HMM
WHAT ARE YOU DOING ...
...URU-MA?
IT'S LATE ...
AND YOU LIVE THE OTHER WAY.
I JUST GOT OUT OF TUTOR-ING.
WHY ARE YOU HERE?
YOU SHOULD GO HO—
WAH

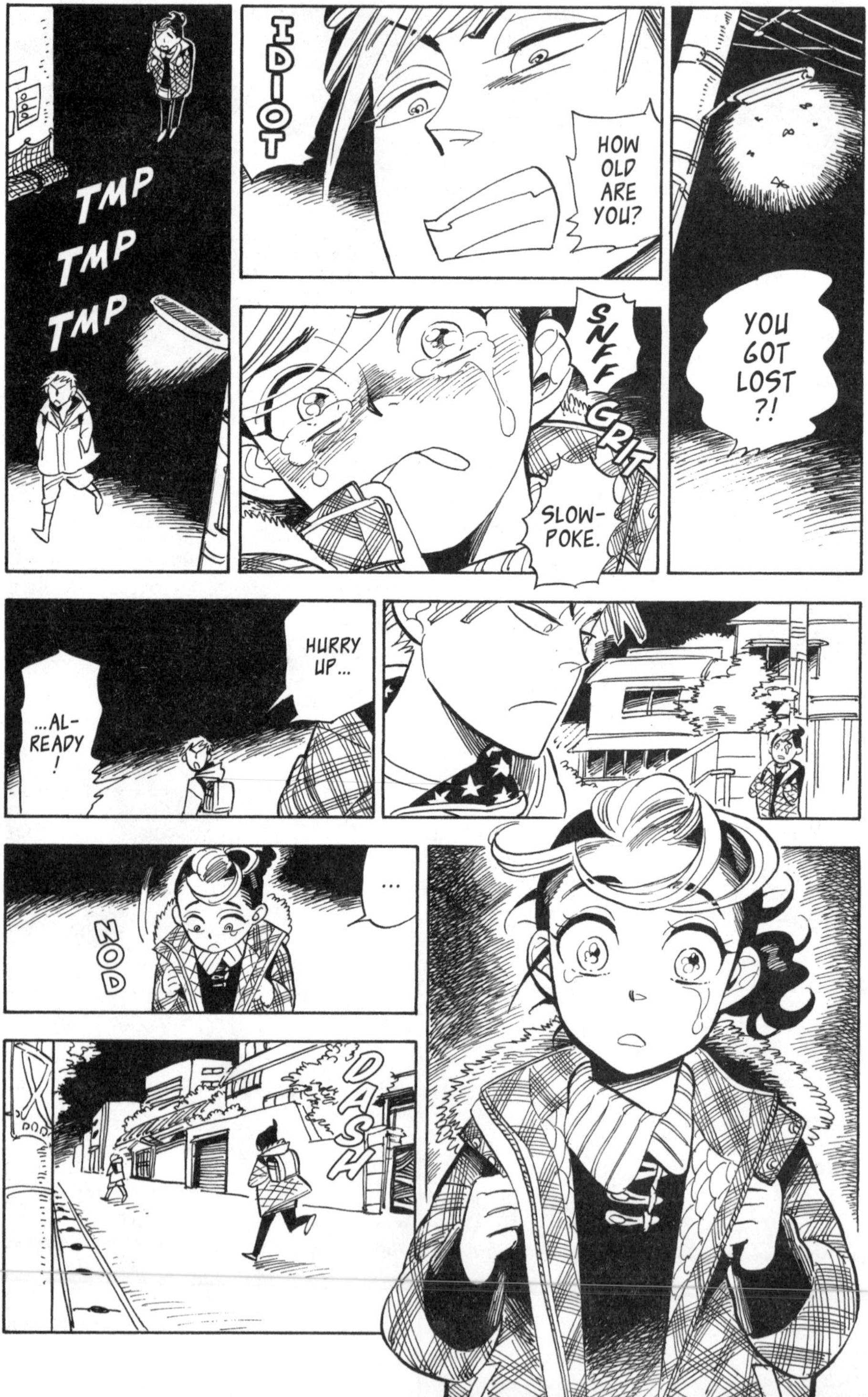

YOU GOT LOST ?!
IDIOT
HOW OLD ARE YOU?
SNFF
GRIT
SLOW-POKE.
TMP TMP TMP
HURRY UP...
...AL-READY!
...
NOD
DASH

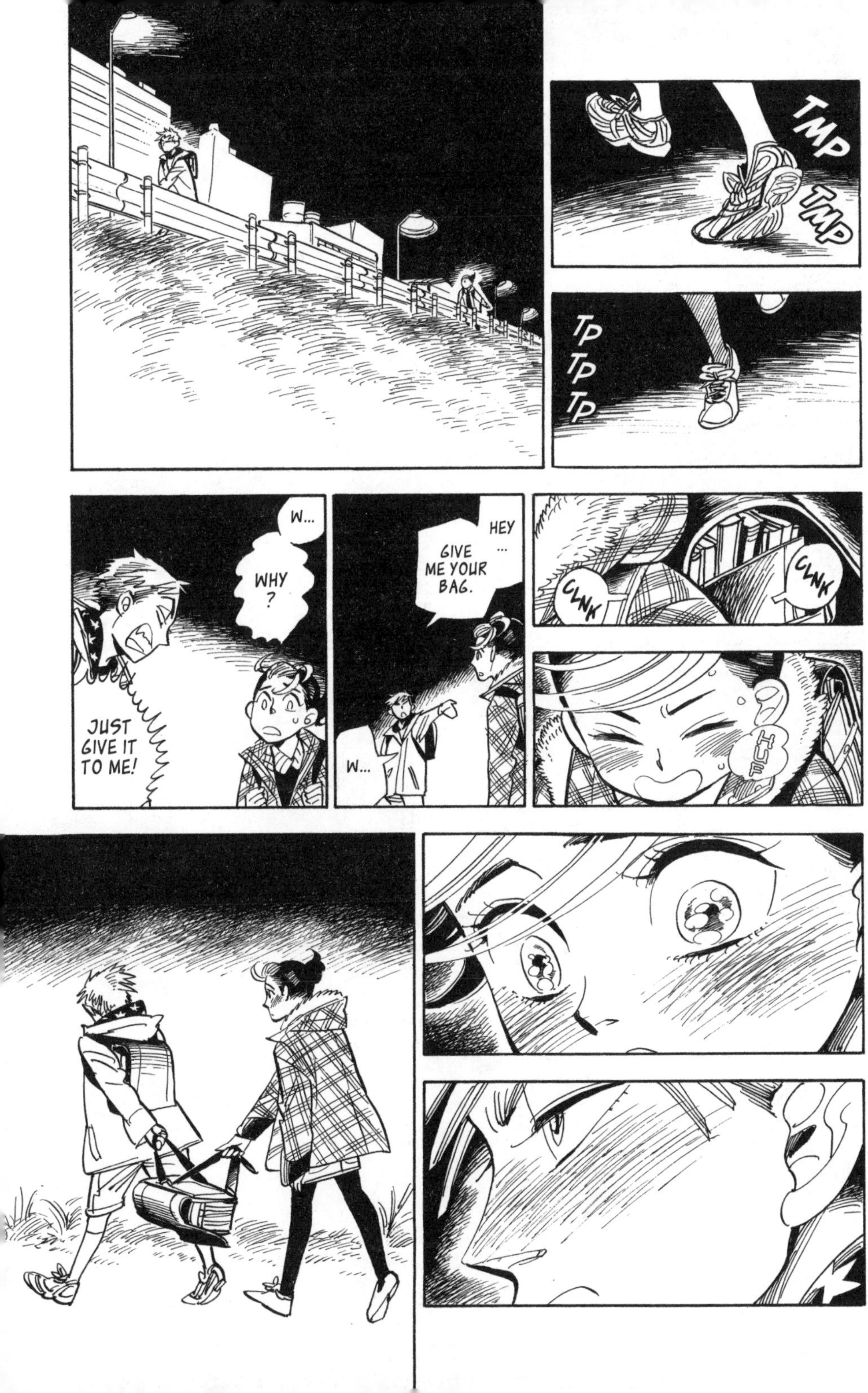
TMP
TMP
TP
TP
TP
CLNK
CLNK
HUF
HEY ...
GIVE ME YOUR BAG.
W...
W...
WHY ?
JUST GIVE IT TO ME!

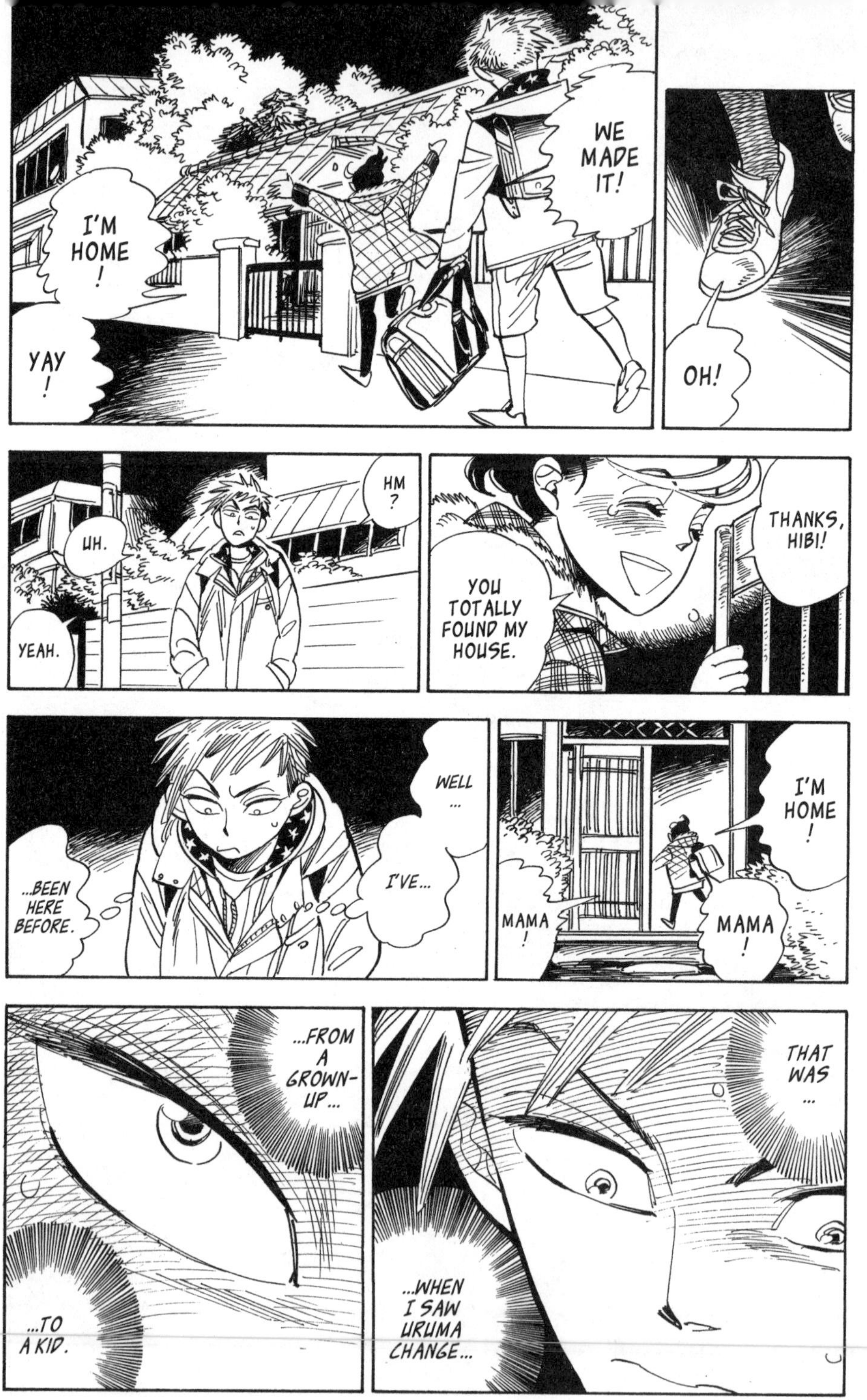
OH!
WE MADE IT!
I'M HOME!
YAY!
THANKS, HIBI!
YOU TOTALLY FOUND MY HOUSE.
HM?
UH.
YEAH.
I'M HOME!
MAMA!
MAMA!
WELL...
I'VE...
...BEEN HERE BEFORE.
THAT WAS...
...WHEN I SAW URUMA CHANGE...
...FROM A GROWN-UP...
...TO A KID.

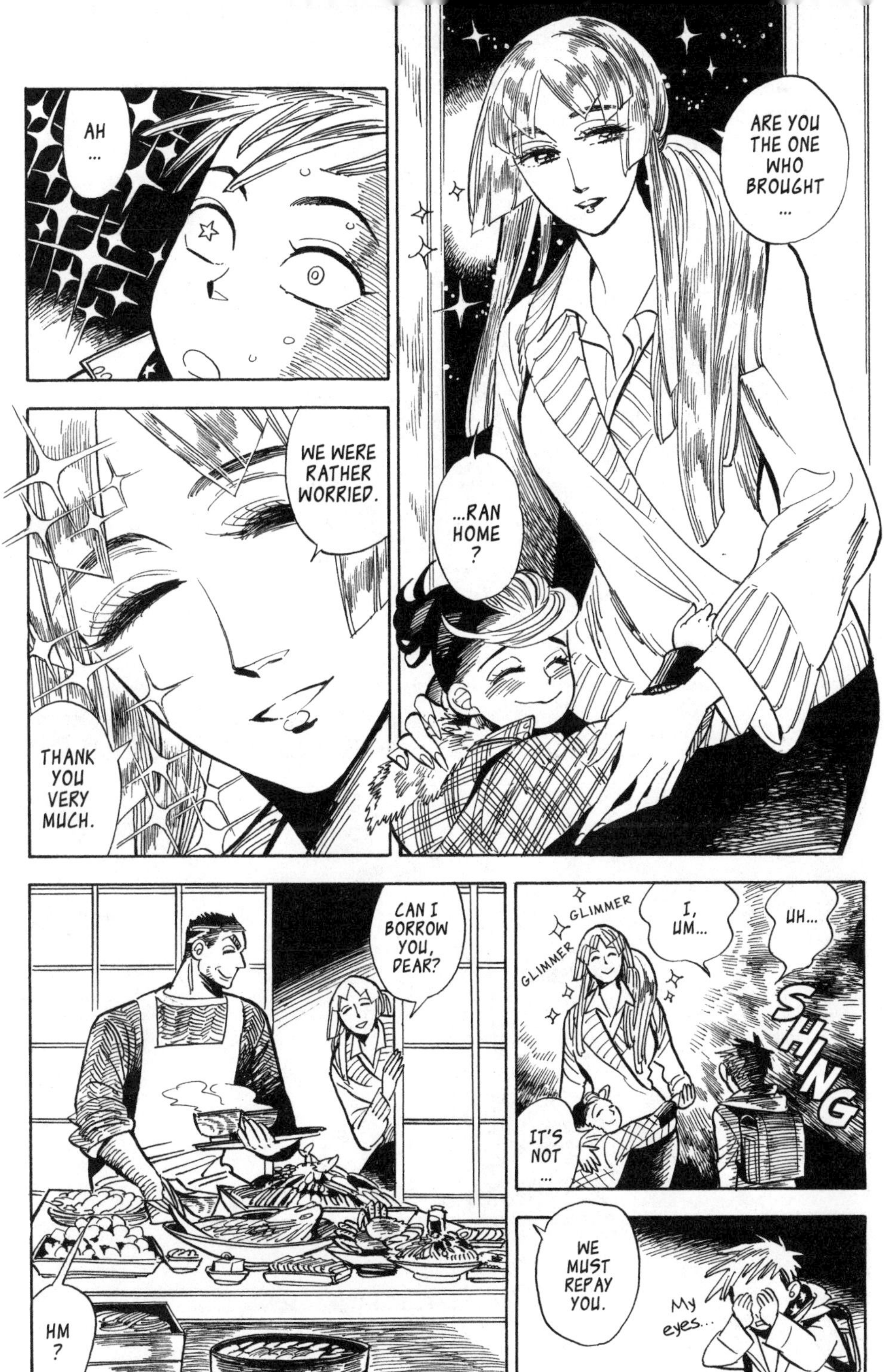
ARE YOU THE ONE WHO BROUGHT ...
...RAN HOME?
AH ...
WE WERE RATHER WORRIED.
THANK YOU VERY MUCH.
UH...
I, UM...
GLIMMER
GLIMMER
SHING
IT'S NOT ...
WE MUST REPAY YOU.
My eyes...
CAN I BORROW YOU, DEAR?
HM?

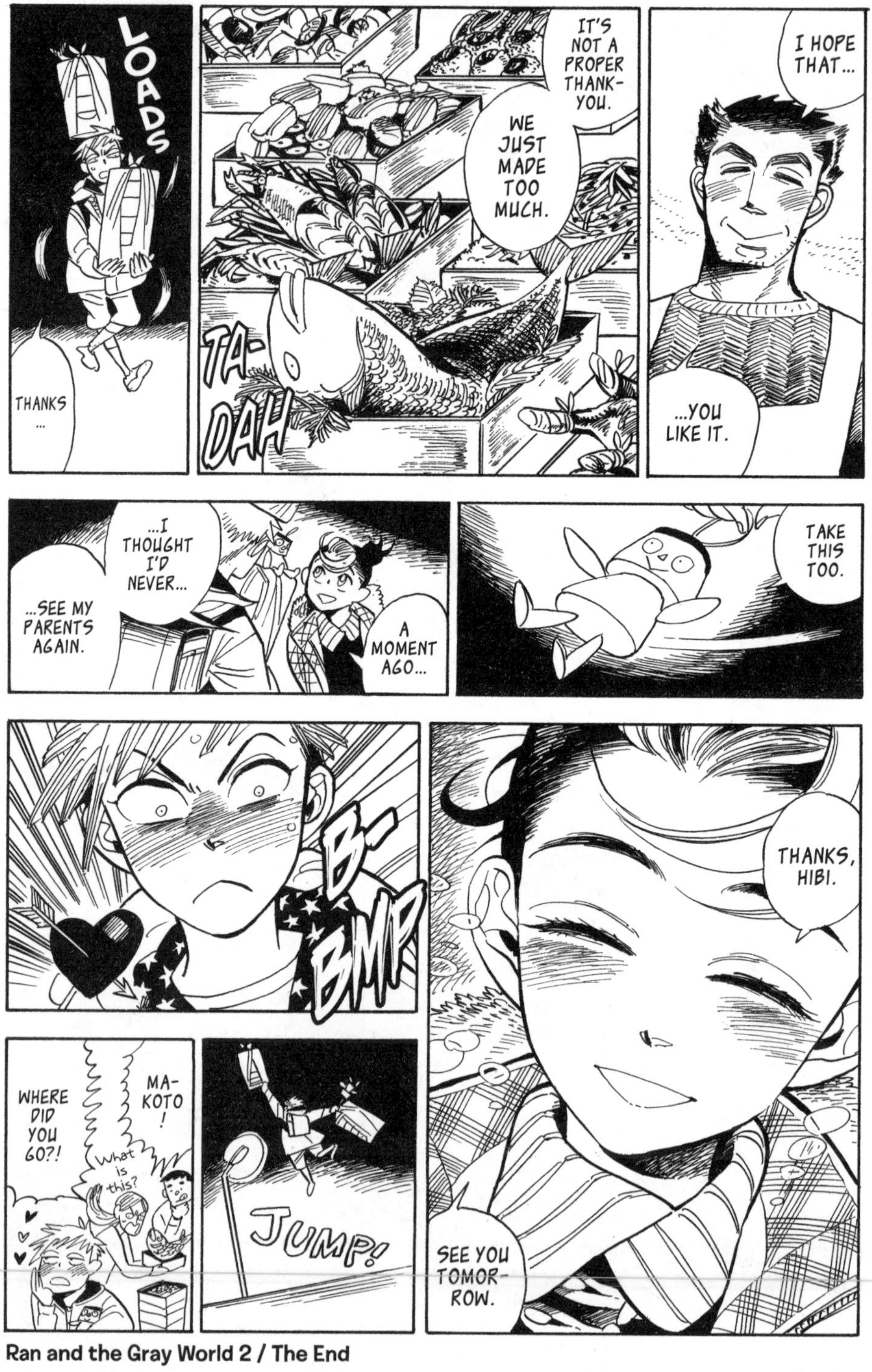
I HOPE THAT...
...YOU LIKE IT.
IT'S NOT A PROPER THANK-YOU.
WE JUST MADE TOO MUCH.
TA-DAH
LOADS
THANKS...
TAKE THIS TOO.
A MOMENT AGO...
...I THOUGHT I'D NEVER...
...SEE MY PARENTS AGAIN.
THANKS, HIBI.
SEE YOU TOMORROW.
B-BMP
JUMP!
MA-KOTO!
WHERE DID YOU GO?!
What is this?

Ran and the Gray World 2 / The End

Aki Irie was born in Kagawa Prefecture, Japan. She
began her professional career as a manga artist in
2002 with the short story "Fuku-chan Tabi Mata Tabi"
(Fuku-chan on the Road Again), which was published in
the monthly manga magazine *Papu*. *Ran and the Gray
World*, her first full-length series, is also the first
of her works to be released in English.

RAN AND THE GRAY WORLD

VOL. 2
VIZ Signature Edition

Story & Art by
AKI IRIE

English Translation & Adaptation / Emi Louie-Nishikawa
Touch-Up Art & Lettering / Joanna Estep
Design / Yukiko Whitley
Editor / Amy Yu

RAN TO HAIIRO NO SEKAI Vol. 2
©2010 Aki Irie
All rights reserved.
First published in Japan in 2010 by KADOKAWA CORPORATION ENTERBRAIN
English translation rights arranged with KADOKAWA CORPORATION ENTERBRAIN

The stories, characters and incidents mentioned in this publication are entirely fictional.

Printed in Canada

Published by VIZ Media, LLC
P.O. Box 77010
San Francisco, CA 94107

10 9 8 7 6 5 4 3 2 1
First printing, February 2019

 MEDIA

viz.com   vizsignature.com